THE
MBA HANDBOOK

We work with leading authors to develop the strongest educational material in business, finance and marketing, bringing cutting-edge thinking and best learning practice to a global market.

Under a range of well-known imprints, including Financial Times Prentice Hall, we craft high quality print and electronic publications which help readers to understand and apply their content, whether studying or at work.

To find out more about the complete range of our publishing please visit us on the World Wide Web at:
www.pearsoneduc.com

THE
MBA HANDBOOK

Study Skills for Postgraduate Management Study

Fourth Edition

SHEILA CAMERON
The Open University Business School

An imprint of **Pearson Education**

Harlow, England · London · New York · Reading, Massachusetts · San Francisco · Toronto · Don Mills, Ontario · Sydney
Tokyo · Singapore · Hong Kong · Seoul · Taipei · Cape Town · Madrid · Mexico City · Amsterdam · Munich · Paris · Milan

Pearson Education Limited

Edinburgh Gate
Harlow
Essex CM20 2JE
England

and Associated Companies around the world

Visit us on the World Wide Web at
www.pearsoneduc.com

First edition published in Great Britain under the Pitman Publishing imprint in 1991
Second edition published in 1994
Third edition published in 1997
Fourth edition published in 2001

© Sheila Cameron 1991, 1994, 1997, 2001

ISBN 0 273 64653 2
ISBN 0 273 65154 4 (Open University edition)

British Library Cataloguing-in-Publication Data
A CIP catalogue record for this book can be obtained from the British Library.

Library of Congress Cataloging-in-Publication Data
Cameron, Sheila.
    The MBA handbook: study skills for managers / Sheila Cameron.--4th ed.
        p. cm.
    Includes bibliographical references and index.
    ISBN 0-273-64653-2 (alk. paper)
        1. Master of business administration degree. 2. Business education. 3. Industrial
    management--Study and teaching (Graduate) I. Title.

    HF1111.C27 2000
    650'.071'173--dc21   00-055111

10 9 8 7 6 5 4 3 2 1
06 05 04 03 02 01

Typeset by 7
Printed and bound in Great Britain by Redwood Books, Trowbridge

Contents

Acknowledgements   xi

INTRODUCTION   1

1 Using this handbook   3
How the book is structured   4
Planning your work on the handbook   5
Chapter structure   8

BEFORE DECIDING ON A PROGRAMME   9

2 What MBAs and related qualifications offer   11
MBA origins   12
The changing management development context   13
Key dimensions of variation   17

3 Choosing a Master's programme   26
Assessing your present position and goals   27
Choosing the best route   29
Choosing between institutions   37

PRE-COURSE PREPARATION   41

4 Preparing for Master's level study   43
Gaining organisational support   44
Managing stress   46
Coping with unavoidable stress   48
Developing assertiveness skills   50
Exploiting information technology   56
Preparatory reading   58

5 **The time problem**   62

   Assessing the problem   63
   Freeing the additional time you need   65

6 **Managing time at work**   71

   Basic time management principles   72
   Putting principles into practice   82

   DEVELOPING LEARNING SKILLS   85

7 **Effective learning**   87

   Finding a place   87
   The advantage of studying at regular times   89
   Developing a study plan   90
   Clarifying your study objectives   92
   Using time effectively   95
   Exercises which can be used during study breaks   96

8 **Learning from learning theory**   99

   What is learning?   99
   Kolb's theory   100
   Learning styles   102

9 **Improving reading skills**   108

   Eye movements   109
   Increasing reading speed   111
   Selecting reading material   113
   Choosing your reading speed   114
   Photo-reading for accelerated learning   116
   Taking notes   117

10 **Using diagrams**   120

   The importance of diagrams   121
   Brain patterns or mind maps   124
   Relationship diagrams   127
   Rich pictures   128
   Systems maps   129
   Multiple-cause diagrams   133
   Other diagramming techniques   134

11 Working in teams   138

Task and process   139
Behaviours seen in groups   140
Choosing a group   143
Group formation   146
Aids to group effectiveness   148
The dangers of group work   149
Becoming a more effective group member   150
The role of informal groups   152

12 Learning from case studies   155

The place of case studies   156
Coping with cases   161
A method for approaching cases   162

13 Using numbers   172

Causes of difficulty   173
Why managers need maths   175
Representing numbers   179
Range   180
Distributions and histograms   180
Bar charts   182
Pie charts   185
Graphs   187
Estimating   189
Rounding   189
Fractions, percentages and ratios   190
Using equations   196
Working with brackets   200
Helpfile: Cracking the code   202

SKILLS FOR ASSESSMENT   211

14 Scoring well in assessment   213

Assessment in context   213
Common causes of failure   216
Assessment as communication   224

15 Writing assignments and reports   228

Assignment planning   229
Developing your material   237
Drafting written assignments   240

Using report format   241
The basics of clear English   248
Helpfile 1: Glossary of terms used in examination and assessment questions   254
Helpfile 2: Spelling (the right word)   256
Helpfile 3: Punctuation and grammar   259

16 Making presentations   264

The risks of presenting   265
Structure   267
Delivery technique   267
Visual aids   269
Handling questions   271
Dealing with nerves   271
Preparation   272

17 Passing examinations   274

Types of written examination   275
Common causes of failure   276
Exam preparation   278
During the examination   284

18 Other forms of assessment   288

The reasons for alternative approaches   289
Portfolio assessment   290
Constructing your portfolio   291
Assessment centres   292
Preparing for assessment via simulation   293
Viva voce examinations   293
Preparing for a viva voce examination   293

19 Projects, theses and dissertations   297

The objectives of a management thesis or dissertation   298
The role of a supervisor   300
Topic choice   301
Generating possible topics   305
Topic selection   309
Literature search   314
Data planning   317
Project planning and control   321
Writing up   327

AFTERWARDS   331

20 Beyond your Master's...   333
Lifelong learning   334
Reassessing your objectives   335
Exploring options   336
Making an effective job application   339
Technology and recruitment   342
Going forward   343

References   345
Index   349

Acknowledgements

Among the many to whom thanks are due I should like to mention in particular:

Peter, for contributions on mathematics and computing, and boundless support;

Hester, Neill and James, for their tolerance (Earth to Mum…);

my Open University students, for all they have taught me.

INTRODUCTION

INTRODUCTION

1 Using this handbook

Objectives

By the end of this chapter you should:

- have identified those chapters which will be of most use to you
- have decided upon the order in which to study these
- Have started to work out a timetable for completing your work on these chapters.

INTRODUCTION

Management careers have changed dramatically during the last twenty years. So too has management development. An MBA used to be a rare qualification, pursued by a small band of ambitious young high-fliers, and treated with suspicion by many employers. Today, MBAs or other management-related Master's degrees are highly regarded by employers and sought by large numbers of managers of all ages.

If you are looking at this book you may have already enrolled on such a programme, and be considering how to prepare yourself for it. Alternatively, you may be wondering whether the time has come for you, too, to gain a management qualification. If so, you may well be wondering which of the plethora of courses on offer would best suit you.

You are right to be thinking seriously about choice of course, and about preparing yourself for the experiences it will bring. Formal management study at this level is a serious undertaking. It will not be easy – it would not be worth it if it were. Some students will inevitably fail or drop out before completing the course. Others will gain the qualification, but leave feeling that the benefits gained do not justify the effort expended. Many, however, will find that their studies not only are fascinating in themselves, but lead to a transformation of their work experience and of their subsequent careers.

This book is intended to ensure that you are in this latter category. It helps you to choose a course which best suits your needs, and once having chosen, to develop the skills that will enable you to gain full benefit from your study. It shows you how to manage your time effectively, how to deal with stress and how to gain organisational support for your study. It covers basic skills (numeracy, written communication, use of IT, team-working,) which may be rusty or new to you. It explores common aspects of management programmes such as learning from case studies, and doing projects or dissertations. It looks at how to fail (and succeed) at the sorts of assessment you are likely to meet. It looks at how to go on developing your skills, and your career, once you have gained the qualification.

Although written primarily for the manager who is studying while working (in Europe, the majority of postgraduate management students are in this position) large parts of the book have proved useful to full-time students, particularly those with an academic background unrelated to management. Many of the skills covered have been useful, too, to those who decide that the time is not yet right for them to seek a qualification. Improved time management, interpersonal and communication skills have helped them to reach a position from which an MBA or similar programme *is* an appropriate goal.

When the first edition of this book appeared, MBAs were the predominant management qualification at this level. Now there are many more Master's level programmes available. For continuity, this remains as 'The MBA Handbook'. But it should prove equally applicable to a wide range of other programmes at this level – if you are studying on one of these programmes I apologise for what may seem over-frequent reference merely to MBAs.

This handbook is *not* a textbook – it is not designed to be read passively. Rather it is closer to an interactive distance learning text: you will gain full benefit only if you work through the activities and exercises provided. Nor are you intended necessarily to use *all* chapters. Management students come from a wide range of backgrounds. Some have PhDs, others left school at 16. Some are engineers, others studied arts subjects. Their needs with respect to learning skills therefore cover a wide range. Your own needs are likely to be some subset of these. If you have already chosen a course, you do not need to work through the chapter on this. Engineers will find the numeracy chapter completely unnecessary. If you have an English degree you are unlikely to need the revision section on writing clear English. You therefore need to select those parts of the book which *are* relevant to you.

Because you may not be familiar with this sort of use of learning materials, and need to work out how best to use the book, this short introductory chapter aims to help you understand how the book is structured, and to relate this to your own particular needs.

HOW THE BOOK IS STRUCTURED

If you refer to the list of chapter headings, you will see that the book falls roughly into three main parts. Chapters 2 and 3 deal with the period before you commit yourself to a course of study. What does postgraduate management study entail, and what benefits can you expect? Given your own particular set of goals and circumstances, is an MBA an appropriate goal, or is some other qualification more desirable? If so, which available course is most likely to suit your needs? Is part-time or full-time study better for you? If opting for part-time, do you need the discipline of regular class attendance, or would the flexibility of distance learning be better? Having decided on a type of course, what questions should you ask of possible colleges or other providers?

The next three chapters deal with preparation you could usefully do if you have time available before starting your course. Many programmes run only once or twice a year. It may take time to obtain sponsorship. Your life may be too full at present to allow study. There are many possible reasons for not starting a course immediately. But if you have decided that you will study at some future point you can start *now* to prepare yourself. This first part of the book covers the general preparatory reading that might be helpful, together with the organisational negotiations and improved time management techniques that may well be necessary to ensure that the conflicting demands of job and study can be managed. The commonest cause of student dropout on part-time courses is the inability to cope with this double workload, so it is worth doing all you can before the course starts to minimise the conflict. If you are planning a full-time course, much of this will be irrelevant to you, although if you have not been on a time management course, the chapter on managing time at work (Chapter 6) could still be highly relevant to your job.

Chapters 7–13 deal broadly with developing the learning skills you will need. While this could be seen as a part of your preparation, usefully done before your course starts, they are in a different category from the more general preparation of earlier chapters. If you have already started your course, you may be hard pressed to find the time to develop these skills. However, they are so important that you might perhaps focus on those chapters where you feel the greatest need, say, numeracy, or diagramming.

Presumably you wish to study management in order to become more effective at work. The section on learning skills will be of great use at work. Organisations are changing so rapidly that the ability to learn is a vital management skill. But obtaining the qualification is also an important goal. In order to get good grades, and pass the course, it is necessary to do *more* than learn. Unless you can *demonstrate* this learning, through your performance on whatever assessment is used on your course, you will not gain the qualification. Assessment is not the same as performance evaluation at work. It will probably involve a selection of written assignments, assessed group work, examinations, and a substantial thesis or dissertation. You therefore need to develop a separate set of skills related to this aspect. Chapters 14–19 deal with this. Even if you have already started on your course you should find this part of the book helps you to improve your grades.

The final chapter is intended to help you consider your career goals after you obtain your qualification, and how you can continue to develop as a manager. In a changing environment continuous professional development is essential for success as a senior manager.

PLANNING YOUR WORK ON THE HANDBOOK

Figure 1.1 shows how work on the various chapters might relate to milestones in an MBA or similar course. You should now study this diagram, and highlight those chapters which you think you will wish to use.

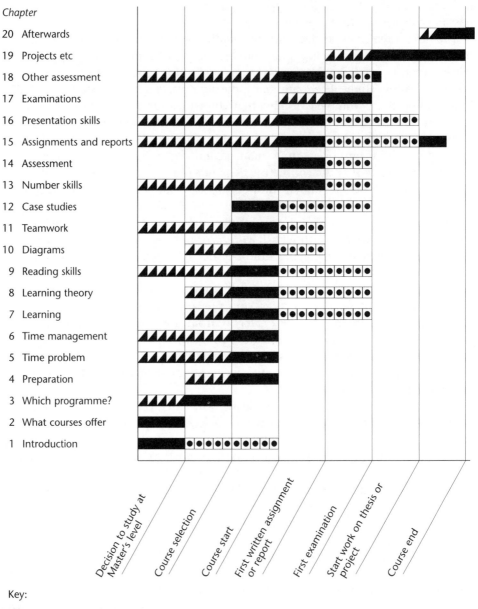

Key:

■ denotes optimal study period

◢◢ denotes scope for bringing study forward

●● denotes period into which study could be postponed if unavoidable

  Fig.1.1 Optimal study times for Handbook chapters in relation to course milestones

ACTIVITY

Spend some time skimming through one or two of the chapters which seem most relevant to your needs. Try to assess how long they would take you to work through if you were to do all the activities thoroughly. Then think about how long you can afford to spend working on them, either before your course starts, or while you are at the same time doing coursework. Try to be realistic in your estimates. If you have focused on more chapters than you know (being honest) you can find the time for, then be ruthless. Discard the least pressing. It is better to set yourself a task you can do and succeed, than to attempt too much, become discouraged, and fail to achieve anything. You can always revise your targets later if you are getting on faster than anticipated.

Now decide on target completion dates for the chapters you have selected. Complete the chart below, or devise a more extended one. Be sure to note your target dates in your diary, too, to ensure that you do not forget to check your progress. You will need to bear your course timetable in mind, if you are already registered for a course, or your anticipated course start date if not.

Chapter	Target completion date	Notes
_____	_____	_____
_____	_____	_____
_____	_____	_____
_____	_____	_____
_____	_____	_____

Comment

The above activity should have introduced you to one of the key ways in which you are intended to use this book, that is, to write on it! By the end of your course you should have absorbed all you need from the book, and need to make only limited reference to it thereafter. So there is no need to keep it in pristine condition. Deface it as much as you like, provided this will help you. Indeed it will be suggested that you deface other printed material, too (provided that they belong to you, not the library), so you might as well start now.

You should not be locked into your plan above. Course demands, or other discoveries, will almost certainly cause you to revise your priorities and assessed needs. When this happens you should revise your plan too. You may sometimes wish to look at parts of the book you decided were not important, in order to check that your decision was right. The fact that your plan will probably change considerably does not invalidate it. Such changes should constitute improvements. Without an original plan to improve on, this will not be possible. The key thing is that you *have* a plan, and that you follow it, modifying it only to make it *more* effective.

CHAPTER STRUCTURE

In skimming through the chapters in which you are interested, you will see that each starts with an introduction preceded by a set of objectives for the chapter. You will probably find it helpful to think about these objectives, and see whether they are what you would wish to be able to do as a result of reading the chapter. If there are objectives which you feel are missing, add these with a question mark. And at the end of your work on the chapter, check whether these objectives have been met as well. (Write to me c/o the publishers if you find significant omissions.)

In order to meet the objectives, you will need to work through any activities and exercises included in the chapter. Activities do not have answers, though the subsequent discussion in the text may draw upon what you have written. Exercises are intended as a check on your understanding of techniques or concepts, and will normally have an answer. These answers are printed at the end of the chapter in which the exercise occurs.

You will find suggested sources of further information at the end of most chapters. Use these at a starting point if you wish to pursue a subject in more depth than the chapter allows. Authors who are referred to in the chapter, but may not be the best starting point, are listed in the references at the end of the book rather than at the chapter end.

There is also a website associated with this book. You will find it at www.booksites.net/cameron and items on this website are shown in the text by this symbol. There you will find additional exercises for some of the chapters and links to other useful sources of information.

You should now have sufficient grasp of the book's structure to start working through sections with the highest priority for you. I trust that this will prove useful.

SUMMARY

- This book is intended to be used selectively, but relevant sections should be *worked through*, rather than merely read.
- Although chapters divide roughly into choice, preparation, learning skills and assessment skills, much of the book can be worked through in preparation for the start of a course.
- Many chapters cover highly transferable skills, just as useful at work as on your chosen course.
- Your plan for working through the book should depend on your priorities, and the timetable of the course you intend to study. It is important that this plan be realistic.
- There is a companion website for this book at www.booksites.net/cameron.

BEFORE DECIDING
ON A PROGRAMME

2 What MBAs and related qualifications offer

Objectives

By the end of this chapter you should:

- understand the original rationale for an MBA syllabus and subsequent developments
- appreciate the range of potential benefits of Master's level study from both student and employer perspectives
- be aware of the range of possible qualifications and key dimensions of variation
- appreciate the different costs likely to be involved in different programmes.

INTRODUCTION

There are now well over 1000 MBA and other management Master's programmes on offer, with huge variation between these. Choosing a programme which meets your particular needs is crucial. The wrong programme may lead to failure, or at best leave you feeling that beyond the letters after your name, you have gained little. Another programme might have the capacity to transform your working life.

Before choosing a course it is important to understand the range of potential benefits that different programmes may offer: you can then decide which of these are most important to you. You also need to understand the other dimensions of variation between programmes, such as length of course, academic level, degree of specialisation and the pattern of time commitment needed. These are likely to be equally important factors in selecting a programme.

This chapter looks at how provision has developed from the original US MBA model to the range of programmes now available, and at the way in which both student and employer perspectives on MBAs have changed. In the UK, and Europe more generally, this change has been – and continues to be – dramatic. Thirty years ago very few European employers had more than a hazy idea of what an MBA even stood for, and tended to think that their possessors were liable to be expensive, arrogant and generally useless. Now, some sort of formal management qualification is widely seen as almost a prerequisite for management success. In the 1970s, only a handful of young, ambitious managers pursued an MBA. Now, some 20 000 graduate annually from the 500 or so European business schools, most of them already with substantial management experience behind them. (This is still a small number in relation to the 80 000 US graduates, but the number is growing rapidly, augmented by increasing numbers of managers seeking more specialist qualifications.)

The reasons for this expansion, and its consequences, provide important contextual information which will help you to consider what you want to do. Costs and benefits of study have changed markedly, and you need to evaluate both when choosing, first, whether or not to seek a qualification of this kind, and subsequently, which qualification to pursue.

MBA ORIGINS

The prototypical MBA originated at Harvard around a century ago. This type of MBA is a high-pressured two-year programme, usually with high entry requirements for students. The first year of such a programme will concentrate on the basic management disciplines: likely courses include control, managerial economics, finance, marketing, organisational behaviour, human resource management, production and operations management. It also covers aspects of the environment in which business takes place, such as government and the international economy. There will be scope, too, for organisational placements, perhaps in the form of consultancy projects, and for study of a range of electives in the second year.

Teaching on such programmes is likely to be heavily case study based – a method pioneered in the Harvard Law programme. Harvard students report being expected to analyse two or three substantial case studies per night – each requiring two to four hours' study – in preparation for class presentations and discussions the next day. The academic level was extremely high, and the atmosphere highly competitive, placing considerable pressure on students.

This distinctive approach to teaching management has many benefits. The first and obvious one for students is the prestige attached to the qualification itself. Entry to the top business schools is highly competitive. Merely being accepted suggests something special. The competitive nature of the programme means that those who survive it are even more distinctive.

Until fairly recently employers would compete vigorously for the graduates of these business schools, offering 'golden handshakes' on starting, and salaries twice or more those offered to non-MBA graduates. The MBA graduates were valued because they had gained a highly analytical approach to managerial problem solving, and the ability to approach new problems in a structured fashion. From the 800 or so case studies they had analysed, they had a 'vocabulary' of types of problem, and a degree of familiarity with a wide range of business contexts. They had a clear grasp of finance, and the ability to use financial models. The competitive approach to teaching developed a high level of confidence in students who survived it. These qualities made graduates particularly attractive to management consultancies and investment banks, the subsequent employers of the majority of graduates.

However, although the first European business schools modelled themselves upon Harvard, several important changes took place from about 1980 onwards. These significantly influenced what managers and employers wanted from a qualification, and how they wanted to achieve it. As a consequence, the 'Harvard' model is no longer the dominant one in Europe.

THE CHANGING MANAGEMENT DEVELOPMENT CONTEXT

The factors which brought about this change are somewhat interrelated. They include government interest in management education, growing employer interest, concern for more relevant and practically oriented programmes, an explosion of 'MBA' courses being offered, particularly via distance learning or other part-time modes, and a change in the type of manager choosing to study. Figure 2.1 tries to show how these factors led to the current provision. It uses a convention (multiple cause) described in Chapter 10. This section is written from a UK perspective, but broadly similar factors have operated, albeit on slightly different timescales, elsewhere in Europe and indeed around the globe.

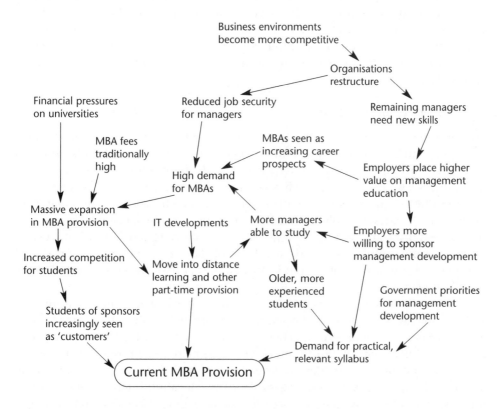

Fig. 2.1 Factors contributing to the current nature of MBA provision

Government influence

To the extent that they fund education, governments are significant stakeholders in the process. During the 1980s the UK government, concerned with industry's apparent competitive weakness, started to wonder if the solution lay in better management training, and commissioned several reports on this. It emerged that management training was seen by employers as an overhead, rather than an investment. Of the 90 000 or so who entered managerial roles each year, most had no prior formal management education, and subsequently received on average only one day of training per year. The USA had only four times the population of the UK, but produced forty times as many management degrees and diplomas.

Perceived reasons for this disparity included possible employer confusion over available qualifications, and a concern that courses were over-academic and non-vocational. In an attempt to produce a clear framework for management development, the Management Charter Initiative (MCI) was launched. It went on to develop a framework of management competences, and qualifications based upon these. These National (or Scottish) Vocational Qualifications (N/SVQs) extend from a basic supervisory level 1 to a level 5 in Strategic Management, and to gain them candidates need to show a portfolio of 'evidence of competence', rather than pursue any particular programme of study.

Although fairly popular at lower levels, these qualifications have not replaced more formal programmes at higher levels. The initiative has, however, probably had two significant effects. First, the MCI raised employer awareness of the importance of management development. Second, it brought into sharp focus a debate which was already starting about the academic and analytical nature of the MBA syllabus.

The university perspective

Concerns were already beginning to surface in the USA about the syllabus. There were complaints from employers that the focus on 'hard' analytical skills neglected other areas crucial to success – interpersonal skills, for example, or creativity. The *Harvard Business Review* itself addressed this issue (see Lataif, 1992). One view, expressed by a leading management writer, Professor Mintzberg, went so far as to suggest that business schools such as Harvard were seriously damaging US business. He claimed that the process of case study analysis fostered a willingness to pronounce on complex issues, from a basis of dangerous ignorance, and that it favoured the ambitious, glib and quick-witted, rather than those committed to the good of their organisation.

At this time, many UK universities were under considerable financial pressure, and saw management courses, for which premium prices could be charged, as an important new source of income. There was therefore a big expansion in provision, with many institutions with little track record in management offering a range of management courses, up to Master's level. During the 1990s this extended to quasi-franchise arrangements, with colleges of further education offering courses under the auspices of (usually new) universities in the region. Undergraduate management programmes expanded massively during this period.

Because of the prestige attached to the MBA qualification, and the high prices that could be charged, almost every management education provider wanted to provide such a qualification. Of course this was a serious threat to that very prestige. In trying to fill the new courses, entry qualifications were lowered, sometimes to the point of non-existence. And in trying to staff the programmes, lecturers were drawn from a wide range of vaguely related programmes, or from industry. It could be argued (indeed I would argue it quite strongly) that the best management teachers are those with current experience of senior management allied to a strong academic background in the subject and experience in, and a love of, developing managers. Unfortunately many of those sucked into this expansion of provision as part-time lecturers did not fit this pattern.

Also in the 1980s, the Open University, the major undergraduate distance learning provider in the UK, realised that many managers could not afford to take two years off to study an MBA full time, and that their well-tried undergraduate methods might be easily adapted to postgraduate management study. Because distance learning students are working while studying, the OU adopted a strong position on the nature of the courses they proposed to offer. While aiming to be based on sound theory, they wanted to be essentially practical, something that would make practising managers *better* at what they did, as well as preparing them for promotion. This emphasis on 'improved management practice' and hence on transferable skills, is now widespread in the UK.

While considerable variation in quality of provision still exists, the expansion in MBA provision has now had time to increase the number of qualified potential lecturers, and organisations have had time to learn about effective teaching of management. While you can still find fairly undemanding (and correspondingly fairly unrewarding) programmes, and need to choose very carefully, there are now many courses that offer good content and competent teaching, and are deservedly well regarded by employers.

To summarise thus far:

- With increased competition for students, universities, which in the 1980s tended towards a 'we know best what's good for you' attitude, have had to become more customer focused.

- With expansion of part-time provision, the typical MBA student is no longer a recent graduate, with little if any management experience. More typical now is someone in their mid-30s, and with considerable organisational experience.

- Such students are good at making clear what they want, and this tends to be a programme rooted in organisational realities, with the practical relevance of what is taught to the fore. This is consistent with government (and employer) emphasis on the importance of transferable skills.

- Although some highly 'academic' programmes remain, the majority have become much more applied, and draw upon the experience represented in the student body rather than relying totally upon case studies.

The employer's view

There is, of course, considerable variation in employer's attitudes towards MBAs, and in what they seek in their managers. While the following general trends seem to be apparent, treat them with caution!

At the outset, as already indicated, many employers viewed MBA graduates with extreme caution, made nervous by their arrogance, salary demands and lack of both practical experience and common sense. It is much easier to solve a case study than a real-life problem, with all its complexities, emotions and power relationships. Attitudes to management qualifications are, however, markedly different today. Contributory factors include: government publicity associated with the MBA; experience with a new kind of MBA graduate; pressure from their own employees for sponsorship; and perhaps most importantly, fairly major changes in business environments and therefore in the skills managers need.

Organisational environments have become far more turbulent in recent years, with fierce competition from new fronts, and major impacts from developing information and communication technologies. One response has been to 'delayer'. While this may mean that some managers are no longer required, those that remain have greater responsibility, and may need to be very flexible in the way they operate. A formal management course which can increase the ability to operate in such an environment is therefore desirable. Furthermore, it is not only the high-fliers who need these skills. With delayering, *all* levels of management may need to be able to operate autonomously, flexibly and with an understanding of strategic issues.

I quote but one employer, Nokia's head of human resources, writing in one of the many publications (in this case Hobsons MBA Casebooks) designed to help you choose/sell you an MBA. As a rapidly growing international organisation, in one of the most turbulent markets of all, Nokia is well aware of the importance of good managers. They value MBAs because they give graduates a strategic perspective and wider vision so that they are not seduced by short-term advantage into avenues that will threaten longer-term success. They value the interpersonal skills which allow total relationship management with customers, seen as crucial. They appreciate a high level of cultural awareness, which will enable managers to operate across the globe (one of their managers to whom I spoke recently had a team spread across three continents, and many more countries). Lateral thinking, willingness to take early responsibility and ability to work under pressure were other advantages cited.

Employers tend to view part-time study more favourably than full-time for existing employees, fearing (not without reason) that if they sponsor someone on a full-time course there is a real risk that that person will leave soon after completing the qualification. For new recruits offering an MBA gained elsewhere, questions are more likely to concern the reputation of the institution where it was gained, the nature of the programme and the level of marks gained. More importantly, they will want to know how the learning has been used subsequently.

Many employers feel that their management development needs are unique, and can be met only by a specially designed programme. While such 'corporate MBAs' can be of a very high standard, they may fail to develop the breadth of view that is one of the advantages of a more general MBA, where you will probably learn as much from the varied organisational experience of fellow students as you will from the teaching staff. A middle ground is the consortium MBA, specifically designed for a small number of different organisations.

The manager's view

In the next chapter you will be exploring your own objectives in seeking a Master's. Suffice it to say here that part of the growth in MBA and other provision has been driven by management insecurity that has followed the radical organisational restructuring undertaken since the late 1980s. This forced many managers to realise that what they had thought would be a 'job for life' could no longer safely be regarded as such. They were likely to need to seek a new position several times during their career, and such openings would be fiercely competed for. A qualification that would make them more attractive to possible future employers, and enable them to operate for periods of self-employment, therefore became very important.

With restructuring, those managers who kept their jobs found themselves with wider responsibilities, and again felt the need for a course that would help them to rise to the challenges these presented.

The increased availability of part-time and distance learning courses made pursuit of a qualification a realistic possibility for many whose commitments meant that full-time study was simply not an option. This goes a long way to explaining the increasing age profile of management Master's students, already described.

KEY DIMENSIONS OF VARIATION

The first questions intending students tend to ask are:

- How long will it take?
- How much will it cost?
- Will I get a place?
- Will I be able to cope?
- How do employers rate this particular qualification?

While these are important questions, there are others equally important, if slightly less obvious, which should influence your choice. These concern the suitability of the delivery mode to your particular circumstances (dealt with in the next chapter), the approach to teaching, and the focus of the content – how strategic is it, how international, how practically oriented?

Length of programme

The Harvard model was for a two-year full-time programme, and many still argue that to take someone with no academic background in management to Master's level in this complex subject takes at least this long. However few students can afford this time, and there has been strong pressure, particularly in Europe, to reduce the course to 18 months, or even 12 months. The two-year programme is now very much the exception, and even in the USA shorter programmes are now becoming available. While some of the reduction in time can be at the expense of vacations and industrial placements (less important for those who already have management experience) some will inevitably be at the expense of learning. For those who can afford it, a two-year programme at a top school is likely to offer significantly more learning than a shorter programme.

For part-time programmes, the content is inevitably spread over a longer period. And the situation is compounded by the expected commitment per week. A two-year part-time programme may have less content than a three- or four-year programme, or may merely require up to twice the number of the study hours per week. Because of this variability, it is worth thinking about two dimensions – duration, relating to how long you will be involved in the programme, and size, relating to the amount of material you will be expected to cover during this period.

Delivery pattern

Because full-time programmes are now in the minority, it is important to understand the other delivery patterns available. 'Part-time' covers several major variations. The original part-time model of regular weekly attendance either in the evening or a mix of daytime and evening is still widely available. However, because many managers have jobs which do not allow of such regularity, either because of frequent travel or because of irregular working hours, two other variants of part-time study have become common.

The first is the 'executive' model, which requires blocks of attendance at perhaps monthly or two-monthly intervals. This is only feasible for managers working in organisations which support this form of development. It has many of the advantages of full-time study – intensity of study, ability to concentrate whole-heartedly on the course, interaction with fellow students, the ability to study overseas for some of the programme, or with managers from other cultures. These are combined with some of the advantages of part-time study – the ability to apply what is learned almost immediately to work, and continuity of employment and salary.

The second variant is distance learning, which removes, or at least greatly reduces, the need to study in a particular place or at any particular time. The flexibility of this mode and the lack of any logistical reasons to limit numbers, together with the high quality of the teaching on some distance learning programmes, has made this the dominant method at present. The Open University had over 6000 MBA students in its programme during 1999, spread throughout Europe and beyond.

The ability to deliver good quality printed material, good audio-visual support materials and a high level of tutor support was until recently limited to a few specialists in this area. However, IT developments have removed many of the 'barriers to entry' to the distance learning market. It is relatively easy to provide text, and offer some sort of academic support, electronically and on a global scale.

Choosing between these variants is addressed in more detail in the next chapter.

Cost of programme

Costs can vary quite significantly, and it is not always easy to find out what all the costs will be. The obvious ones are course fees, cost of travel, accommodation costs, living costs if full-time, cost of books, PC and any other materials and equipment. You may additionally need to budget for the cost of getting into the school of your choice. You may need to take the GMAT test (at your own expense), to travel for interviews. There may be costs for processing your application. There may be examination fees, and perhaps additional costs for studying overseas. You will be able to find information about fees fairly easily from the Internet or one of the MBA guides listed at the end of the chapter, but may need to ask specific questions to elicit the full picture.

As a rough guide, the costs of study in 2000 range from something in excess of US$100 000 if you include two years' tuition, living expenses and loss of salary, through to about £10 000 for a good distance learning programme which allows you to continue earning, or even less for some part-time face-to-face courses.

You may be lucky enough to persuade your employer to pay your fees. After all, the organisation should benefit considerably from your improved efficiency. If not, it may be possible to obtain a loan to cover your study. In the UK, government-backed Career Development Loans may be used for this purpose. Alternatively, if you are studying for an MBA approved by the Association of MBAs (AMBA) you may apply to their loan scheme. Other schemes may be available to you if you live elsewhere in Europe. Terms for such schemes are more favourable than for a standard overdraft, so they are worth investigating. A very few scholarships are also available. Business schools, banks and the World Wide Web are the best starting point for current information on current sources of finance.

Entry requirements

Requirements for entry vary enormously, with the top business schools requiring a high GMAT score (for sources of further information on this *see* the end of the chapter) together with a strong academic record and evidence of other achievements (as well as the ability to pay high fees). Indeed there are organisations devoted to helping you (for a fee) make a successful application to one of these schools. At the other end of the spectrum you may find programmes which will accept you with any class of degree, a professional qualification, or failing that, evidence of management experience. While in some cases this is out of a desire to attract sufficient students to make a programme economically viable, you cannot assume that low entry requirements imply a low standard of teaching.

Three factors allow programmes to be flexible over entry qualifications. The first is that no academic background in *management* is required. Unlike a Master's degree in, say, mathematics, where you would be expected to start with a high level of knowledge of the subject, MBA courses assume the general intellectual level of a graduate, but no subject specific knowledge. Successful managers are likely to be able to operate at this level, even if for some reason they do not hold a BA or BSc.

Second, there is a different cost to failure on a part-time programme. It would be highly irresponsible to accept someone on to a full-time programme if there was doubt as to their ability to pass the course, particularly if they were giving up their job in order to study. Failure would, for them, be a disaster. But for the manager who continues to work while studying, failure, while painful to the ego, is less catastrophic. Part-time programmes can therefore afford to take risks with students lacking the normal qualifications (though they should make it clear to applicants in this category that they *are* perceived to be at risk, so that they can decide whether it is a risk they wish to take).

Third, whereas on face-to-face programmes large classes are undesirable, and limits therefore need to be set, the reverse is true of distance learning. The larger the student body, the more likely students are to find others on the programme living near them, and for local tutorial provision to be feasible. Distance learning materials are costly to produce, too, and if the cost can be spread over a larger number of students, fees can be kept lower. Thus there are good reasons for distance learning programmes in particular to be more relaxed about entry requirements.

The entry requirement factor relates to management experience. This is linked to the shift in emphasis that has taken place in most European programmes. Once an MBA is seen as an active learning process, rather than mere passive absorption of information, then a student needs to have experience of management if full benefit is to be gained. There are still MBAs which do not presume management experience, and more specialist Master's programmes tend not to require any. If you do not yet meet your preferred institution's experience requirement you can either wait until you do, or select a programme elsewhere which is designed not to need it. (I must admit to a preference for the former option. While purely academic study in a management subject can be intellectually challenging, and good preparation for an academic career, there is little to match the excitement of studying a subject you have already *lived*, in the active learning mode – described later – that this allows.)

Degree of specialism

The prototypical MBA, although allowing limited specialisation via second-year electives, was essentially a generalist management qualification. Many (including some of the major accrediting bodies) still feel that all MBAs should remain generalist qualifications. It is a contradiction in (their) terms to talk of an MBA in Marketing, in Technology, in International Tourism or in the Music Industry. But these, and many other specialist 'MBAs', are currently available.

Furthermore, there are now a great many specialist Master's programmes that are not described as MBAs, but which do contain a varying degree of general management content in addition to the specialist material.

Obviously within any given 'size' of programme, only so much material can be covered. Specialist material will be at the expense of more generalist topics. This is obviously a factor you will need to take into consideration, selecting a programme that covers what you think you are likely to need most for the next few years.

Content specialisation is one dimension. Contextual specialisation, as in the corporate MBAs already described, or programmes for the public sector or specific industries, is another kind of specialism. Again, such a programme is by definition of restricted applicability. Its relevance to your needs will depend upon your future career plans as well as your current job.

Degree of strategic focus

Traditionally, MBAs were distinguished by their strong strategic focus, this being perceived as essential for senior or would-be senior managers. For managers at lower levels certificates and diplomas, or specialist professional qualifications, were available. These concentrated upon developing the functional skills such managers were deemed to need.

Organisational restructuring has blurred the distinction between junior and senior management in many organisations. And a substantial proportion of intending MBA students today, while experienced, do not expect rapid promotion to Board level. MBA programmes today therefore offer a mix of functional skill development and strategic understanding, although there is considerable variation in balance between these. Indeed a clear divide seems to be emerging between institutions offering a highly strategic traditional MBA, frequently to younger full-time students, and those offering a more practical, less strategic programme, often to slightly older, more experienced part-time students.

In the flatter, more flexible organisations in which many managers currently work, all managers need an appreciation of strategy. This is something that employers value (*see* the views of one employer mentioned earlier in this chapter). But they also need practical skills. Given size constraints, this is a difficult balance to achieve. Consideration of where a programme lies on this dimension, and how this relates to your current and likely future job situation, will clearly be important.

Internationalisation

Given the global nature of much business today, most MBA programmes will claim to prepare graduates to operate internationally, through international faculty, an international student body and/or a curriculum which is deliberately international. Language teaching may be included, as well as visits to, or work experience in, another country.

If this is an important variable, you need to look carefully at the likely effectiveness of a programme in meeting your needs. The extent to which you may benefit may be surprisingly limited, particularly if you are studying part-time. Language skills are indeed important, but difficult to develop. An extended placement where you operate in another language will be invaluable, if you already have the basic skill level to take advantage of it. But at the other extreme, it is unlikely that the minimal language teaching some programmes offer will take you beyond the point of being able to order a beer or ask the way to the station. Similarly, a one-week 'field trip' abroad with a group of fellow students, while enjoyable, is likely to do little to improve your understanding of how managers operate in another culture. 'Size' is a real programme constraint.

Students generally claim to learn as much from fellow students as from the curriculum. If the student body is international, and there is a lot of time for interaction, this can be invaluable. But there may be limitations. If the overseas students are recent graduates they may contribute little in terms of cross-cultural management experience. On part-time programmes outside the major cities there may be few non-local students.

Many distance learning programmes now operate over a wide geographical base: more than half their students may be non-European. But this will only provide benefits if students who live far apart have opportunities to interact, perhaps electronically or at residential schools. Many remote students find such contact, limited though it may be compared to following a full-time programme together, to be extremely helpful.

Programme credibility

All of the above factors, and others, will influence the credibility of a particular qualification. Given the diversity of MBA and similar programmes, their different content and the variation in standards expected, concern over 'whether this MBA is a good one, which employers will respect' is justified. In the USA 'rankings' of business schools are published by both *Business Week* and *US News and World Report*. Although there are arguments about the validity of the methods used, such rankings are influential. There is as yet no equivalent ranking for European schools.

In the USA, business schools also need to gain accreditation. The main body performing this is the AACSB, which now operates in Europe as well. In the UK, where universities are deemed to be of an acceptable standard, accreditation is not essential although non-universities *will* need to have programmes validated. Because of the variability of MBA programmes, the fact that a programme has been accredited is valued by potential students, and therefore sought by universities. The best-known UK body is AMBA. This also accredits some programmes elsewhere in Europe. As well as being widely recognised as a 'seal of approval', AMBA accreditation gives students access to the special loan scheme already described, and provides networking opportunities and other services through an active alumni association.

Accreditation is a developing field within Europe. The US-based International Association for Management Education, the AACSB, has extended its operations into Europe. Perhaps in response, the European Foundation for Management Development (Efmd) has launched EQUAL, an international association of quality assessment and accreditation agencies in the field of European management development. EQUAL has developed a European Quality Improvement System (EQUIS),which has developed a system of quality benchmarking which can be used for audit, or as a 'stamp of approval' through an accreditation process.

In the UK, intending students can gain information about the general credibility of a business school by finding how it scored in the most recent Research Assessment Exercise, and how it was rated in the Higher Education Funding Council's assessment of teaching. Schools that have received high scores will tend to include this information in publicity material. You need to treat such information with a degree of caution. The research will not necessarily inform the teaching you receive, although academics may argue strongly to the contrary. And while schools receiving bad teaching assessments are best avoided, given that the assessment teams vary from school to school, and it is difficult therefore to calibrate assessments, the difference between very good and satisfactory ratings may be elusive.

Indeed, you need to use all 'official' information about credibility with a degree of caution. A business school with a high US ranking, or a top research ranking, while undoubtedly credible, may still not be the best programme for you. A school with a lower, though still good ranking might offer a programme more suited to your situation, or provide more of the sort of support that you need in order to do well.

Employers, too, may have their own preferences with respect to MBAs. Those which influence sponsoring decisions may be different from those which influence hiring ones. It is impossible to predict what these will be – there is no alternative to doing a little research. In-company values, preferences and prejudices should be fairly easy to elicit. If you are aiming at an eventual job in another organisation or sector you may need to do some investigating for yourself.

Teaching approach

The approach to teaching will depend greatly upon the location of a programme on the dimensions already outlined. If the programme is highly academic there may be a strong emphasis on the relative merits of different theories and different methods, with a strong reliance on input from lecturers or textbooks. If there is a more practical orientation the programme may focus more on the application of such theories to the real world, and on the development of transferable skills. If so there is likely to be more discussion of students' own experience, and assessment is more likely to be based on real situations encountered by the students.

There is an increasing emphasis on transferable skills in higher education generally. A possible list of such skills which any MBA programme might develop, albeit in different proportions, is:

- numeracy and analytical skills – through case studies and projects
- written presentation skills – through assignments and project reports
- oral presentation skills – through presentations on group work
- team skills – through group work on cases and projects
- IT skills – through use of word processing and graphics, spreadsheets, databases, the World Wide Web, and electronic conferencing
- negotiation and other consultancy skills – through an in-company project
- personal skills (self-organisation and time management) – through meeting programme demands
- learning skills and self-awareness – through a continuous process of challenging assumptions and reflection on practice.

Your own needs with respect to these skills will form an individual profile: an ideal programme will match this fairly closely.

Another element of teaching approach which will be important is the degree of 'spoonfeeding'. There are two aspects to this, one good, one bad. If you are told what to think, and what to reproduce in exams, this is not good. An MBA should be developing your ability to think for yourself. But some institutions are very much better than others at providing you with the information and materials you need in order to study efficiently, and this sort of 'spoonfeeding' is all to the good for the majority of pressured students.

Teaching media

Although in one sense a subset of teaching approach, the use of media in teaching is so important it warrants a separate section. Information and communication technologies (ICTs), in particular, have become a transforming force in management and management education, the full effects of which have yet to be envisaged. These developments have had an effect on the curriculum, with e-commerce and knowledge management courses highly popular at present. More importantly, they have impacted upon almost all the basic components of conventional teaching.

Consider the traditional 'building blocks' of education. Information was transmitted by a lecturer or in a textbook. Understanding was increased through questions to the lecturer and seminar discussion, and tested in examinations. The physical presence of student in lecture room or library was essential.

Distance learning allowed this physical presence to be dispensed with. 'Lectures' were transformed into printed workbooks and/or video and audio tapes, and necessary readings often collected into specially compiled books and mailed to students. Telephone and letters allowed students to receive answers to specific questions. There might be 'telephone tutorials' with several students linked to tutors.

As noted, developments in ICTs are taking this tentative step towards distance very much further. E-mail is now a standard communication channel between students and tutors, far easier than waiting outside someone's door or playing telephone tag. Instead of printed texts, materials can be distributed electronically. Web pages can hold tests which you sit at your leisure, and from which you receive automatic feedback. You can submit substantial assignments electronically and receive tutor comments almost immediately. Computer conferences allow synchronous or asynchronous 'discussion' between students, and it is now fairly easy to add an audio component, making such interaction much closer to a traditional seminar. Via the Internet you can attend 'lectures', and access not only the equivalent of a first-class library, but also an almost infinite variety of more transient and current (albeit often less reliable) materials.

Opinions are at present divided on how best to exploit the technical options for teaching. The latest ICT developments can be sources of frustration as well as excitement. Equipment or software incompatibilities may waste hours or even days of valuable time. Searching the World Wide Web without some guidance can positively devour time, and produce results ranging from amazingly good to worthless. Trying to study quantities of material directly from a screen is for many far more difficult than working from good quality print. Conferencing with fellow students round the globe can produce fascinating insights, but on the whole is less exciting than a good face-to-face debate followed by a visit to the pub.

Because your own situation and preferences are important here, and things are changing so quickly, this is another dimension which you will need to research carefully when making your choice. Bear in mind the quality of materials and interaction in the media used, the likely learning efficiency, and whether you will feel comfortable with, and enjoy using, the different media on offer.

SUMMARY

- MBAs and other management Master's programmes vary in length (duration and size), degree of specialisation and strategic focus.

- The original US MBA was generalist, analytical, strategically focused and highly competitive.

- In Europe a clear split has developed between programmes like this, normally offered full-time, and more practical skills-oriented programmes, aimed at slightly older, more experienced managers, and normally offered via distance learning or other part-time mode. The latter type is now dominant.

- Increasing numbers of specialist MBAs or other Master's programmes in specialist management areas are now available.

- ICTs are transforming management education in many ways, but not all of these are universally perceived as improvements upon more traditional media.

- Transferable skills you can reasonably expect an MBA to develop include: learning skills, numerical and analytical skills, written and oral presentation skills, problem-solving skills, leadership and team-working skills, IT skills, consultancy skills, personal management skills and perhaps entrepreneurial skills.

Further information

Bickerstaff, G. (ed.) (1999) *Which MBA? A critical guide to programmes in Europe and the USA* (11th edn), The Economist Publications.

Kelly, F.J. and Kelly, H.M. (1986) *What They Really Teach You at the Harvard Business School*, Grafton Books. This is an entertaining read, giving a good flavour of a traditional programme and introducing many of the concepts you are likely to encounter.

MBA Casebook 99 (1999 or later editions), Hobsons International. This has substantial editorial material relevant to those considering MBA study in a range of countries, with (promotional) information about a wide range of schools.

The Official MBA Handbook 1999/2000 (15th edn) (1999, or later editions), Financial Times Prentice Hall. This is the guide to business schools produced by AMBA, and again has useful editorial content as well as a CD-ROM.

Robinson, P. (1994) *Snapshots from Hell: the making of an MBA*, Nicholas Brealey. This is also entertaining, though it may risk discouraging you from pursuing a traditional programme.

Useful websites are given on the companion website at www.booksites.net/cameron.

3 Choosing a Master's programme

Objectives

By the end of this chapter you should:

- see the extent to which obtaining an MBA or similar qualification could help you achieve your wider life objectives
- understand the constraints limiting your freedom of choice concerning management courses
- have identified the most important features, from your particular perspective, of a management course
- be in a position to make an informed choice of course in the light of your analysis.

INTRODUCTION

If you have already registered for a course of study, skip this chapter. If, however, you have not yet decided whether an MBA or similar programme is a good idea you need to think hard before reaching a conclusion. A management qualification requires an enormous investment of effort. Unless your employer supports you financially, it represents a large cash investment too. To maximise the return on that investment, you should first think very carefully about your own objectives in seeking a qualification, and the type of course which is most likely to enable you to meet these objectives.

You will need to decide, first, whether an MBA or a more specialist Master's degree is the best route to your objectives. Whatever qualification you choose you will need to decide between full- and part-time study. If the latter, you will need to compare the relative merits of face-to-face or distance provision. Once you have decided on the mode of study, you will wish to evaluate possible institutions, to see which offers a course, and support, best suited to your needs.

ASSESSING YOUR PRESENT POSITION AND GOALS

From the previous chapter you should now be aware of the shifts taking place in the management development environment, and of the range of programmes that have developed in response to these. The dimensions of variation in these are so many that choice is far from straightforward. However if you think carefully about *why* you want to study it will help you decide upon what is best for you. Most of the rational problem-solving and planning techniques taught on an MBA are elaborations on the simple theme of:

- establish where you are now
- decide where you want to be
- identify possible routes from the first to the second
- select the best route
- follow it.

So common is this model, and so frequently does it appear wearing but slightly refurbished clothing, that I have come to think of it as the 'Universal Management Paradigm' (the UMP). A final step of checking progress may be added.

In this case 'where you are now' does not mean merely what job you are in, though this is probably an important element. It encompasses *all* relevant aspects of your life, your management experience, qualifications, knowledge, strengths and weaknesses, family environment, sources of finance, leisure interests, and anything that could affect, or be affected by, your proposed studies.

ACTIVITY

Take a large sheet of paper and find some way of representing your current situation as it relates to management study. The diagramming chapter (Chapter 10) of this Handbook gives some ways of mapping information if you feel this request is difficult, or Fig. 3.1 shows one potential student's attempt.

Having mapped features of your current situation, think about what it is important to you to *achieve* in the medium term, say the next seven years. Again do not restrict your consideration to your career. You may find that some of your objectives can be broken down to show sub-goals which need to be reached in order to achieve the higher-order objective. A useful technique for representing such hierarchies of objectives is the *objectives tree*. Such trees look like the familiar organisation chart, but show goals instead of management roles. They are drawn from the top downwards. You start with what seems to you an important goal and put it at the top of the tree. Then you think about all the things that you need to achieve in order to realise your main goal, and put them in at the next level down. For each of these you consider necessary sub-goals and so on downwards until you have gone as far as it makes sense to go. Figure 3.2 gives an example.

You will probably have a number of different objectives in life, and for each of these you can construct a different tree.

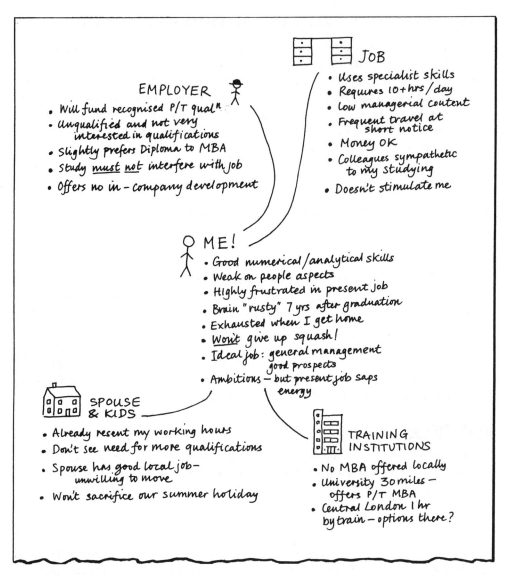

Fig. 3.1 Student map of factors relevant to choice of a Master's level programme

---

ACTIVITY

Take more large pieces of paper, and draw objective trees for all the major goals in your life. Highlight any conflicts between sub-goals, either on a single tree or between trees.

Conflicts between objectives are common. For example, you might have one goal of getting into the squash club's first team, which would require a lot of practice and coaching, and another of obtaining a part-time MBA which would also be very time consuming. If a third objective is to obtain rapid promotion at work, which will mean making a heavy input to your job, then there is an obvious conflict.

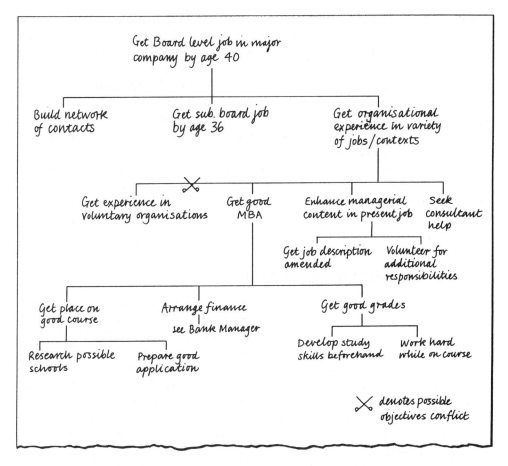

Fig. 3.2 Hierarchy of career-related objectives for an intending Master's level student

You will need to think about how to handle such conflicts. One whole set of objectives may need to be put aside until another is achieved. Figure 3.2, for example, showed an example of a single objective tree related to career.

CHOOSING THE BEST ROUTE

Having constructed your objectives trees you are now in a position to ask yourself how central a postgraduate management qualification is to your most important objectives, and whether it will conflict with some of these. You may also be able to see alternative routes to your objectives that might generate fewer conflicts. For example, if the main block to achieving your objectives is the attitude of your current employer, a judicious change of jobs might be a quicker, and cheaper alternative. If you are unsure about your academic abilities, it might also be safer.

Any management qualification, and this is particularly true of an MBA or other Master's level study, demands a certain amount of pain and self-denial. It is likely to take over your life for the duration, allowing little space for food and sleep, let alone the higher pleasures. It should be undertaken only if you are absolutely sure that it is important enough to you to obtain the qualification that the sacrifices required will be worthwhile. If this book causes you to realise that you do not really want an MBA, it will have saved you hundreds of times its purchase price.

Of course, my livelihood, and that of many of my friends, depends on large numbers of managers being convinced that they really do want a management qualification, so I hope that you will wish to proceed. Naturally I cannot claim to be unbiased in this, but the vast majority of my students claim that the effort is indeed enormously worthwhile.

If you *are* convinced that a management qualification will help you achieve your longer-term objectives, you need first to decide whether to start with a certificate and/or diploma, to obtain a professional qualification or to enrol on a direct entry MBA or a specialist Master's programme at the outset. Relevant considerations are described below.

Your academic background and ability

If you have not studied at university level before, you may find it difficult adjusting to the pace of study. You will be thrust into the demands of course content at the same time as having to develop new learning skills. This is particularly likely if you choose one of the more academically focused programmes. Even if, by heroic effort, you gain the qualification, the effort and stress involved may be disproportionate to any benefits gained in terms of self-development. An MBA which offers the alternative of a more practically based diploma as its first part might take a little longer or be less strategically focused, but you might gain far more from the experience. During the more skills-based early part of the programme you would be developing a wide range of transferable skills, including learning skills that will make the remainder of your MBA courses much more rewarding.

If you are in a specialist management role, such as finance, human resources or marketing, and planning to continue in that area for several years, one option is to gain a relevant professional qualification. Many of the professional bodies have revised their syllabuses, expanding their general management content. Where this is the case the qualification may not only serve as meeting the entry requirements for an MBA programme, but also, if overlap in content and teaching method is sufficient, count for some credit exemption. If you are undecided, check both with your own organisation as to which they would find most useful, and with likely business schools regarding their position on recognition of your intended professional qualification. You may wish to consider a specialist MBA or an MA or MSc in your specialism.

If your background already includes a Diploma in Management Studies (DMS) or a management-related professional qualification, you will obviously want to explore the extent to which this will gain you exemption from parts of the course duplicating your previous study. This will vary from institution to institution, and will depend on the recency of your qualification, as well as the structure of the MBA you are considering. Exemptions will be less likely for the more strategically focused MBAs than for the 'top-up' variety.

You may know that your background includes specific areas of weakness. (Mathematics is one such area which bothers many potential students, though this Handbook will attempt to convince them that this concern may not be justified.) If so, you will wish to explore the extent to which compulsory components of possible MBAs will require you to be competent in the areas about which you are most worried.

Your managerial experience

If you have *no* managerial experience (note that job title is not a reliable guide here – many managers are not labelled as such, but still perform a managerial function), you may wish to defer your studies until you have spent a year or two struggling with the problems that constitute a manager's job. It is perfectly possible to teach management as a theoretical subject – indeed undergraduate management degrees now attract large numbers of students. But those who study management *after* they have gained some managerial experience find their studies far more exciting than do those lacking such experience. If you have grappled with a seemingly intractable problem for some time, and are then offered a conceptual tool which will help you out of your difficulties, you are extremely grateful for that tool. If you didn't know about the difficulty, the concept may be seen merely as one more thing to learn.

If you *do* decide that an MBA is the best route out of a non-managerial job and into the career you always wanted, you would probably find that, paradoxical as this may seem, a more theoretical and strategically based MBA will suit you better. Practical skills development on an MBA is most effective if you can practise the skills in parallel with the course. Part-time and distance courses offer splendid opportunities for practice for those already in managerial jobs. These are rather wasted on students who are not in a position to take advantage of them. For non-managers there are definite advantages in considering a full-time course, if this is at all feasible. The disadvantage relative to other students will be less (though even on full-time courses their prior management experience will be a tremendous asset). Also full-time institutions, especially the longer established ones, tend to offer more help with finding jobs after the course, an important consideration in times when management openings are restricted, even for MBA graduates.

Your career objectives

If you are fairly new to management, or you are an experienced middle manager, wanting primarily to improve your current performance, rather than to progress with all possible speed to a position as Chief Executive, you will probably be happier with one of the more practically orientated courses, and one on which the majority of students have a considerable degree of managerial experience. However, if you are seeking intellectual stimulation, and particularly if you are aiming at senior management, you would need to check that any practical orientation was not at the expense of adequate consideration of strategy.

If you are sure that your future lies within a specific function, organisation or sector, then one of the more specialised MBAs, or even a management-related MSc, may be your choice. The price you will pay in terms of reduced 'portability' may be more than compensated for by the added depth to which an area can be studied. The more generalist MBAs are strong on breadth, and excellent for those who do not know in which ways their career is likely to develop, but those with specialist interests may find that their coverage of favourite areas is necessarily somewhat superficial.

If you are strongly ambitious you will need to look seriously at the small number of 'prestige' MBA institutions in this country, or indeed consider going overseas. Although there is a fair degree of consensus as to the 'best' MBAs, different employers may have slightly different orders of preference, and you might wish to find out the prevailing views of the organisations which you would most like to join. You would certainly wish to ensure that your chosen MBA had a strong strategic focus.

Your preferred mode of study

The three main options, full-time; part-time face-to-face; and distance learning, also part-time, were outlined in the previous chapter. In the following discussion 'part-time' will normally be used to refer to the face-to-face variety, unless indicated to the contrary.

Full-time study has major advantages in terms of allowing you to immerse yourself single-mindedly in the course. You will normally be studying at an institution with ready access to all the library, computing and other facilities that you are likely to need. There will be ample opportunity for contact with faculty members, and even more contact with fellow students. Their backgrounds will depend on the admissions policy of the institution, but they are likely to constitute an enormously rich resource in terms of information and organisational experience, they may come from many different countries, and there should be plenty of scope for you to benefit from this.

Traditional teaching methods of lectures and case study discussion can be employed, and you may, additionally, be seconded to a co-operating employer for some part of the course, sometimes overseas, thus allowing you to gain valuable insight into how another organisation operates. If the course emphasises skills development there will be ample scope for role play and other simulations.

You will get to know many of your fellow students very well. This can form the basis for mutually supportive networks throughout your career. Indeed, when Japanese companies started to sponsor employees on US MBA programmes the two reasons they gave for this were to improve their spoken English, and to develop networks and contacts with potentially influential Americans. Networks may traditionally have been less central to business in the European culture, but they are now becoming increasingly important.

Employers will normally advertise opportunities within the school or visit to interview potential graduates. Or your secondment may develop into a job offer.

Full-time courses can be very hard work, but are usually stimulating and rewarding, and some types of learning can be highly effective on this type of course. There are, however, some fairly obvious disadvantages.

Few employers will finance more than a handful of their highest-fliers on full-time courses. You are therefore likely to have to take leave of absence or resign. This means that you will have to find the substantial fees charged while forgoing your normal salary. Loans can be obtained fairly easily for this, but if you have dependants the decision to take such a step can be a difficult one. It is no longer as easy as it once was for new MBA graduates to find suitably challenging and rewarding jobs. Even if the financial considerations do not concern you, you may not wish to leave a job that you really enjoy.

Full-time study, particularly at a distance from home, may entail considerable dislocation of family life. Although a year is not long, it can seem an eternity to a partner or child left at home with little support while you are having an exciting, stimulating, developmental experience elsewhere.

Less obviously, while full-time study lends itself admirably to the gaining of knowledge, it does not allow you the opportunity to experiment with concepts and techniques in a real working environment. Case studies offer few advantages in this respect when compared with on-the-job experience as a vehicle for developing the more competence-based aspects of the course. They do not allow students to *apply* their learning within a short period of acquiring it.

It may be for this reason that past full-time students often say that there is much of their MBA which they have *never* put into practice. While this must to some extent reflect the relevance of their syllabus, at least part of the reason may be that if the more difficult techniques are not practised while 'fresh', there will be insufficient impetus ever to make the effort of applying them. By the end of a year's full-time course a student's head may feel completely stuffed with all that has been covered. It is not surprising that some of this material may be pushed to the back, never to appear again.

Thus, although full-time study has many advantages, it is not *necessarily* the best route, even for those with indulgent employers or for whom money is not a major consideration. To decide whether this route is the best for you, you will need to reflect on how well the characteristics of full-time learning match your personal situation, and your most important objectives, as mapped in the earlier activities.

Part-time face-to-face teaching is a method adopted by many business schools with established full-time programmes. It allows them to increase the accessibility of their courses, attracting students within reasonable travelling distance who are not in a position to give up their jobs in order to study. The teaching approach is normally similar to that on full-time courses, although with lectures concentrated into a shorter period, perhaps one afternoon and evening a week, there will necessarily be less opportunity for group working and discussion.

Advantages are that regular attendance imposes its own discipline, and allows a reasonable amount of contact with faculty and other students. Library, IT and other facilities will be available, although opening hours are not always suited to part-time students. The fact that you can continue to perform your normal job not only protects your income but also allows tremendous advantages in terms of making possible the immediate application of what is taught on the course. (This advantage obviously applies equally to distance learning.)

Disadvantages are that your job must allow regular attendance, usually at least some of this during normal working hours. Many employers are unwilling to allow this, or your job may be prone to crises or require frequent travel. In either case, it may be impossible to ensure that you will be free on a regular basis. The need for regular attendance also means that if there is no suitable course nearby, a lot of time may be needed for travelling to classes.

Less obvious disadvantages include the possibility that the course may not be taught by the same lecturers as the full-time course, as they may be unwilling to work the unsocial hours required. While the alternative lecturers may be excellent, this is not always the case. You would need to find out about the quality of teaching if at all possible.

Executive programmes are a variant of part-time face-to-face provision. Such programmes concentrate the teaching into longer, more widely spaced blocks than the normal weekly part-time offering. There is wide variation in the length of the blocks. They might be two days, or a month, or occasionally even longer. Between the face-to-face blocks you are expected to work alone, while continuing with your normal job. Obviously there is considerable disruption to your regular job with this form of provision, and it is not feasible without full employer support. The disruption is less than with a full-time course, however, and does allow some of the advantages of full-time study. There is more room for intensive contact with faculty and other students, and students from a much wider geographic base can be assembled. It is possible for a UK manager to study on a French executive programme, or for an Italian manager to study on a UK programme.

The limited face-to-face teaching on either form of part-time course will need to be supplemented by considerable private study, which will require self-discipline, and will be prone to disruption by conflicting demands from the job and elsewhere. If the main focus of an institution is full-time teaching, there may have been little thought given to the support part-time students need to ensure that their private study is effective. The 'give them a reading list and let them get on with it' approach is still all too frequent. But part-time students have little time to chase books that are not readily available. Often if the book *is* located, it turns out that only a small part of it was relevant after all, and that part not particularly good. There may, too, be little attention given to study skills development. (It was precisely this identified need that led to the production of this Handbook.)

One of the biggest disadvantages is, of course, the continual conflict between course and job demands. Part-time students *cannot* be single-minded in their studies. Good time management can help, but the problem will never go away entirely. The other inevitable problem is that the course will necessarily take longer than a full-time course covering the same ground, so motivation will need to be sustained over several years.

If you are fairly sure that part-time study *is* the most appropriate route to satisfying your objectives, you will obviously want to check out the syllabuses of possible courses. You might additionally wish to ask possible institutions any of the following questions which are not clearly answered in their brochures:

■ What attendance is required? (Not just for classes, but for any residential component, examinations, etc.)

- What additional costs will any residential requirement incur?
- Who actually teaches the courses?
- What flexibility is there if you hit a prolonged crisis at work or home?
- What support is there if you find any part of the course difficult?
- What additional study time is likely to be needed over and above class attendance?
- How many books etc. are you likely to need?
- Will these need to be bought, or are there sufficient copies in the library?
- Will you need your own PC and modem? If so, what software will you need to run and how powerful a machine do you need?

As a check on the answers you receive, you might also enquire about dropout rates, and pass rates in previous cohorts of students.

Distance learning is the most dramatic development in management education in recent years. Indeed, the majority of part-time MBA students are now on distance learning programmes. You may not feel that full-time study would be appropriate. A suitable part-time course may not be available locally. An executive programme may be impracticable or unattractive. You may be in the sort of job where demands are unpredictable or variable. It may be simply that you are not yet convinced that these more traditional types of teaching are exactly what you want. In any of these cases you should think seriously about the possibilities of a distance-taught MBA.

A good distance learning course will provide you with all the materials you need for your study, saving you hours of time wasted in chasing elusive materials. Furthermore, these materials should be written specifically for the course. Good distance learning materials are designed in such a way as to make individual study as easy and rewarding as possible. They are well laid out, to avoid eye-strain; teaching objectives are made very clear so that you know what should be achieved by the end of the part of the course being worked upon; material is broken up into 'chunks' which can normally be studied at a single sitting; a study calendar is provided so that you know what should be achieved by each point of the course. Most importantly, the material itself is as interactive as possible, asking you at regular intervals to think about what has just been read, and apply it to your own job context. There should also be regular exercises and self-test questions, with answers provided, so that you can ensure that you understand each part of the material before progressing to the next.

Written text will be supplemented by video and audio materials, either to allow 'expert' lectures (a video has the advantage of allowing replay of any difficult bits!) or as a vehicle for providing case study materials. There will probably be software provided, and there may be CD-ROM based materials. You may additionally have access to on-line databases via the Internet, and the opportunity to participate in computer conferences with other students and teaching staff.

In addition to teaching materials, a good distance course will provide substantial personal tuition, with assignments submitted to a tutor who will provide written comments in return, and someone, ideally that same tutor, who is available by phone to help you with any difficulties encountered, whether in the course material or the assignment requirements, with more general study problems, or to provide support and advice if the clash between course and other demands becomes unmanageable. Ideally there will be deadlines for the submission of written work. Flexibility is great in theory, but without interim deadlines many students find that they are unable to maintain the pace of work required, and may fail to complete the course.

While some courses may be capable of being taught solely at a distance, in many areas of management education there is much to be gained from at least some face-to-face teaching. It would be difficult to learn how to interview, for example, with *no* face-to-face component. And any business policy course which did not provide opportunities for discussing options with other students would be greatly impoverished. While such interactions can take place electronically, most students prefer at least some of this discussion to take place in groups. Good distance-taught courses will therefore include a limited face-to-face component, either in the form of one-day workshops or shorter tutorials, with probably a small residential component as well.

The advantages of distance learning include the obvious one of flexibility. You are not tied to regular class attendance, and can pursue your studies whether on a plane to the States or sitting on an oil rig in the North Sea. If you know that you have periods at work when all hell breaks loose and you are working 16 or more hours per day every day, then you can get ahead in your studies in the slack periods, and put them to one side during the times of high demand.

A major advantage for your employer (and for you if your employer doesn't believe in management development or qualifications) is that no time off work is required, except perhaps for examinations and any residential course component. Distance learning should be compatible with any job that does not make totally unreasonable demands on your time.

There is also the major advantage, shared with other part-time courses, that you are instantly able to put into practice what you learn. In this way new ideas and techniques will become part of your way of working as you go through your course, rather than mere theory to be learnt for an exam and then forgotten. Some distance providers would argue that this means that they were developing competence at work long before NVQs were established!

The worries that many people have before starting distance learning concern the difficulty of sustaining motivation when working alone, and the lack of interaction with fellow students. The motivation problem can be minimised by well-designed materials. Students on courses with high student numbers may well find others on the same course living near to them, so that it is possible for them to make their own opportunities for face-to-face interaction. Computer conferencing offers further interactive possibilities. However there may still be less interaction than some would like.

Possibly more of a problem is the cost of distance courses. While it is *possible* to produce cheap materials, by relying heavily on existing textbooks and offering little by way of tuition or student support, such courses are likely to suffer from high dropout rates, and are unlikely to be appropriate to the competence development emphasis that is becoming more important today. The cost differential between part-time face-to-face and distance learning becomes less significant if loss of working time is added to the cost of a part-time course. The differential then vanishes. Part-time courses are in any case increasing in price at a rate rather greater than distance courses. But if you are paying for yourself, then loss of working time is not a compensating factor, and you might choose a part-time course on financial grounds alone.

Distance-learning courses have particular problems for students not currently working as managers. Because much of the traditional case study discussion work may be replaced by assignments requiring you to analyse aspects of your own organisation, you will have difficulty if you do not work in a suitable organisation, or if your position in it is such that access to information is difficult. If you are in this situation you should discuss requirements carefully with any intended distance provider, to see whether you would be at an unreasonable disadvantage.

If you are considering distance learning, you might find it helpful to ask possible institutions the following questions in addition to those listed under part-time face-to-face:

- What proportion of the materials are specially written?
- What is the quality of the specially written materials? (Inspect some of this if at all possible.)
- How many students are enrolled, in what area? (This will determine whether you will have a chance of working informally with students.)
- How much face-to face contact is there?
- What use is made of electronic communication?
- How much feedback is given on written assignments?
- Do you have access to telephone, fax or e-mail help in cases of academic difficulty?
- Is there any local support available, and if so, what?

CHOOSING BETWEEN INSTITUTIONS

Once you have a clear idea of what you are looking for in general terms, you will need to decide which institution offers you the best programme. It is not always easy to obtain the information you want, but several avenues are open. Most institutions will be happy to answer questions by phone, though you may need to persist in order to go beyond the routine enquiry clerk and contact someone who can answer the more detailed, less administrative, questions that you wish to put. Present and past students can be very enlightening. See whether there are any within your own organisation, or ask the institution how you might contact students. Syllabuses and prospectuses can give some information, but they are primarily written to sell you the course, rather than convey detailed information. And while prospectuses are not dishonest, they are unlikely to go out of their way to highlight possible disadvantages.

It *is* important to check on the credibility of your intended course. While rankings are available for US business schools, there is no accepted ranking system for those in Europe. Nevertheless European business schools vary widely in the quality, as well as the nature of what they offer. Qualifications from some will be highly regarded, whereas those from others will be deemed worthless by the majority of informed employers.

You can obtain a range of 'guides' to business schools, but some of these are little more than collections of promotional material. As all the schools featured sound wonderful, they are little help in evaluating relative credibility.

There are two sources of information in the UK. The Higher Education Funding Councils assess business schools on their teaching quality (across all the programmes they offer). You can ask schools for information on their assessment. This will provide some guidance, but is a fairly blunt instrument. Employers are not greatly concerned with quality of teaching, though it may impact upon your experience of the course, and upon quality of graduates, so it does have an indirect effect upon credibility.

You can also ask for information about their research rating – again this is assessed at intervals. A high rating in research *does* tend to be associated with business school credibility, though it may not be associated with quality of teaching! Teaching and research may be done by different people.

One useful source of information is the Association of MBAs (AMBA). This accredits some programmes, and employers may ask if your MBA was from one of these. Furthermore if studying on such a programme you will have access to certain loan schemes not generally available, and on graduation will be eligible to join AMBA and attend local meetings. However, at present AMBA accredits only generalist MBAs. You might need to look carefully at a non-accredited generalist MBA, but non-accreditation of a specialist programme is no indication of poor quality.

Others accrediting programmes in Europe include the AACSB, the primary US accrediting body, and EQUIS, the quality improvement arm of the European Foundation for Management Development (Efmd).

Useful information sources, including the guide produced by AMBA, are listed at the end of the chapter. Because this is an area where information changes fairly rapidly you will find it invaluable to seek for information electronically. Guides will give links to home pages of programmes featured, so that you can be sure that your information is as up to date as the information currently being shown by the institutions concerned.

In choosing between institutions, quality and credibility will be as important as the nature of the programmes offered, and therefore something you need to research carefully. The 1990s saw a major expansion in the number of institutions offering postgraduate management courses, MBAs in particular, often under franchise arrangements from other institutions. Not all of these arrangements have yet settled down. Some overseas 'universities' award qualifications on very dubious authority. Given the significance of the investment you are considering you really do need to investigate possible course providers thoroughly. This will ensure that the course you choose will be an exciting developmental experience, and the qualification you gain will be widely respected.

SUMMARY

- You should think carefully about whether postgraduate management study is the best route to your own personal objectives.

- You should decide whether you want a more traditional, academically based course, or one emphasising competence development.

- You should consider whether a generalist or a specialist qualification is more appropriate.

- You should consider the relative merits of full-time, part-time face-to-face or distance learning before coming to a decision.

- The experience, reputation and track record of any institution should be an important consideration.

Further information

Bickerstaff, G. (ed.) (1999) *Which MBA? A critical guide to programmes in Europe and the USA* (11th edn), The Economist Publications. This gives a wider, albeit more expensive view.

The Official MBA Handbook 1999/2000 (15th edn) (1999, or later editions), Financial Times Prentice Hall. This gives detailed information on AMBA-accredited MBAs, and includes a CD-ROM.

Useful websites are given on the companion website at www.booksites.net/cameron.

PRE-COURSE PREPARATION

4 Preparing for Master's level study

Objectives

By the end of this chapter you should:

- understand the relationship between your course and your job, and thought how this might best be exploited
- recognise the symptoms of stress and be aware of techniques for managing it
- be aware of the distinctions between aggression, avoidance and assertion, and have a plan for developing your own assertiveness
- have assessed the adequacy of your computing skills and be developing a plan to address any inadequacies.

INTRODUCTION

You should now be fully aware of the size of the step you are taking in starting on a Master's level management programme, and of the investment of both money and personal effort involved. While the potential gain is enormous, so too are the risks, both to your self-esteem and to your credibility at work, if your study is public knowledge. You may have time before your programme starts, whether because it will take time to arrange sponsorship, or because the course does not start for some months, or for some other reason. If so, you will probably wish to use that time to maximise your chances of success on the programme, both in terms of extracting the maximum learning from the experience, and of gaining the qualification.

Most of the rest of the book, as a quick scan in Chapter 1 will have shown you, can be used to help you prepare for success. Rather than try to anticipate subsequent chapters, here we address four important areas not covered elsewhere. The first of these concerns gaining the support of your organisation. This can make your path through the course much smoother and more productive, even if it does not include financial support. The other areas concern personal skills not restricted to management study, but highly relevant to them. The first two, managing stress and assertiveness skills, will be invaluable to you at times when demands of course and work conflict. The third, IT skills, are of near-universal importance, but will almost certainly be called upon if you are to take advantage of learning resources on your course. While it is obviously beyond the scope of a single chapter to take you from PC illiteracy to a high level of skill, the chapter aims to explain to the minority who need it why it is important that they take the necessary steps themselves. Finally there are suggestions as to things you might usefully read while waiting for your course to start.

GAINING ORGANISATIONAL SUPPORT

Your motivation for studying is likely to include a desire to improve at your job, and a significant part of your learning is likely to be directed towards learning to apply concepts to organisational contexts, prime among which must be your own organisation. Chapter 5 on 'The time problem' argues forcibly for negotiation with your superior to ensure that you will have time available for study for the duration of the course. But there is much more than this to be gained, for you and for your organisation from a closer involvement of your organisation if this is possible.

Of course, it may be that you are studying secretly, or overtly but with no support from your employers. In this case, you will probably be unable to follow the suggestions in this section. But if your employers are interested in your studies, and particularly if they are sponsoring you in these, then it is worth devoting at least some of your preparation to discussing ways in which organisational support might be made available.

Potential sources

There are at least four obvious sources of organisational support:

- the HR or training manager
- your own manager
- a mentor
- your team.

As the person with an interest in management development in the organisation as a whole, the training or HR manager should be in a position to support you in many ways. This may be by arranging access to others in the organisation when you need information for assignments, by discussing possible projects, by taking your part if your line manager starts to overload you once the course has started, by helping you to obtain any resources you may need, or by putting you in touch with people in your organisation who have gained, or are currently working towards, an MBA. There may be supplementary short courses which you could usefully attend. Just keeping in touch, and making sure that you are getting on satisfactorily and not encountering any serious problems can be helpful. It is therefore worth keeping in close touch with your management training department from the point at which you start considering an MBA or other qualification. Discuss with them the sorts of help which the organisation can offer, and keep them in the picture as your course progresses.

Your immediate boss is another source of potential help, not merely in avoiding overload, but in helping you to see how what you are learning relates to your organisation. You may well be working at a level below that at which strategy is developed, and a perspective from slightly higher up the organisation may enable you to link theory with practice in your own case. If your boss is sympathetic to your pursuit of a qualification, then keep in close touch, trying, if possible, to schedule regular discussions on your progress, as well as getting permission to raise particular queries as they arise. There are several potential benefits to your boss. First, this should help you to gain more from the course and thus to be a more useful subordinate. Second, the discussions about how to apply the course should be beneficial to both of you. If your boss has a qualification, supporting you may act as a useful reminder of previous learning, and a stimulus to its continued application. If not, there is scope for shared learning ...

You may find, however, that the relationship you have with your boss does not allow this sort of discussion. The boss–subordinate relationship can be fraught, and many people do not feel comfortable about relaxing, and being completely honest, with the person who may have power over their career. If this is the case, there is much to be said for the use of a *mentor*. Your organisation may well have a mentoring scheme in operation. If you already have one, you should take pains to involve your mentor from the start in your thinking about an MBA.

If you do not have a mentor yet, see whether you can be assigned one, even if your organisation does not have such a scheme. Discuss with your training manager whether the idea might be used as a source of support to you during your studies. Mentoring means that you are linked to a particular senior manager, at least one level above you, but not in a line relationship. Thus you gain the advantages of being able to discuss your personal and career development with someone higher in the organisation.

Because of their senior position, mentors can be expected to have a better understanding of the organisational context, and of policy development issues than you do yourself. But because a mentor is not in a direct line relationship to you, you avoid the disadvantages which stem from trying to discuss developmental issues (and by implication your weaknesses) with someone directly responsible for your performance. A mentor from a slightly different part of the organisation will also avoid the narrow perspective that might arise if these discussions took place with your own immediate superior. Thus a mentor takes an interest in your progress, and at the same time is senior enough to help you to increase your understanding of organisational issues. Again because of their relative seniority, mentors are often able to gain you access to other senior people in the organisation if you need it.

Meeting regularly with this mentor to discuss your course, how it relates to your organisation, and how you might apply what you are learning to your job, can make the whole process of learning far more effective. It is thus in your organisation's interest to provide this sort of support, and you may find that even if the concept is new, it is welcomed.

Many managers find their own subordinates benefit greatly from involvement in their study, as well as acting as useful sounding boards. If your organisation uses

360° appraisal then you may be used to this sort of communication. If not, it may be worth experimenting to see whether your team are prepared to provide feedback on your ideas and assignments. One of my students used his own MBA as a framework for developing his team. He shared course concepts with them as he learned them, and then made opportunities for all to use them.

MANAGING STRESS

Managing stress is a fashionable topic, but none the less important for that. While definitions of stress vary, a useful way of looking at it is to say that stress occurs when pressures on an individual are such that health and/or performance are impaired. Note that implicit in this definition is the possibility of variation between individuals in the level of pressure that constitutes stress, and of stress being caused by pressures that are too low as well as too high. Both these factors contribute to difficulty in predicting and detecting stress.

Let us examine the second point first. One of the most stressful periods in my life occurred when I started a new job, and was given nothing to do for weeks on end except 'familiarise' myself with a heap of files. You may well have experienced similar causes of stress. Indeed, for many people, holidays are very stressful! Thus an increase in pressure is welcomed. It is seen as a challenge, the job becomes more exciting, and the satisfactions to be gained from doing the job increase. Even very high levels of pressure can be positive, provided they are short term. Working through the night to meet an impossible deadline, and succeeding, can generate a tremendous high.

If the short-term crisis is extended, however, the positive aspects are rapidly overtaken by negative. Similarly, if there is a gradual increase in pressure over time, there will come a point where, if you stop to think, you will realise that your job is no longer an exciting challenge, but rather something to be endured. The trouble is that one of the many bad effects of stress is to make us less able to stop and think, both because we no longer have the time, and because our thought processes become somewhat impaired. Besides, the process may be so gradual that we are never aware of it. We go home a little later, and a little later … We cut back our running to twice a week, then once, then miss it altogether. Our partners are no longer keen to go out to dinner with us because we are too tired to be good company, and learn their own strategies for coping with our decreasing involvement at home.

As was said earlier, the fact that stress sets in at different levels for different people makes the situation worse. If we see others thriving on more work than we are coping with ourselves, we feel that we should *not* be stressed. Organisations may have cultures demanding that all managers exert the same superhuman efforts as their exceptional chief executives. Admitting to what might be seen as weakness is unacceptable in many working contexts.

The first stage, as with any problem, is looking in more detail at the situation. How, though, can you see whether you are stressed or not, given the difficulties described? The surest guide is how you feel. Also useful is assessment by others close to you.

ACTIVITY

Think of the last time you felt really good about your job, waking up each day looking forward to the challenges ahead, and arriving home at night looking forward to the leisure activities you had planned. Now think about how you felt this morning, and how you felt when you got home after work. It can't be *too* bad, or you would not have felt up to working on this chapter, but is the difference significant? Ask your partner, if you have one, if they think that you are under more stress than they think is ideal. Ask your colleagues if they think that you are ever irritable, or perhaps make errors of judgement, because of pressure. Think about your health. Do you have a number of minor ailments, perhaps more than you used to? Headaches, respiratory and digestive disorders, sleep problems, asthma and eczema are among ailments which can be made worse by stress. What is your alcohol intake? If you need a couple of drinks when you get home to help you relax, this suggests a fairly high stress level. Can you turn off thoughts of work when you are at home? Or do you continue to toss problems around half the night? Do you tend to eat too much, or find difficulty eating enough to maintain a reasonable weight?

Comment

Your answers to the above questions should make it possible for you to assess your own stress level, and to be fairly honest with yourself as to whether this is something you should be tackling even before the course starts. Even if stress is high but not excessive, you should perhaps be thinking about developing techniques for handling the increased levels once your course starts.

*If there is no problem, skip to the next chapter. If there **is** a potential problem, more analysis is needed. This should focus on the **causes** of the stress levels you are experiencing, and on the possible ways open to you for **coping** with stress when it is unavoidable.*

Common causes of stress include simple overload, in that you are being asked to do, or expecting yourself to do, more than is reasonable over a sustained period. If you feel that this is the source of most of your pressure, work carefully through Chapter 6. More effective use of your time at work, together with clear thought about your objectives, should do much to reduce your problems.

Another common reason is role ambiguity. You are not at all sure about what you are being required to do, or what your boss sees as a reasonable effort, or the goalposts seem to shift every time you are in a good position to shoot. Again, Chapter 6 will be of some help here, but if the fault lies in ambiguity further up the organisation, a solution may be beyond your grasp. You may either need to look for another job, itself a source of considerable stress, or set your own objectives and define your personal sense of success or failure in terms of these.

A simple clash of objectives can be almost as stressful as ambiguity. This may be between yourself and someone higher in the organisation, or between you and your subordinates, or between you and your family. They may well feel that your priorities do not include family life sufficiently high on the list. The clash may have moral overtones, for example if your company starts to operate in a way that is inconsistent with your personal value system.

ACTIVITY

Assess the major sources of stress in your life. Divide them into those that you can reduce, and those which you can do nothing about. (You will probably want to write this list privately.)

The next step is to find ways of reducing stressors which *can* be reduced. This will depend so much on your personal situation that discussion here would be inappropriate. In order to think as creatively as possible about options, you may find it helpful to discuss your situation with a good friend.

Once you have thought of action you could take, set yourself deadlines for actually *doing* something. And check that you are keeping to your deadlines. If you have involved friends in this, they will be helpful as progress chasers.

COPING WITH UNAVOIDABLE STRESS

The remaining action needed is to find ways of coping with unavoidable stress. These fall into three main categories: attitude change; relaxation techniques; physical change.

Attitude change

An old prayer asks for the strength to change what can be changed, the patience to accept what cannot, and the wit to know the difference. This is, in essence, what you need. There is no point in wasting energy trying to change the immutable. The knack is to find a way of thinking about it that allows you to work at a level that is not damaging to you, without loss of self-respect. To achieve this, you need to value yourself sufficiently to accept your own definition of what is reasonable, even if this is at odds with what goes on around you. You may lose your job, but this is unlikely. It is far more likely that, by not recognising your own limitations, your performance will gradually decline to the level that your job is threatened anyway, with additional detriment to your health. This topic is developed further in Chapter 6.

The following technique drawn from Neuro-Linguistic Programming (NLP) might help you reduce negative feelings. It uses visualisation to reduce the intensity of feelings about a situation or event which has happened to you. While it may seem strange at first if NLP is new to you, it is worth a try if the 'patience to accept' is proving difficult.

Think of such a situation, trying to see it unfolding as a film, complete with images and sounds. Next, deliberately select theme music which *mismatches* the prevailing mood of the 'film'– perhaps a ridiculous or joyful tune. Replay the film in your mind with the new music sounding loud and clear. If you then revisit the images *without* the music you are likely to find your unpleasant feelings have greatly diminished. (To neutralise them completely, repeat the exercise a few times more, each time using different, but still inappropriate, music.)

Relaxation techniques

Such techniques need to be *learned*. You cannot suddenly relax on demand if you have not developed the necessary skills. Popular techniques include yoga, meditation, or relaxation using an audio-cassette as a prompt. Flotation tanks, which impose a high level of sensory deprivation, are also used for relaxation purposes. Different techniques suit different people, but ask your friends to see what they find helpful if you have not already developed your own techniques. See what classes are available locally if you have some considerable time before your course starts, or look for a weekend course if time is short. If nothing is available, seek advice on a good cassette.

If you wish to start practising relaxation before finding a tape, sit or lie in a quiet, dimly lit room. Start to think about your breathing, trying to keep this fairly slow and regular. Gently discard any other thoughts that intrude, returning to your breathing each time. If you prefer, you can concentrate on a visual image, a blue water lily, rippling water, or any other thing for which you can form a clear image and which means peace to you. Or repeat a short phrase over and over in time with your breathing. Again, a phrase with peaceful overtones should be chosen, although the exact content is not important. With the image or the phrase you should again try to put aside other thoughts as they occur, gently, and without irritation. Practise for about five minutes at a time to begin with, gradually building up to 15 or 20 minutes. You should find that with practice you will be able to keep your thoughts increasingly focused on your chosen object, and that you will feel greatly refreshed at the end of the period. At the end of your time, move around gently before getting up, and do this slowly.

If such approaches do not appeal to you, but you find listening to music or other leisure activities relaxing, take steps to increase the time you devote to these. Flying kites is found to be an excellent relaxation by many. As one source of stress is often friction from those with whom we live, see whether a form of relaxation which involves these people can be found. If the friction persists, then the activity will not have a stress reducing function, but if it can be relaxing *and* companionable, you may be able to reduce stress in two ways at once.

Physical exercise

The merits of physical exercise will be referred to on a number of occasions in the Handbook. If you are not already an exercise convert, or doing a physically demanding job, think seriously about building more exercise into your routine as part of your pre-course preparation. If you have not developed the habit *before* your course starts, your chances of doing enough exercise during your course will be extremely slim. It is not important what exercise you take. Any exercise which raises a sweat and which you can do at least two or three times a week for half an hour or so will do. The effects on your health and your ability to study should be significant.

To stick to regular exercise, it is important that you *enjoy* it. If you do not currently exercise you will not enjoy it at first, but by starting gently should soon begin to do so. Think about what you *used* to enjoy as a guide, or something you like the idea of. Your chosen activity should be convenient. If major arrangements are needed, and a lot of planning, you may find it difficult to get into the habit. Nor will you be able to continue exercise that takes a lot of time. Your time will be at a premium during your studies. This is why jogging is so popular. No preparation time is needed: all the time you devote to it goes into the exercise. It can be done in most weathers, and little cost is incurred. You can usually find a friend to run with you, too, which will increase the chance of your making the effort when you do not really feel up to it.

By spending no more than 20 minutes, two or three times a week, you can make a significant difference to your chances of success. This is not a sales pitch, although it may sound like one. Some people *hate* running, but love swimming, or squash, or fast walking. Choose an activity to suit your circumstances. But do choose one, unless there are health reasons for not doing so.

If you are new to exercise, force yourself to set exceedingly modest targets to begin with. There is always a challenge to run farther or faster, or play squash against a better opponent than is ideal. But if you injure yourself, it will set back your plans considerably. Even if muscles and tendons survive, over-exercising can build up a psychological resistance to further exercise that no amount of will-power will overcome. Starting *below* your capacity, and increasing your exercise only very gradually, will be both more enjoyable and more effective overall.

ACTIVITY

Decide on a plan for introducing a modest amount of exercise into your life, if you do not already exercise. Set targets, and review your progress against these. Again, involve a friend or member of your family if you can, as this will increase your motivation significantly.

DEVELOPING ASSERTIVENESS SKILLS

How assertive do you think you are? If you are already overloaded, and asked to take on more and more work, and you tend to say 'Oh, all right. I suppose I can do it', you are likely to have problems with finding time for your studies. If, in a group, you tend to keep quiet if you do not agree with what the others are saying, or stop defending a particular point as soon as there is any dissent, you will probably not enjoy the group work on your course. Nor will you make a very positive contribution to it.

In both the above examples you would probably be aware that you were being insufficiently assertive and avoiding conflict at whatever cost. If you are sure that this is not your problem – you have absolutely no inhibitions about telling people they are wrong, or about telling them precisely what you think about them for dumping work on you – you may still have something to learn from this section. Aggression is not the same as assertion, and may be very much less effective. Figure 4.1 shows this.

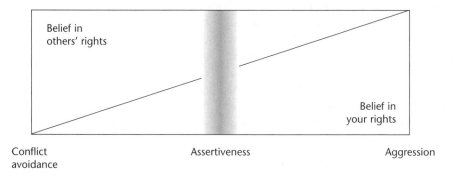

Fig. 4.1 Assertiveness – the balance of rights

The essence of assertion is to stand up firmly for your own rights while giving due regard to the rights of others in a situation. In avoiding all conflict you may be respecting the rights of others, but totally ignoring your own rights. It is clear that you are likely to suffer for this. Your needs will not be met. You may end up working on a weekend when you had much more attractive plans. It may be assumed that you will take on all the jobs that no one else wants and projects that you would really have liked may be given to others. Your boss may not see you as MBA material, and fail to support your request for sponsorship. In the long term your mental or physical health may suffer.

But the damage goes beyond this. If you are failing to make the contribution to the group that you are capable of making, whether at work or on your course, the group is missing out. You may disagree because you have information that no one else possesses, or because you have interpreted information differently from others – and perhaps better. Even if your disagreement stems from a misunderstanding, perhaps because your background is different, it may point to an area where careful explanation is needed in any presentation.

If your response is aggressive rather than assertive, you may be being less effective than you think. Aggression tends to arouse either matching aggression or defensiveness in others. Neither is likely to lead to constructive problem solving, nor to future positive relations between the parties concerned. If you are aggressive to a superior, he or she will be equally aggressive in response, the communication will become a contest, with both sides trying to win, and your superior is likely to emerge the victor. Nor will you have gone up in your superior's estimation as a result of the episode. With subordinates the damage may be less obvious, as a defensive response is more likely. This may mean that you never find out why the conflict really arose – there will be excuses rather than a genuine attempt at finding reasons – so things are unlikely to be better next time. There will be other effects that you may be totally unaware of, as subordinates will find their own, possibly counterproductive, ways of avoiding future conflict. Again there may be long-term damage to your health.

In a group, if you tend to dominate through aggressive behaviour such as interruptions, sarcasm or put-downs directed at other members or similar behaviour directed at ensuring that your point of view is accepted whatever others think, you will do more than prevent the group from coming to the best solution. (It may seem impossible, but this may not necessarily be the one that you are convinced is right!) You will find that if the group does not become demotivated – to the detriment of everyone's learning – it will find a way of controlling what it sees as the damage you are doing, and this can be very uncomfortable for you.

The benefits of assertion, rather than aggression or avoidance, go far beyond helping you to control your workload and to make a positive contribution to group work on your course. At home, as well as at work, assertiveness can lead to constructive outcomes rather than conflict in a wide range of situations. Whether it is a matter of coaching your subordinates (and giving and receiving praise benefits from assertiveness skills just as much as does giving and receiving criticism), discussing how to handle a crisis, negotiating an expansion of your role to allow you to use newly developed skills, or deciding on where to go for your next holiday, assertiveness skills are relevant. You do not therefore need to wait until your course starts to begin to develop them. Indeed such development can start immediately.

EXERCISE

Classify each of the following responses as aggression, assertion or avoidance:

(a) 'You always blame me when things go wrong. It was Fred who accepted the contract.' _____

(b) 'That's all right. I'll see if I can find something for you to use as an ashtray.' _____

(c) 'I find it very difficult to feel I am making a contribution when I am never allowed to finish any sentence.' _____

(d) 'Well I suppose I could go to the meeting, though I am a bit busy at present.' _____

(e) 'I need to work on my report this afternoon if I am to meet our agreed deadline. Do you think that the meeting is so essential that I should go despite this?' _____

(f) 'Why are you always so critical?' _____

(g) 'Never mind. If you all think the main problem is cash flow I'll go along with that.' _____

(h) 'It seems to me that we are focusing exclusively on the financial aspects of this case, and ignoring fairly important human resource implications.' _____

(i) 'You are right. The first section is unclear, though I don't think this criticism applies to the subsequent analysis. Perhaps next time we could discuss what is needed in a background section in a bit more detail before I start the report. _____

(*The correct classification is given at the end of the chapter.*)

In developing your assertiveness skills you need first to appreciate the nature of assertiveness – that it is an adult, self-confident, rational rather than emotional, straightforward and constructive response in a situation. The discussion thus far should have made this somewhat clearer. You can reinforce the message by observing interactions around you, at work and at home, and classifying responses in the same way as you did in the above exercise.

Believing in your rights

You first need to work on your own confidence, and think about *your* rights in any situation. It is easy to say that assertiveness is about respecting your own rights, but too many of us undervalue those rights, and underestimate the worth of our own contributions. If you wish to become more assertive, you need to *believe* that you do have rights in a situation. These could be described as:

- *The right to ask for what you want, or to make clear what you do not want.* Your wants and needs in a situation, whether a desire for time off, for recognition for what you have achieved, or a chance to use valued skills, are valid information. If you do not make your wants clear, others may be totally unaware of them, or fail to appreciate their strength. Even if aware of them, they will find it easier to ignore your wants if you leave them unstated.

- *The right to be listened to and respected.* There is no reason why you are not worth as much as anyone else. If you are not being respected as a person, this reflects badly not on you but on those who are failing to respect you. In any situation, a key element may be the difference between the various perspectives that interested parties bring to bear upon it. By representing part of this diversity you are making a valuable contribution. You may feel that your experience is inadequate and your view in a debate therefore worthless. This is likely to be far from the truth. You can be more analytical about a discussion if you are coming to it fresh. You are less contaminated by preconceptions and assumptions which may be widely held but not necessarily right. A problem may seem insoluble precisely because the shared view of it is so strong that no one can escape from it to a creative solution. So value your own contribution, particularly if it *is* different from those of the rest of the group. And stand up for your right to make it.

- *The right not to know, or not to understand.* You have a perfect right not to be omniscient. The trouble comes when you are reluctant to admit to a lack of knowledge or understanding. In consequence you may fail to make a contribution, or misdirect your efforts. If you do not know or don't understand, admit to it and ask for help from those who do. Sometimes you may be the only one who has seen a flaw in a line of reasoning, and they may not understand either. Sometimes once you have clarified something you may be able to use that knowledge more effectively than those to whom it was already familiar.

- *The right to make mistakes.* There is, of course, a corresponding duty to learn from your mistakes, but no obligation to be infallible. Again, it is usually far more damaging, and takes far more effort, to attempt to conceal mistakes than to face up to them and learn from them. In some organisations mistakes are recognised as evidence that you are trying to push back the boundaries.

- *The right to change your mind.* All too often it is seen as a sign of weakness to move from a position once you have adopted it. But if subsequent exploration of a problem shows it in a new light, it is only by changing your mind that the best solution can be found. A group will never reach its full potential if any position is defended to the death by its original protagonists, regardless of what emerges in subsequent debate. Sometimes the most significant contribution you can make to a group discussion is to say that you have changed your mind about something and explain why. At work you may have taken a decision in the light of imperfect knowledge (the normal condition for taking decisions) and subsequent events may have shown that a better course of action would be better. Again, it is a sign of strength rather than weakness to revise your decision, though again information about the reasons for this will be useful to others who are involved.

CWS

ACTIVITY

During the next two weeks observe those around you. Note any situation where assertiveness might be appropriate. Think about whether those involved in the situation are acting as if they believe they have the above rights, and whether they are respecting similar rights in others. Observe your own reaction in such situations. Which of your own rights do you have the most difficulty in respecting? (It is important to be honest with yourself here.) Discuss with someone whom you trust reasons why this might be, and why the right is important.

Expressing assertiveness

You will have noted from the earlier exercise that the words in which you express yourself are important if you are to assert yourself effectively. Once you have started to work on believing in your rights, you will need to practise using assertive forms of words.

The essence of assertiveness is clarity, objectivity (though your own wants and feelings are valid data), calmness rather than emotion, firmness, a refusal to be sidetracked, and the pursuit of a positive and constructive solution rather than a victory. The words you use will therefore be characterised by at least some of the following:

- use of phrases such as 'I prefer ...', 'I think ...', rather than 'You ...', 'He ...'
- use of phrases such as ' ... could ... ', and '... might ... ' rather than ' ... can't ... ' or ' ... shouldn't ... '
- checking that you have understood before responding – 'I think your argument is ... '
- asking for more detail if you are not clear – 'Could you give me another example ... '
- acknowledging the other person's feelings – 'I know that you have been hoping ... '

- saying what you feel – 'I feel very frustrated … '
- calm repetition, possibly using the same words each time, when it is clear that you are not being listened to
- the absence of apology (unless justified).

Body language is as important as the words you use. If you avoid all eye contact, speak with your hand over your mouth, cower into your chair or lean as far away from the other person as possible, you will find it harder to use assertive phrases, and their effect will be diminished even if you succeed. If you raise your voice, clench your fists, stare the other person down, and get *too* close to them, the effect will be aggressive whatever you say. So get into the habit of observing first the body language of those around you and then your own, and of ensuring that your body language is reinforcing your words, rather than giving a conflicting message.

Preparation

The final important step to assertiveness is to prepare for any anticipated conflict situation. Think about what you want to achieve and why. If you feel in danger of undervaluing your rights, discuss the situation with a supportive colleague to reinforce your beliefs. Think about the other person's likely response. If your colleague, or a friend, is willing to co-operate, act out the scenario in a range of possible ways, trying always to be calm and assertive, rather than avoiding issues or becoming aggressive.

If a situation is thrust upon you with no warning, it is often acceptable – and extremely useful – to ask for thinking time, so that you prepare yourself at least a little rather than trying to respond while in a state of mild shock. A response such as 'This is a complete bolt from the blue. I had no idea you were feeling like this. Could you give me five minutes to think about it …' may lead to a much more constructive outcome to the encounter.

Assertiveness skills take time to develop. So too does the skill of knowing when to be assertive. Aggression has its (limited) place, and there will be times when avoidance will be an appropriate response. You can, however, become considerably more effective in a wide range of situations where assertiveness *is* appropriate through preparation beforehand, use of the sorts of phrases that are most effective during the encounter, and reflection as to your success afterwards, with a view to further development of your skill in this area.

The above discussion is necessarily no more than a brief introduction to the subject. If you want more help there are good books on the subject (*see* Further information at the end of this chapter). Even better is to go on a good course. If you start developing your skills now, and review your progress at intervals, your job performance, your studies and your relationships outside work should all benefit.

EXPLOITING INFORMATION TECHNOLOGY

Almost all managers now use IT in some form. You probably have a computer at work which you use for e-mail, word processing, spreadsheets and accessing databases and information available via the Internet. If so, you probably have all the IT skills you will need on your course and all the preparation you need do is check that you have access to a suitable machine and the Internet for your study. (Some organisations do not allow use of their machines for non-work purposes, and may have fire-walls that prevent you from using them for communication on your course.)

What follows is aimed primarily at those few managers who are not as happy with IT as they will need to be for their chosen course. Rather than trying to give them 'training', it discusses the sort of use that is likely to be made of IT on a management course, and the importance of developing the necessary skills beforehand.

Why courses require IT use

Management programmes tend to require students to use IT for a number of reasons. First, because most managers need to be able to use IT in their jobs, institutions feel that any of their students who lack basic IT skills should develop them before they gain a qualification. Thus you would be expected to be able to use spreadsheets, as they are almost universally used in business for all sorts of purposes, and to understand databases and their use. Basic keyboard and file management skills would also be expected, as e-mail and electronic file transmission are similarly universal.

Such basic skills development is likely, however, to be only a minor part of the reason for the prominence of computing and communications requirements. Organisations increasingly use IT for communication and team-working between staff who are widely separated geographically, and to allow remote staff to access information held centrally. These uses are also of great benefit on many programmes, particularly those taught at a distance.

Finally, with e-commerce a major growth area, some of your programme is likely to address strategic issues relating to this growing market. It will be essential for you to be familiar with the medium if you are to appreciate these issues.

This section will concentrate on the likely immediate practical uses of IT within your programme.

Writing assignments

There are important practical reasons why you are likely to need IT skills. Assignments which are word-processed tend to be of a much higher quality than handwritten ones, because of the ease of redrafting. Graphics will also be far better, as it is now easy to produce clear diagrams and incorporate them, together with numerical data, in the text.

You will find it an advantage to work in such a transient medium, too. 'Writer's block', discussed in Chapter 15, is far less common now that successive drafts are easy to produce. 'Cutting and pasting' from notes or other sources is also easy. (Electronic organisers which allow data transfer to your PC can be invaluable for taking notes.)

Some distance learning institutions now require you to submit written assignments electronically, and they will be returned, marked, by the same route. If you live in a country with an unreliable postal system this can be invaluable. Even in the UK it can mean that assignments are returned to you perhaps four days earlier than they otherwise would be, and feedback on your work will be the more valuable the fresher it is in your memory.

Accessing information

You will have access to far more information if you can use the electronic resources which your institution's library is likely, increasingly, to have in place of paper. Even 'distance learning' students are likely to be able to access electronic library resources – thus overcoming one of the difficulties they experienced in the past if they did not live near a suitable university library.

You will be able to access all sorts of non-library information via the World Wide Web, as well. You will have found this already if you used the suggested web sites as the start of a search for information about suitable MBA programmes. Later in your course you are likely to find Internet searches invaluable when researching projects or for a dissertation (*see* Chapter 19).

Communicating with students and tutors

Even if you are studying full-time, you may find e-mail is the most convenient way to communicate with tutors. If you are a part-time student, particularly studying at a distance, then it may be far superior to other routes. But the possibilities go far beyond simple e-mail. A distance learning programme is likely to use a computer conferencing system that will allow you to 'discuss' with other students, and perhaps tutors as well, issues related to the course. Indeed you may be required to work collaboratively on some of your assignments, exchanging thoughts, data and drafts electronically. While much of this work may be 'asynchronous' – as with e-mail, messages are posted, to be read when someone else logs on – systems are developing which allow real-time interaction, through voice and/or video links, together with 'shared screens', where changes one person makes to the image on the screen are seen by all taking part. The scope here is considerable, and the technology may significantly alter the nature of distance learning.

You are likely to be given training in any system used on your course. Such communications are mentioned here only to alert you to the sorts of possibilities, and to strengthen your resolve to ensure that you have the necessary machine and communication links operational well before the course requires them. (There are all sorts of reasons why getting computer and modem working may take longer than you think, and it can be a real setback if you do not join conferences until they are well under way.)

Preparatory steps

The first necessary step is to find out precisely what use will be made of IT on your intended course. You then need to arrange access to a suitable machine and, if necessary, modem and Internet link. Be very careful if you are deciding to buy a PC for use at home. There seems a relentless drive towards ever more sophisticated software, requiring an ever higher specification of machine. It usually makes sense to buy the highest specification you can afford to allow for updating of requirements during your programme. But seek advice on this from a range of friends who are addicted to computers as well as from your intended institution.

Once you have arranged access, practise using any of the software with which your course will require you to be familiar. The more comfortable you are with it before the course starts, the less likely it is to interfere with the learning it is intended to mediate. Make sure that you can word-process efficiently. Practise your keyboard skills. Find out how to draw graphs from figures and produce other diagrams and incorporate them into text. Make sure that you can check grammar and spelling, and count words on the machine. The quickest way to learn is from someone who is already comfortable with the package you are using. Work out what you want to be able to do. Find out what you can do by trial and error. Then take your remaining problems to an expert friend. Failing that, buy one of the many 'Idiot's guide' type books available. They are usually infinitely more helpful than the official manual.

In particular, if you are not used to searching the Internet, practise this, focusing on information that is likely to be useful to you in preparation for your studies. Even if you have chosen your course, you will find useful general information about MBAs on the Hobson website, for example. If you do not take the *Financial Times*, find the electronic version. Take management topics which interest you, and see what you can find out. Practise bookmarking useful sites so that when you want to refer to them during your studies you will be able to get there easily. Practise extracting information from sites and pasting it into notes on the topic that could be useful in future.

Any time that you can spend in this fashion will contribute to success in your studies.

PREPARATORY READING

Many intending students feel that as soon as they sign on for a course they should rush out and obtain the textbooks they will be using, and start to read them. While it is an excellent idea to start preparing yourself as soon as you have decided what you are going to do, textbooks are not always the best idea. Without the supporting lectures or distance-teaching materials, they can be unrewarding. Other forms of preparation may be preferable.

Of course, you should ask your chosen institution what preparation they recommend, but if they are less than forthcoming, and you are left to work it out for yourself, then you might wish to consider the following.

First, it is most important that you develop the study skills that you will need, so you should give priority to working through those parts of the Handbook that are relevant. Second, your course will be more stimulating if you have started to develop a strategic perspective, that is, to think about the higher-level decisions taken by organisations, and the context in which they are taken, and their implications. Rather than reading textbooks, you will find this information readily available in the business section of your newspaper, in the *Financial Times*, in the various management publications, and in radio and TV programmes devoted to the subject. You may find your local main library takes relevant business publications, or that they are available within your organisation. Reading these, perhaps in conjunction with the chapter on effective study, should be useful preparation. There are also many good management-related websites. Develop your Internet search skills by seeking some of these.

You can also usefully start to explore your own organisation's policy and strategy formulation. Ask your manager, or your mentor, or your training officer, or indeed anyone in the organisation who might know, what information is available, and where. Some of it may already be passing across your desk, but merely skimmed, or not read at all. Start taking it more seriously, trying to see the organisation from the perspective of those who are developing policy, rather than merely cursing the effects of that policy when it starts to impinge on your job.

If you do wish to read books, then there are countless general management books. Some of these are excellent, some of little value. Again a library should have a reasonable supply (few of them stand re-reading, so it is probably not worth investing other than in paperbacks). Autobiographies of senior industrialists, although needing to be taken with a pinch of salt, can be enjoyable reading and give you the perspective of a decision maker. You will probably find the array of management books available in a good bookseller rather bewildering. It is easier to shop at airports, or the larger railway stations, which often have an excellent, though not too large, selection of management books. Some suggestions are listed under 'Further information' at the end of this chapter, but this list is by no means exhaustive. It is merely a starting point. Of course, all the books listed under Further information elsewhere in this book would also be good preparation.

As you will discover later in the book, it is not usually a good idea to be too ambitious. Think about your priorities in preparing yourself for the course, work out a realistic plan that will enable you to meet at least the highest of these, and follow the plan. It is far better to decide that you will work through two chapters in detail, talk to your training manager, and start reading the business pages, and *do* these, than to buy a heap of books, and decide that you also need a lot of study skills development, and sit there never doing anything because the whole task seems so forbidding. So opt for preparation that will not be too onerous, and enjoy it.

SUMMARY

- Your own PC and modem can be an enormous asset on an MBA course, and may be essential.

- If purchasing, you will need to consider compatibility of hardware and software with both office and business school, and seek advice.

- You may need to allow considerable time for developing the skills required, particularly word-processing, information search and communications skills, to use your PC to best advantage.

- Organisational support, beyond the provision of time and fees, can make your course much more effective.

- Support can be sought from training manager, immediate superior and/or mentor, and these should be involved from the start of your planning. Subordinates can be a further valuable resource.

- You can start to develop assertiveness skills now, to the benefit of both your job and your studies.

- Stress will normally be increased by your studies. In addition to working on your time management skills, you should think about the sources of stress in your life and reduce what can be reduced. Techniques for coping with inevitable stress should be developed *prior* to the course if at all possible. They will probably include attitude change, relaxation techniques and regular exercise.

- Useful preparation can also include developing a more strategic perspective.

- Rather than reading textbooks, you can exploit media business coverage, material on the Internet, more general management books and resources within your own organisation.

Further information

There is a wealth of books on the personal skills covered in this chapter. Some are very superficial, some rather irritating. Those that follow are my personal choice. You are advised to browse and find one that suit you. Different things irritate different people!

Andreas, S. and Franklin, C. (1996) *NLP. The New Technology of Achievement*, Nicholas Brealey.

Back, K. and Back, K. (1999) *Assertiveness at Work* (3rd edn), McGraw-Hill.

Bishop, S. (2000) *Develop Your Assertiveness* (2nd edn), Kogan Page.

Clegg, B. (2000) *Instant Stress Management*, Kogan Page.

Kellaway, L. (2000) *Sense and Nonsense in the Office*, Financial Times Prentice Hall. A strictly non-academic book that could arm you with a healthy degree of cynicism about what you will meet on your course.

Lifeskills International (1999) *Staying Healthy at Work*, Gower. This addresses stress, physical health, interpersonal relations and lifestyle planning.

Roberts, B. (1999) *Working Memory: Improving Your Memory for the Workplace*, London House.

If you have time and wish to read for more general awareness raising, starting to develop your mental fitness and preparing for the finance part of your programme (if this is the part that terrifies you), the following are recommended.

The Economist.

Financial Times.

The 'business pages' of any quality newspaper.

Butler, G. and Hope, T. (1995) *Manage your Mind: The mental fitness guide*, Oxford University Press. This covers stress, study skills and memory.

Cramer, S. (2000) *The Ultimate Business Library: 75 books that made management*, Capstone.

Drucker, P.F.: just about any of his books!

Gibson, R. (ed.) (1998) *Rethinking the Future*, Nicholas Brealey. A set of highly accessible contributions 'from today's most highly regarded thinkers' – which will provide a good preview of a range of issues and 'names' that you are likely to encounter in your course.

Glynn, J.J., Murphy, M.P. and Perrin, J. (1998) *Accounting for Managers* (2nd edn), International Thomson Business Press.

Greising, D. (1998) *I'd like the World to Buy a Coke. The life and leadership of Roberto Gorzueta*, Wiley.

Handy, C. (1999) *Inside Organisations*, Penguin, plus any other of his management books.

Huczinski, A. (1996) *Management Gurus. What makes them and how to become one*, International Thomson Business Press.

Israel, R., Whitten, H. and Shaffran, C. (2000) *Your Mind at Work: developing self knowledge for business success*, Kogan Page. This includes some excellent examples of diagrams relevant to Chapter 10, as well as material useful in preparation.

Kakabadse, A., Ludlow, R. and Vinnicombe, S. (1987) *Working in Organisations*, Penguin.

Kind, J. (1999) *Accounting and Finance for Managers*, Kogan Page.

Nutz, K. and Freiberg, J. (1997) *Southwest Airlines Crazy Recipe for Business and Personal Success*, Orion Business Books.

Pizzey, A. (1998) *Finance and Accounting for Non-Specialist Students*, Financial Times Pitman Publishing.

Answers to Exercise

(a) aggression   (f) aggression
(b) avoidance   (g) avoidance
(c) assertion   (h) assertion
(d) avoidance   (i) assertion
(e) assertion

5 The time problem

Objectives

By the end of this chapter you should:

- have estimated how much time you have available, and how much you will need
- understand your current pattern of time usage
- have identified your personal 'prime time'
- have an initial strategy for freeing time by different use of non-work time, and know what additional time will need to be released, either by a negotiated reduction in workload, or by more effective time management at work
- be starting to test the accuracy of your estimates of available time.

INTRODUCTION

The commonest problem encountered by part-time students, and the most frequently quoted cause of dropout of failure is 'not enough time'. While full-time students also find time a problem, the remedies are different. This chapter is concerned only with the problems of students combining study with a full-time job.

The size of their time problem is not altogether surprising. Few busy managers (and it is the busy ones who sign on for courses) have the hours required for Master's level study currently uncommitted. Are *you* sitting doing nothing for up to 15 hours each week? Somehow this time has to be 'found', whether by ceasing to do some things you are presently doing, or by doing some things more efficiently, or both. You need to work out a strategy, and negotiate it with work colleagues and family, if you are to avoid divorce, dismissal or physical and mental decline while still gaining your qualification.

Developing such a strategy is a significant task. Some of the time will be released from your leisure, some will probably have to be found through more effective time management at work. This is dealt with in the next chapter. To work through these two chapters will itself take some considerable time, perhaps as much as ten hours, in addition to the time required for practising any techniques you choose to adopt.

'Lack of time' is the excuse many busy managers give for not improving their time management. Regard these two chapters as a test of your commitment to your future success. They will profoundly influence it, *provided* you are prepared to make the necessary time investment in the first place. Merely reading this part of the book is not enough. You *must* work through the activities carefully.

ASSESSING THE PROBLEM

As with any managerial problem-solving exercise, it is important to explore the nature and size of the problem facing you before you consider the options available for responding. You need to consider at least three aspects: how much time you expect to need for your selected programme, how much time you have available in your current lifestyle; what situational factors may be obstacles to bridging the gap.

How much time do you need?

This question cannot be answered in the abstract. The answer will depend on the demands of your chosen institution and on your own capacity for getting through the work at speed. Even with both these held constant, there may be variation within the period of study, with some parts of the course being far more time consuming than others. Projects and dissertations are notoriously demanding in this respect.

Do you have a problem?
- *How much time will you need?*
- *How much will you have?*
- *Can you bridge the gap?*

If you are working through this book prior to starting your course, it is worth attempting to gain a rough estimate. (If you have already started, you will probably be all too aware of how much time you need.) Your first source is obviously your chosen institution. Their publicity material probably includes estimates of necessary study time. If not, they should be happy to provide these on request. Make sure that estimates include *all* likely activities: attendance at face-to-face sessions; work on provided study materials; any additional required reading or Internet use; preparation of assignments; any residential periods; any computer-based conferencing or other work; use of any audio and video materials; and any other time needed for completion of the course.

As institutional estimates are sometimes at variance with those of their students, it is worth trying to make contact with several current or past students to check on the information provided. I have come across several managers who chose their course because it offered the quickest qualification available, and then found that the workload was far beyond what they had been led to expect. In consequence they were faced with a choice between giving up or persuading their employers to allow them to cut back their workload, effectively to part-time, so that they could keep up with their studies.

As a rough guide, many students on full-time MBA courses claim to work for up to 70 hours a week during a one-year course. If a part-time course were to aim to cover the same ground in two years you could find you needed up to 35 hours' study a week to reach the same standards. As another ball-park figure, the Open University estimates that honours graduates taking its direct entry MBA will need to study an average of at least 10 hrs per 50-week year over three years.

All mentions of study hours in contexts such as this refer to the mythical 'average student'. The extent of variation from this average is demonstrated by a survey I did of students on a distance learning 'Managing People' course. The course was rated as 100 hours, and the average was indeed close to this, but student estimates of the time actually taken ranged from 70 hours to 150 hours.

The extent to which you should regard yourself as 'average' will depend on how fast you can assimilate material, how quickly you can write assignments, and how much of a perfectionist you are. It will also depend on how much you are wanting to gain from the material itself. If it is a subject that interests you, and which you wish to go into in depth, it will obviously take you longer than something which you are studying only because it is compulsory, and for which your objective is no more than to obtain a passing grade.

You can gain some idea of your degree of variation from the amount of effort you found necessary in any previous studies. If these were far removed from management education, say in pure mathematics or philosophy, this will be only a faint indication, however. You will need to combine your assessment of whether you are generally quick or slow to learn with a factor indicating whether you are merely trying to pass, or aiming to be the best student ever. And your assessment of how long you will need must also take into consideration whether or not you are familiar with studying management-type material.

Once you have come to a first estimate of your time need (and you can always revise it later), the next stage in exploring the problem is to estimate how much time you can fairly easily make available.

How much time do you have?

Whatever your estimated time need, it is likely to require major reorganisation of your life to make this time available. Although you do not sit around doing nothing, there may be some activities which could be sacrificed altogether for the period of your studies, some which could be reduced, and some which could perhaps be done more efficiently. Others may be capable of being combined with your study. In order to decide which activities fall into each of these categories, it is necessary to conduct a rough time audit.

The first step to this is to produce an instant estimate of time usage. Complete the activity on pp. 66–7 before reading further.

More reliable than estimates are observations of actual behaviour. If you have a while before your course starts, keep a *time log*. Concentrate on your non-work time. Working time will be analysed later if this proves necessary.

Identifying your prime time

All time is not equal. The time between 7.00 am and 8.00 am is likely to have a *different value* from, say, that between 2.00 pm and 3.00 pm, and that between 11.00 pm and midnight. We all have daily biorhythms: alertness and energy levels fluctuate throughout the 24 hours. Although few people are alert in the depths of the night, and many have a 'low' in the early afternoon, individual patterns of fluctuation vary considerably.

The value of the 'time that you have' thus depends upon *when* you have it, and you may be able to increase its value by rescheduling. To do this you need to have identified your good and bad times. You may already be aware of these. I know that I can achieve far more, time for time, in the early morning than between 4.00 and 7.00 pm. If you have not, however, thought much about your own rhythms, you might like to map them while you are keeping your time log. To do this, jot down at regular intervals how alert you are feeling, and how well you think you would be able to cope with study at that particular time.

FREEING THE ADDITIONAL TIME YOU NEED

There is room for some creativity here. Many students find that fairly minor changes in their habits can free significant slots for study. Taking a slower but less crowded train could yield three hours a day of ideal study time for the extrovert who works best with a degree of external stimulation, and who is having to spend time commuting in any case. Flying time provides many students in mobile jobs with hours of potential time to work on their course materials. Replacing a meal by a (healthy) snack can be good for the figure, as well as freeing a worthwhile total of hours per week.

Cutting down on TV watching or leisure reading are obvious routes. More painful, but for many students a necessity, is to cut down considerably on an active social life.

In thinking about potential time savings, you must avoid setting yourself a timetable that is unrealistically demanding. If you live with people, then they have rights to your time, and you probably have a need for time with them. It is very important to involve those close to you in discussing your time-finding problem. They must feel that your solution is their solution too, and takes their needs into account. If not, they may well indulge in effective (though perhaps unconscious) sabotage of your efforts to work on your course, at a time when you are in need of their support to keep you going.

Do not assume that because many of the world's most successful people claim to manage on four hours of sleep a night you will be able to do likewise. It is worth experimenting with *gradually* cutting back on sleep. You may find that your brain still functions and you feel well. You may, however, feel dreadful on such a regime. Do your experimenting prior to the course start if at all possible. And remember that if you routinely cut sleep to a minimum, there will be less room for burning the midnight oil as an emergency measure. If you feel overtired or irritable on reduced sleep it is probably not worth persevering with the regime. An MBA is primarily a test of endurance. It is not worth risking your ability to last the course.

For the same reason, you should include some of the things that make life worth living (at least in your view). *Schedule* some relaxation and treats for yourself. These need to be actively planned. Otherwise their effect will be destroyed by guilty feelings that you should really be working. Knowing that there is a treat coming up may make it easier to stick to a piece of difficult work. So make sport and active relaxation (yoga, meditation or your favourite TV comedy – suit yourself) a positive part of your strategy for effective study. Even if you do not actively exercise at present, you might like to think about building some form of exercise into your schedule, as suggested in Chapter 4. If you are reasonably fit you may well find that you can use study time more effectively.

ACTIVITY

Jot down estimates of time spent per week, using the categories given as prompts. They are in no sense intended as a definitive list, and you should add any other significant categories at the end.

   (Ignore the right-hand column for now. You will need this later.)

	Hours	
Work Time at work		
Time travelling to and from work		
Time spent on work brought home		
Time on physical maintenance Sleeping		
Eating and other necessities		
Exercise		
Other		
Time on mental maintenance Leisure (list activities)		
Meditation etc.		

Time spent on social activities With partner and children (if any)	Hours	
Other social activities (list)		
Time spent on 'environment' maintenance House		
Garden		
Car		
Other maintenance (list)		
Other activities (List any significant other use of time, e.g. TV)		

Comment

*Having provided this instant estimate, you must next, a more demanding task, check it. Estimates are notoriously unreliable. There are several possible checks. The first is to ask your partner, if you have one, to do a similar estimate of your time usage, and then to compare their estimate with yours. You may find some interesting discrepancies. Then go back over your diary for the last few weeks, and see whether this is consistent with what you have written. Finally think carefully about **last** week. How did you spend your time then? In what ways was this atypical? Modify your estimates in the light of these checks.*

ACTIVITY

Log your usage of time when not at work, for a period of at least a week, preferably two weeks. A simple format to use is that of the large office diary, which divides the day into periods, though in this case for times outside normal working hours. Log waking time and activities until arriving at work. Log your time of leaving and activities thereafter until you go to bed. You can either record events, i.e. the start time of each new activity, or time usage. For this you will need to make an entry each hour, estimating use of time within that hour.

Depending on the imminence of your course start, you may wish to sample random days, or even random weeks, for time logging. Watch out, however, for seasonality effects. If, for example, your course has a summer break, and you are working through these activities during the summer, ask whether your time patterns will be sufficiently representative to be worth the effort of logging.

Do not continue beyond the point at which you feel you have sufficient information about actual time usage to progress. If your log differs significantly from your instant estimate, you might like to highlight areas of difference and reflect on these.

You should now work from a combination of your estimate and log. Categorise the activities listed, and start to estimate how much time could be fairly easily freed.

ACTIVITY

Use the spare right-hand column on your list of time estimates to write down a realistic estimate of weekly time that could be freed for study without detriment to health, relationships or time spent at work. Total these, and check against your estimate of time needed.

If you are still well ahead of your course start, you can check your estimates for feasibility. Draw up the sort of timetable you will need to fit in the level of work you think your course will require, using the time that you have estimated could be freed. Then for a period of about two weeks, use these times to do activities similar to study. These might consist of working through the preparatory sections of this Handbook, doing suggested remedial work, for example on your mathematical skills, or reading and taking notes on relevant management literature, doing exercises to increase your reading speed, or even getting ahead on personal business (tax, letters, or similar) so that you will not need to devote time to this once your course starts.

Comment

Obviously the closer your chosen activities are to the sort of mental activity your course will demand, the more reliable the test. Getting ahead with gardening or DIY might save time later, but would not test your ability to keep to the timetable you propose. While you may be able to slap paint on walls at 1.00 am, your ability to read, absorb and evaluate management literature at that time might be much reduced.

This trial will indicate whether your estimates of available time are realistic. See whether there is scope for rescheduling activities to make more 'prime time' available for study. If a significant reduction in 'at work' time is needed, you should work through the next chapter, on 'Managing time at work'.

Reducing work demands

You might also wish to consider negotiating a reduction in work demands for the duration of your course. Unless you are doing the course secretly, with the aim of getting a new job as soon as possible, you should discuss your studies with your organisation.

If you are being sponsored, it is in the organisation's interest that you should gain as much as possible from your course. You will not be able to do this if job and course demands add up to a load which places intolerable stress on you. In order to avoid this, you should negotiate as soon as possible an agreement that workload will be kept at a level compatible with your studies. If you enter this negotiation armed with a clear idea of time requirements, and an action plan for freeing a substantial amount of your own time, your position should be fairly strong.

It is important that your own immediate manager and his or her superior are parties to any agreement. Training managers may make generous promises, but these may fail to translate into reality if your own direct superiors are not committed to them.

Your negotiated agreement might include your attendance at a good time management course. Although the next chapter makes every effort to help with this, you probably *know* the basics of good time management already. Most managers would be far more effective if they put into practice the principles that they already know. A good short course can give you the motivation to start applying what is taught. Indeed, I met someone on such a course recently who had attended many such courses, because he said he needed 'booster shots' at regular intervals!

Beware promises of time off work for study if they are not associated with reductions in workload. If any leave taken involves putting in the equivalent amount of time either before or after the leave, in addition to any normal work, it is a dubious benefit. Many managers are in this position. Work does not go away, but merely awaits their return. While a promise of time off for attending any classes or residential component is a prerequisite, and revision or thesis-writing time can be a great advantage, you do need to consider whether any promised study leave will involve you in excessive overtime to compensate.

If you do not feel any need to reduce working hours, it might still be prudent to discuss the time demands your course will make with your superior. If at all possible you should try to gain agreement that there will be no attempt to increase your workload once the course starts. This is all too frequent an experience. No one can prevent your boss going sick, and you would probably be loath to reduce the probability of promotion during your course, but more controllable, and less desirable, increases in workload should be avoided if possible.

When the unexpected does occur – and mergers, restructurings, the installation of new computer systems, etc. are so common as almost to be expected – you may need to be assertive in order to avoid serious threat to the viability of your studies. By this time you, and perhaps your organisation as well, will have made a significant investment in your course, whether of time or effort or money. You should therefore be allowed to continue with it if at all possible. But you may well need to assert your rights, and to be unpopular for doing so, in order to achieve this.

If all your attempts at finding ways of bridging the gap between your estimate of the time needed and the time that you can make available are insufficient to make the two match, and the gap is still significant, you should think seriously about the viability of your plans. There is little point in committing yourself to a course knowing that you will not be in a position to benefit from it to the full. The potential effects of the stress of overcommitment on your personal life, your job performance and even your health should not be underrated.

However, before you abandon your plans, you should consider whether additional time *could* be made available by more effective time management at work. This might allow you to reduce the length of your working day without detriment to your performance, thus freeing time for study. Indeed, even if you think that you will be able to fit in enough study with your existing work pattern, it is probably still worth looking at the next chapter. Many of the time management techniques described are applicable to your study as well as your job, so they could be of benefit. Furthermore, your estimates might be wrong, and better time management might allow you to create a time reserve for contingencies. Finally, good time management should make you more *effective* in your job, as well as saving you time, and this is presumably one of your goals. Otherwise you would not be considering an MBA or other qualification.

SUMMARY

- Ensuring that you have sufficient time available for study is a prerequisite for success on an MBA or other qualification.

- To estimate the size of the problem this presents, it is necessary to analyse your current time availability and compare this with the time which you estimate will be needed. The value of time can depend upon your biorhythms.

- To reduce any gap between the two, you need to think about reducing some of your non-working activities, creative use of potential time such as that spent travelling, and a possible reduction in demands on you at work.

- If, after this, a gap still remains, you should look at more effective use of your time at work.

- If this is not possible, you should question the viability of pursuing a course at this point.

6 Managing time at work

Objectives

By the end of this chapter you should:

- know the principles of good time management
- have identified key objectives of your job
- be allocating your time according to established priorities
- be directing your efforts towards the efficient achievement of your objectives
- have reduced ineffective use of your time by others
- be monitoring your time use and adjusting plans accordingly.

INTRODUCTION

'Eight out of ten managers work late at the office and 47 per cent take work home', according to a survey by Philips Dictation Systems.

'Very few were prepared to say "no" to their bosses about taking on extra work,' says the survey. 'Taking work home and working late at the office are symptomatic of the late 1980s culture ... these practices are unnecessary and caused by poor time management, failure to set priorities, setting unrealistic targets – or all three.' Thus spoke *Personnel Management* in January 1989 (p. 9). Evidence suggests that managerial workloads actually increased during the 1990s.

You might wish to argue about whether bringing work home *is* a sign of poor time management, but it is fairly incompatible with part-time study. If you regularly work late, and/or bring work home, then you will probably need to change your habits or abandon thoughts of a qualification by this route.

If you have by now successfully negotiated a reduction in workload, all may be well. But if this was not possible, either because your employer was unsympathetic, or because fear of the effect of raising the subject on your job prospects kept you silent, you will need another solution.

It is potentially more rewarding, and of far more lasting benefit, to learn how to achieve the same results without using time that you will need for your studies. Someone I interviewed recently told me that the most valuable benefit of his own part-time MBA did not stem from the course content, useful though this had been. Far more significant was the fact that combining study with work had *forced* him to practise good time management. By the end of his course the habits were so well established that they remained, and he continued working far more effectively than had been the case prior to his course.

This chapter will tell you little that you do not know already. As was said earlier, you probably know many ways in which you *could* make better use of your time. The problem is that breaking old habits and establishing new ones is not easy, as you will know if you have ever tried to stop smoking, overeating or drinking too much, or to substitute running for TV watching. But if you want to do something enough, it can usually be achieved. Your previous analysis should have established the need. This section will provide a framework for starting to change your habits now that the need to do so is more pressing. Nothing can make the process *easy*. New ways of working will inevitably be uncomfortable at first. You can expect a difficult period while you are consciously trying to do things differently, perhaps to the surprise or resentment of colleagues. But the difficulty will be temporary, and eventually you will wonder why you ever functioned in your old fashion. The assertiveness skills which you have started to develop as a result of working through Chapter 4 (unless you already possessed them) will be essential to you in achieving some aspects of improved time management.

Your chances of making significant change to your ways of working will be enormously improved if you can work through this chapter with a small number of colleagues. This will bring the experience much closer to that of going on a short course, and will considerably strengthen your motivation to do the necessary work. It will also provide you with a wider range of ideas, and improve your colleagues' performance as well as your own. You may find that you can talk your employer into regarding the exercise as an in-house course, allowing you to get together during working time.

This chapter requires you to carry out a series of activities. You will gain little benefit from merely reading it. The answers to the activities will often be fairly lengthy, so it is suggested that you start a time management file for your responses, and for your subsequent work on the topic.

BASIC TIME MANAGEMENT PRINCIPLES

Guidelines for good time management

- Direct your effort *appropriately*, i.e. towards the things that are most important.
- Direct your effort *efficiently*, i.e. maximise your achievements for time and energy expended.
- Stop *wasting* time.

To achieve the above you will need a continual awareness of time as a scarce and non-renewable resource. It is necessary to plan all your use of time, and to monitor this usage on a continuing basis to ensure that bad habits are not creeping back.

ACTIVITY

Start your time management file by thinking about your last full working week, and writing down answers to the following questions:

- Were you absolutely clear what objectives you were trying to achieve?
- To what extent did you achieve them?
- How many hours did you work?
- How many of these hours were directly spent on work towards your objectives?
- What proportion of your desk surface was clear when you arrived at work each morning?
- Of the time directed towards objectives, how much was spent working as effectively as possible?
- What prevented full efficiency?
- How often were you working on something when you knew there was something more important that should have been tackled?

In addition to the above, think about how your time was divided, and write down estimates of the percentage of your working time devoted to different activities: reading; writing; formal meetings; informal meetings; travelling; on the phone; in other activities (add all those which are relevant to your job).

Directing your effort appropriately

To direct your effort appropriately, you need to allocate your time in accordance with the importance of the different tasks facing you, spending more time on those crucial for success, less on those which are less significant. Work that is unnecessary should not receive any time at all! This may sound obvious, but it is surprising how often managers work on low priority jobs (perhaps because they are ones they like doing) while a high priority job is waiting. They may supervise subordinates far more closely than is necessary, or indeed desirable, or do work themselves which could be delegated. They may aim at perfection when something far less would be 'good enough', for example reading documents in close detail when a quick scan would suffice, or spending hours composing an informal e-mail. Another inappropriate use of effort is to agree to work on something new when already fully committed.

Direct your effort more appropriately:
- *understand why you overcommit*
- *plan more effectively*
- *concentrate on important work*
- *delegate*
- *do things 'well enough'*
- *stop doing unimportant things*

ACTIVITY

Identify your own key job areas. Think about your job, and list up to seven key objectives. If you find this difficult, refer to your job description, and discuss it with your boss. Your last appraisal report might also be helpful. For each objective identify the tasks needed to achieve it. These may be ongoing or one-offs. Place your list of objectives and tasks somewhere convenient for easy reference – in your desk diary, in your newly formed time management log, or on the wall. You will need it for future reference.

ACTIVITY

Identify your current misdirections. Look back at your answers to the previous activities, and think about your time usage in relation to the objectives you have just identified as important. List those aspects of your own behaviour which contribute most strongly to misuse of time.

Remedial action if you suspect misdirection of your effort

The action needed will depend on what you have identified as your most pressing faults, but some or all of the following will probably be helpful:

- **Plan your time**. When you next get to work, and daily thereafter, review your key objectives, and think about how you can best use the next working day to achieve progress towards these. It will be necessary to allow time for such routine as is inevitable, and to plan a margin for the unexpected, but aim to make some progress towards at least some key objectives each day. When you do your planning depends on your job and your preference. Many managers find it helpful to spend 15 minutes or so at the *end* of each day, reviewing progress and planning the next day's work, so that they arrive at work with a clear idea of what they will be doing. Indeed, they may find it helpful to leave themselves a note of this on their desks. Others find early morning, before they have read the post, better. Others use travelling time. If you are now inseparable from your electronic organiser you will find it very easy to set, review and revise objectives no matter where you are. Whichever time you choose, it is important that the planning is done regularly. Experiment to find the time of day that makes it easiest to build this planning session into your daily routine. A major planning problem for many managers is under-estimation of the time required for task completion. This 'planning fallacy' often stems from a genuine and confident belief that *this* task will proceed without the delays and other glitches experienced in the past with similar work. This type of optimism is typical of poor time managers. If you suspect yourself of this fallacy, log your estimates for tasks, and the actual time taken. The stark evidence of a mismatch may help you improve your estimating.

- **Delegate more**. Delegation requires an initial time investment in training your subordinate(s). Perhaps even more of a hurdle, it requires absolute clarity on your part as to the objectives of the work, a reasonable final deadline, and suitable points at which progress should be reviewed. All this must be clearly communicated to the person who is to do the work, together with an idea of how the work relates to other departmental work and objectives. This understanding of the context in which the work is required will make the job far more meaningful for the subordinate, and will make it likely that any discretion needed will be exercised in an appropriate way.

  'Busy' managers often cannot find the time to develop their subordinates. They do not *think* clearly enough about what is required for successful completion of a piece of work, let alone communicate this to the subordinate. As a result the work is poorly done, the subordinate learns nothing, and the manager's view that 'It's quicker to do it myself', or even 'I'm the only one who can do it properly' is reinforced.

ACTIVITY

Within the next week, identify at least three areas of work which could be delegated. Plan any staff development necessary for this delegation to be successful, and take steps to set this in motion. Once it is complete, start to delegate work. Ensure that objectives are understood, and agree targets and review points. Leave the subordinate to get on with it between reviews. Put a note in your diary for six weeks hence to review the success with which you are delegating.

- **Understand why you overcommit.** We nearly always connive at our own overload by agreeing to do more than is reasonable. We may have got into this position because of the planning fallacy described above, which has caused us to underestimate either imminent demands from our current workload, or the requirements of the new task. Another problem may be that we are insecure. We feel afraid of being left out, and need to prove that we are essential to the organisation. Being busy, or being involved in everything, can thus reduce our anxiety. Sometimes the new task may simply have looked too interesting to refuse. Often there is a culture within the organisation of saying 'yes' to every piece of work assigned, so agreeing to overcommitment avoids adverse notice. Or sometimes it may be that non-working life offers few rewards, and working long hours is preferable to facing the demands of the family, or to time spent alone.

  Whatever the reasons, overcommitment is seldom the best solution. It can lead to high levels of stress, which may be physically damaging. This in turn leads to less efficient work because of chronic fatigue, and may result in low quality work and missed deadlines, thus negating some of the reasons for taking on the work in the first place!

ACTIVITY

Identify the reasons for your own overcommitment, and make a private note of any personal weaknesses they reveal. For each of these, think of at least one step which you could take in the near future to improve the situation. Decide when you will act, and note review dates in your own diary.

- **Practise saying 'no'.** Assertiveness skills, as discussed in Chapter 4, are necessary for many of the remedial actions listed in this chapter. They are of particular importance here. You need to know what is reasonable, and to accept that you have a right to this. You then need to be able to persist calmly, and with explanations, in asserting your rights. Calmness and persistence are likely to succeed where anger and defensiveness will not. If you do wish to accept an interesting new assignment, then you will need at the same time to say 'no' to some of your existing work, i.e. negotiate a reduction in existing load.

ACTIVITY

From now on keep a record of all new tasks which you are asked to do, and try to refuse them unless they are accompanied by a reduction in existing work. Set a suitable review date in your diary to assess progress in this.

- **Renounce perfection**. Much of our early training emphasises thoroughness, and the aim of doing things as well as is possible. Anything less is regarded as not being a source of satisfaction. While there are times when it is essential to achieve a result as close to perfect as you can manage, there are many more times when this is totally unnecessary. If a quick handwritten note will achieve the same as a typed one that has had to be proofed and corrected twice, then use the hand-written one. If brief minutes of a meeting, noting action points and not much more, will do as well as something approaching a verbatim record, then opt for the shorter version. It will save other people's time, as well as your own. Current definitions of quality emphasise fitness for purpose, and it is worth heeding this.

ACTIVITY

Evaluate the last four pieces of work that you completed to decide whether a lower standard would have been equally effective. If so, identify the ways in which you are doing unnecessary polishing. Is it in terms of excessive detail, or better presentation than is strictly required? Set review dates in your diary at monthly intervals to assess your progress away from unnecessary perfection.

Do be careful in the above to preserve the *necessary* perfections. You must, for example, be fully prepared before conducting a disciplinary or appraisal interview, and cannot afford to skimp if you are drawing up a project contract, or entering into negotiations with a trade union!

- **Stop doing things**. Think carefully about how you described your use of time in the previous activities, particularly about the way in which you spend the largest fractions of your time, and those jobs which are routine. How many jobs could be omitted without disaster? Are you filing things which you will never need to refer to again? Are you routinely circulated with, and reading, materials from which you gain little? Are you attending meetings at which your presence contributes little? It is all too easy to accept demands on your time, particularly those which are part of the accepted routine, without ever questioning their necessity.

ACTIVITY

During the next month question yourself at the start of each activity as to whether it is really necessary. If there will be little ill effect if you omit it, then do so. And take steps to avoid ever doing it in the future. Ask your secretary to bin some types of material directly, or to remove your name from mailing lists. Withdraw from working groups or regular meetings, and so on. List all the activities you already know to be unnecessary, and add to the list as the month goes on.

Effective effort

Once you are sure that you are directing your efforts towards the right things, you need to work at making those efforts as effective as possible. One common problem is procrastination, leading to effort being wasted worrying about what things you have to do, rather than actually getting on with it. Another is lack of organisation, so that time is spent hunting for lost things, or important deadlines are missed, or activities necessary before other tasks can be commenced forgotten. Other inefficiencies come through tackling tasks in a less than ideal way because of inadequate planning, or trying to do demanding work when you are not at your best, because you have devoted the times when you were at your best to trivial jobs. Interruptions can also reduce your efficiency when you are working on something difficult. Trying to do more than one thing at once is another common problem.

> *Make your effort more effective:*
> - *organise your working space*
> - *avoid procrastination*
> - *use prime time for prime jobs*
> - *clarify objectives*
> - *set deadlines*
> - *do one thing at a time*

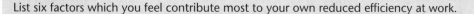

ACTIVITY

List six factors which you feel contribute most to your own reduced efficiency at work.

Remedial action if your efforts are not fully effective

Again the remedial action you take will depend on your particular weaknesses, but it is likely to include at least some of the following.

- **Organise your working space**. It is extremely hard to concentrate when surrounded by a mess, so aim to keep your desk and floor clear. A simple but effective system for this is to use a set of stacking trays with one for 'Do today', one for 'Do this week', one for 'Awaiting information' and one for 'Out'. You will also need a set of drawers, boxes, or whatever, in which you keep together all documents and notes you are ever likely to need when working on each of your key job areas. Electronic 'clutter', while less obvious to the casual observer, may be as great a threat to your effectiveness as physical disorder.

  The system you choose is unimportant. That you *have* a system is vital. And a major component in any system will be your wastepaper baskets, real and virtual. If you are not sure where to put something, put it in the bin. If it does not need action, and does not relate to a key area of your job, you probably do not need it. If you are daunted by the magnitude of the task of organising yourself (and I can sympathise – recently someone who uses the same 'horizontal' filing system as I favour gave me a beautiful sign for my wall which read, in magnificent gothic script, 'A tidy floor is a sign of a sick mind'), then enlist the help of a good secretary or Personal Assistant. (Secretaries usually understand the principles of filing, whether paper or electronic, far better than managers.) Once you *are* organised, you may be pleasantly surprised by the time you have to spare, now that you are not continually having to sort through things to find the piece of information that you need, and how much better you feel, working at a clear desk.

■ **Stop devoting effort to *not* doing things.** As my grandmother was irritatingly fond of pointing out, procrastination is the thief of time. Certainly it uses an enormous amount of energy, not only in thinking of reasons for not starting a piece of work and finding alternative activities, but in coping with the feeling of doom and oppression induced by work hanging over you. Even work which has been put off for excellent reasons can absorb effort, particularly if you keep thinking about it while working on something else. To avoid this, you need to decide when you *will* start the work, note this in your diary or work planner, put it in the appropriate file, and then forget about it until the scheduled time. The simple act of 'booking work in' to some future date makes it much easier not to worry about it in the meantime, as well as easier to start it when the scheduled time arrives.

Procrastination is usually associated with tasks which are either distasteful for some reason, or so big as to be rather frightening. If a task is one you are *not* looking forward to, it can help to supplement the 'booking in' by scheduling a reward for tackling it. You could arrange lunch with a congenial colleague on the day you have set aside for budgets, or a trip to a part of the organisation you enjoy visiting on completion of a major report, or even a stiff whisky after the disciplinary interview which you did not really want to conduct (provided you are using public transport).

For large tasks, a 'divide and conquer' approach may be effective. Split the larger task into sub-tasks which are more manageable, set deadlines for these, and book them in individually. You will see that this is the approach recommended in a later chapter for your thesis. One of the pioneering organisations in training managers in this area, Time Manager International, classifies such jobs as 'elephant' jobs, using the splendidly graphic, albeit distasteful, image of eating an elephant. This would be impossible to achieve at a single sitting, but might eventually be accomplished if you sat down to a plateful each day.

Indeed there is considerable value in tackling some part of larger jobs on an almost daily basis. The anticipation is usually far worse than the reality, and increases as time passes, until resistance to the work may become so great that 'booking in' is no longer sufficient remedy. Even a small amount of work each day or two will prevent the build-up of this negative anticipation.

Another form of 'not working' which can be a drain on energy is 'not working at home', i.e. taking work home and then not doing it. This can cast a blight over the entire evening or weekend. You will have enough to do towards your MBA at home, so should get out of the 'taking work home' habit *now*. If extreme circumstances force you to break this rule, 'book in' the work to a specified time slot in the evening or weekend, and do your best to forget it for the remaining time.

■ **Use prime time for prime jobs.** As noted in the previous chapter, we are all subject to daily biological rhythms that mean that at some times of day we function more effectively than at others. For many managers there is a tiredness factor building up as the day goes on, and superimposed upon these rhythms.

It is not good use of your prime time to fritter it away on routine activities. These should be reserved (if they cannot be omitted altogether) for times when you are less effective. In planning your work, schedule demanding work for your personal 'prime time', even if this means saving all but the most urgent items in your in-tray until after lunch. Block this time out in your diary, ignore your e-mail, close your door and direct phone calls in order to make best use of this valuable time.

ACTIVITY

Unless your work on Chapter 5 allowed you to identify your own prime times, do this now. During the next two weeks note down all times at which you have a feeling of working really well, and those when you seem to be minimally effective. From this identify your own 'prime times'.

- **Make sure that you know what you are meant to be doing**. If you are at all unclear about the objectives of any activity, it is highly likely that you will waste effort. If you are writing something, it is important to be clear who will read it, and what you wish them to learn from it. When you ask a subordinate to come and see you, it is essential to work out what you want to achieve by the meeting, and to jot down beforehand the points that you wish to cover. If you are making a phone call, a similar checklist should be made, and unless developing your relationship with the person called is one of your objectives, extraneous conversation should be curtailed.

  It is essential to spend time at the start of each task thinking about your objectives, and how best to achieve them. This will enable you to plan all the resources that you need, thus saving considerable time later. You can also save time by thinking *around* the task, about the possible effects of other factors upon it, and the implications of the likely outcome of the task itself. Planning for these at the outset can reduce the chances of this job creating further work later on.

- **Work to deadlines**. Deadlines tend to concentrate the mind wonderfully and to focus effort. You will find out how necessary they are in your studies, as well as in your job. Harness this effect by creating your own deadlines for tasks that do not already have them, and interim deadlines for tasks with a long time-span. Treat these deadlines as *real*. They will indeed *be* real, as your time planning and 'booking in' systems will disintegrate if work spills over into time allowed for other activities. Your deadlines may need to be in advance of external deadlines on some pieces of work, in order to balance workload. Few managers can write four major reports in a single week, for example. In such cases your personal deadline will be more important than the external one: if you fail to meet the first, you are likely to miss the second. You must, therefore, resist any temptation to see the more distant external deadline as a reason for taking your own shorter-term deadline less seriously.

- **Work on one thing at a time, aiming to finish it**. Too often a feeling of being rushed makes us flit from one job to another without finishing any, or to work on more than one thing at once – for example, trying to write a letter while on the phone. Split attention is tiring, and almost never effective. Discipline yourself to concentrate on one thing at a time. It is a good idea to keep a notebook to hand, so that any ideas about other jobs, which surface while you are working on something else, are not lost. This will help you resist the temptation to drop what you are on and start working on the job to which the idea relates. You will know that you can ignore the idea until the end of the present job without losing it.

Reduce time wastage

Many managers act as if everyone else has more right to their time than they have themselves. Keep reminding yourself that your working time is *yours*. It is your scarcest resource, and the responsibility for its effective use lies with you. You should not allow others to cause you to use your time in non-productive ways. It will make a nonsense of your time planning, and considerably reduce your effectiveness. Meetings may be one of the greatest thieves of your time. It is a salutary experience while sitting in a meeting to calculate the cost of that meeting, and consider whether it will achieve enough to justify this. If your mind is wandering sufficiently to do this calculation, the chances are that your contribution is not justified, for a start! I heard of one organisation which had a special clock for meetings. When the number and status of participants were entered, the clock showed not the time, but the cost of the meeting so far. Apparently meetings became much shorter following its introduction.

Reduce time wastage:

■ *cut down on meetings*
■ *keep control of your diary*
■ *reduce interruptions*
■ *shorten informal meetings.*

Another source of 'stolen' time is casual conversation with people who drop in, or are encountered when you are on your way somewhere. Such informal communication can be invaluable, a part of the networking that tends to be associated with management success. But you need to ensure that only productive conversations intrude on your time. If very busy you may need to curtail even these.

ACTIVITY

During the next week, without consciously trying to reduce lost time, log all time devoted to activities not contributing to the direct achievement of your key objectives. Identify the major sources of time loss, and plan action to reduce these in future. Log non-productive time for the following fortnight, aiming for a steady reduction throughout the period. Thereafter, check non-productive time on occasional days, to ensure that you are not slipping back.

Remedial action if time wastage is a problem

Again you will need to suit the remedy to the disease, but the following prescriptions are available:

- **Reduce meeting commitments**. For all meetings you chair, think carefully about the objectives of the meeting, and whether the meeting could be run differently to achieve these. Do the objectives justify meeting with this frequency, and for this duration? Is the attendance of all the participants necessary? Although your main effect in this is likely to be saving others' time, there will be some effect on your own as well. For meetings which you do not chair, ask whether your attendance is really necessary. Could someone else represent you, if representation is needed? Could you persuade the chair to schedule meetings less frequently? Are the meetings well run?

  For any meeting you attend, you should know well in advance when the meeting will start and finish, its purpose, and what you need to do in order to be prepared to contribute effectively. The meeting should be well chaired, in order that all may make appropriate contributions, and discussions be orderly. Decisions need to be reliably recorded, and someone needs to take the responsibility for ensuring that action is taken to implement decisions. If these conditions are not met, then everyone's time has probably been wasted. You could argue that you have a right to leave a meeting at its stated finish time, and to stay away if papers are not sent to you in advance.

- **Keep control of your diary.** One common problem is an electronic diary which allows others to have access to your schedule and the *right* to book time in it. You need to find out how you can retain control over your time. While it may be very helpful to others to be able to set up meetings without the need to consult participants, the right to your time should remain with you.

ACTIVITY

Review your time for the last two weeks and the next two. How much of your time is scheduled for meetings? How reasonable is this?

- **Reduce interruptions**. It has already been suggested that you protect your 'prime time' from interruptions, but you may also need to cut down the total volume. By breaking into your concentration, and requiring you to spend time afterwards picking up the lost threads, interruptions can cost you far more time than their actual duration. Use your secretary as a filter. A good secretary may be able to deal with many of the interruptions, perhaps with a little training, or to direct people to someone who can help them at least as well as you could. If not, your secretary can at least ensure that you are disturbed only during whichever part of the day you have set aside for this.

  You will obviously wish to remain accessible to your staff in the case of real problems, so you need to make sure that they do not feel 'distanced' by your change in practice. If they understand *why* you are trying to alter your schedule, this is less likely to happen. If you compensate by encouraging contact at times when it will not be disruptive, such as coffee breaks, or a *short* regular meeting to discuss ongoing concerns, you may even achieve better communication than previously. Perhaps your subordinates could be encouraged to apply the same principles of time management to their own jobs.

Bosses may present a greater problem, but again careful explanation of what you are trying to achieve should go a long way towards bringing about improvements.

■ **Shorten unavoidable interruptions**. You may not wish to go so far as those managers who ostentatiously start an egg-timer when a visitor walks into their office, but you should make sure that those who interrupt you for informal meetings make their objectives clear at the outset. Ask them what it is that they want to talk about, and how much of your time they think they need. If you anticipate a visitor staying longer than you would wish, do not invite them to sit down, and prime your secretary to ring you after, say, five minutes. If you feel that the meeting would be more efficiently conducted if you were better prepared, arrange a time to meet later.

PUTTING PRINCIPLES INTO PRACTICE

The activities in this section should have started you on the route towards improving your time management, but it is essential that you make time *now*, not next week or some time after that, to plan a systematic approach to better practice. Unless you at once set a deadline for completing the planning phases, and commit yourself firmly to meeting that deadline, all that this section will have done for you is to provide something else about which you can procrastinate, and thus constitute a further drain on your energy!

Your plan will depend on the particular weaknesses that you have identified, and upon the demands of your job. Only you know what you need to do, and when you can realistically expect to have done it. Do discuss your plan with someone else if you can. This could be the colleagues who have been working through this chapter with you, your boss or your partner. Such discussion will strengthen your commitment to your plan, and increase the likelihood of your putting it into action.

If you do not already keep one, starting a time management file for use at work will be important. This can be electronic, or a simple ring-binder. You will need a section for each major job objective, and pages for each task within it. You will also need an overview chart at the start, which can show all the deadlines you are working towards, and review pages for regular completion. These will help you to monitor your time usage, and its effectiveness, using the sorts of points covered in the above discussion. A simple file can be more effective than a specially designed leather portfolio organiser because you can design its contents and format to suit your particular needs. An electronic organiser is better still, as this is both more flexible and more portable.

An example of part of one manager's planning process for implementing the principles described is shown in Fig. 6.1.

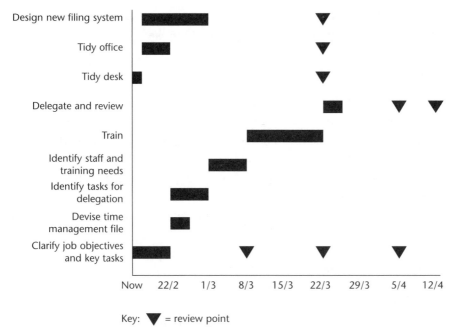

Key: ▼ = review point

Fig. 6.1 Part of one manager's planning process for improving time management

ACTIVITY

Drawing on the work you have done in all the other activities, draw up a complete action plan for improving your time management at work. You will probably need about six weeks to implement this fully, but choose a time-scale to suit your circumstances. Build in review dates for all planned changes.

Whatever approach you adopt to implementation, it is important that you adopt the following habits:

- *think* each day, before post, telephone and unscheduled visitors start to intrude upon you, of what it is that you wish to achieve
- *check* at some point each day that you are progressing satisfactorily towards deadlines
- *review* your time effectiveness at intervals
- *alter* future plans or ways of operating if your review shows this to be necessary.

It is also important that you do not become obsessive about time management, and make your subordinates feel that they can no longer look to you for support, or that they have no call on your time. Nor should you miss out entirely on the informal communications that are one of the most valuable sources of information in an organisation, generate some of the social rewards that help make a job enjoyable, build the contacts that you may need in the future, and keep people loyal to the organisation. In planning your strategy you should value these factors, and make sure that you find a way of retaining them. Remember, time management is an aid to better **management**, not an end in itself.

SUMMARY

- Time is a scarce resource which must be managed.
- All time must be planned for, and effectiveness of time usage monitored.
- Improving your time management means breaking ingrained working habits, both your own and your colleagues'.
- It therefore requires considerable discipline, a plan devised to help you make necessary changes, and frequent reviews to assess progress.
- Working with others to develop your time management skills can generate better ideas, and sustain motivation.
- Time management depends on three key elements:
  – effort needs to be directed *appropriately*
  – effort needs to be directed *efficiently*
  – time-wasters must be eliminated.
- Action needed is likely to include clarifying objectives, setting and meeting deadlines, planning to use your best time for your most demanding work, controlling interruptions, organising office, desk and diary, delegating more, and avoiding needless perfection.
- A secretary can be a great asset in helping you manage your time better.
- Assertiveness skills are important for effective time management.
- It is important to start improving your time management *now,* and to monitor your progress continually.

Further information

Bird, P. (1998) *Teach yourself Time Management*, Hodder & Stoughton.
Caunt, J. (2000) *Organise Yourself*, Kogan Page.
Clegg, B. (1999) *Instant Time Management*, Kogan Page.

DEVELOPING
LEARNING SKILLS

7 Effective learning

Objectives

By the end of this chapter you should:

- have considered and evaluated possible study locations
- be able to develop a study plan
- appreciate the importance of developing good study habits
- know how to use breaks etc. to increase the efficiency with which you study
- have developed techniques for focusing your study of a set of materials, and for learning more effectively.

INTRODUCTION

Once you have freed time for study you need to think about how to use it to best effect. There are two aspects to this. The first concerns very practical considerations of when and where to study, and how to develop a study plan. While this may seem fairly basic, such issues can have a significant impact on the effectiveness of your study. Careful planning may make the whole process far easier than it might otherwise be.

It is also important to think about what is meant by 'learning' in a management context. This chapter introduces different sorts of learning that may be important to managers, and appropriate study techniques for each. In the next chapter ideas about management learning are developed further, and some relevant theory introduced.

Taken together, the two chapters should help you to become a much more effective learner. While the application to your studies is obvious, the wider application to learning throughout your career may be even more significant.

FINDING A PLACE

If study can become a regular habit, you will find the process relatively easy. But if each study session involves prolonged debate with yourself as to whether you work now or later, and where to do it, you can use up an enormous amount of energy before ever starting to achieve anything. Students without the study habit can sit in

A study location needs:
- *peace and quiet*
- *storage facilities*
- *comfort for reading and PC use.*

front of their books, get up and do something, sit down again, decide to move elsewhere, decide that some of the materials they need are where they were in the first place, and before they know it an hour will have passed, they will feel exhausted, and nothing will have been achieved.

The first step towards making study a habit is to establish a habit of place if this is at all possible. This is something which you can usefully do as part of your preparation, prior to the course start.

If you are a part-time student there are obvious practical advantages to having a place devoted to study. You will be accumulating a significant volume of materials, and will be working on substantial assignments that may take weeks to complete. You need to be able to store your materials and your 'work in progress' in an organised fashion, readily accessible so that you do not need to spend time searching for, or shuffling through, heaps of books and papers. They also need to be safe from the attentions of dogs, cats, children and cleaners. For on-line work you will need a phone point near your PC. The place needs to be one in which you can work without being subjected to too many distractions. As you will be spending a lot of time reading and at a PC, ergonomic considerations are important. Check that you have adequate lighting for reading and PC work, that chairs are the right height for you, and that screen and keyboard are in the right positions to avoid eye and wrist strain.

The ideal is a room of your own, used exclusively for studying, and with the layout designed for your particular requirements. If, however, such exclusivity is impossible, time separation can be a good second best. Provided your study time does not overlap with other usage, and there is a cupboard or something similar for easy storage of materials, a kitchen or dining room can work perfectly well.

Some students prefer to study in their office, provided they have access outside normal working time. Others have found more creative solutions, using garden sheds, spare rooms in friends' houses, and even in one case adapting the back of their van and working in the office car park for an hour or two early in the morning and again through their lunch hour.

It will be extremely helpful if you can have your study plan pinned to the wall where you can see it from your desk (study plans will be discussed shortly). This will enable you to check your progress easily. If no suitable wallspace is available, keep a copy in the front of your working file. Either way, make sure that you can check the plan regularly.

ACTIVITY

Spend 15 minutes designing your ideal study. Now think of what is available to you in reality. Note the ways in which your best available option departs from the ideal. Think of as many ways as possible in which you can improve your proposed location, and set the improvements in motion. Once completed, use this location for further work through this book, so that you start to develop the place habit.

Having a place where you normally study is a tremendous advantage. But if you travel frequently, you may have chosen part-time study, probably of the distance variety, precisely because it does not require you to do all your studying in a particular location. In this case it is worth thinking about how you can gain some of the advantages of a habitual study place while on the move. The first advantage, that of having everything to hand, can be approximated by careful packing before you leave, and perhaps having a special 'course briefcase' in which you keep current materials, in order to make the packing easier.

The second advantage of a dedicated study place, that you instantly slip into 'study mode' on entry because it has become a habit, is harder to duplicate. Some students swear by a special piece of clothing to wear while studying, or a special mug for coffee, or other ways of giving themselves a visual cue that this is study time. You might find that the sight of your materials is sufficient. If not, you will need to find an appropriate portable cue.

> *Studying is easier with:*
> - *scheduled times*
> - *clear cues*
> - *family co-operation*
> - *sustained discipline.*

THE ADVANTAGE OF STUDYING AT REGULAR TIMES

Possibly even more important in developing the study habit is to study at regular times. Again, this may seem to contradict the advantages of flexibility claimed for part-time study, but where regularity *is* possible, students find that it takes away much of the pain of deciding whether or not to study on a particular occasion. It becomes automatic, after a time, to go to your study on Tuesdays, Thursdays and all of Sunday, or whatever pattern you have chosen. No decision is necessary. Family and friends know the pattern and what to expect, and that you will be available to them at other times. Indeed, if family and friends helped you devise your study pattern, and feel part ownership in your plan, they may act as 'police' rather than 'saboteurs'.

If regularity is impossible because your life just isn't like that, then follow the practice recommended in the section on time management at work, and 'book in' your study time. This will gave the same advantages that it had there. You need not worry about the work when you are not doing it, because you know it is under control, and when the scheduled time arrives, no decision is needed as it has already been taken.

Of course, with either approach you will need to be prepared to adjust your schedule when study is genuinely impossible. If you have a temperature of 105°F, or the cat has just been run over, or an old friend has dropped in *en route* from Alaska to Zaïre, then it would be unreasonably obsessive to insist on continuing to study. Lesser interruptions should, however, be firmly resisted. You will often feel a bit tired and disinclined to study. If you start to make this an excuse you will never complete your course. Similarly, you can see your next-door neighbours on another night, and if you forgot to feed the cat it will probably not die of starvation before you finish your scheduled study session.

A schedule which you stick to under all reasonable circumstances, whether it is a regular weekly schedule or one which you draw up each week or fortnight to suit prevailing circumstances, will considerably reduce the effort required for study.

Procrastination is probably the greatest threat to successful course completion, and scheduling should help you to avoid it.

In drawing up your schedule, you will need to make sure that you do not make unreasonable demands upon yourself. It is highly unlikely that you will be able to study effectively for six hours at the end of a demanding day at work. Shorter sessions during the week are far more likely to be effective, and longer sessions should be reserved for weekends or any study leave.

Think, too, about the best times of day for you to study. The concept of 'prime time' was introduced in Chapter 5. You may already have used it to improve your time management at work. It is equally applicable to study time. If you are getting up early to study on some mornings, this time may be better than the late evening slots you have programmed on other days. In your search for possible study time you will almost certainly have included some times when you will be in a good state to study, and others which will be less good. You may find in devising your schedule that you can find ways of expanding the 'prime' periods, and of reducing the others.

ACTIVITY

Devise a study schedule for the period between now and your course start, aiming to work through relevant sections of this book or to do other preparatory work in the slots you identify. This need not be as heavy a schedule as you will need once your course has started, but it will help you to get into the habit of working regularly, and in at least some of the periods which you intend to devote to your course. If the course has already started, draw up a schedule and start working to it forthwith.

DEVELOPING A STUDY PLAN

The study schedule you draw up, whether of regular study times that will be available to you, or the times you scheduled on a weekly basis if your life itself is too irregular to allow a fixed regular schedule, provides the framework within which you will construct your study plan. The process involved, not unnaturally, is very similar to that of work planning described earlier. Although it is possible to think about your schedule in the abstract as part of your preparation for the course, you cannot draw up your plan in advance: it depends upon specific course requirements. You may therefore wish to omit this section if you have not yet started your course. If this is the case, make a note in your diary for the time your course begins, reminding yourself to revisit this section and draw up a study plan as soon as you have the necessary information.

Plan for:
- time
- materials
- achievements
- motivation.

Study planning involves deciding, for each study topic, what material you will need to cover as a bare minimum, and how long this is likely to take. It is also helpful to know what additional material would be worth studying if time allows, and how much time would be required for this. You then need to plan which scheduled study sessions you will devote to which work, in order to do all that is necessary before any submission deadlines, or any deadlines that you set yourself in order to balance workloads. Your planning must include ensuring that you acquire any materials not already in your possession in time for their anticipated use.

This may all sound blindingly obvious, but it is surprising how many managers, excellent though they may be at scheduling tasks and resources at work, neglect to adopt the same approach to their studies. They seem victims of a particularly seductive manifestation of the 'planning fallacy' – the belief that somehow, shortly before a deadline, time will miraculously expand to allow the necessary work to be fitted in, and that all the references they require will be sitting in the library ready for their use, despite the fact that everyone else on the course is wanting to borrow them at the same time. Whenever you feel this nice, warm feeling of security creeping up on you, stamp it out fast. It is particularly common for work with a distant deadline. (Chapter 19 on managing theses and dissertations offers techniques for handling it.) Sit down at once, and draw up a realistic schedule, making sure you have included *all* the interim tasks that will be needed in order for you to meet the deadline with a good piece of work. Remember, too, to build sufficient slack into your plan to allow for the unexpected.

If you are a distance student, much of the scheduling may have been done for you. The Open University's Business School, for example, provides students with *all* the materials they need, and divides the work into study sessions for which rough time indications are usually given. A printed study calendar is provided showing exactly what the student should have achieved by each week in the course. But even if this is the case, you will still need to modify the plan to take account of demands in your job and personal life. If your chosen course leaves most of the planning for you to do yourself, it is especially important that you tackle this task carefully.

Devising, or adapting, an overall study plan is perhaps the easy part. Far harder is to plan each individual session so that it is effective. To do this, you will need to be very clear about your objectives in covering the material. Focusing on what you aim to *achieve* in each session, rather than merely on how long you plan to spend, is crucial. There are many ways in which you can learn, and many things that can be learned. The next chapter looks at some of the simpler ideas about how managers learn. These may help you to improve further the effectiveness of your own study. In the meantime, consider the advantages of keeping a study log.

One of your challenges will be sustaining your motivation through many study sessions. A useful motivational technique (though it has many other uses as well) is to keep a study log. For each of your study sessions, log date and duration, and the material on which you have been working. Make notes on the significant points absorbed, and the sources from which they were derived. Note any queries raised which will need pursuing at a later date, and any interesting points you might wish to raise with your tutor, or in class discussion. Make a particular note of anything that looks potentially relevant for forthcoming assignments. Comment, too, on any difficulties encountered in maintaining concentration, and on how accurate your time estimates are turning out to be.

CLARIFYING YOUR STUDY OBJECTIVES

At this point, it is worth starting to think about the 'what' of learning: the next chapter will take this topic further. You might be learning facts, such as the content of a particular piece of employment legislation, in which case memorising is appropriate. But some students think that this is the only type of learning, and try to learn *all* their course materials by rote. This is not appropriate to a subject like management. Although some things will indeed have to be learned by heart, there are many different sorts of learning which are more important.

Learning to apply techniques will be central to your study. You may need to know, for example, how to calculate the weighted average cost of capital or the net present value (NPV) of possible projects to allow comparison of expected future benefits. In these cases, you need to know what to include in the calculation, and how to do the mathematics. Some of this comes fairly close to rote learning. But additionally, you will need to *practise* doing the calculations until you know which buttons to press without thinking. You also need to know what the answer *means*, and when you would need to calculate it, and how you would use it in decision making, and when it may give you a misleading impression. You need to know, too, what alternative approaches might be considered and when they might be preferred. All this requires that you understand what you are learning, and its significance. To achieve this sort of understanding requires much more than learning by heart. It requires you to *think* about what something means, to try it out against things which you already understand, to think about some of the things which it implies if you have understood it correctly, and to see if these make sense. If not, you need to work out where you have gone wrong. A colleague told me that the difference between the USA and the UK in their approach to management study is neatly demonstrated by the different approaches to NPV calculations. In the US approach, it is the resulting *value* that is deemed significant. In the UK it is the *process* of arriving at that value that is of interest: one could plausibly arrive at almost any desired value by making the appropriate assumptions. Apart from suggesting caution in using this book outside the UK, this neatly illustrates the richer type of learning that your course may aim for, and the different time requirements likely for the different types. When you are trying to learn techniques, your study plan should therefore allow for you to practise them until you are confident in their use. If you are trying to understand their application, or indeed anything else, then you need time for thought, for experimenting with the consequences of your thought, and ideally discussing them with others.

Theories

You will often need to study *theories*. These are ways of describing complicated sets of phenomena more simply, in a way that will allow you to make sense of what is happening, and predict what is likely to happen if you make certain changes. Take a theory that you may well have already encountered on short courses, and if not will probably meet early in your MBA. This is the Herzberg 'two-factor theory of job satisfaction' (Herzberg, 1966). In a nutshell, this asserts that there are two sets of job-related factors. The first, which includes items like pay and working conditions, contributes to employee job *dissatisfaction*. He calls this set the hygiene factors. The second set, including responsibility, achievement and the work itself, contribute to employee *satisfaction*, and he refers to these as *motivators*. The essence of Herzberg's theory is that while *dissatisfaction* can be reduced by improvement of hygiene factors, such improvements will not generate job *satisfaction* or motivation. To achieve this, it is necessary to make changes to motivator factors. The most frequent change made by adherents of the theory is to increase responsibility levels, a process referred to as *job enrichment*.

In learning a theory, merely learning the 'facts', or what the theorist is asserting is of limited value. You also need to know the *significance* of the theory. What is it explaining that is not explained by other theories? What new predictions would it cause you to make? (In the case of Herzberg's theory, that attempts at improving motivation by altering pay are doomed to failure.) What sense would this enable you to make of things that concern you in your own job? (Perhaps your own subordinates show such low levels of motivation because they have so little responsibility.) Where does the theory contradict your own experience? (Perhaps you have just introduced a payment by results scheme which has had wonderful effects on output, and by inference, motivation.)

Also relevant is the *evidence* on which the theory is based. If it is merely the result of armchair pondering, or (as in the example above) based on a fairly limited questionnaire study capable of other interpretations, it needs to be viewed differently from a theory based upon extensive observations and varied tests of its predictions.

Theories can be enormously useful in helping you make sense of a complex situation, but they *are* only theories, not God-given truths. Herzberg's may be famous, but there are other theories which make more sense of motivation at work. For any theory you will need to go beyond learning, and into thinking about believability and usefulness. Is the theory logically consistent? Does it fit all the data the author quotes? Are all its predictions plausible? You will find your own managerial experience offers plenty of scope for applying the theory, and thinking about whether it is useful. You should get into the habit, even if course materials do not demand this, of testing everything against your own experience. You will find that your study is much more interesting if you do so. You will also find theories, or other concepts, much easier to learn if you have already linked them to your personal reality. You should also aim to start *using* the ideas to help you function better at work. This may take a little working time, but apart from improving your job performance, it will mean that you do not have to *learn* them when you come to the exam. They will already have become part of your personal conceptual toolkit.

Methodologies

Another category of learning to which you will be exposed will be that of methodologies, or ways of approaching problems. Again, this will be far more rewarding, and interesting, and have more effect on your managerial practice if you go beyond rote learning of content, and into an understanding of why the methodology is offered, what it can and cannot do, what advantages and disadvantages it has compared to alternative approaches, and when it would be suitable. This applies whether you are talking about a simple approach, such as the framework for looking at a competitive environment via analysis of social, technical, environmental and political (STEP) factors, or a more complex approach such as the Checkland Soft Systems Methodology, a set of stages designed to help you address organisational problems from a systems perspective. Again, you should, if at all possible, go beyond understanding, and start using the methodologies whenever suitable opportunities present themselves in your job.

Understanding context

Gaining an understanding of *context* and its importance is crucial at Master's level. The STEP factors just referred to constitute a simple classification of factors in the *external* environment which are likely to be important. For departmental level problems the wider organisation will constitute an important *inner* environment. Much of your learning will involve coming to appreciate the importance of both types of environment, understanding their likely impact, and becoming more sensitive to all the relevant factors in any particular problem which you may have to face.

Rote learning will have little part to play in this. Instead, you will need to think about what is happening in the cases with which you are presented, and start to become more aware of general trends, such as political ones, which influence business. You will need to concentrate particularly upon those environmental factors to which your own organisation is especially sensitive. This sort of learning should be a continuous process, once you are sensitised to the issues involved.

Becoming critical

Perhaps the most important category of learning which an MBA programme is intended to produce is the development of your critical faculties. During your career you can expect to encounter all sorts of new fads and theories. You will be faced with many reports from consultants or others, arguing for various investments or changes. You will need to be able to evaluate these critically. Some may be worthless, others highly significant. Much of what appears in the management literature is of limited usefulness. The ideas may be old ones, thinly disguised in new jargon. Or the content may be primarily the author's opinions and prejudices, even wishful thinking, rather than based upon hard evidence or sound reasoning. It is important that you approach all your study materials critically, rather than assuming that the fact that they are in print automatically ensures that they are worth reading. Otherwise you may replicate their errors in your own thesis, and finish the course without developing the important transferable skill of being able to critically evaluate papers written by either academics or consultants.

Objectives and planning

In planning any single session, you should be clear first of all about your objectives. Are you aiming to learn this material by rote, or is it theoretical, needing evaluation, or a technique which you wish to become competent at using? Is the material intended to change your perspective? If you are working on a paper in a journal, for example, it is a good idea to set down at the beginning what you would ideally like that paper to tell you about the topic it addresses. Then when you have finished it you can check what it *did* tell you (if anything). Be clear as to how this fits in to course requirements. How much detail are you expected to absorb about something? What assignments does this material relate to? What other courses might it be relevant to? You will often find interrelationships between the concepts in different courses, and it is worth noting these in your study log.

If you plan your work for each session noting your objectives, and the extent to which these are achieved in your study log, together with any insights gained from testing the ideas against your work experience, you will find your study time exciting and productive. This is unlikely to be the case if you regard your study periods as something to be endured (much as children see their music practice), during which something of value may, if you are lucky, rub off in a passive sort of way. You can gain further benefit by using your log to record the effects of your attempts to apply course ideas and techniques while at work.

USING TIME EFFECTIVELY

It will already have become apparent that the principles of good time management at work apply equally to effective use of study time. Strong time and place habits should reduce any tendency to procrastinate. You can further reduce the risk by making a point of *always* starting to work exactly when you scheduled yourself to do so, thus preventing any bad habits from starting to develop. This means making that cup of coffee *before* your study session is due to start. And it means completing, or ignoring for the duration, all those other tasks like fixing the shelf, or cleaning the oven, that have a way of becoming terribly urgent just when you are about to start work.

Just as it is important to keep a time management file at work, the need for a study log and working file is clear. Instead of key objectives, you will have *courses* as your main dividing categories, subdivided by learning objectives and study tasks. Your study plan should schedule these tasks so as to ensure that all course deadlines are met, and workloads kept even, or fitted in with other conflicting demands. Again, regular review of your effectiveness is crucial. Your study log, by recording what you have achieved, difficulties encountered and thoughts about future tactics, will enable you to gain insight into your own study skills and their development. It helps motivation because of the satisfaction derived from recording achievements on each occasion.

Another important factor, if you are to be fully effective, is to take account of your own body rhythms, and plan your work in accordance with your personal good and bad times. Even if you were able to schedule most of your sessions to take advantage of 'good' times, as suggested above, there will almost inevitably be occasions when you have to study even though you are not at your best. In this case, as at work, you should make sure that you schedule demanding tasks for your better times, leaving more routine work for times you are not at your peak.

Even at your better times you should not try to force your concentration too far. For most people an hour is about as long as concentration can be maintained without strain. You are likely to make far more effective use of your time if you schedule short (five- to seven-minute) breaks every hour or so, using this time to have a drink, move about, or get some fresh air. A few brisk exercises, or even a very brief walk can do wonders for concentration, as well as easing the strain caused by sitting still. You may have your own favourite exercises already. If not, friends who do yoga could give you suggestions. Alternatively you can simply experiment by yourself to find movements that make you feel good. If you are short of ideas, you may like to try the following exercise suggestions. Remember, the point of the exercises is to make you feel good, not to cause pain. Stop at once if there is any discomfort. And if you have back or other physical problems, consult a doctor first.

EXERCISES WHICH CAN BE USED DURING STUDY BREAKS

Stretch
Stand with feet slightly apart, and reach as high as you can towards the ceiling. Hold this position for 10 deep breaths.

Hang
Keeping feet in the same position, and legs straight, hang forwards from the waist, with head and arms loose. Only rest your hands on the floor if this is totally comfortable. Aim for a slight pull behind the knees. Hold for up to 10 deep breaths, then unroll upwards slowly, from the small of the back, imagining that you are putting your vertebrae back in place one by one.

Shrug your shoulders
Do this up to 10 times, exaggerating the movement as much as possible, perhaps including a circling motion.

Circle your head
Drop chin onto chest then let your head roll in a large circle towards your shoulder, backwards, over other shoulder and back to chest. Repeat in the reverse direction.

Massage your back

Lie on your back on the floor, knees drawn up loosely towards your chest, hands clasped above them. Pull your knees gently towards your chest five times, feeling your lower back pressing slightly into the floor. Then place one hand on each knee and move your knees together in small horizontal circles, again feeling the movement of your back against the floor.

Twist your spine

With knees still drawn up, let legs flop apart slightly (think of a baby lying in a pram) and wriggle a bit. Then stretch arms out to each side, along the floor. Keeping both shoulders firmly on the floor, flop both knees over to the left, so that your left leg is on the floor, the right resting gently upon it. Increase the twist by turning your head to look along your right arm, and sliding your right leg a little further down and across your left leg. Hold for up to 10 deep breaths, then do it in the opposite direction.

Relax

Spend about a minute deep breathing, and trying to keep all your muscles relaxed, and your mind as clear as possible. Get up slowly after this, taking at least five deep breaths to become vertical.

ACTIVITY

If you have been working on this book for at least 40 minutes, try the above exercises, or others, now. Otherwise wait until you have been working for 40–60 minutes and try them then. Before you start, note any parts of your body where you are aware of tension or discomfort. Check to see whether any remains after the exercises. If so, experiment with other movements to relieve it.

Try to do exercises after each of the next five hours of study you do. Only then can you feel justified in abandoning them if they still seem not to be working.

It is important that you schedule the end of any study breaks, as well as the beginning. This allows you to enjoy the time afterwards, and relax properly. If you finish your planned task in less time than you anticipated, you might even stop early.

In addition to scheduled breaks, you should stop if you are finding it totally impossible to concentrate at any point. It is a waste of time to sit in front of a page without registering it in any way. If you have clarified your study objectives, are taking notes as suggested later, and having regular breaks, you should not find this problem arises, unless you are ill, overtired, have serious worries, or the material is extremely badly written. Take 10 minutes to explore possible causes. If no obvious reason can be found and remedied, try some exercise or fresh air, and try again. If concentration is still lacking, try a different activity. If that fails too, admit defeat and terminate your study session rather than wasting time. Log the problem in your working file. If it recurs, look for a pattern that might help you identify the reason. Before stopping, remember to reschedule the missed time.

The above fairly practical points, combined with good planning techniques similar to those which you should by now be using at work, should help you to make effective use of the study time that you have freed, perhaps at considerable sacrifice. The following chapters on more specific study skills should further enhance your effectiveness.

SUMMARY

■ It is important to develop habits of time and place if at all possible, as this will reduce the effort wasted by procrastination.

■ Study periods should be broken by brief scheduled rest periods in order to improve concentration. Exercise may be helpful here.

■ Time management techniques are equally applicable to work and study. In particular, you should actively plan your study in order to achieve objectives and meet deadlines.

■ Part of this planning should be done with a clear understanding of what it is that you are trying to learn, and why. Different approaches will be needed for facts, techniques, theories, methodologies or material intended to broaden your perspective, or heighten your awareness.

■ Your study will be more effective if you adopt a critical approach and make a habit of testing ideas against your prior work experience, trying to use as many course ideas, techniques and methodologies as possible in the practice of your job.

Learning from learning theory

By the end of this chapter you should:

- understand what is meant by learning styles, and the learning process
- have an idea of your own preferred learning style and its strengths, and how to develop less preferred styles
- have a deeper appreciation of how learning can be made far more effective through integration with work experience.

INTRODUCTION

This is not a psychology textbook, and it is not the intention here to give you an exhaustive treatment of learning theory. Nevertheless, the previous chapter referred briefly to different sorts of learning that you might need, without exploring this in any detail. In this chapter we look at how ideas about management learning have shifted some way beyond earlier ideas of managers needing to *absorb* knowledge imparted by tutors. Competences, or the ability to *do* things, have come into the frame. And now, with the growth of interest in knowledge management, managers' ability to *construct* meaning and knowledge is coming to be seen as the essence of management learning. This is seen as necessary for success in a complex and rapidly changing organisational world. An understanding of how this type of learning is best achieved will enable you not only to benefit from your course, but to continue learning from the experiences that you have thereafter.

WHAT IS LEARNING?

Long, long ago I went for an interview for a job at the Civil Service College. It was a typical Civil Service panel interview, with – I think – seven panel members. About half way through the interview, the then head of the college asked me aggressively what I thought I had learned from my experience as an Open University tutor that might be relevant to the job in question. I enthusiastically replied that the one thing it had convinced me of was that if you wanted to change the attitudes or behaviour of adults, learning needed to be participative. He looked at me disdainfully, and said, 'But Mrs Cameron, we are not trying to change people's attitudes or their behaviour.' At that point I stopped wanting to work there (I'm still not sure why I accepted the job!) as I couldn't see what on earth they *were* trying to do in the name of training.

As discussed in Chapter 2, the emphasis in management development was originally on the transfer of 'knowledge', but shifted towards a focus on management *competence*. Recently there has been a further shift towards the more conceptual end of management skills. Knowledge management has become an area of increasing interest, and some of the ideas from there are highly relevant to management development.

The argument runs thus. The role of management is changing, and changing rapidly. The world in which managers operate is fluid – prediction is difficult, competition often fierce. 'Information' proliferates as IT becomes ever more sophisticated. For many senior managers neither 'facts' nor 'competences' are enough. In such an environment the ability to 'make sense' of a complex and rapidly changing world, and to learn continuously from experience, is crucial. Learning is seen as going beyond the absorption of facts and theories into developing the ability to actively *construct meaning*.

The integration of theory and experience is crucial to this process. One of the advantages of part-time study (noted earlier) is that it ensures a continuing supply of experience. Kolb, Rubin and MacIntyre (1974) developed a simple framework suggesting how this integration might be achieved, and Honey and Mumford (1986) built on this to provide suggestions for practical steps which students could take to make their own learning more effective.

KOLB'S THEORY

Kolb suggested that learning should be viewed as a circular process, whereby experience was followed by attempts to make sense of that experience through reflection and conceptualisation, followed by experimentation with the concepts so developed, followed by further experience, reflection, and so on, as shown in Fig. 8.1.

There are a number of points to derive from this. First, learning is very much an active process: mere experience is not necessarily enough. You can do something wrongly for years, if nobody has told you to the contrary. You can continue to do something poorly indefinitely, if you do not reflect on what you are doing, try to understand it, and experiment with ways of doing things better. In either case, experience is likely to teach you almost nothing. Similarly, purely theoretical knowledge, if not related to experience, and itself experimented with, is unlikely to be productive of useful learning.

Your course is likely to help you to use all the stages in the cycle, thus accelerating your learning. You are likely to be encouraged to reflect on your own experience (or that of others as described in case studies). You will become more aware of the 'theories' that you have, perhaps unknowingly, been using, and will be offered a wide range of alternative frameworks which you will be encouraged to use. Your 'reflection' will therefore become a more deliberate, and much richer,

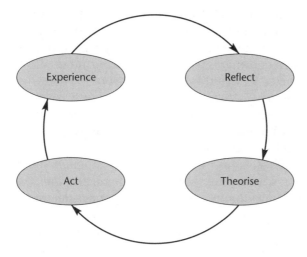

Fig. 8.1 The learning cycle (adapted from Kolb)

process of making sense of what happens in organisations. It will also become established as a habit which will remain with you throughout your career. But some courses have yet to adopt this approach fully. If this is the case with your chosen course, you can make your learning much more effective by consciously looking for links even where they are not suggested, and always testing concepts against your experience, as was suggested in the last chapter.

You can do this very usefully in informal study groups, as this will enable you to draw on a wider range of experience for the testing process. It may be that something does not seem particularly useful to you because some part of your own experience has been limited. By hearing how others find the concept helps them, you will become more aware of its possibilities and uses.

As well as testing each concept you encounter against your experience, Kolb's theory suggests that you should get into the reverse habit of becoming more reflective about your experience. If something *always* seems to go wrong, try to analyse why, and how it differs from fairly similar things that go right. Is there anything in your studies that can throw light on this? What about aspects of your job performance with which you are fairly satisfied? Are there ways in which, by thinking about what is actually happening and trying to understand it, you can see ways of building on your strengths and reducing your weaknesses? Such reflections do not need to be limited to what is covered in your studies, although such links should be sought out and built upon.

Improve your learning:
- *test concepts against experience*
- *discuss your 'sense making' with others*
- *reflect continually on experience*
- *keep a learning log*
- *develop less preferred learning styles (see later).*

In your attempt to undertake active learning, your superior and your mentor can both prove useful. A formal appraisal system may offer opportunities, but you will probably achieve more, and do so more flexibly, through informal discussions. You can also profitably discuss problem areas of work with colleagues. Perhaps they have made more progress in understanding the situation than you have, in which case you can benefit from their insights, or at least start to experiment with their ideas to see if they work for you too. If they are as uneasy as you are, discussing the issue and sharing your different perspectives may enable you jointly to come to a clearer understanding of what is really the problem, and to find ways of being more effective. Subordinates are a further source of ideas.

In organisations which take learning seriously, review sessions are a regular feature. Through these, teams working on a project can take time to learn from what is happening, both from what is going smoothly and from hitches, and can discuss ways whereby practice might be improved in future. You may be able to introduce course concepts into these discussions (though you may need to tread carefully so as not to antagonise people in the process), but it is not essential. An appropriate concept may provide a short cut to understanding, but you should be able to use the general approach developed in your course, and a version of the UMP to make progress if not. If your organisation does not currently encourage review sessions, you might think about whether they would be an advantage in your context. If so, think about what you could do to encourage their introduction.

For learning to be effective, people must be confident enough to admit to less than perfection. If review sessions turn into ways of shifting blame away from each person onto others, then they will be highly counterproductive. But if people are prepared to accept that nobody is expected to be perfect, and that it is a sign of strength to be able to recognise possible areas for improvement rather than a weakness, then active review with the aim of learning from experience can be extremely useful.

For your own individual learning, you will need to be prepared to admit to your own areas of possible improvement. Even privately this may be slightly uncomfortable. We often feel that we should be perfect, and hate to admit to ourselves that we might not be. To admit it to a boss is even more difficult, to subordinates, worse still. But if handled positively, this can increase your standing in others' eyes, rather than diminish it. Care *is* needed, though, if this is not normal behaviour in your organisation. Thorough groundwork may be needed to ensure that everyone involved understands, and agrees to, the change in approach.

By involving others in your organisation you may be moving it towards a more learning-oriented approach, which is likely to have major benefits in the increasingly fluid situation of the twenty-first century. Chapter 2 suggested that employers are increasingly becoming aware that continuous development of staff is the only way in which the organisation can remain competitive. One of the spin-offs from your course of study might be a move towards developing a culture in which this continuous development can more readily take place.

LEARNING STYLES

Kolb's cycle involves phases of activity, reflection, conceptualisation and application of those ideas. Honey and Mumford (1986) have suggested that different individuals prefer to learn in different ways, broadly related to Kolb's four phases, and have developed a learning-styles inventory to help people identify their own preferred learning style.

ACTIVITY

Tick the statement most characteristic of your own reaction to a learning situation.

1. 'I'm game to try it, let's get started.'   ☐
2. 'I need some time to think about this.'   ☐
3. 'What are the basic assumptions?'   ☐
4. 'What's this got to do with my job?'   ☐

The above statements give only the broadest of indications. If you are really interested in your learning style you should obtain, and work through, the full learning-styles inventory. But the above gives you a flavour of what is meant. The following descriptions relate to the four learning styles identified.

- **Activists.** These are open-minded, and involve themselves fully in new experiences. They are not noted for their caution, nor for their tolerance of boredom. They love short-term crisis fire-fighting, and the challenge of new problems, brainstorming and finding solutions. They are weaker on implementation, consolidation and anything requiring sustained effort. They are highly sociable and like to be the centre of attention. If you favoured Statement 1 you are probably an activist.

- **Reflectors.** These are thoughtful and cautious, preferring to consider all possible angles, and collect as many data as possible before coming to a decision. They prefer to observe others rather than take an active role themselves, and will adopt a low profile in discussions, adding their own points only when the drift of the discussion is clear. If you preferred the second statement you are probably a reflector.

- **Theorists.** They approach problems logically, step by step, and adapt and integrate their observations into complex but coherent theories. They like to analyse and synthesise, and to establish basic assumptions, principles, theories and models. They are often detached, and dedicated to rational objectivity. They are uncomfortable with anything that doesn't fit into their theoretical framework, and hate subjectivity, uncertainty, lateral thinking and a flippant approach. If you chose the third statement you may well be a theorist.

- **Pragmatists.** These thrive on new ideas, provided they can put them into practice. They like to get on with things, and are confident about trying to apply new ideas. Open-ended discussions are seen as highly frustrating 'beating about the bush'. Problems and opportunities are seen as a challenge, and they are sure that there is always a better way to do anything. If you preferred the fourth statement you could be a pragmatist.

As with most simple categorisations (and you will encounter a lot of them during your studies), this is an oversimplification. Examples of 'pure types' may exist, but you are likely to have found elements in more than one category that you felt applied to you. The analysis is useful, however, because it is clear from each of the 'styles' that every strength has associated weaknesses. By being alert to these, you can take steps to minimise the effects of weaknesses, and arrange your learning activities so as to build on your strengths.

If you have *activist* tendencies, your open-mindedness, energy and creativity will be enormous assets. But you will need to find ways of sustaining your motivation during the course. You will also need to discipline yourself to plan adequately for assignments, and to ensure that you are meeting requirements fully. Your tendency will be to get excited about something, and leap in without exploring all the other possibilities. You will thrive on new and diverse experiences, and on short exercises such as role-playing, competitive team activities and business games. You will love learning in groups, and volunteer to chair meetings, give presentations or lead discussions.

But other group members may resent your leading role, and feel they are prevented from making a full contribution themselves. Lectures will strain your concentration. And you will find it hard to learn from other people's experiences. You will also be unlikely to think sufficiently about your learning objectives before a task, and may be poor at assessing what you have learned afterwards. Dissertations are potentially a major problem, as they require both careful planning beforehand, and sustained work thereafter to carry them through. Neither of these comes easily to an activist.

If you are a *reflector*, your strengths will be in careful analytical work, and detailed, painstaking research. You will consider the full picture, never neglecting important background features. You should find a dissertation the most enjoyable part of your course, provided you do not spend too long planning, thereby leaving yourself insufficient time for data collection. You will be excellent at observing groups in action.

However, many characteristics of MBA work will be uncomfortable for you. You will hate to be asked to reach conclusions on the basis of insufficient data, will hate being forced into chairing groups or making presentations, and will find the conflicting demands of work and study particularly hard to reconcile. Indeed, you may hand work in late, because you spent too much time perfecting it. If you fail an exam, it will probably be because you used the time to produce excellent answers to rather fewer questions than were required.

If your strongest tendency is as a *theorist*, you will thrive on the more academic aspects of the course, such as evaluating competing theories, perhaps even coming up with improvements, organising data into neat frameworks, and looking for interrelationships between factors in a situation. If your MBA includes a course on Systems Thinking, you will probably enjoy this enormously. Provided objectives are clear, and the situation well structured, you will be able to handle complexity well. Concepts will excite you, whether or not they are relevant at the time.

You will be highly uncomfortable, however, if you are asked to participate in activities without the context or purpose being clear, and particularly if you have to take part in situations where emotions or feelings are significant factors. In a dissertation, your methodology section will probably be brilliant, but you may risk adopting a more complex methodology than was strictly necessary, and will find it hard to cope if you are forced to work with less than the perfect data you had planned. You will also be reluctant to include qualitative information.

In group work you will be infuriated by the less considered approach of the activists in your group, and may find it difficult to work effectively with them.

If you are mainly a *pragmatist*, and the majority of MBA students seem to tend this way, you will find your course enormously exciting provided you can see how to use it in your job. If choosing an MBA, you should seek a programme which has embraced the 'competence' approach to the full. Case studies showing how other organisations have solved problems will be a better source of learning for you than theoretical discussion. You will enjoy any skills development parts of the course, provided you get good feedback on your performance, and will do well at learning any techniques which will help you do your job better. Part-time and distance learning are particularly suited to pragmatists, because of the opportunities they offer for practising skills and applying concepts to their job as soon as they are learned.

You will be highly frustrated by any lecturers with no practical managerial experience, or indeed by any material presented without guidelines on how to put it into practice. In project work or dissertations you will leap into solving a problem, probably coming up with excellent and practicable solutions, but a lack of emphasis on the conceptual underpinning of what you are doing may cause you to receive low marks. You will also tend to apply solutions from one situation to another, preferring something which has been shown to work to something totally innovative. This may limit your options on occasion. Creativity is not usually your strong point in any case.

Whatever your preferred style, and however strong your preference, you will on occasion be required to take part in learning activities unsuited to your natural style. It is possible to increase your capacity to benefit from these by developing aspects of those styles which do not come easily to you. This will have potential benefits at work, as you will be better able to go through all the stages in the Kolb cycle, as well as helping with your course. A 'fully competent learner' operates comfortably at *all* stages of the cycle, and you may need to work on your less preferred styles to become one.

ACTIVITY

From the following list of activities designed to develop aspects of the different styles, choose at least six which you feel would be useful to you, and practise them. Write a note in your diary one month from today to review progress.

To develop activism

1. Do something totally out of character at least once a week (e.g. talk to total strangers, wear something outrageous, go somewhere totally new …).
2. Force yourself to fragment your day, switching deliberately from one activity to another.
3. Force yourself to be more prominent at meetings. Determine to make at least one contribution in the first 10 minutes. Volunteer for any chairing or presentational role.
4. Practise thinking aloud. When you are trying to solve a problem, bounce ideas off a colleague without thinking before you speak.

To develop reflection

1. At meetings practise observing behaviour and interactions, and analysing what is happening (Chapter 11 will help).
2. Keep a diary, reflecting each evening on the day's events and what you have learned, or enter this in your study log.
3. For your next piece of written work aim for perfection, doing more drafts than normal, and polishing it as best you can.
4. Undertake to research a topic of concern at work, investigating in as much depth as possible.
5. Before actions or decisions, force yourself to draw up a list of pros and cons, looking as widely as possible for potential results and effects.

To become more of a theorist

1. Spend at least 30 minutes daily reading something heavy and conceptual, trying to analyse and evaluate the arguments involved.
2. Find a complex situation at work and analyse how it developed, and what might have been done differently.
3. Before acting, clarify your objectives, and try to structure the situation to make the outcome more certain.
4. Look for inconsistencies, dubious assumptions and weaknesses in others' arguments.
5. Practise asking probing questions, persisting until a clear, logical answer is received.

To become more of a pragmatist

1. When discussing problems, make sure that you do not conclude before devising action plans for yourself and any others involved.
2. Put as many techniques as you can into practice (e.g. time management, forecasting, making presentations, drawing up budgets).
3. If possible, seek feedback from experts on the above task.
4. Tackle some DIY project (but *not* if you have already started your course!).

Whatever your preferred learning style, there are advantages in making active links between your studies and your work experience, and you should do all that you can to ensure that you get into the habit of doing this. Discussions, whether with fellow students, colleagues or interested others, will be very helpful in this. Also useful is to record your reflections on your daily learning experiences in your study log. Comments on how your way of *making sense* of work situations has altered as a result of your study will be particularly useful. What assumptions have you become aware of? Which of these have you deemed unhelpful and changed? What additional factors/relationships have you become more aware of? What are you doing differently as a result of such changes in thinking? Your note-taking should always highlight links between theory and practice and in assignments you should be actively seeking to use theory to inform your analysis.

These points recur throughout the book, but it is worth taking time now to think about how you can develop the habit of making linkages, and actively interpreting experience in the light of theory or concepts (developed by yourself or offered as part of the course), until it becomes second nature. If this occurs, you will gain more from your study than specific learning. You will have developed the capacity to learn from everything that you do and experience, throughout your working career. This could be of far more benefit to you than anything else that you learn on the course itself.

SUMMARY

- Learning can be viewed as the active construction of meaning.
- It is usefully seen as a continuous cycle of experience, reflection on experience, and the development and testing of concepts.
- Individuals vary in their preference for activist, reflector, theorist or pragmatist learning styles.
- Each style has strengths and weaknesses.
- Aspects of non-preferred styles can be strengthened.
- Learning to learn, whether from theory or experience, is perhaps the most valuable outcome of MBA studies.
- For optimal learning you need to be comfortable with all four styles in order to use the four styles in the learning cycle.

Further information

Butler, G. and Hope, T. (1995) *Manage your Mind: the mental fitness guide*, Oxford University Press.
Honey, P. and Mumford, A. (1986) *The Manual of Learning Styles*, Peter Honey.

9 Improving reading skills

Objectives

By the end of this chapter you should be able to:

- decide *what* you need to read
- use different reading *techniques* as appropriate, in order to make the most effective use of your time
- take useful notes on what you have read.

INTRODUCTION

Your management studies will almost inevitably involve extensive reading. Most people read inefficiently. The purpose of this chapter is to show why reading is normally slower than it might be, and to suggest exercises which will enable you to improve your own reading speeds if you so desire. Although there is a common perception that speed reading can achieve miracles, you should not expect the effect on your reading of major materials to be enormously improved. There is an old Woody Allen joke, where he stated that after a speed-reading course he was able 'to go through *War and Peace* in 20 minutes. It's about Russia'. Obviously, you will wish to retain rather more than this from many of the materials that you read. But there will be times when rapid scanning will be useful, perhaps in deciding which of the hundreds of theses in the library would merit serious attention, and techniques for this will also be covered.

If your background is in the arts, you may already have developed your reading skills to a point where you can afford to skip this chapter. If you are a scientist, an MBA may make you feel as if you are drowning in a sea of paper unless you do something to improve your reading speeds. If materials are distributed electronically you may have even greater problems without the paper. It is difficult for many people to absorb large amounts of information from a screen. Many resort to printing quantities of it themselves, which rather negates the intended benefits of electronic transmission.

As you will frequently need to take notes on what you are reading, this chapter also covers note-taking skills.

EYE MOVEMENTS

Most readers are unaware of their eye movements while they read, assuming, if they think about it at all, that their eyes are moving steadily along each line before moving to the next. If this were the case, and if you read at one line per second, which most people who are asked assume to be a reasonable speed, you would be reading at 600–700 words per minute. At this pace, you would find you could easily cope with the volume of MBA materials you are likely to encounter. Eye movements when reading are far more complex, however. The eye makes a series of extremely rapid jumps along a line, with a significant pause, 0.25 to 1.5 seconds, between each jump. Furthermore, many readers do not move, albeit in this jerky fashion, straight along a line. Instead, as Fig. 9.1 shows, they indulge in frequent backward eye jumps, fixating for a second, or even a third time on a previous word, and at intervals their eye may wander off the page altogether. With erratic eye movements like this, and forward jumps from word to adjacent word, many readers achieve reading speeds of only 100 words per minute. At this rate of reading, the volume of work for an MBA is likely to prove an impossible task.

At the purely technical level, it is possible to achieve reading speeds of up to 1000 words per minute by:

- reducing the number of fixations per line, stopping every three to six words rather than every one
- eliminating backward movement and wandering
- reducing the duration of each fixation.

If you wish to reach this level of improvement, you will need to work at it. It will require concentration and considerable practice. But as well as improving your

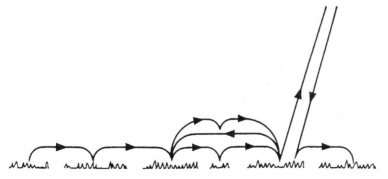

Fig. 9.1 Typical unskilled eye movements when reading

ability to get through your course materials, and reducing eye fatigue in the process because of the reduction in eye movements that you will make, you will also be able to get through your reading at work more quickly, making your use of time better there, too. The investment will therefore pay off handsomely. Also, although it is often feared that comprehension will be reduced by rapid reading techniques, the reverse may well be the case. The pattern of a sentence, and its meaning, may emerge much more clearly, and be more readily absorbed, if the sentence is read in phrases, than is the case if it is read one word at a time. Your interest is more likely to be maintained if ideas are coming at you more quickly, and your motivation will be higher if you feel you are making rapid progress, so the rewards of improved reading techniques are many.

If practice is all that is needed, you may wonder why we are all reading so slowly. Surely we have been 'practising' reading most of our lives. Unfortunately, we have been practising our existing bad habits (in the process establishing them more firmly), rather than practising rapid-reading techniques. You will find that it takes much more effort, at least at first, to read at increased speed, and improvement will be made only through the practice of exercises specifically designed for that purpose. Even when you have developed efficient reading techniques you may still find that you have to make a point of consciously practising them at intervals, to prevent yourself from falling back into less efficient habits.

ACTIVITY

Look at your watch again and note the time ___. Now note how long it is since you last noted the time ____. There were approximately 700 words in that piece of text. Divide that figure by the number of minutes elapsed in order to find your reading speed in words per minute. Write this down __.

EXERCISE

Now check your comprehension by answering the following questions, saying whether each statement is true or false according to the preceding text. Do not glance back at the text.

		T/F
1.	Poor readers fixate once per word.	_____
2.	With practice a poor reader can increase from a speed of 100 to 1000 words per minute.	_____
3.	A speed reader will fixate only once per line.	_____
4.	Once you have mastered speed-reading techniques they will become second nature.	_____
5.	The only drawback to rapid reading is that it tends to reduce comprehension.	_____
6.	The duration of each fixation can range from as little as 0.25 of a second to as much as 1.5 seconds.	_____

Comment

Answers are at the end of the chapter. If you got more than one wrong, you should be aiming to improve your retention skills since you were specifically instructed to try to retain the information in the passage.

A reading speed of 250 or more words a minute, with reasonable retention, is an adequate basis on which to start your course. If your speed was significantly less than this, or at your present speed you are not absorbing enough, you may find the following exercises useful.

INCREASING READING SPEED

The following practice activities are developed from those suggested by Tony Buzan. They will enable you to make significant improvements in your reading speed, provided you are prepared to invest the necessary time and effort in your practice. You will need to spend 20–30 minutes a day for several weeks if you wish to reach the full speed of which you are capable. This will allow you to do some of the activities several times per practice session. To keep up your motivation, and to see when your rate of improvement is beginning to level off, keep a graph of your progress. Using a single book, to control for ease of reading – material varies enormously in difficulty – set a timer, and read for five minutes, noting start and finish points. Then count the number of words read. Aim to remember significant points in each piece of text. Check your speed during your first practice session, then every five to seven sessions thereafter. Plot your speeds on a graph, so that you have a visible record of progress. If you choose to use this book, then you can use your earlier speed as the first point on the graph. When you have reached the speed you want, or progress seems to be minimal, cut back to one practice session per week for a while, and then one per month. Check your reading speed monthly there-after, and resume more frequent practice sessions if your speed starts to fall off.

Many of the practice activities which follow require a way of measuring speed. Counting chimpanzees, or whatever you usually do in the absence of a clock, will not work, as it will interfere with your reading. A metronome, which will allow you to vary the speed of your cue, is ideal. If you do not have one, it may be possible to borrow. Failing that, your PC can probably be made to emit regular beeps, or find a clock with a loud tick. You will not, in that case, be able to alter the interval. A kitchen timer that can be made to ring at intervals of from one to five minutes will also be invaluable.

You will also need suitable practice material of various density of text. This Handbook could be regarded as medium density on average, although there is variability between sections. A light novel would be low density, an academic management textbook heavy density.

For all the activities you will need an 'eye guide'. You will use this to coax your eyes to fixate less often and more rapidly, by pointing with it to where you wish to fixate, and moving it after the duration of fixation you require. A finger will do, but since the comprehension exercises which follow this section suggest highlighting key points, you might prefer to get used to reading with highlighter in hand, moving this, just *above* the surface of the page, to indicate stopping points.

Reading practice activities

1. Muscle exercise

Fixate alternately between the top left-hand and right-hand corners of the page, moving your eyes between them as quickly as possible. Then alternate between top and bottom, and between diagonals. Aim to speed up slightly at each session.

2. Page turning practice

Practise rapid page turning. Turn pages at a rate of three seconds per page, increasing to two seconds per page after about 10 sessions. Move your eyes rapidly down each page, aiming to absorb *something*, though it will not be much at first. Do this for two minutes at a stretch.

3. Reducing fixations

Practise fixating less often. Start by pointing at every third word, or every second one if you find three too difficult, and moving your pointer every 1.5 seconds. After a few sessions gradually increase both the speed at which you move the pointer, and the distance you move it, until you eventually can fixate once per line, for one second only. If you can eventually do this quite easily (and it is likely to be some time before you can), experiment with more than one line per fixation, though it is unlikely that you will be able to read at these speeds during most of your study.

4. Speed reading

Still using your eye guide, practise reading as fast as you can for one minute, regardless of comprehension. Mark start and finish points. Then read for a further minute aiming for comprehension of significant points, noting your end point. Count and record words per minute. This exercise can be done several times per session, varying the density of the material.

5. Progressive acceleration

Using light- to medium-density material, and starting with your fastest comfortable 'reading with comprehension' speed, increase your speed by about 100 words per minute, and read for a minute, then by a further 100 words per minute for a further minute, until after four minutes you are reading for a minute at approximately 500 words per minute faster than your starting speed. Calculate the speed at which your eye guide must move to achieve these speeds. Then read for a further minute, aiming for the fastest 'with comprehension' speed you can achieve. It should be higher than in exercise 4.

6. Pre-scanning

Using fairly light-density material, start at the beginning of a chapter. Estimate approximately where 10 000 words will take you, and put a marker there. Scan read to the marker, taking two to four seconds per page. Then go back to the beginning and read for *some* comprehension, at a minimum of 1500 to 3000 wpm. (Use the lower speeds in early sessions, increasing with time. You might also increase the density of material over time.)

The above exercises, if practised regularly, should increase your speed of reading without loss of comprehension. It was suggested that it might even increase comprehension. You can, however, make a more direct attack on improving the effectiveness, rather than merely the speed, of your reading. In parallel with the fairly mechanical exercises described above, you need to develop study strategies that will enable you to read more *effectively*. To do this you need to know *what* to read, what speed it is appropriate to read it at, how to absorb and think about significant points, and how to take good notes to supplement recall. It is also helpful to index these notes for later reference.

These ideas were briefly introduced in the last two chapters, but will be developed further here.

SELECTING READING MATERIAL

Knowing what to read is critical. Even if you are a distance-learning student and provided with everything you need in carefully measured packets (and this is not the case on all distance courses), you will need to make some decisions about what to omit if short of time, or what additional reading to do in areas which really interest you.

For most other part-time students there are fairly major decisions to take. There may be huge reading lists, and selectivity will be essential, especially if there are several texts on a single subject, any one of which looks as if it would do. On projects and dissertations *all* students are faced with major choices of what to read.

This Handbook can do no more than suggest a systematic approach to an answer that will suit your particular circumstances. It is, naturally, a variation on the 'Universal Management Paradigm' (UMP) described in Chapter 3.

Define the problem

What are your objectives? Why do you want to read something in this area? What do you *really* need to know? Is it facts, ideas, alternative approaches, background information, or something else that you are seeking? Is the information a requirement for an exam, necessary or potentially useful for an assignment, or just for your own clarification or interest? Refer back to the discussion of the different types of learning in Chapter 7.

Identify options

What sources exist? Look at references at the end of recent or key papers on the topic. Seek a librarian's help in identifying and searching relevant databases. Use the same keywords to search the Internet more generally. Look at reference lists in recent theses on the topic. Ask teaching staff and other students or knowledgeable colleagues for ideas. Check government publications and websites, in-company resources, etc. Browse in a good bookstore. (Note: there is more guidance on literature searching in Chapter 19.)

Identify your measures of effectiveness

Coverage relevant to your purpose is obviously crucial. Availability is important, with price and order time also significant. Reputation is crucial. The level at which something is written is also a factor to consider. You do not want something trivial, but nor should it be so specialist that it is impenetrable. It helps if something is well written. Has the author used substantial evidence, or extensively surveyed published material, or is the piece written on the basis of opinion and prejudice? When was the work published? You will need to consider in each case which of these factors are most important for you. If using material 'published' electronically be particularly cautious. It may not have been subject to the scrutiny given to papers in refereed academic journals.

Selection

Selection will be difficult unless you have access to possible materials, and can inspect them. With even brief access you can scan materials rapidly to gain an idea of their likely usefulness. Otherwise you will need to accept advice, or use other clues. Always ask a tutor or project supervisor for as much help as you can get in the vital area of identifying materials which are worth the effort of obtaining and reading. In evaluating possible materials, check whether the author's objectives are compatible with your own. Particularly in North America, where academic tenure depends largely on the length of a lecturer's publication list, there is enormous pressure to publish, regardless of whether the person has done any research or had any ideas worth reporting. Whole books may be written around a single, fairly basic idea, filled out with anecdotes drawn from the author's consultancy experience. These may be interesting, but may not score highly on relevant measures of effectiveness.

Going through the stages of the UMP should help you to make a sensible choice of materials. Having done so, you need to consider the appropriate reading speed for the materials selected.

CHOOSING YOUR READING SPEED

Sometimes you will be looking for a highly specific piece of information. Did this research use a particular technique? What sample was used? What does this author say on a particular point? If your purpose is to find something like this, a full reading of the book or article, at whatever speed, will be unnecessary. Instead, use the index, plus rapid scanning of the material to identify the part you need to read in detail. Just as you can hear your name being mentioned at the other side of a crowded room (the so-called cocktail party effect), so can you bring selective attention to bear upon written materials. You can scan the page too rapidly to read it, but still notice the word or phrase that you are seeking. In the photo-reading technique you will be scanning pages even *more* rapidly. Scanning requires concentration, and a determination not to be sidetracked by interesting points irrelevant to your purpose. Of course, if you *can* spare the time, such digressions can be rewarding, indeed, some would say they are what study is all about. Alas, they will often be a luxury.

The next fastest type of reading after scanning is that aimed at getting a picture of the overall pattern of a book, chapter or article. To obtain this kind of mapping of material, you need to focus first on any contents lists, then introductions and summaries, and main headings and subheadings. Diagrams and tables of results are also useful. You may find that several rapid passes through the material will help you to map it better than will a single, slightly slower pass. It is useful at this stage to note any specific questions you would like the material to answer, together with any aspects which arouse your curiosity more generally.

Slightly slower again is speed reading, using your fastest comfortable speed. This may be suitable for lengthy materials, where the level of relevant content is fairly low, or for background reading. You will be aiming to absorb the author's main arguments and the extent to which these are based on relevant and reliable evidence.

Much of your study will need to be at a slower rate. This is not to say that speed-reading techniques are a waste of time. You will still benefit from eliminating redundant eye movements, and from more rapid reading of any non-critical parts of the texts. But there will be materials where there is little redundancy. Almost every word will be important, and concepts will require active thought, particularly to assess the extent to which they fit, and help make sense of, your own experience. For this type of study you will need to take notes, both to aid comprehension, and for later recall, and you may need to stop reading to think, or even to consult other sources, before coming back to the main materials. You may need to practise working something out, if it is complicated. If you are trying to understand the basics of linear programming, for example, speed reading will not be appropriate.

Slowest of all, is reading to learn by heart. If you need to be able to reproduce an equation, or a diagram, or a set of categories, you will need to spend time on the item itself, committing it to memory and ensuring that you fully understand every detail, and its significance, particularly in relation to the sorts of things you are likely to use it for. You will probably need to practise applying the thing learned, preferably to a variety of situations. It has already been argued that there is little point in learning something if you do not at the same time learn how, and when, to use it.

You may find that once you have gone over all the details, relationships and possible uses, you will have *learned* the material in question. But other things may prove more elusive. If so, try to devise a mnemonic. I still recite the colours of the rainbow, on the rare occasions when this is requested, by remembering the phrase from my childhood, 'Read out your green book in verse', and go through the entire 'Thirty days hath September . . .' rigmarole to feel sure that there really is an August 31st. In either case, this is a fairly long-winded procedure, and you might feel that the learning by rote, or constant repetition, in the way that tables used to be taught, is more efficient. If speed of recall is important, such as when you need to know what 7×9 is in the middle of some mental arithmetic, then indeed straight learning may be preferable. But mnemonics are extremely useful for information that you might not need for several months, as they will enable you to drag from the recesses of your memory material that would otherwise be inaccessible.

An alternative to devising a phrase is to make the initials into a pronounceable word, such as Checkland's CATWOE, to describe the elements of the root definition that his methodology requires you to produce. This is totally memorable, although trying to remember the elements of his definition without it, apart perhaps from 'actor' and 'transformation' which are fairly obvious, would be difficult. Many authors help, by going out of their way to come up with things that are in themselves memorable. The uncharitable might say that this, rather than the merit of what it is that they are enabling you to remember, is what has made them so popular. You will almost certainly encounter the 7 Ss, the 4 (or more) Ps, and many more of that ilk. Rhyming is also popular. The 'form, storm, norm, perform' sequence is used in Chapter 11 on working in teams, and there are several other such formulations in different areas. If authors have not been so helpful, you can have fun devising your own mnemonics.

Guidelines for effective reading

- Establish purpose in reading
- Select appropriate material
- Scan entire text rapidly to establish structure and coverage
- Refine purpose – what key points/questions are of interest?
- Read relevant parts of text at fastest appropriate speed
- Capture understanding by diagramming structure of arguments, highlighting text and/or note-taking
- Review against purpose
- File notes carefully.

PHOTO-READING FOR ACCELERATED LEARNING

One system claiming to enhance your ability to learn from printed materials uses an ultra-rapid scanning stage called photo-reading, incorporated into an approach similar to that already described. In (very) brief outline, this requires that you first clarify your objectives in approaching the text, as you should with any study. Then, again as suggested, you preview the text, getting the gist of it, looking for trigger words that catch your attention, looking at a contents list. Then the method departs slightly, in an attempt to put the brain into a receptive state and to absorb material without being aware of it. To achieve this you need to 'enter an accelerated learning state' through relaxation and visualisation. Music may also be helpful. While in this state you 'photo-read', with your eyes focused on something behind the book (if you can vaguely see two lines between the pages, not one, you have it right). With this 'fuzzed' focus, breathing evenly and maintaining your relaxed state you turn the pages steadily, once per second or so. On finishing, set the text aside for a while, then deal with it through normal effective reading and note taking. It is claimed that you will absorb far more because of the photo-reading stage.

If you want to experiment with this, you probably need to read more about it: achieving the relaxed state is not all that easy. As with other techniques, this will require practice, but it may be something you wish to try if you are going to have to read a lot during your course.

TAKING NOTES

There are several reasons why note taking is important. If you are working with borrowed books, then apart from the parts that are so important that you photocopy them, you will need something that you can refer to once the book has gone back to the library. If you are working with your own materials, then taking notes can be helpful *while* you are studying, as it can maintain your concentration, can help you to sort out the essence of what an author is saying, and can give you something that is much easier to use for revision than the full volume of materials.

Furthermore, your notes can be *more* helpful than the original materials, as they may be easier for you to understand. You may have managed to represent the original materials in a way that makes more sense to you, and included relevant other material, such as cross-references to key parts of other courses that have a bearing on the point, or comments on how the material relates to your own experience. Because they are briefer than the originals, your notes may be easier to refer to, and to revise from.

The most useful type of notes will depend on the purpose for which you are taking them. Notes on borrowed materials will normally need to be more detailed than those on materials you own. For borrowed materials you may well need to copy out the most quotable phrases and diagrams, as well as any references that look potentially useful, and may need to go into detail on the actual content.

With materials that are electronically available there may be a strong tendency to copy huge chunks, because it is so easy. While this may provide you with material for future reference, you still need to be able to extract and absorb key points, in the same way as with printed material, if you are to make effective use of the ideas and information contained therein.

The most basic form of note taking with your own printed materials is to highlight key points or concepts. (You may also be able to highlight electronic materials.) This will in itself ensure that you are *thinking* as you read, continually striving to extract the main ideas. This form of interaction with the text helps you to absorb more, and to maintain your concentration more easily, than with passive reading.

Also, when you return to the materials you will be able to extract the key points very quickly by reading the highlighted text. If you have made brief notes in the margin to supplement the highlighting the process will be even easier. Such notes might be brief 'labels', explanations of points that took you some time to grasp, examples from your work which exemplify the idea, or cross-references to other materials.

If your course does not provide one, you may wish to construct a glossary, or other digest of the course, defining and explaining each major idea, and cross-referencing or adding relevant notes from your reading. As you will need to add to this glossary continually, it has to be in flexible form. An electronic organiser which you can take to libraries is ideal, or you can transfer rough paper notes to your PC. Either way the material will be readily accessible for future assignments.

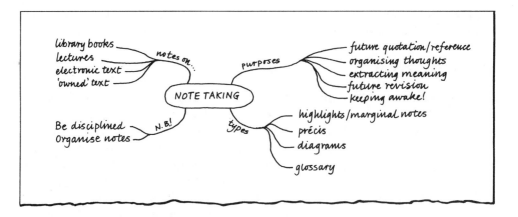

Fig. 9.2 Diagrammatic notes on note taking

In all your notes, paper or electronic, it will be very important to note relationships between materials, whether on the same course, or between different ones. Although most Master's courses are taught as a series of discrete modules, the problems you encounter as a manager are unlikely to fit within such boundaries. In your work, in analysing general case studies, and in your final project, if there is one, you are likely to need to draw on a range of different courses for relevant concepts and techniques. This will be much easier to do if you have made a practice throughout your studies of noting how different topics interrelate, or have the potential for interacting. The best way of ensuring that you do this is to highlight such relationships in your notes. Notes in the form of diagrams can be extremely useful both for establishing the structure of arguments and for showing other relationships between components. Diagrammatic notes can also help you remember what you have read. The process of drawing a diagram forces you to *think* about the structure of text in a way that a précis of points made may not. The resulting picture may be much easier to remember than words. A useful type of diagram for such note taking is described in Chapter 10, but Fig. 9.2 gives you an example of what you might have produced if taking diagrammatic notes on note taking itself.

How ever you take your notes, whether on your computer, on cards, or on sheets of paper in a series of ring binders, it is important that you are disciplined about filing them. A series of organised notes can be invaluable. A collection of scruffy pieces of paper scattered all around the house is useless. Part of this organisation should consist of keeping a good index to your materials, so that you can instantly put your hands on the notes on a particular topic if an assignment or a project requires.

Efficient reading skills and good note taking should increase your capacity to benefit from your studies many times over, a benefit which should be apparent in your assessment grades. The skills should be equally applicable at work. The time needed to develop them is therefore potentially an excellent investment.

SUMMARY

■ Reading speeds can be considerably increased if you are prepared to spend time on the exercises described.

■ The decision as to what to read is important, and requires you to be clear about your objectives, as well as knowing what is available.

■ There are several sources of help, including lecturers, librarians and colleagues.

■ Different reading speeds are appropriate for different purposes, ranging from rapid scanning to slowly working through materials.

■ Note-taking skills are important, and whether you work on paper or electronically, notes should reflect purpose.

Further information

Buzan, T. (1989) *Use Your Head,* BBC Publications.
Buzan, T. (1997) *The Speed Reading Book*, BBC Publications.
Giles, K. and Hedge, N. (1994) *The Manager's Good Study Guide*, The Open University.
Rose, C. and Nicholl, M.J. (1997) *Accelerated Learning for the 21st Century*, Piatkus.
Russell, L. (1999) *The Accelerated Learning Field Book*, Jossey-Bass Pfeiffer.

Answers to Exercise

1. False. Poor readers fixate more than once on some words. This backtracking is a major cause of slowness, and you should have remembered this.

2. True, provided it is specially designed practice.

3. False, according to the text, which claimed three to six fixations per line, although it may well be true, as later text will show. You may have *known* that the statement was really true, but it is often necessary to note what is actually in a piece of writing, even if it conflicts with what you think is true.

4. False. You would still need to practise the techniques at intervals to maintain high speeds.

5. False. Rapid reading may increase comprehension. This was another very important point.

6. True.

10 Using diagrams

Objectives

By the end of this chapter you should:

- appreciate the importance of diagramming in managerial problem solving
- be using a variety of appropriate diagrams for a range of purposes
- be able to interpret critically any diagrams you encounter.

INTRODUCTION

In analysing management situations you are frequently dealing with a large number of interrelated factors, where the interrelationships are as significant as the factors themselves. It is extremely difficult to represent such a situation other than by the use of diagrams. By a diagram I mean any representation where position on the page is significant, and lines and possibly symbols are used to add further meaning. Linear text is not at all suited to describing relationships in a variety of directions, nor is it at all easy for the pattern of those relationships to emerge without the use of diagrams.

This chapter is in the part of the book devoted to study skills because diagramming is an invaluable tool when sorting out an argument, whether your own or that in text, and for exploring relationships when you are analysing case studies or other problem situations. But you should not restrict your use of diagramming to study alone. Diagramming techniques can be invaluable when you are presenting your findings, whether in a written report or in an oral presentation. They can also be a great aid to group problem-solving work: it is very much easier to share perceptions through the medium of diagrams, particularly if shared conventions are used, than through the rather more ambiguous medium of speech. This chapter will therefore look at diagramming for all these purposes, rather than limiting the treatment to diagramming for study use alone. The ability to use diagrams effectively is a highly transferable management skill.

 For further information on creating diagrams, refer to the companion website www.booksites.net/cameron.

THE IMPORTANCE OF DIAGRAMS

Speech, especially when written, is characteristically linear. Word follows word in a one-dimensional sequence. But management situations are extremely complex, and *relationships* between factors are of crucial importance. It is extraordinarily difficult to describe multiple interrelationships using only words. Understanding such descriptions is even more difficult! Imagine trying to describe the London Underground network without recourse to the little map in your diary. And then consider how much more complex are many of the managerial situations you will be analysing than the Underground map.

Diagrams use symbols and spatial relationships to supplement words. (On the Underground map, the use of colour is significant, as is the relationship of one station to another, though distance between them on the map is not significant.) Patterns between elements can be readily shown and understood on a diagram, though there must be an agreed convention between 'artist' and reader as to the meaning of patterns. Similarly, symbols will increase the information which can be usefully conveyed only if the meaning of those symbols is agreed beforehand.

Diagrams, whether bar or pie charts, maps, or those using other agreed conventions, can be an enormously useful aid to communication, whether incorporated in reports, or used as visual aids to a spoken presentation. They can be drawn so as to make clear those relationships you wish to emphasise, with extraneous material omitted. From a large table of figures, for example, it is possible to draw a bar chart of monthly, or annual values for a key variable, so that any trend is readily apparent. This would be totally obscured by all the other figures on the table if the raw data were presented. An organisation chart can clearly represent reporting relationships: these would be confusing if described in words alone, particularly if the organisation is structured on matrix lines. In all these cases, diagrams are being used to communicate something which has been worked out beforehand, and is understood by the sender, in such a way as to be easily understood by the receiver.

> *Diagrams can:*
> - *clarify perceptions*
> - *develop understanding*
> - *emphasise relationships*
> - *simplify situations*
> - *show different perspectives*
> - *aid communication.*

Simplifying situations

Even more powerful is the role diagrams can play in helping you to understand a situation or an argument, and to work out by yourself or in a group the complexity of relationships contained therein. In trying to understand a lecture or article, you will find that diagrams can be an invaluable aid to teasing out its structure, as well as providing a form of notes that will be useful for future reference or revision. In case study analysis, where complexity can be considerable, diagrams can help you explore how situations arose, and represent the complex dynamic of inter-relationships that will need to be taken into consideration if the likely results of a possible solution are to be anticipated. In planning a report or a presentation, you can use diagrams to clarify and structure what you want to say. When planning your dissertation you will find you can use diagrams to move from an original vague idea of your intended topic to a detailed series of questions to be answered and approaches to answering them. Other diagrams such as bar charts and networks will help you schedule your research activities and monitor progress. In group work, the construction of joint diagrams can be an excellent way of developing a shared understanding of the situation, and of highlighting differences in perception between the various group members.

Diagrams can be used in a divergent or a convergent fashion. They can be used to tease out all the possible strands of a single theme or topic, as in dissertation planning, or when representing your first ideas of what *might* be relevant in a report you are going to write. Or they can be used in a more convergent way, to impose structure on something where structure is not immediately apparent, such as your first ideas on a topic, or a somewhat convoluted argument in an article.

Presentation

Diagrams can be rough working tools, in which case the rougher the better. You will want to feel free to modify them repeatedly as your ideas develop. Students are often inhibited from using diagrams because they doubt their artistic skills. But when you are using diagrams for analysis, artistic skills can be a positive disadvantage. The more finished a diagram looks, the less it invites modification. Yet diagrams are so powerful as analytical tools precisely because they can be regarded as tentative, disposable models. Your diagrams are a way of making explicit your current perceptions and of making it easier thereby to examine those perceptions and improve them by experimenting with variations. So the inartistic are at an advantage when using diagrams for analysis. If you *are* an artist and using diagrams to help develop your thinking, you should resist the temptation to make them too beautiful!

There will, of course, be occasions when a polished finished product is called for. When you are using your diagrams for communication, you will want them to be as clear and attractive as possible. If you are writing a report for the Board, or even a dissertation, high quality graphics can contribute considerably to the overall impression of quality of your work. But artistic skills are no longer necessary. Computer graphics can be easily incorporated in a report. For oral presentations they can either be printed on transparencies or be projected directly from the PC.

However, a caution concerning 'art' is in order even here. I have had many heated discussions with graphic designers who have 'beautified' diagrams I have produced for use in texts. Their versions were indeed more attractive and professional looking than mine, but by making things symmetrical that were not intended to be, or by turning diagrams into quasi-3D that were intended as straight 2D ones using generally accepted conventions, such as for engineering diagrams, they frequently reduced the clarity of my originals, and sometimes even altered the meaning of the diagram. Computer graphics present even stronger temptations to elaborate and beautify.

Your first goal should always be to communicate *clearly*. If you have sophisticated techniques at your disposal, you should think very carefully before you sacrifice clarity or meaning to appearance. The whole point of a diagram is that it enables you to grasp a pattern, or gain an instant picture. If this pattern is obscured by spurious symmetry or over-elaboration, the communication value of the diagram becomes zero.

Symbols and conventions

Symbols and conventions are an invaluable aid in diagrams. If a convention exists, and your reader is likely to be familiar with this, then all that is needed is to say what convention you are using, and stick to it resolutely. If no suitable convention exists, then devise one, give a clear key as to what arrows or other symbols mean in your diagrams, and stick to your usage so that your reader can become familiar with it. Imagine a series of Ordnance Survey maps where each one used symbols in its own way. With a key to symbols on each map, you *could* use them. But the process would be much more laborious than with the standard convention which allows you to become familiar with the symbols used, and to understand them at a glance without frequent reference to the key, regardless of whether you are in the Lake District or Surrey.

As well as increasing the amount of information that can be easily communicated, conventions serve a further purpose for the diagrammer. In drawing a diagram, you are trying to produce a useful model of a situation. Models are characterised by being simplifications of a situation, and by being capable, normally, of manipulation. The simplification is where the increase in your own understanding may first arise. The situation is almost always very complex. By using a particular diagramming convention, say one that focuses on causal links, or one that looks at flows within the situation, you are being forced into a particular kind of simplification.

It may be difficult to represent the situation in just this way, and you may be tempted to take liberties with the convention. But the discipline of keeping within the rules can generate a creative tension between your understanding of the situation and the needs of the diagramming convention. This may in fact advance your understanding in a way that using the convention less rigorously would not. If you find, therefore, that the conventions described here are frustrating, stick with them despite this.

It is worth remembering that every way of seeing is a way – or many ways – of *not* seeing. This is as true of diagrams as of anything. But by drawing a *series* of diagrams from different perspectives, and looking at different aspects, you can gradually accumulate understanding. If a series of conventional diagrams still seem inadequate, you can always draw additional diagrams to a less rigorous convention. In this way you should gain full benefit from the diagrams in terms of increased understanding, as well as generating diagrams readily understood by others familiar with the convention. Indeed, although you may need to persevere for a while to get to this stage, particularly if you are not used to thinking spatially and are diffident about your drawing skills, there should come a time when you find diagrams indispensable. You will find yourself reaching for paper and pencil whenever you are talking to someone, or trying to sort out a problem at work, as well as using diagrams as a matter of course to improve your assignments.

BRAIN PATTERNS OR MIND MAPS

Perhaps the most versatile diagramming techniques in the 'helping you to think' category are the brain patterns described by Tony Buzan (1995). Variants of these appear in a variety of contexts, variously described as mind maps, spray diagrams, relevance trees and fishbone diagrams.

In constructing a mind map (the catchiest general title), you normally start in the *centre* of the page with a word or phrase indicating your main idea or central theme, and then branch out, with each sub-theme taking a separate branch. These branches divide further into sub-sub-themes.

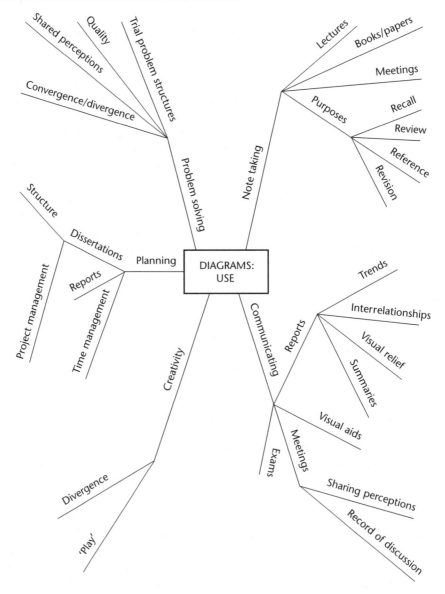

Fig. 10.1 Mind map showing uses of diagrams

Figure 10.1 shows a Buzan-type mind map for the possible uses of diagrams as described in this chapter. (Figure 9.2 was also an example of a mind map.) You can often 'illustrate' your diagram with small sketches to make it more useful/ memorable. Colour may help to distinguish different types of element, too. Buzan highlights the following advantages for this type of diagram over linear note taking:

- the central idea is more clearly defined
- position indicates relative importance – items near the centre are more significant than those nearer the periphery
- proximity and connections show links between key concepts
- recall and review will in consequence be more rapid and more effective
- the structure allows for easy addition of new information
- patterns will differ from each other, making them easier to remember
- when using the patterns creatively (divergent use), the open-ended nature of the pattern helps the brain make new connections.

The above list comprises a convincing argument for the use of such diagrams in note taking, although if taking notes in a lecture you may wish to supplement your mind map with more narrative notes, perhaps using one page for diagrams, the facing page for narrative. Mind maps are useful in a variety of contexts, from analysing a problem situation to generating a thesis topic. Because of their deliberately divergent form, they can lead you out from a central idea into a variety of subsidiary ideas that you might not otherwise have thought of, and at the same time can form the basis of the structure of anything you might write on the topic.

An alternative format with many of the same advantages as mind maps are relevance trees. These were developed primarily for research and development management (Jantsch 1967) but are applicable on as broad a front as mind maps, to which they are functionally equivalent. Figure 10.2 gives an example of a relevance tree for the early stages of a research project.

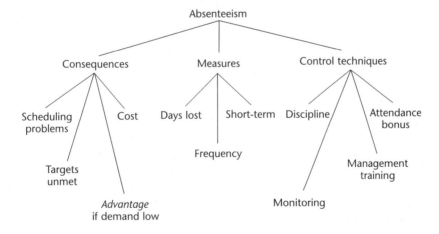

Fig. 10.2 Relevance tree for the early stages of a research project

The main advantage of this format is that you avoid the 'budgie syndrome' incurred by having to tilt your head at every conceivable angle to read the various twigs. Disadvantages are that the width of the page will rapidly limit the number of 'twigs' possible, and that the more formal, less playful appearance is less likely to stimulate creativity.

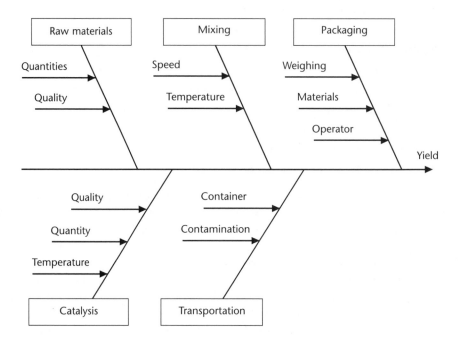

Fig. 10.3 Ishikawa-type 'fishbone' diagram used in quality analysis

The fishbone diagrams widely used in Quality Circles (an approach to generating suggestions for quality improvement through the use of voluntary groups of employees meeting to discuss problems reflecting the quality of output) are also devised to have parallel twigs, and are therefore similarly tidier than mind maps. Again, the tidiness places constraints on the branching that is possible, and makes it harder to add to the diagram, thus reducing its usefulness for creative purposes. Figure 10.3 shows a diagram of this kind.

Although, as Buzan emphasises, 'messy looking' diagrams are a positive advantage at the note-taking or thought-clarification stage, they can be quickly 'tidied-up' into something fairly respectable. If you *are* using them as a note-taking device this is worth doing, as it is hard to sort out a lecture structure while listening to it, and you will probably have needed to modify your diagram somewhat as you went along. Making a tidied-up version will have two benefits. First, the tidying-up process will consolidate your learning. Second, you will find the tidier version easier to use for reference or revision.

Even in their tidy form, such diagrams are best seen as primarily for your own consumption. Unless your audience knows and loves the technique, it can be dangerous to include mind maps in written work. In any case, once your ideas have become clearer through drawing the diagram, most of the information can usually be translated into the major and minor headings of a report. If you do wish to use a diagram showing your structure, then one of the parallel versions is most likely to communicate effectively to an uninitiated audience.

Despite the above reservation, Buzan does make one interesting suggestion about possible public use of this kind of diagram. In planning or problem-solving meetings, he says, points are often lost, and the chair may have difficulty in keeping discussion to the point. If the person organising the meeting uses the mind map structure as a basis for running the meeting, such problems may be avoided. A board should be presented to the meeting, with the central theme shown, and perhaps two sub-themes. As each member concludes a point, he is asked to summarise it, and show how it fits into the map. This ensures that all contributions are recorded, keeps speakers more to the point, means that a shared perception of the structure of the discussion will be built up, and allows participants to have a copy of the resulting pattern to take away as a record of the meeting. Use of magnetic write-on shapes, or more prosaically 'post-its', allow structure to be revised as the meeting develops. Some conferencing systems allow participants' PC screens to be used in a similar fashion during 'virtual' meetings.

You might like to experiment with this approach during group work on your course. Once convinced that the method works, and once you feel comfortable operating in this way, you might try it with colleagues. Remember, though, that you should gain participants' agreement to this method of working *before* the meeting, rather than springing it upon them when they arrive.

RELATIONSHIP DIAGRAMS

Mind maps are useful in the early stages of your thinking about a topic. A similar technique, also useful in the early stages of analysis, is the use of relationship diagrams. These differ from mind maps in that they do not require you to start with the main idea. This can be a considerable advantage if you are not sure what the central theme is (e.g. when you first meet a case study).

A relationship diagram consists of 'words' sometimes enclosed in blobs, denoting factors in a situation, and 'lines' showing some sort of relationship between them. By constructing such a diagram, it is possible to identify key groupings of factors, which may help you to go on and draw a mind map, or a systems map or other appropriate diagram.

On relationship diagrams it is best to minimise the crossing of lines. If not, you may end up with something resembling a children's puzzle, and this may lead to difficulty in 'reading' the diagram. It can be helpful, too, to distinguish strong from weak relationships, perhaps by use of thicker lines for the former. Other than this there are few rules, apart from the general one applying to all diagrams, that once complexity reaches such a point that clarity is lost, it is worth thinking about drawing more than one diagram, rather than trying to cram too much onto a single

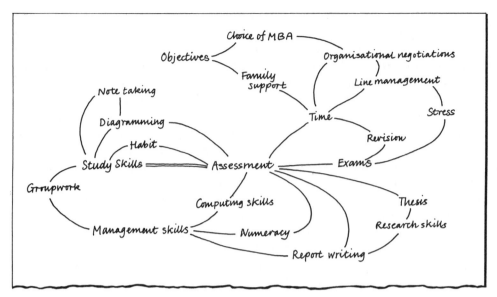

Fig. 10.4 Relationship diagram drawn in the early stages of Handbook planning

one. Figure 10.4 shows an example of a relationship diagram drawn in the early stages of planning this book. It convinced me that my intended simple structure would not accommodate the complexity of interrelationships between the topics to be covered, and that something slightly messier would be needed.

RICH PICTURES

A more graphic and amusing form of relationship diagram is the 'rich picture' devised by Peter Checkland for use at the problem-exploration stage of his soft systems methodology. This supplements the words and lines of the basic relationship diagram with cartoon-like pictorial symbols to show the nature both of the things the words represent, and the relationships the lines indicate. This type of diagram is particularly suited to group work during the early stages of investigating a problem. Using large sheets of paper such as flipcharts or wall boards, everyone can join in drawing the diagram, and there is usually much discussion of the relevance of possible items and relationships. There is no fixed convention as to symbols, though crossed swords are often used to indicate conflict, ££s for money, and sketch graphs to indicate trends. Stick men abound, with bowler hats for the managers, cloth caps for the workers. Beyond that, part of the fun is devising the symbols. Figure 10.5 shows a rich picture drawn in the early stages of a case study analysis.

Whether or not your syllabus includes a course on systems, and you learn how to use the other stages in Checkland's approach, rich pictures have many advantages. They can be a great aid to individual analysis (I know one student who at the planning stage of his project lined his downstairs loo with flipchart paper and added to his rich picture on each visit...). Even more useful is to draw a rich

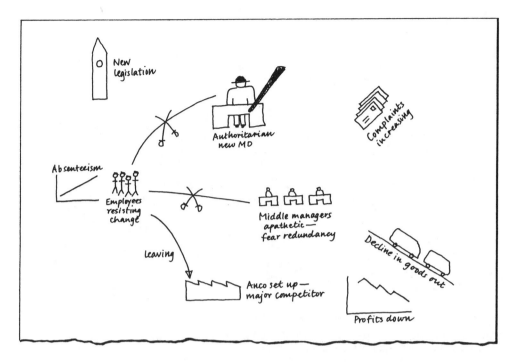

Fig. 10.5 Start of rich picture constructed in the early stages of case study analysis

picture in a group. The pictorial element encourages participation and creativity and is *fun*. And it allows you to gain an appreciation of a much fuller and more complex set of potentially important factors than either a written description or a simple relationship diagram would permit. While you may later choose to exclude some of these factors from your investigations, it is always easier to narrow down than to broaden your base once you are half way through. In general, breadth at the outset will be an advantage, though selectivity will be necessary as your analysis proceeds.

As with mind maps, rich pictures are best seen as for author's eyes only. You will risk being seen as eccentric or worse if you include them in a report addressed to those unfamiliar with the method, although Fig. 10.6 shows a splendid example of a rich picture successfully included in an MBA dissertation. If you have the personal presence you *may* be able to use rich pictures successfully face to face. Indeed, because rich pictures have so many strengths, and because they are easy to explain and use, you will usually find that you can introduce the concept to a group which has never used them before, without any need for expert guidance. Try it in your syndicate group, or when you are in a group at work that is finding difficulty in coming to grips with a problem.

SYSTEMS MAPS

You cannot expect to gain full benefit from systems maps unless you have been exposed to basic systems concepts, but since many management courses include

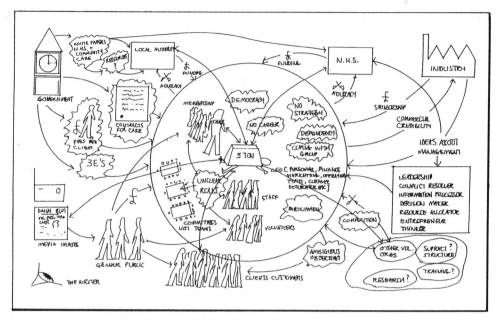

Fig. 10.6 Rich picture used in a successful MBA thesis
(with thanks to C. Bolton and de Montfort University)

systems teaching, and since students find these diagrams far more difficult than the simplicity of the convention warrants, they are included here. Skip them if you do not need to use them now, coming back if they turn out to be necessary later.

Systems maps are a variant of the Venn diagrams now taught as part of primary school maths. Venn diagrams are blob diagrams where the blobs represent classes of things, so that where they overlap it shows that items are members of both sets concerned, and when one blob is totally contained within another, all members of the first set are also members of the second. Figure 10.7 shows an example. Think about what might be represented by the overlap in this case.

Although systems maps look like Venn diagrams, the convention is slightly, but significantly, different. In a systems map a blob represents a *system*, i.e. a group of components that have in some sense a group existence. Components in a system are interrelated to such an extent that if a component were to leave the system both component and system would be altered in some way. Thus a battery full of chickens would be a system if all the parts which contributed to chicken

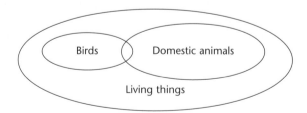

Fig. 10.7 A simple Venn diagram

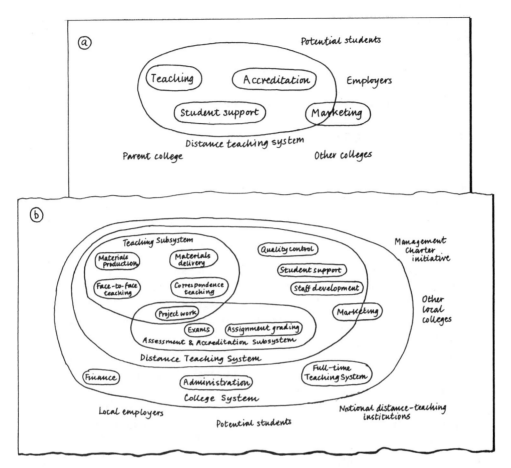

Fig. 10.8 Systems maps: (a) Simple map for a distance-teaching system; (b) a more complex systems map

production, such as food supplies, temperature regulation, etc. were included. The mass of chickens might be seen as a component of that system, though not as a system themselves, as they do not by themselves constitute a viable unit. This is in contrast to a Venn diagram, where chickens might well constitute a set of objects deserving of a blob to themselves.

On a systems map, any elements grouped within a blob should be a system. They could be the system you are looking at, or a subsystem of it, i.e. something which could itself be regarded as a system if the level of analysis changed, but in this case is contained within the system you are choosing to explore. The line around the blob is the system boundary, a rather more complex concept than a physical or geographical boundary. It is better thought of as a rule for deciding on inclusion, and could have a number of dimensions.

Figure 10.8 shows an example of a simple systems map drawn at the stage of planning a move into distance education for a business studies department. There is an elaboration of this first simple map shown below it, showing what the author felt would be needed for successful delivery of such education.

Points to note about these diagrams include:

1. As just described, they are not simple Venn diagrams. Many students asked to draw a map would have shown staff, buildings, students, etc. as components. Indeed, they would not be wrong; at one level this is important information. But by looking at the system *structure*, particularly subsystems and the relationships between them, a much clearer picture emerges. It is all too easy to draw a systems map of an organisation showing every sort of employee, for example in the above case to show lecturers, administrators, students and so on, as components. But this is unlikely to add to the author's or the reader's understanding of how that organisation functions. Indeed, it may show *less* than an organisation chart. It is the effort of *imposing* a new structure, in terms of functional systems and subsystems, systems to *do* various necessary things, that aids conceptual development.

    This element of 'does it *do* something?' (and if so, what) is perhaps the strongest test of whether something should be regarded as a system. Indeed the system title should reflect what it is that the system does, and should be clearly indicated on the diagram. In deciding whether or not to include a particular component, the acid test should be 'will this system do what its title suggests without the inclusion of this component?'

2. A simple diagram usually communicates far better than a complex one. While you may wish to go far beyond even the level of complexity in the second diagram for your own purposes, for communication you should always aim to keep your diagrams as simple as possible. If complexity is essential, start with a simple diagram first, showing the basic structure, following this with more elaborate versions.

3. Overlaps are used sparingly, as they reduce clarity. Whereas on a Venn diagram it is incorrect not to overlap in the case of shared membership of sets, on a systems map there is no such compulsion. In the example given, in the case of project and assignment work, learning and assessment functions may conflict, so it is important to highlight this. Also the fact that marketing of the courses is under the control of the wider college system is important. But the relationships between student support and teaching and assessment, or quality control and staff development, do not need to be indicated by overlaps. Because these are all shown as system components they are by definition interrelated, and overlaps do not need to be used to emphasise this point.

4. Things which the system cannot control, yet which have the capacity to influence it and therefore need to be taken into consideration in planning, are shown as in the system *environment*, i.e. outside the boundary of the system, but still there. It is not necessary to draw a further line around the environment. It is unlikely that the set of factors capable of influencing the system will themselves constitute a system, although sometimes your target system will be a subsystem of a wider system, and so can usefully be shown as totally contained within it. In this case, there will often be environmental factors outside the wider system which will also need to be included.

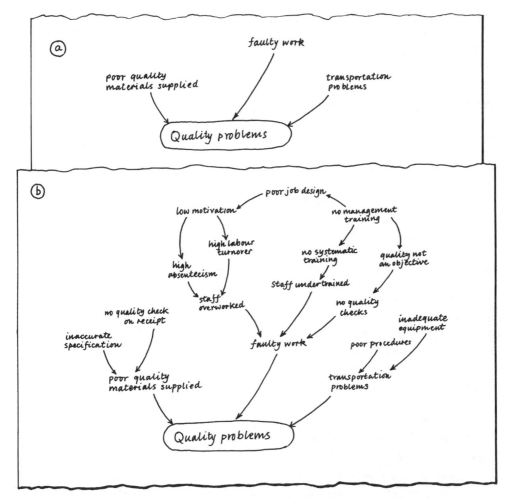

Fig. 10.9 Multiple-cause diagram showing factors leading to quality problems in an organisation

MULTIPLE-CAUSE DIAGRAMS

All the diagram types so far described are representations of things, and of the relationships between them. Frequently you may wish to understand *events* and why they happened. Multiple-cause diagrams are a powerful tool for this. In drawing a multiple-cause diagram, you use phrases and arrows. Starting with the event you wish to understand, you move backwards, looking at factors contributing to that event, factors contributing to these factors, and so on. Figure 10.9 shows an example of a first analysis of factors contributing to quality problems in an organisation.

Provided that you remember to start with the end event and work *backwards* (and it is surprising how many students forget this simple point), and that you look for contributory *events* or states, not things (in the example it is not management that is the contributory factor, but its untrained state), then you should have no problems. Even weak causal factors may be worth featuring. An arrow leading from A to B need not mean that A *causes* B, merely that it is one of the factors contributing to it.

OTHER DIAGRAMMING TECHNIQUES

There are many other techniques which you will encounter in your studies if you are not familiar with them already. Various forms of flow charts, algorithms or other engineering diagrams are commonly used. Systems maps may be elaborated into influence diagrams by the addition of arrows from major influences to the things influenced. You will almost certainly be taught the use of networks and bar charts for planning and project control, and Chapter 19 gives an example of their use in theses and dissertations. Chapter 13 shows how diagrams such as histograms and graphs can be used to represent numerical information. This chapter has concentrated on the diagramming types most useful for note taking, the preparation of assignments and general problem solving. To attempt much more would have deserved a book in its own right. Nevertheless, you will find that if you become competent in the diagramming types described, you will also find the use of other diagrams easier. It is partly a matter of confidence, partly the development of the habit of looking for patterns and the skill to represent these diagramatically, using space, convention and symbol to advantage. This applies to all types of diagram.

General diagramming guidelines

- Working diagrams should always be spaced out as much as possible. Take large sheets of paper, and use the whole sheet. Space will allow easy addition and modification, and will make your result much clearer. When using diagrams for communication, you should also avoid cramped diagrams. Again, space will aid clarity.

- Try to avoid mixing types of diagram. Avoid events on a 'thing' diagram such as a systems map, or 'things' on a dynamic diagram like multiple-cause.

- Start with simple diagrams, developing more complex ones from these only if the complexity is necessary. The simpler the diagram, the clearer will be the pattern.

- Always give each diagram a title to say clearly what kind of diagram it is and what it represents, and use a key if necessary.

- Experiment with different versions of diagrams, and different diagram types, to develop your thinking about a situation. Remember, diagrams are models, and their full value is apparent only when you play with them.

ACTIVITY

During the next month, each time you encounter a problem situation where the solution is not immediately obvious, try using different diagrams to clarify your thought. If possible, once you have drawn your diagrams, ask a colleague to 'read' the diagrams back to you, i.e. to translate them back into words. When the words do not match your intent, think about how you could have made your diagrams clearer. Note below points learned in the process.

_____

_____

_____

_____

_____

_____

ACTIVITY

Also during the next month, use mind maps when planning reports or presentations, or as a method for taking notes on any presentation you attend or article you read. Again, note any learning points below.

_____

_____

_____

_____

_____

_____

EXERCISE

Identify as many faults as you can with the following diagrams. (Answers are given at the end of the chapter.)

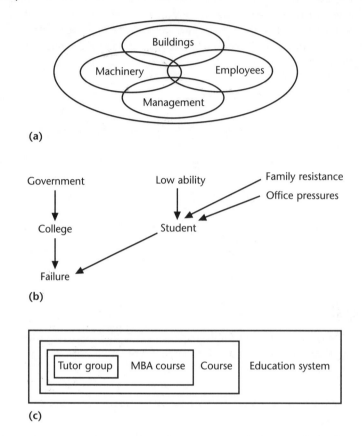

(a)

(b)

(c)

SUMMARY

- Its non-linearity makes diagramming a powerful analytical and note-taking tool, better suited to representing complexity than is text alone.

- Diagrams are also a useful vehicle for communication. Good diagrams can give an impression of overall quality. Use of position, symbol and conventions allows patterns to be explored, and increases the amount of information which can be easily handled.

- Diagrams may be convergent or divergent, dynamic or static. It is best to avoid mixing types on a single diagram.

- Mind maps are particularly good for note taking and for exploring the structure of arguments, or developing your own structure.

- Relationship diagrams and rich pictures are also useful for early exploration of problem situations, system maps for slightly later analysis.

- Multiple-cause diagrams are particularly useful for understanding how events or states of affairs came into being.

- Space and simplicity aid clarity. Titles are essential, and consistency in the use of symbols is important.

- Although you may find an initial resistance to using diagrams, with practice you will come to find them invaluable.

Further information

Buzan, T. (1995) *The Mind Map Book*, BBC Publications.

Carter, R., Martin, J., Mayblin, B. and Munday, M. (1984) *Systems, Management and Change – a graphic guide*, Harper & Row in association with the Open University. This paperback provides an excellent and entertaining introduction to the use of systems ideas, as well as including many examples of diagrams.

Morris, S. and Smith, J. (1998) *Understanding Mind Maps in a Week*, Institute of Management.

Answers to Exercise

(a) Both the system shown and the diagram lack titles. This is a serious omission. There is nothing shown outside the boundary. It is highly unlikely that a system is not susceptible to influences outside itself. There is no attempt at breaking the system down into functional subsystems, i.e. subsystems that *do* something. This is essentially a list, not a systems diagram. It is unclear what grouping the components within a boundary adds. The overlaps add nothing save confusion.

(b) Words on a multiple-cause diagram should be *events* or *states*. Student, college and government are *things*, not events. Arrows should mean 'this event contributes to this event'. Office pressures don't 'cause' a student!

(c) You can see why blobs are preferable to squares. It is much easier for the eye to distinguish them. Lots of parallel lines are very confusing. Nesting these 'systems' *might* be helpful, though it is hard to imagine why … It would be more informative, I suspect, to look at fewer levels of system in more detail.

11 Working in teams

Objectives

By the end of this chapter you should:

- understand the difference between managing the task and managing the process in a group
- recognise the sorts of behaviours helpful and unhelpful for task and process
- know what to consider if choosing members for an effective group
- be aware of the stages groups go through in becoming effective
- know how a chair can help and hinder a group
- understand the dangers in group working, and how unhelpful outcomes may be reached
- know how to record group activity
- understand how to give constructive feedback on group behaviour
- realise your own strengths and weaknesses in a group, and how to work with these.

INTRODUCTION

Managers have always attended meetings, but organisational restructuring has increased the importance of both teamwork and networking. Furthermore, not all teams actually meet. 'Virtual' teams may operate over great distances, using electronic means of communication. The skills that you will need in order to learn effectively as part of a group are therefore highly transferable to your role as a manager.

Effective teams can take decisions which are far better than those an individual could achieve, and commitment to making these decisions work is likely to be higher. On the other hand, if groups are working ineffectively, large amounts of time can be wasted, individuals can be thoroughly demotivated, poor decisions may be reached, and resentments generated which may poison working relationships for years to come.

On most full-time management programmes there is a large amount of syndicate work. On part-time courses, and particularly with distance learning, the proportion is likely to be smaller, but there may be possibilities for supplementing official group work by informal self-help groups. This will increase the scope for you to benefit from each other's experience. Understanding what makes groups effective will make your group work more satisfying, and your results of a higher quality. You will also be able to use the group work exercises as a vehicle for developing your own skills, thus enormously enhancing your effectiveness in teams at work.

TASK AND PROCESS

Groups can have many purposes. The following discussion concerns groups formed to carry out a specific task, as these are the sort of groups most likely to be encountered both during your course and at work. These days such groups may seldom meet face to face; indeed members may be in different continents, linked by video and/or computer conferences. The same basic principles apply to both face-to-face and remote group work.

ACTIVITY

Think about a group which you have belonged to recently, which you enjoyed belonging to and felt was effective, and another which was much less satisfactory. Try to think of at least three ways in which the groups concerned differed, and list these below.

'Good' group   **'Bad' group**

_____   _____

_____   _____

_____   _____

_____   _____

Comment

There could have been many reasons why your identified groups differed. Size might have been a factor, or the compatibility of the individuals concerned, or quality of leadership, or clarity of task, or any number of different factors. But it is likely that ultimately the factors you listed affected you either because they interfered with the group's achievement of its task, or because somehow they stopped the group working well together. Perhaps members were not in sympathy with each other, did not feel valued by the group, or even true members of it, and so did not work together effectively. If so, the **process** was wrong, with consequent detrimental effect on the task.

For a group to work as a _team_, that is, to achieve synergy, and to be in a sense _greater_ than the sum of its parts, the social needs of members must be met. (In this context 'social' does not mean pleasant if aimless chatter over coffee, but the satisfaction gained from feeling that you are making a contribution to a group task, and that you and your contribution are recognised and valued by other group members.) Unmet social needs can drive people to act in non-helpful ways. You have probably encountered many group members in your career who insist on talking for a far larger proportion of any meeting than the value of any contribution they might make could warrant. The less the group appreciates their input (and the signals can be crystal clear) the more determined they are to monopolise the floor. If the group refuses to reward them for membership, they can at least claim the reward of forced attention, even, in extreme cases, the perverse satisfaction of annoying their colleagues! Action in pursuit of one's own social needs can disrupt group process. Behaviour which recognises and supports the social needs of others tends to help group process.

In considering aspects of group effectiveness, it is worth having the 'Universal Management Paradigm' at the back of your mind. As with any task, the group is likely to need to:

- define the problem
- clarify and agree objectives
- generate possible options
- evaluate options and select one.

The group may sometimes need to go on to:

- implement that option
- monitor implementation.

Managing the *task* requires that each of the above stages is gone through systematically. The first two stages are of course crucial. Unless all members are committed to an agreed set of objectives, they will not function as a team. Nor will they be motivated to progress the task. (Naturally if the problem is wrongly defined, even if all agree with this definition, effort will be misdirected.)

It is equally important that the group *process* is managed well. Otherwise motivation is unlikely to be sustained, and many members may be unwilling or unable to make their full potential contribution to the task. When working remotely it is easy to forget process issues, but they are if anything more important when members do not physically meet.

Many classifications of group behaviour have been proposed; you will doubtless encounter several during your studies. The following is not intended as definitive in any way, though it is fairly widely used. Take it as a starting point, if you like, for developing your own classification, if you wish to explore this area thoroughly.

BEHAVIOURS SEEN IN GROUPS

Behaviours serving *task* needs

These are as follows:

- clarifying objectives
- seeking information from group members

- giving relevant information
- proposing ideas
- developing ideas or proposals suggested by others
- summarising progress so far
- evaluating progress against objectives
- timekeeping
- for each decision, ensuring that someone is identified to ensure its implementation
- setting up a review mechanism to check implementation is progressing.

Behaviours serving *group* needs

These are as follows:

- encouraging members to contribute
- rewarding individual contributions (with praise or agreement)
- checking that you have understood a point before giving any reasons against it
- resolving conflicts in a positive way, without either party feeling rejected
- changing your own position to one closer to the group's view
- ensuring that those who contribute too much are kept under control (again in a positive way)
- praising group progress towards objectives
- dissuading group members from negative behaviours.

Behaviours interfering with task or group needs

These are as follows:

- contributing too much, or otherwise seeking attention
- reacting emotionally to points raised
- defending one's own position excessively
- attacking the position of others by ridicule, or other unreasoned statement (e.g. 'It won't work')
- interrupting or 'talking over' another group member
- raising a totally different point when discussion is in full flow
- holding private conversations during the meeting
- not concentrating on others' contributions so that ground has to be re-covered
- using excessive humour
- introducing red herrings
- withdrawing ostentatiously from the group (the pushed back chair, crossed arms and determined silence ...).

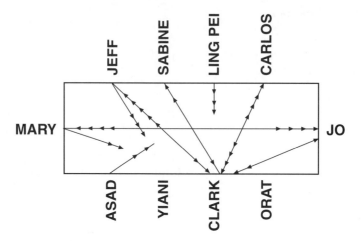

Fig. 11.1 One way of recording group interaction

You may find it enlightening to observe some meetings at work with these behaviours in mind. There are various ways of recording what goes on. The simplest is merely to chart interactions. In meetings members often address their remarks to individuals, rather than to the whole group. One aspect of process can be recorded by mapping these interactions. Figure 11.1 gives an example. Each arrowhead represents a separate interaction. Arrowheads to the centre mean remarks addressed to the group as a whole.

If you wish to get more sophisticated, you can categorise the behaviours involved, and record each instance against the person generating it. There are too many categories in the list above for easy recording. The specimen chart in Fig.11.2 gives an example of a possible recording form. With either approach it is worth looking at those who contribute little, and asking whether this level of contribution is appropriate. With the second method you will be able to see whether there is a lot of interrupting by other members, perhaps causing a more diffident member to cease in mid-contribution. You can also see whether the unhelpful behaviours are contributed by a limited number of members, or more widely distributed. If you notice a change in the proportion of unhelpful behaviours at some point, you may also be able to think back and consider what could have caused this.

A simpler recording method focuses on progressing the task, and uses the stages of the problem-solving paradigm, logging the time at which each stage is started and completed. There is unlikely to be a single pass through. Stages are often 'revisited' several times, sometimes effectively, because understanding has deepened, sometimes merely because of poor task management. You may find that some stages are omitted altogether, or undertaken surprisingly late. I have often observed student groups who, after much heat and little progress ask each other plaintively, often in the last 10 minutes of an exercise, 'What are we really meant to be doing?'.

Such occurrences are not uncommon in real life, either. Perhaps the most

	JEFF	SABINE	LING PEI	ASAD	YIANI	CLARK	JO
Clarifying objectives							✔✔✔
Giving/seeking info.						✔✔✔✔✔	
Proposing/developing			✔✔✔	✔✔✔		✔✔✔✔	
Summarising	✔						✔✔✔✔✔
Timekeeping	✔✔✔						✔
Encouraging/rewarding							
Conflict reduction		✔✔✔✔					✔✔✔
'Gate keeping'							✔✔✔✔✔
Interrupting/overtaking			✔✔✔✔ ✔✔✔	✔✔✔✔✔✔		✔✔✔✔	
Attack/defence			✔✔	✔✔✔			
Changing the subject					✔✔		
Excessive humour		✔✔				✔✔	
Withdrawal		✔			✔		

Fig. 11.2 Example of a simplified form used in recording behaviours in a group

dramatic I encountered was a meeting to discuss the commissioning of research. Several fairly senior civil servants were present, together with a large number of more junior specialist advisers. Many proposals were discussed in great depth, with impressive intellectual skills being brought to bear. After about two hours someone had the temerity to ask the size of the research budget remaining, as this would rather determine how many of the projects under consideration could go ahead. After some rather embarrassed debate it emerged that almost none of the budget remained: it had all been committed many months previously!

While I hope that your observations will show nothing as dramatic as this, it can be enlightening to see which stages of the approach are habitually rushed, which laboured over, and how many loops indulged in, and to relate this to the quality of decision reached. From your various observations, you should become much more sensitive to the dynamics within groups, and to how these could possibly be altered for the better in order to arrive at better outputs.

CHOOSING A GROUP

You may find yourself assigned to a group, in which case you will have to work within the constraints imposed by your particular group's composition. But if you do have a choice, there are several factors you may wish to consider.

Group size

Size can have a powerful influence on effectiveness. The optimum size will depend on the task, but four to eight will usually be the best range. A larger group gives you potentially greater resources of knowledge and experience to draw upon, and allows for division of labour on large tasks. However, the compensating drawback is that the larger the group, the smaller the scope for individual participation. Larger groups can also present logistical problems as it may be difficult to find meeting times convenient for all members. More formal approaches tend to be necessary to manage a larger group. Parkinson, in addition to formulating his famous 'law', suggested that maximum inefficiency was reached in a group of 21, as once this size was reached, a group member had to stand to be heard, and once on his feet found the temptation to make a speech irresistible.

Expertise

The range of expertise contained within the group is important. While you may find it comfortable to work with a group of similar background, and therefore similar perspective, to your own, many tasks demand a range of expertise, as indeed do many tasks at work. You are likely to gain more benefit in the long run, therefore, from joining a group with skills complementary to your own. Try to arrange that all the basic management disciplines are covered if possible.

Objectives

People seek management qualifications for many different reasons. Your own objectives will be an important factor in choosing fellow group members. Here, similarity rather than variety is desirable. If you are highly ambitious, and aiming to do as well as possible in the course, you will find it frustrating to be in a group whose main concern is to do the minimum necessary to pass. If you have taken the perfectly valid decision to be one of the latter category, you will find a bunch of high-fliers equally unrewarding to work with.

Group type

People tend to prefer to play a limited number of roles within a group. The best groups consist of a mixture of such preferences. It is helpful therefore that, as with expertise, you aim for variety of preferred group type if possible. At the start of your course you are unlikely to know other course members well enough to be aware of their preferred role type in groups, and their strengths and weaknesses in this way. The behaviour categories listed above can in theory be performed by any group member, but Belbin (1981, 1993) suggested that for a group to be productive nine team role types need to be present. Different individuals will be stronger in some roles, weaker in others.

The types (or roles) suggested for effective group functioning are:

- **Co-ordinator**. The co-ordinator clarifies goals and promotes decision making, is a good communicator and social leader, and a good chairperson. Co-ordinators may, however, be seen as somewhat manipulative, and too prone to let others do the work.

- **Plant**. The plant comes up with original ideas, is imaginative and usually very intelligent. But others may see plants as careless of detail, and prone to resent criticism.
- **Shaper**. Shapers are task minded and dynamic, and stimulate others to act. But they may be impulsive, impatient and intolerant of vagueness.
- **Monitor-evaluator**. These assess the qualities of ideas or proposals, being good at dispassionate, critical analysis. They may, however, be seen as lacking warmth and imagination, and have a damping effect on others' enthusiasm.
- **Resource investigators**. These are good at bringing in resources and ideas from outside. They tend to be extroverted and relaxed, but not overly original. The team will usually have to pick up their contributions and run with them, as their enthusiasm wanes rapidly.
- **Team worker**. Such people are very important in holding the team together through focus on the process side. Sensitive, good at listening and at defusing friction, they may be indecisive and too keen to avoid conflict.
- **Implementer**. Their strength is in practical organisation, and turning ideas into manageable tasks. They bring method to the team's activities, but may be inflexible, and resist changes to plans.
- **Completer-finisher**. They are good at checking details and chasing deadlines, so are essential for group performance, although they may make themselves unpopular in the process.
- **Specialist**. Specialists provide rare skills and expertise and are focused and self-motivated. But they may see only a narrow segment of the situation, and lack communication skills.

Although the above may read like a list of stereotypes, it is firmly based upon Belbin's work with groups within organisations, and his finding that groups with a mix of roles consistently performed better than groups that were more homogeneous (in role terms).

Several things are worth noting. If you think about the above in terms of personality types it may seem depressing – at work in particular you are often stuck with a particular group. But if you think of it in terms of roles to be performed for effective group working (and you will readily see the links to useful group behaviours in Fig. 11.2) then it can give you another route into thinking about why a group is, or is not, working well.

If you do have a free hand in choosing a group to work with, it may be worth seeking to form a group where preferred roles are balanced. If not, you might wish to discuss how to handle the imbalance and deliberately allocate roles which do not come naturally to any members. This will help you all to develop your less-preferred roles, and therefore become more versatile group members.

If you are in a group where some of these functions are not being carried out, it may be helpful to comment on this.

GROUP FORMATION

It is rare for a group to be effective from the moment of its formation. Members are unsure of each other at first, and do not know what will turn out to be acceptable and unacceptable behaviour within the group. How formal will it be? Will disagreement be acceptable? Is everyone going to be far better informed, more confident, more experienced and a great deal more intelligent than they are? Different groups have different 'norms' of acceptable behaviour. And members fit into groups in different ways, playing different roles and having different status depending upon the circumstances. A popular (because easy to remember?) description of the stages of group formation was formulated by Tuckman in 1965. It suggests that groups go through four stages.

- **Forming.** This is when individuals try to establish their identity within the group. Behaviour is often tentative at this stage, and extreme politeness may prevail. A leadership pattern may emerge.

- **Storming.** All the positions established at the earlier stage are now challenged. There may be considerable conflict. Personal agendas emerge. Status battles may ensue. A group can disintegrate at this stage. Alternatively, if the conflict is constructive, it can generate greater cohesion, a realistic commitment to objectives and trust.

- **Norming.** This is when the group develops norms for how it will operate. Acceptable behaviour within the group is established.

- **Performing.** Only when the earlier stages have been passed through is the group in a position to operate effectively.

If group members are aware of the need for the earlier stages, they are less likely to be disturbed or discouraged by them, as might be members who enter the group expecting instant 'performing'. Instead, they will pay attention to managing the group process through the early stages, so that conflicts are used constructively, appropriate norms emerge, and the performing stage is reached as painlessly as possible.

'Adjourning' is sometimes added as a fifth category to highlight the need for attention to be paid to the way in which a group is disbanded. If members have worked closely together there may be feelings of sadness or dissatisfaction if this stage is ignored.

The need for a chair

Many groups which have floundered are likely to say at the end of the exercise 'If only we'd had a chair'. The advantage of having an agreed chair is that there is someone in the group with the *responsibility* for achieving progress towards objectives. It is accepted that it is the chair's job to manage both task and process issues, and behaviour directed towards achieving this will be accepted by the group. The chair has the *right* to silence an over-verbose member, to push people towards expressing agreement with what seems to be emerging as the group view, to instruct individuals to carry out follow-up work, etc.

With a chairperson who is skilled in managing groups, and good at both task and process issues, a group can be highly effective. Indeed, with a newly formed and temporary group, which will not have time to go through the processes of group formation, a designated chair is essential. This is also the case for most groups larger than about eight, and any formally constituted group. However, as with most benefits, there are associated costs. A good chairperson can be a tremendous asset, but a poor one can be a powerful liability. Because it is the *chair's* responsibility to manage the group, members take no responsibility for this themselves. Few chairs are equally good at managing task and process (indeed, you will note that Belbin saw the chair's role as primarily co-ordination, rather than the combination of many of his roles commonly expected).

Some chairs are singularly poor at *both* aspects. Perhaps they use the position to satisfy their own social needs for attention and the exercise of power, and monopolise the meeting, driving their own preferred conclusions through regardless of the views of other group members. Under such a 'tyrant chair', group members rapidly cease to feel any commitment to the group and see no point in trying to make a contribution. Instead, they gain what little satisfaction they can from criticising the chair behind his or her back.

Perhaps more common is the 'willing but weak' chair who would *like* to help the group to be effective but lacks the skill to do so. He or she may know they *should* control the over-wordy, but be insufficiently assertive to achieve this. They may be incapable of gaining a sufficiently firm grasp on the arguments flying around to be able to summarise effectively. Under such a chair, members will be equally frustrated, if less angry.

In either of the above cases, group members will see the group's failures as the chair's responsibility, seldom blaming themselves for failing to assert their own rights as group members to effective chairmanship, or to recognise their own responsibilities for managing aspects of task or process clearly beyond the reach of the chair.

If a group genuinely chooses a chair because they think the person is capable of filling the role, then problems are likely to be few and those that arise can be discussed openly because the chair knows that she or he has the group's support.

Hardest is the case when a chair is forced upon a group, perhaps by virtue of seniority. This used to be standard practice in the Civil Service, and it was readily apparent that chairmanship skills were *not* a prerequisite for promotion. With an imposed chair, group members feel far more inhibited about taking on aspects of the role which the chair cannot handle. Yet there is no real reason why they should not assume these roles. If done skilfully this can be a great relief, both to the chair and to the other group members, and can turn an ineffective group into one which feels it is getting somewhere.

If the chair is self-assumed, the situation may be very difficult to resolve. Members sometimes volunteer to chair because they know they have the necessary skills. More often it is because they are very task-oriented, and want to start 'getting on with the job, rather than wasting time talking about how to tackle it'. Such chairs are often strong on task management, but weak on process. Worst of all, the volunteer may be an incipient tyrant, with strong needs to dominate, and equally strong, though not necessarily right, views on what 'the answer' is. Such a chair will not allow group members to play a role in managing the group, or indeed any role at all other than that of audience.

In such circumstances, group members will have the choice of allowing the chair his or her head, or voicing their unhappiness, and expressing the need for a change of style. The one sort of poor chair who is not necessarily a liability is the chair who knows his or her limitations. If, for example, you very much wish to develop your own skills at chairing because you know these to be weak, let the group know that you would like to play the role. With their help, and with feedback on your performance, this can work very well.

By offering your weakness as material for analysis, you can help the whole group to learn from how you handle the role. Because you have admitted to your shortcomings before you start and asked for help, the group will be happy to take some of the responsibility for ensuring that the task is progressed. The comments about the dangers of a poor chair should not therefore make you reluctant to take this opportunity for skills development in a relatively protected environment.

Because of the risks associated with vesting all the management roles in one individual, some working groups choose to share roles between members. With a long-established group, well into the performing stage, this may be done informally. Less assured groups, or those with a complex task, may prefer more formal allocation of roles, with individuals agreeing to take the main responsibility for timekeeping, or for making sure that everyone has a chance to contribute, or for summarising at intervals or checking against objectives. If your course involves much group work, or if you can become a member of a self-help group, you may be able to experiment with different ways of working, sometimes having the chair, sometimes designating and allocating different roles, sometimes trying to be completely informal about it. Eventually you should be able to choose the best approach for any given task and set of members; both will be important considerations.

AIDS TO GROUP EFFECTIVENESS

There are some very practical factors which can have a marked influence on group working. Seating arrangements are critical. Members tend to interact with those with whom they can have eye contact. With a rectangular arrangement they will therefore talk to those opposite, rather than adjacent to them. Circular arrangements are often, therefore, to be preferred (unless you wish to *discourage* interaction between certain members).

Physical comfort can help. If a room is stuffy or cold, or members are hungry or thirsty, the quality of the meeting is likely to suffer. Indeed, chairs have been known to gain agreement to unpopular decisions by making sure that they are low on the agenda, and are discussed at 1.20 pm, when the strongest concern is with getting lunch before the canteen closes rather than fighting a particular decision.

Stamina is limited. Full involvement in group work requires intense and sustained concentration. After about two hours, sometimes less, effectiveness is likely to diminish if there is no break for relaxation. It is important, therefore, to have an agreed end time for the meeting, and to have a number of interim deadlines so that the business is progressed at a rate which will allow this end time to be adhered to. With practice it will become clear how much can be attempted with a two-hour or other length of meeting.

For a new group it is well worth providing name cards, big enough to be read by all members. This ensures that people are not using all their concentration to remember who is who. Use of name cards can significantly increase effectiveness in such cases.

Just as a group goes through a series of stages over time, any single meeting has a number of identifiable stages which need to be understood if the meeting is to be fully effective. The first is *nurturing*, a slightly off-putting term for making people feel welcome and valued. Offering coffee, and encouraging members to talk to each other, having greeted them on arrival, can help this stage. Then there is the *energising* phase, when members gradually get 'up to speed'. It is inappropriate to tackle major tasks in this phase, though fairly routine items, on which easy decisions are possible, can speed the energising process. *Peak activity* occurs in the next stage, when major work should be undertaken. The final stage is *relaxation*, when the group unwinds, and achieves a feeling of completeness, having finished. It is important not to omit this stage, or members will feel slightly dissatisfied, and the sense of achievement generated in the earlier stage can be somewhat diminished.

If you are setting an agenda for a meeting you should bear the above stages in mind when doing so. If you are working in a case study syndicate, it can still be helpful to steer the group towards finding small but useful activities that can act as energisers, and trying to manage to include a relaxation phase at the end.

> *Meetings go through stages of:*
> - *nurturing*
> - *energising*
> - *peak activity*
> - *relaxation.*

THE DANGERS OF GROUP WORK

A group can have a very powerful effect on its members. Being approved of by the group may come to be enormously important, while being rejected by the group may be psychologically damaging, or at best very painful. If the group is firmly agreed on something, members feel that it *must* therefore be true. These aspects of group membership lead to some of the potentially unproductive outcomes of group working.

The first such negative outcome is called *groupthink*. Often this involves extreme optimism and a willingness, because of the feeling of group invulnerability, to take undue risks. The group disregards any external evidence which contradicts its view, and any member

> *Beware:*
> - *groupthink*
> - *scapegoating.*

rash enough to suggest that there *is* evidence of a problem will receive a clear message from the group that the suggestion is unacceptable. The suggester realises that if he or she wishes to remain in the group then they should stop acting in such a disloyal fashion. In such circumstances, the desire for group cohesiveness and sense of belonging are acting counter to task needs. If you find yourself in this position you will start to think that you were wrong, rather than insisting on your point of view. This phenomenon is very common within organisations facing serious problems. Boards may refuse, long beyond the time that it is glaringly obvious to everyone else, to accept that they have a problem. They will question the understanding of anyone who suggests otherwise, and refuse to believe the clear implications of any sets of figures with which they are presented. If the group is aware of the possibility of groupthink, they *may* be better able to resist it, although the tendency is a strong one. The rejected member can at least suggest that they examine the possibility that groupthink is taking place.

Another form of group behaviour which interferes with group learning is *scapegoating*. If a group performs poorly it will seek an individual to act as scapegoat and accept all the blame for the failure. ('Blame the chair' is a mild version of this game, 'blame the tutor' another.) This can be a painful experience for the group member concerned. It also removes from the group any perceived responsibility for what happened. There is, therefore, no felt need to look at how *the group* contributed to what happened, to learn from this, and to make changes that will increase the chance of future success.

BECOMING A MORE EFFECTIVE GROUP MEMBER

To work on your personal effectiveness, you need to know your own strengths and weaknesses.

ACTIVITY

Think about your own behaviour in the last two groups you were a part of at work, either as chair or member. Use the behaviour categories listed previously as a basis for identifying your own strengths and weaknesses in groups, and list these below.

Strengths

_____

_____

_____

Weaknesses

_____

_____

_____

If possible, check your perceptions with those of someone you trust. Ask them to observe you in a meeting soon, and give you feedback on aspects of your behaviour which they feel contributed to the meeting, and aspects which reduced your effectiveness. Indeed, if you are in a group of students who work reasonably well together, members might agree to nominate an observer for each meeting for a while, so that you all get feedback on your behaviour, and can support each other in increasing your personal effectiveness, as well as the effectiveness of the group as a whole.

If you become more aware of your strengths and weaknesses you will be much better able to work out ways of improving. It may be that you can make simple changes in the way you phrase your contribution. You may realise that you have strengths, for example in summarising, that you are not exploiting as much as you might.

Many people, whether as chair or as member, are less effective than they might be because they are insufficiently assertive. Either they do not realise the difference between assertiveness and aggression, and avoid the former for fear of the latter, or they have never developed assertiveness skills, so the phrases that would help do not come readily to their tongues. They may simply never have thought about their rights in a meeting. If you recognise yourself in this description, and have not already done so, work through the section on assertiveness skills in Chapter 4.

Support is absolutely essential in improving group performance. It is very easy to give feedback in a 'holier than thou' fashion, which carries the message that the observer is infinitely superior to the observed, and in possession of secret knowledge of all the observed's faults. Since our social interactions are an area in which most of us feel vulnerable, such feedback can be highly destructive. The group needs an agreement beforehand on how it wants feedback given, and a commitment to supporting its members in their efforts to improve in the light of feedback. If this works, it can provide one of the most important developmental aspects of your whole course. In our jobs we are seldom allowed scope for detailed feedback on this important area of performance. This is odd when you consider the enormous potential for organisational damage caused by poorly managed meetings and task groups.

The potential for psychological damage means that if the opportunity for personal feedback is to be used in a positive way, you *must* pay attention to developing feedback skills, and to getting feedback on your feedback. I was exposed, back in the 1960s, to one of the rather nasty 't' groups then in fashion. Fairly typically, it was run in a totally non-directive fashion, and members seemed to think that the purpose of the group was to be as unpleasantly truthful as possible about each other's shortcomings. I certainly learned nothing from the experience, apart from to keep quiet in that group. Those less cautious will, I am sure, carry the scars to this day. It is easy to focus review and feedback on what is *not* working. While it is obviously important to identify such things, and to do something about them, it is equally important to look at what *is* working well. If at the end of a meeting, for example, you review the progress you have made as a group, and highlight achievements, the group will feel 'rewarded', and be motivated to future effort. They will also be more likely to use any behaviours identified as contributing to that success on future occasions.

Giving feedback is a skill, and you cannot learn it from a book. That is why it is important to obtain feedback on your feedback. The following points should be remembered:

- Feedback is less threatening if it focuses on the behaviour shown, not on the person behaving: 'That remark about ... might have been interpreted as an attack on ...', rather than 'You were very aggressive'.

■ Feedback should focus on good aspects even more than bad ones. This will reinforce strengths as well as making the recipient feel strong enough to face up to a limited number of weaknesses without becoming instantly defensive.

In addition to reviewing individual effectiveness, a short period at the end of each meeting devoted to thinking about group effectiveness may prove useful in pointing out areas of potential improvement.

Guidelines for effective team working

■ select members with appropriate skills, knowledge, and, if possible, a mix of preferred team roles

■ ensure that all members understand and accept the objectives

■ pay attention to both task and process

■ accept that feelings may run high during early 'storming'

■ value all contributions

■ review both task progress and group process at regular intervals

■ reward success

THE ROLE OF INFORMAL GROUPS

Well-managed groups can generate powerful learning experiences, as well as being a source of support, information and expertise. If your chosen programme provides few official opportunities for group work, perhaps because you have chosen a distance course, or a part-time one heavily based on lectures, it is important to create unofficial opportunities.

Distance learning students have for many years been exploiting the possibilities of self-help study groups. These range from the highly formal group with a co-ordinator, regular meetings, agendas circulated beforehand and minutes afterwards, right down to the much less formal 'at the pub, every other Friday' sort of meeting, or the agreement among two or three students to ring each other for support or encouragement when they feel the need.

However students choose to operate, they find such groups a rich source of ideas, help with course material, and moral support. Although part-time students may feel slightly less need for such groups if they meet regularly at classes, they may be underestimating the potential benefits of self-help. If you are in this position you should see whether there are others with whom you could meet, even if only occasionally, for additional discussion. If there are, try having a few meetings before rejecting the idea.

When there are several people from the same organisation enrolled on a course they can form their own group, perhaps meeting for lunch if they work on the same site. At their meetings, some of the time can be devoted to discussing how to apply course ideas to their own organisation. Indeed, this is such a powerful way of 'tailoring' a course to a specific organisation's needs that many employers deliberately arrange such meetings, perhaps with an in-house trainer as facilitator. If your employer is sponsoring several from your organisation and has not yet realised the value of such a provision, you might suggest it. That way you may be able to have your self-help group meetings in working hours.

Whether your group is in-company, or you all come from different organisations, and whether working face-to-face or remotely, you may find the following guidelines helpful. They are derived from various sets of guidelines available within the Open University, for use by students and tutors but are potentially of use in a wide range of collaborative learning situations.

> ### *Guidelines for running study groups*
>
> ■ Nominate a meeting co-ordinator. This need not be permanent – the role may rotate, but someone needs to take the initiative for the first few meetings.
>
> ■ Decide where and when to meet, and for how long, and ensure that everyone knows how to get there.
>
> ■ Decide on an agenda. This need not be formal, but everyone needs to know the purpose of the meeting, what they should bring, and what preparation, if any, would be useful beforehand. Possible topics include discussion of the next assignment, comparing members' experience of organisational practice on a particular issue, role plays and so on. Start with fairly simple objectives for your first few meetings.
>
> ■ Remember the nurturing! Arrange a comfortable meeting place, where refreshments are available (not possible for remote meetings).
>
> ■ Check your objectives at the start of the meeting, and review the extent to which they have been met at the end. Consider whether this has implications for the way future meetings will run.
>
> ■ Bear in mind all the information in this chapter about effective group working.
>
> ■ Fix your next meeting before you leave.
>
> ■ Share phone numbers and e-mail addresses so that interactions can go on outside meetings.

SUMMARY

■ In managing group *tasks* the 'Universal Management Paradigm' can be a useful framework.

■ Behaviours concerning clarification, information giving and seeking, proposing, summarising, evaluating, timekeeping and identifying further action are important.

■ In managing group *process,* behaviours of agreeing, encouraging, praising and resolving conflicts are important.

- Group observation, and feedback based on that observation, can give valuable insights.
- Group members should ideally share goals, but have a range of expertise and preferred group roles.
- Groups normally go through stages of 'forming', 'storming' and 'norming' before 'performing', and a single meeting will need to go through a cycle of 'nurturing', 'energising', 'peak performance' and 'relaxation'.
- A good chair can manage both task and process issues, but these need not all be the chair's responsibility, and not all groups need chairs.
- Groups can exhibit negative features, such as groupthink and scapegoating.
- Feedback must be supportive to be helpful.
- Informal groups can usefully supplement those which are formally required.
- Group working skills developed during your course can markedly improve your performance as a manager.

Further information

Hardingham, A. (1995) *Working in Teams*, Institute of Personnel Development.

12 Learning from case studies

Objectives

By the end of this chapter you should:

- understand the strengths and weaknesses of case studies as a vehicle for learning from the teacher and student perspectives
- be prepared for the main difficulties encountered in working with cases
- be able to approach case study analysis in a systematic and effective way.

INTRODUCTION

The central role of case study analysis in traditional MBA programmes was discussed earlier. Case studies are still widely used in postgraduate management study, as vehicles for both learning and assessment. In studying management, the content of the concepts, theories, frameworks and techniques that you encounter, while significant, is far from all you need to know. Being able to apply these techniques to the situations managers encounter is equally vital, and successful application depends upon appreciating the context of the application. Case studies, which are representations of organisational situations, provide that context.

By working through a number of cases you will become better able to recognise types of problem situation, more skilled at extracting key features in these and better able to work out root causes and possible actions. There are never 'right answers' to organisational problems, but through cases you may become better able to think your way through to ones which are not totally wrong!

As well as providing the context for you to use concepts from the course, cases offer the opportunity to practise a wide range of transferable skills. These include reading and note taking, diagramming, analysis of information, coping with complexity and ambiguity, group working, time management and written and oral presentation. They also place more of the responsibility for learning on the student than do lectures or seminars.

Given this, it is not surprising that case study work poses considerable challenges. This chapter is directed at helping you make full use of the learning opportunities that case studies present. It will also help you to do well in case-based assessment. It first outlines key features of case-based learning, and then offers a method for approaching cases. While understanding the former will help you manage your learning, you could, if pressed, move straight to the method.

THE PLACE OF CASE STUDIES

The case study teaching method was first used at Harvard Law School in 1869. Since then it has been widely used, particularly in management education. Looking at how (and why) cases are used goes a long way to explaining their popularity. More importantly, if you understand *why* you are being asked to work in a particular way, you are more likely to benefit from that work.

The case method

In the case method of teaching you are presented with information about an organisational situation. Normally much of this will be in the form of written description of that situation, together with relevant quantitative information. Thus you might receive a few pages, written by a case author, saying what was going on in the organisation and what was problematic, together with, say, financial information in the form of tables. Some cases may include very much more than this, including 'original' information such as press cuttings, copies of internal memos, survey reports – the possibilities are endless. Some of the information might be in the form of video or audio material, perhaps including interviews with key protagonists. Sometimes a case may be enormous, 60 or 80 pages long. Sometimes it may be fairly short.

Whatever the nature of the case with which you are presented, you will be required to 'analyse' it. This means working out what seems to be happening, and why. You might be asked merely to explain a situation, you might be asked to evaluate actions that have already been taken or you might be asked to consider possible future actions and compare the likely effectiveness of these. In doing so, you will be expected to use ideas that you have been taught in your courses, thus exploring the usefulness of theories and techniques in different contexts and gaining practice in linking idea to situation.

> *Case studies:*
> - *are interesting*
> - *introduce 'real' situations*
> - *allow use of concepts and techniques*
> - *are a good basis for group work.*

You may be asked to analyse the case single-handed (particularly for a written assignment or exam, where your analytical skills and conceptual grasp are being tested). More commonly, particularly if the objective is to increase your learning, you will be asked to work in a group. In this case you will typically be asked to stand up and present your analysis and conclusions to the rest of the class (assuming a face-to-face context). The following discussion assumes a group context, but most of it will be relevant to individual case study analysis).

Intended learning

When faced with a case study, your first reaction may be, 'Help! What am I supposed to do with this?' Some time later you may feel you are drowning in a sea of so-called information, which is doing little to inform you about anything you want to know. You may be barely speaking to some of your group, who seem not to be pulling their weight or even deliberately obstructing your efforts after progress. The whole thing may seem a total waste of time, and certainly not a source of any kind of learning at all.

Perhaps this will remain your view. But if you reflect back upon your objectives in studying, it may become clear that the value of the approach stems from its capacity to generate precisely these sorts of frustration. Let us assume that you realise that letters after your name are unlikely to be enough to make you more effective as a manager and accelerate your career. You therefore seek to develop the skills that will achieve this. Many of these skills will be conceptual ones, and of a fairly high order at that.

Managing is not easy. The situations you encounter are likely to be different from those encountered in the past. They are likely to be complex, with many interrelated factors, and different views as to what is happening and should happen. Some important factors may be unknown, perhaps unknowable until it is too late. You cannot hope to walk in with ready-made answers – 'When they had this problem at X they solved it by doing Y, so we should do Y'. The chances are that at X there were key differences: what worked there will not work here. Indeed they may not really have had 'the same' problem. In many situations it is difficult to know just what the problem *is*. Frequently a situation will be construed as a particular type of problem when deeper investigation identifies something completely different.

The skills that you will need to take appropriate action as a manager in the face of complex, unfamiliar and uncertain problem situations include:

- identifying those with an interest in the problem situation – the stakeholders – and their different perspectives;
- understanding the wider context within which the situation is located – how it links to other problems (and other non-problems), what is changing outside the area of immediate concern that may impact upon it, what constraints will be imposed by the context;
- figuring out what information you have, or can obtain, that will cast light on the situation, and how reliable this information is likely to be;
- becoming aware of assumptions that are being made about the situation – by yourself and by fellow group members, as well as by key actors in the case; these may be leading to misperceptions about the problem, or limiting what is seen to be possible by way of improvements;
- living with ambiguities and uncertainties, as you will never have full information;
- 'making sense of' the problem situation, so that you feel that you have an understanding of what is 'really' happening – the key issues in the situation, the factors which contributed to their becoming issues, and the causal relationships involved, and/or the likely effects of recent and possible future action;
- given this understanding, working out what needs to be done;

- convincing anyone who needs to be convinced that this is indeed the appropriate course of action;
- making sure that all those involved in this action are committed to the action and are enabled to implement it.

Dealing with complexity

Case studies are not reality – more of their limitations in this respect shortly. But they are a pretty good half-way house. They are complicated, and difficult to make sense of, and the difficulties they present allow you to develop the conceptual skills which feature in the list above. Of these, that loosely called 'making sense' is perhaps the hardest of all. Working out what the issues are, when faced with a seeming 'mess' of information, feelings, different perspectives and interpretations of 'the problem' presents major challenges. The same is true of working out the causal factors and relationships involved.

Critical application of ideas

Since much of the academic content of your course will consist of ideas intended to *help* you make sense of organisational complexities, and you cannot do this without something to make sense *of*, the centrality of case study work is not hard to understand!

One skill not explicitly mentioned above, though implicit in 'making sense', is choice of suitable frameworks and ideas to help with this. The ideas taught in your course will not in any sense be 'solutions'. But by using them in a situation, you may find that they lead you to suggestions that will improve things. This point was nicely made by one of my students recently, when he said: 'What is different about this course is that all my previous management training has purported to give answers: this one is giving me the questions.'

Different ideas are of more or less use in different situations. You need to be able to work out which will be useful in any particular situation, and then to derive benefit from using them. Furthermore, you are likely to be faced with new theories and concepts throughout your life, and will need to be able to critically evaluate these, too. Are they logically consistent? Are they based on reasonable evidence? When are they likely to be useful? In what ways? When are they likely to be of little value?

By now you should see the importance of those features of case study work that are most likely to drive you to despair – complexity, uncertainty, information unreliability and/or overload, and 'woolliness' of what you are being asked to do. These are precisely the features of real working life that are most difficult to cope with as a manager. It is these aspects of cases that will help you develop the necessary conceptual skills.

Groups, assumptions and communication

The potential value of case study work goes beyond the purely conceptual, though. If used in the group context described above, cases simulate real contexts well enough to give you the opportunity to practise *all* of the managerial skills listed earlier. The group is important – your group work on the case allows simulation of the team-working and negotiation with colleagues that you would need in dealing with complex problem situations in reality.

Communication skills will be practised in two ways. You will obviously need to communicate with members of your team while working on the case. There will usually be a great deal of heated discussion about interpretations and significance of information, and the virtue of different courses of action. Your ability to make your points in a way that others can understand, and to argue clearly and coherently, will be important. Furthermore, through presenting your analysis and conclusions, orally and/or in a written report, you will develop the communication skills that you would need if you were to gain approval for a particular proposal.

Some of your most heated debates are likely to stem from different underlying assumptions and values, whether about the case situation or about organisations in general, or about life as a whole. One of the greatest areas for potential learning is becoming aware of such assumptions, your own and those of others. They can have a profound effect on how you conceptualise problems and evaluate solutions. Yet if you are unaware of these assumptions, the negative effects can go far beyond shouting matches. You may come up with views of a situation that do not correspond to those of any other stakeholder, and 'solutions' which aggravate the situation. Or you may fail to realise the potential of a whole set of possible options.

Contextual awareness

There is one more area of potential learning. The importance of context was stressed above, and the context is part of the case. Your analysis of any particular case will develop your understanding of the importance of specific contextual features. By studying a large number of cases you will also develop an appreciation of the range of contexts that exist, and their characteristics. It will not give you the same understanding as you would gain from working in a wide range of different organisations, but it will help to broaden your understanding of the world of business, of the sorts of situations that can be problematic, the kinds of factors likely to be relevant to these, and the wide range of possible options that might be considered.

A caution is in order, however. Cases are simplifications. The greatest challenge to managers in real life often comes from the parts that are 'simplified out'. The messy interactions between people, resistance to change, power and its manifestations, the amount of time needed for communication – the list of such things is endless. But if you become better at dealing with those aspects that *are* a frequent feature of cases you should have more time and energy to deal with these other, trickier aspects.

Other advantages of cases

In addition to the advantages in learning terms outlined above, there are other attractions to the use of cases. In assessment, they provide an effective way of testing the ability to apply concepts to a situation – it is easier to compare answers if all address the same situation, and such assessment is likely to be seen as 'fairer' than questions based upon a student's own organisation.

Cases are seen as 'easy' to use. There are many case studies published, so that it is easy for lecturers to select appropriate ones. The students do a lot of the work themselves. Tutors can reinforce their authority by offering a 'solution' to the case. (I would argue that this 'advantage' can be hotly debated. To help students learn from cases requires a high level of tutor skill, the ability constantly to 'diagnose' progress, and give inconspicuous direction, and the even greater ability to draw all the potential learning points out of student experience.)

Cases are acceptable to students. They use a different style of learning from other methods, thus adding to the variety of the learning experience. They give the impression of 'reality' and therefore of validity, of access to privileged information, of learning what *really* goes on. Particularly for students with limited organisational experience this can be seen as highly valuable.

Limitations of cases

The limitations of cases have been hinted at already. The tendency to equate a case with reality is at the root of the main limitation, together with the particular selectivity just discussed. Tutor inexpertise underpins most of the other difficulties you may experience.

Cases are *not* real situations, even if they are derived from them. They have been filtered by the case author, who chose what to include, and what to exclude, and how to describe what was included. This is a frequent source of frustration. You may find that you lack vital information and are forced to base your analysis on assumptions about key aspects. Or you may be swamped with an oversupply of data (though remember that developing the skill to select relevant information from such a mass is important).

Such frustrations, while annoying, can actually enhance your learning, so are not really limitations. But if the case is taken as a 'model' of how things should be done (and the practice of giving 'solutions' may enhance this), then equating case with reality is positively dangerous. Case descriptions are biased snapshots of a point in time, or perhaps a period up to such a point. The bias may lead you to a particular interpretation that would not have been valid even in that situation, and may be even less so in seemingly similar situations.

The 'historic' nature of cases is also problematic. 'Success' may be transitory. It is fairly tempting to analyse the factors contributing to a favourable situation and assume that you have found a universal recipe for success. But what is successful one year may fail the next. We once made a marketing course where every 'exemplary' firm we filmed for the accompanying video was in serious, and public, trouble, even before the first students saw the video! Nor were we unusually unlucky or ill-advised. Clutterbuck and Kernaghan's (1990) study of organisational failure included a throw-away comment in the foreword to the effect that within three years of a study of successful companies (Goldsmith and Clutterbuck (1984)) one-third of the companies from which the authors developed their formula for success were in severe difficulty. Any 'answers' or 'recipes' you are tempted to derive from case studies should therefore be treated with extreme caution!

This is linked to the dangerous nature of 'solutions' that may be offered. First, even if the solution consists of what the organisation actually decided, you are not to know if it was the right decision. This is the difficulty with complex situations. There are so many things you do not know. You may find out that a decision was fairly clearly *wrong*, if disaster follows rapidly after. Even then, the decision may have been the most likely to be appropriate, given the information and probabilities facing the organisation at the time. But normally there are more ambiguous outcomes: the changed situations may be deemed better by some, acceptable by others and not as good as the original by a few. In such cases it is very difficult to evaluate the decision. Since so many organisational situations are of this kind, the possible use of case studies to suggest that it is appropriate to seek for 'the solution' could be argued as a limitation.

COPING WITH CASES

Although cases vary enormously, it should by now be clear that analysing any substantial case is likely to present a wide range of challenges. These include rapid reading, managing and interpreting large amounts of information, living with ambiguity, working effectively in a team, using abstract ideas to help with analysis and synthesis of something approximating messy reality, coping with time pressures, presenting information orally and in writing and managing your own learning, to a greater or lesser extent. The links to most of the chapters in this book are fairly obvious. Most will help you in case study work. This chapter addresses two aspects of cases not dealt with elsewhere, the emotional dimension and the problem of where and how to start when faced with a forbiddingly complex situation.

> ### Guidelines for case study analysis
>
> - clarify task requirements
> - skim read
> - read more slowly, highlighting issues
> - explore the case and its context, identifying themes
> - formulate problem statements
> - identify solution criteria and constraints
> - analyse, using course concepts to help find root problems
> - work out recommendations
> - craft analysis and recommendations into a clear presentation.

Earlier it was hinted that case study work can sometimes be a source of dissatisfaction. Sometimes it can generate a high level of negative feelings. A sense of failure is likely to be the cause of such feelings. It may be failure at having 'got nowhere' with the case. If so the 'method' offered shortly should help. It may however be a sense of having done less well than other groups, of having 'lost' some kind of contest. It helps to be aware of the possibility of such feelings, to understand where they come from and to know how to avoid them.

Failure and dissatisfaction

Most managers seeking a qualification seem to have a high need to achieve, and are also fairly competitive. Many also feel that getting things 'right' constitutes achievement, and giving a more impressive presentation than another group constitutes 'winning'. But note the caution given earlier about whether 'right' answers *can* exist for complex cases. And think about why you are working with a case. It is not (except in an examination) to come to a right answer. It *is* to develop all the skills listed earlier, that is, about *learning*. Learning requires feedback. Experiment with using ideas to sort out a case, and learn both from your own work and group experience, and from seeing what others achieved that perhaps you did not. Then no matter how 'well' you did this will constitute not failure, but very real learning success.

A sense of failure can get in the way of learning. Defensiveness sets in. 'Scapegoating' can occur, with one group member (or perhaps the tutor) blamed for the 'failure'. This will prevent any learning. Alternatively the group may indulge in a kind of 'groupthink', deciding that they *did* do brilliantly, despite what people said about their analysis – others just did not understand its merits! It is important that you are alert to the possibility of these responses. And if you start reacting in these ways, or see the group reacting thus, try to stand back and ask the following questions:

- What were we doing anyway – why does it *matter* to be best?
- How can we learn from what we have done?

If you can address these questions with your group, you will be able to transform your experience of the exercise, and also the extent to which you learn from it.

A METHOD FOR APPROACHING CASES

There are three strands to the method for approaching cases. The first strand concerns practical aspects of managing the task and materials facing you. The second is more conceptual, and concerns the best way to deal with complex problems. The reason for the suggested sequence is that unless you put enough effort into understanding the root causes of a problem, your subsequent analysis may be misdirected. The early stages discussed below are therefore vital. Resist any temptation to skimp them and get on to the 'real work'. (The third strand, that of working effectively in a group, was dealt with in Chapter 11, so is not discussed here.)

One practical issue concerns the sheer volume of many cases. If you are issued with a case in advance of the session at which it will be discussed, avoid the temptation to put it to one side and forget it. Plan enough time to familiarise yourself with the case and its contents. Allow time for a solo pass through at least the first two stages below. If you do not do this, your learning, and that of fellow group members, will suffer, and they may see you as a passenger, and resent this.

1. Understanding the task

One of the first things you need to do is understand what is being asked of you. Are you supposed to adopt a particular perspective, or slant your analysis towards a particular 'client'? What sort of outcome is being asked for? Is it an evaluation of something that has happened, or recommendations as to what should happen? If the latter, how far down the path to a detailed action plan are you expected to go? Are there particular parts of the course you are supposed to draw on, or particular techniques you must use? What form of presentation is asked for? Are there constraints on this – word or time limits for example? How long do you have to work on the case?

If you are unsure about the meaning of words in the question, consult the glossary (Helpfile 1 at the end of Chapter 15). If you are still unsure, or other aspects of the brief are unclear to you, talk to the person who assigned you the case. Misunderstandings about what you are expected to do are in no one's interests. Once you are working in a group you need to check that your understanding of the task matches that of others in the group, and reach a shared understanding of the task.

2. Scanning the case

Once you know what you are meant to be doing, you need to get a 'feel' for the situation in the case. Speed-read the case, trying to get a general idea of what it is about, and the sort of information with which you are presented. If any questions occur to you at this stage, or points 'jump out' as significant, jot them down when you get to the end.

Having done this, go through the case slightly more slowly, using a highlighter or taking notes of points which seem important. If there are sets of figures, try to see what they might mean in general terms. (Effective reading techniques, covered in Chapter 9, will be invaluable in case study work.)

3. Description – exploring the situation and identifying themes

Although in scanning you will already have started to impose structure on the situation by jumping to the conclusion that some things are important and others are not, try to do this as little as possible. It is far easier to narrow your scope later than to widen your perspective once you have imposed limits. If you are by now working as a group, you will find rich pictures (*see* Chapter 10), to be really useful in helping you to come to a shared perception of what is going on. (Relationship diagrams do this too, but tend to be less fun.) Try to identify and represent all the things that could possibly be relevant to the situation. From these you will be able to construct the web of interrelated issues that cause the situation to be worthy of analysis. Make sure that you look at factors outside the immediate problem context, as these may be significant. If different views emerge, try to find out the reason for differences. Have some people seen things in the case that others have missed? Or do they bring different sets of assumptions to the group? Either may be important.

Once you can agree on a fairly broad representation of the situation, look for 'themes' – linked sets of factors that seem to contribute to one aspect of the situation. For example, there might be one strand to do with perceived poor quality, another to do with changes in competitor behaviour. Within each such strand there might be groups of sub-issues.

At this stage you are looking for a useful way of *describing* the situation. If you are looking at a problem situation it may help to think of what you are doing as analogous to a lawyer interviewing a client, or a GP asking a patient, 'What seems to be the trouble?' Note that 'seems'. You are looking for presenting symptoms. What is actually happening? You have not yet worked out what *is* the problem.

Finding out what is happening may involve some fairly deep digging into the information provided. Are there any trends in figures? Graphs may help show these. Avoid digging too deep, however. Until you have moved into the next stage, and worked out why things are happening, too much detail can cloud the issue, or you may spend time on things which your subsequent diagnosis shows to be marginal. A degree of moving back and forth between this stage and the next (diagnosis) may be necessary. As you find out more information about the problem your ideas of important factors and relationships will become clearer. As they do, you will realise that you need to look more deeply at some of the information to clarify your ideas about what is actually happening. As some of your investigative work may take considerable time and effort, you may need to plan how to divide it between sub-groups, and how to share the results.

4. Diagnosis – working out *why* things are as they are

The diagnosis stage is probably the one to which you should devote most of your effort, though its success will depend upon the adequacy of the previous stages – an unclear task can thwart you, as can an imperfect or overly narrow grasp of the situation concerned.

You need now to start imposing structure on the mass of information in the case. There are several approaches to structuring, the most important being to use course ideas and frameworks. One useful way to bring these in is to take each of the themes you have identified and brainstorm potentially relevant course concepts. This will provide a useful reference list in the heat of later moments.

Another way of forcing you to look at concepts from an early stage (and of ensuring that you look at all the layers of the problem) is to structure issues vertically, from those concerning individual employees, through the group or section, to the organisation as a whole, and finally to its wider environment. You can thus produce a matrix of main issues, and their related problems, and think about relevant concepts for each 'layer'. You may wish to add a final column for recommended actions, but if you do so, this should not be filled in until later.

This approach can be somewhat mechanistic – an apparent attraction if you are faced with a big and messy problem. The danger is that it may lead to a somewhat superficial investigation of causes and premature categorisation. Use it as one form of prompt, if you feel you need it, but not as your main approach.

If you are trying to find out how a situation arose, try drawing multiple cause diagrams (*see* Chapter 14). These are excellent for helping you to broaden your thinking away from 'obvious' diagnoses, and into the layers of interrelated causes that are a feature of most organisational situations.

If you are trying to explore relationships between parts of an existing problem situation, try using relationship diagrams or systems maps. Both can help you to gain a clearer view of the situation from different perspectives.

Make a deliberate attempt to sort out evidence from assumptions, and to ask both how sure you are that your assumptions are correct, and how important it is to your diagnosis that they are.

Use frameworks as 'shopping lists'. For example if you have been taught that key features in the competitive environment are political, economic, social and technological, and one of your issues concerns this environment, make sure that you have looked at all of these sets of factors.

Use the predictive power of theories. For example, if the case involves poor motivation and you have been taught that motivation depends upon the perceived links between effort, performance and reward, look at these links, paying particular attention to where they may be lacking, and at the values staff place on the reward. The theory would predict that the problem would lie in weakness in one or more of these areas.

Remember to go back to the case information, and look more carefully at things that become important as your diagnosis proceeds. You will need to produce *evidence* to support your diagnosis.

Use the data provided. What *information* can you derive from the data? Are there trends? Where are they leading? Are there discontinuities in trends? If so, what are they associated with? Are some figures out of line with others, for example are your selling expenses out of line with those of your competitors, or is one product line contributing much more (or less) than others? You may need to do some calculations in order to turn data into information which answers the sorts of questions you are asking. The data will seldom be given in the form you want!

Above all, try to avoid thinking about 'solutions' at this stage. While it is good, as your ideas evolve, to move between the second and third stages of tackling cases (scanning the case and describing it), to move on to solutions before you are sure what the problem is risks a 'solution' to something which is not the problem, and which may even exacerbate it.

Produce problem statements

It is very helpful at this stage to produce a written statement of your perception of the key problems. This will act as a reference point during future discussions. It will also form a basis for improved statements of problems if your understanding of the situation deepens during subsequent discussions, and will be useful in preparing your subsequent presentation. It is surprising how often in the heat of discussions you can forget what it is you are trying to achieve, and wander off in some different direction. Even if this is a productive redirection, which has come about because your perceptions have become clearer, it can be confusing if not everyone knows what the redirection is. If it is an inadvertent redirection, the scope for misplaced effort is enormous. A clearly written problem statement can be an excellent way of avoiding this.

If you have more than one problem, it is helpful to prioritise them. If you have time to tackle only some, it would be sensible to focus on those with highest priority. Useful criteria for selection include:

- *importance* – what will happen if the problem is not addressed?
- *urgency* – how quickly must this problem be solved?
- *hierarchical position* – to what extent is this problem the cause of other problems?
- *solvability* – can you do anything about it anyway?

Decide on criteria for a solution

It may seem out of order to think of how you will choose between solutions before you have thought of any, but there is method in this. Once you have thought of even one solution there is a danger of becoming wedded to a particular idea, and slanting your criteria for choice in favour of this particular one. This point is discussed further in Chapter 19, in the context of dissertations and theses, where similar considerations apply.

It is, therefore, safer to think about criteria for solutions as soon as you are clear about the problem structure. In one sense criteria follow on. If the deepest problem identified is to do with culture, for example, then solutions must be likely to influence this for the better. But if there are also financial problems, then there will be criteria associated with these as well. Indeed, whatever the problem, financial criteria are likely to be important.

If you list the characteristics of a 'good' solution at this stage, you will have a set of yardsticks against which to measure your options, yardsticks that relate to your identification of organisational needs, not merely to your particular set of options. As well as identifying the positive aspects to be sought from a solution – the ability to reduce costs, or to generate capital, or whatever – it is also worth looking at the constraints that will limit the possible option range. Is there an absolute budget for a project? Are there national union agreements that must be honoured? Are there legal constraints? By identifying these as well, you will have mapped out the field within which solutions *must* lie, as well as the part of the field in which it is most *desirable* that they fall.

Generate alternatives

Once you have a clear idea of your objectives in the exercise, have decided upon the problem areas which you wish to address and are reasonably sure you have analysed their root causes, you will need to think about options which could be used as a way out of the problem situation. You will again be drawing heavily on course concepts to suggest better ways of operating. Other useful sources of ideas might be information you have gained from other case studies, from reading the business press, or from each other's past experience. This last source is perhaps your richest resource of all, and in your discussions you should always be aware of what other members have to offer, and ensure that their contributions are encouraged where they can be of value.

You may also find it helpful to use creativity techniques: the broader the range of options you generate, the better. You will probably be familiar with brainstorming already. This is one of the longest established techniques habitually used by managers. Although you may already be using it at work, and will almost certainly cover it at some point in your course, a very brief description is included here in case you are not familiar with the approach and need it before you are taught it. If you have been taught other creativity techniques, use these too.

Brainstorming

Brainstorming is intended to disable the censors which habitually operate within our subconscious, suppressing ideas unworthy of attention before they ever surface. The method aims to create a climate within which silliness and unserious behaviour are the norm, thus freeing participants to voice those normally suppressed ideas. Among these may be the germ of a totally new approach which offers a way out of an existing deadlock. Furthermore, one person's silly idea may spark off a new train of thought in another person, which may itself lead somewhere.

Thus in running brainstorming sessions you try to create a climate of fun, and to free people from their inhibitions. You also aim to capture and display *all* ideas voiced so that they can act as a stimulus to further thought, as well as being available for further consideration after the exercise.

To reduce inhibitions, the group must agree to voice *no* criticism of any idea expressed, and contribute *all* ideas that occur to them, no matter how bizarre. The weirdest ideas may be the most valuable. To get the group into the mood, start the session by spending a few minutes brainstorming a manifestly silly topic, such as what to do with a dead parrot or how to terminate an endless visit from your in-laws.

To ensure that all ideas are captured and displayed, it is normal to work in a room with writing surfaces all round, whether whiteboards or sheets of flipchart paper stuck to the walls. One of the group members writes down all ideas as they are called out, using writing large enough to be easily read by everybody.

The group then agrees on the topic to brainstorm, and starts shouting ideas. The only allowable criticism is that of people voicing criticism! The group continues until it runs out of steam. Only then is any attempt made to evaluate the collected ideas. This is often done by a smaller group, who may group ideas, look for totally impossible ones and see how they might be made possible, or merely look for the best among the bunch. Your group could decide on the best way of handling ideas, given the task in hand.

Other techniques

Other idea generation techniques try to ensure that all group members make a contribution; sometimes quieter members may not give all their ideas. Nominal Group Technique, for example, involves a rather bureaucratic taking of turns in contributing ideas, and voting on the best. This is not likely to reduce inhibitions, however, so where a totally new solution is sought it is probably not appropriate. Other approaches make conscious use of analogy and metaphor. You think of the problem 'as if' it were something else, or consciously look for similarities and differences between your problem and something completely different as a way of stimulating your thoughts out of their habitual channels. Synectics is one well-known approach of this kind.

How ever you choose to become creative, it is important that you do generate a sufficiently broad range of options. You are unlikely to walk out of a chain store with an exclusive designer suit, nor are you likely to end up by choosing an option better than the best among those you generate.

You may need to go through successive cycles of divergence and convergence in generating options. The first pass may generate a huge variety of widely different possibilities. After focusing on one broad class, you can be creative again in deciding on options within that class, narrow down, broaden out at the next level, and so on. This is a common way of approaching product design, but is also applicable to the design of organisational solutions, though with the proviso that the interrelatedness of organisational problems may sometimes mean that the extremes of focusing which this method produces can be insufficiently holistic.

Figure 12.1 shows how the method can be thought of as the generation of part of a tree, along which you travel by way of ever smaller branches and twigs. It is

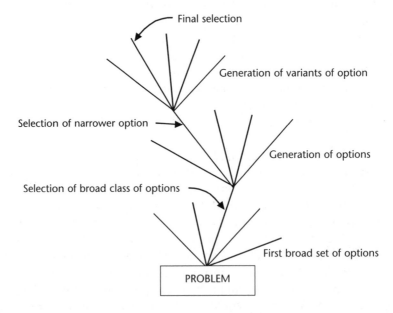

Fig. 12.1 Option selection by successive choice of divergence

important if you are using this method that you ensure that each set of branches or twigs consist of mutually exclusive options. If not, by choosing one path you may be neglecting whole areas that might be highly relevant.

Evaluate options and select the most appropriate

If the solution tree approach is adopted, there is already an element of choice at the generation of options stage. With other methods there should usually be a variety of options generated, as few problems have a single possible solution. The next stage is, therefore, to evaluate the options, in order to see which option, or combination of options, is likely to be most effective.

In evaluating options you will need first to forecast their likely effect, not only on the focal problem, but on interrelated problems, and indeed on the organisation as a whole. If these relationships are not understood, and the possible implications of each option thoroughly teased out, there is a risk that the cure will be worse than the disease. Since forecasts are always guesses, it is important to have an idea of how likely your forecast outcomes are. And, as before, it is important to know how sensitive your forecasts are to your assumptions.

Once you have teased out the likely effects of your options, you can test these against the criteria you decided upon earlier. If there is a single criterion the process is relatively simple. If there are several criteria which you feel to be important, then you may wish to weight these, giving more emphasis to the most important criteria. If you are using quantitative criteria, then it may be sensible to multiply scores on each criterion by the weighting factor, and derive an overall weighted score. If more qualitative factors are important (and qualitative factors should never be excluded merely because they are harder to deal with in analysis) you will need to find some other way of handling the different aspects of your predicted outcomes. One fairly robust technique is to construct the sort of table found in *Which?* magazine, where goods are rated on a number of criteria, being given dots, rather than a number score. Figure 12.2 gives an example of this technique. This allows an 'at a glance' evaluation to be made of the table. The use of dots rather than numbers avoids giving a spurious impression of accuracy. This tabular approach is just as effective with policy options as it is with washing machines.

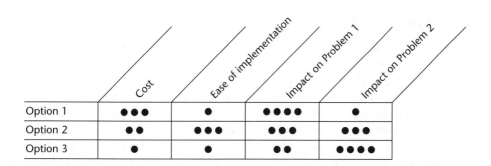

Fig. 12.2 Schematic for a 'which'-type approach to option comparison

Design an implementation strategy

In real consultancy you would be thinking about implementation issues as you worked through your analysis, even if this was not strictly within your remit. In case study analysis within a course, you may not be required to consider this aspect. After all, you will not usually be in a position to implement any of your recommendations. Nevertheless, it is important that recommendations are implementable, and you may well be asked to produce an action plan as part of your assignment. Successful action is much more likely in real life if implementation has been considered from the earliest stages. Whether or not you are strictly required to make recommendations for implementation of your chosen option(s) it is, therefore, worth at least thinking about how they *might* be implemented.

For successful implementation in general, it is important that those who will be affected feel involved in the decision to make changes, rather than the changes being something wished upon them from on high. This is not just good PR. Those involved are likely to have genuinely useful contributions to make to the decisions, as they will have relevant knowledge and understanding not available elsewhere. Although you will not be able to set up consultative mechanisms, it is worth thinking about who would be involved, and what contribution they might make were this possible.

The other vital element is extremely careful planning, with all necessary steps taken into consideration. It is no use planning a highly sophisticated new information system, and forgetting to plan for the considerable staff development needed to make it work. This would have to involve not only those inputting data, but also those intended to benefit from the outputs, and is absolutely essential if the system is to be of any real value. Such planning *can* be done in the context of a case study, and if you are required to do it, should be given due emphasis. It is all too easy to see the decision itself as the important thing, and not to plan time to allow for thought as to how this decision can be made effective. Critical path analysis may well be helpful, but the real work will lie in thinking about the decision in relation to the organisation. What are its different implications for all those involved? This will enable you to identify the steps that will be needed to ensure that positive effects are fully achieved, and as many of the negative ones avoided as possible.

Present your findings

In presenting your findings you will want to convince your audience that you have thoroughly understood the problem, that you have obtained all the necessary information to reach a decision, that you have analysed this information in a sensible fashion, and that the conclusions you have reached are to be trusted. These conclusions should be presented clearly, so that your audience is convinced that your recommendations should be followed.

For class-based discussions, it is likely that you will need to make an oral presentation. Chapter 16 deals with the basics of making an effective presentation to a group, and you should work your way through this before making your first case study presentation, or as an aid to analysing the presentations made by others. Of course you will not need to do this if you are already an expert in this field.

In real-life consultancy, you may often be called upon to make a presentation, but you will *always* need to make a written report on your findings. If you are analysing the case for assessment, then, too, you will need to produce a written version of your findings. Chapter 15 deals with written reports, and Chapter 17 touches on case study-based answers in examinations. You should refer to these as appropriate.

SUMMARY

- Case studies are a vehicle for practising the application of skills, knowledge and techniques learned in courses to quasi-real situations.

- At the same time they increase awareness of the business context in which students are likely to be operating.

- Group interaction, time-management and presentation skills can be developed at the same time as conceptual/analytical skills.

- Difficulties are encountered because typically students are given more responsibility for managing their own learning than they are used to, because tasks may be somewhat unclear, and because case studies frequently contain an over-abundance of information. Group dynamics may also hinder progress.

- Case study analysis can be usefully structured by the use of relevant course concepts, together with an overall structure based upon a national approach to problem solving: explore situation; define problems; decide criteria; generate options; evaluate options; present recommendations.

Further information

Easton, G. (1992) *Learning from Case Studies* (2nd edn), Prentice Hall. This gives much more detailed guidance on case study analysis than is possible here.
Kneeland, S. (1999) *Thinking Straight*, Pathways.

13 Using numbers

Objectives

By the end of this chapter you should:

- see why mathematical tools are important to managers
- understand some of the reasons for your resistance to mathematics
- understand the basic 'language' of simple maths
- feel comfortable using a calculator to perform simple calculations
- recognise some of the situations in which mathematical tools can be useful
- feel confident in your ability to communicate data graphically.

INTRODUCTION

As a manager you will frequently be faced with information presented as numbers. The ability to use these numbers to advantage, to perform simple calculations, to use basic models in order to forecast, or to use statistical procedures for testing the reliability of evidence will be an enormous asset to you in your job. The ability to manipulate and interpret numbers and equations is a key managerial skill, yet one which many managers lack. If you can become skilled in this area you will therefore be at a tremendous advantage. You will not, like many of your colleagues, draw faulty conclusions from figures, or fail to detect important messages which they carry. Nor will you be at the mercy of consultants who produce mathematical-looking reports. Instead of accepting these without question because they look 'scientific', you will be able to evaluate them, and detect any flaws which they may contain.

Most MBA programmes will aim to develop your skills in this area. The mathematics used is often not at all complicated. Indeed, with a calculator or computer a few key presses can generate extremely useful information from raw figures. Yet instead of being excited by courses which offer such advantages, a significant proportion of students regard any course where 'maths' creeps in with almost pathological horror. Indeed, some potential students decide not to attempt an MBA at all because they think they are so 'hopeless at maths' that they will fail. Alas, some students *do* fail because they fail an accounting or other compulsory quantitative course. Those who pass may gain just enough to scrape through, but not enough to be able to use the techniques with confidence at work. This is all because they lack the basic mathematical skills needed to make light work of these subjects.

Working with such students, it is clear that for some the fear of numbers, or of anything with an '*x*' or an '=' in it, is so powerful that as soon as an equation appears on a page, some sort of shutter slams down in their brain. This makes further comprehension impossible, even of perfectly normal text which may surround the offending equation. If you recognise yourself in the above, this chapter may need to be supplemented by considerable help from a numerate friend, and a lot of practice, before you can regard numbers as allies rather than objects of dread. You will certainly need to work through all the exercises in this chapter (answers to these are given at the end), and may need to invent further exercises to supplement these.

If you are in the larger group of students who have a rational rather than an irrational fear of numbers, based on an awareness that you lack basic skills, then this chapter should be sufficient preparation for the more quantitative parts of your course. You will, however, need to work through all the exercises given in those parts of the chapter where you know yourself to be weak.

If you are fairly happy about your mathematical skills, you should move straight on to another chapter. You will have little to gain from the very basic treatment of mathematics here.

The chapter is intended to set mathematics in context, rather than *teaching* maths, and to show that playing with numbers can be easy, even fun, rather than tedious or difficult.

CAUSES OF DIFFICULTY

Why is it that the sight of an equation scrambles some people's brains? I do not know the answer but this chapter may suggest a few thoughts on the subject. Consider, for example, how it is that children seem remarkably adept at working out how many weeks' pocket money it will take them to save up for the plastic object of their desire. They know exactly when they have had less than their fair share of anything, no matter what it is, or the size of the group they are in at the time. They know how much change they should get when they buy sweets. But somewhere along their educational road, this becomes 'mathematics', and therefore 'difficult'.

It used to be the fashion to teach mathematics as a series of techniques to be learned rather than understood. Thus children learned to go through the mechanics of long multiplication or division, with absolutely no understanding of what they were doing. I remember being taught an incredibly complicated method for finding square roots by hand (although even in those benighted times, printed tables of square roots existed. Now, praise be, even the cheapest calculator has a square root button.

Such a form of learning was both difficult and boring. No wonder children subjected to it made frequent mistakes, and came to regard themselves as failures at anything to do with maths, avoiding any further contact with it in consequence. They were thus handicapped for life. It may seldom be necessary to work out square roots, but even in everyday life it is helpful to be able to calculate how much paint, wallpaper or floor tiling you need, or whether one size of packet is cheaper than another. At work you will probably encounter more complex sets of numbers.

The more modern approach of letting children discover mathematical relationships for themselves *should* be more fun. But if teachers lack any real understanding themselves of what maths is about, the results can be even worse. 'Discovery learning' requires careful planning and guidance if it is to be effective. Without this, children risk learning nothing, not even the mechanical techniques in which they would have been drilled under the old system.

ACTIVITY

Think about the numbers that have passed across your desk during the last week. List uses you might have made of them if you had been happier in dealing with them.

_____

_____

ACTIVITY

Think about your experience with maths at school. How do you think your teacher rated your ability?

_____

_____

Underline those of the following which you felt confident about doing when at school:

simple arithmetic; simple algebra; plotting graphs; working out averages; working with fractions; differential equations.

Double underline any of the above which you felt you fully understood.

Cross out any which you think you have forgotten by now.

Comment

The above should have helped you get a feel for the size of the task facing you in coming to terms with the maths you will need to use to benefit from your course. Use the information in planning how much time to devote to this topic.

WHY MANAGERS NEED MATHS

There are many ways of thinking of mathematics. At its simplest, it can be seen as a language with a set of symbols instead of words, and rules for combining these symbols equivalent to grammar. At this level it can provide a clear, unambiguous and concise way of describing some sorts of relationships.

Descriptive equations

You will often find mathematical expressions used in a purely descriptive way in the management literature. After a complex description, an equation will appear. This may be even more complex than the description, involving lots of mathematical symbols and lots of different letters, the meanings of which have to be explained in a lengthy key. So, in addition to any problems caused by the unfamiliar symbols, you are forever flicking back and forth to the key to see what each symbol means.

Provided the equation is not the first step in constructing a model, you can usually afford to ignore this kind of equation. The author's intention may be to clarify the text. For those familiar with the higher reaches of mathematical notation this may work, although *they* may be uncomfortable with such an equation if they realise that many of the symbols in fact represent things for which it would be virtually impossible to find numerical values. If the author's intention is merely to make the argument more convincing and scientific looking with such equations, then they will probably be just as unhelpful to the mathematically inclined as they are to you. Either way, rather than putting down the paper with a feeling of failure, ignore the equations, and see what you can derive from the text alone. Short, simple equations may clarify, and make something much easier to remember, and this sort of descriptive use is extremely helpful. But the more complex, confusing versions can be discarded without guilt.

You will be in good company in this approach. Roger Penrose, a mathematics professor at the University of Oxford, suggests if you encounter a formula:

> a procedure that I normally adopt myself when such an offending line presents itself. The procedure is, more or less, to ignore that line completely and to skip to the next actual line of text! Well, not exactly this; one should spare the poor formula a perusing, rather than a comprehending glance, and then press onwards. (Note at the start of *The Emperor's New Mind*, Oxford University Press, 1989.)

Lucy Kellaway (2000) is more terse, expressing herself in another formula:

> 'F + M = P*R where F = formula, M = management, P = pretentious and R = rubbish'!

Modelling

Going beyond purely descriptive uses, maths can be seen as a way of *modelling*. A model is something which has enough key aspects of the real thing to allow you to answer questions about it, but more easily or economically than would be the case if you were forced to experiment with the thing itself. Thus an architect might construct small simplified models of alternative designs which would allow a client to gain an impression of each in order to make a choice. Or a CAD system might be used to produce the same result with a 'three-dimensional' representation on a computer screen, without the need for scissors and paste. Indeed the latter would be a better model in many respects, as it is easily altered. Minor modifications can be simply made, and the results compared. 'What if we extend that wing?' 'What if we add a further storey to this bit?'

Very simple (as well as very complex!) mathematical equations can be used to give answers to 'what if?' questions. What would be the staffing implications of this change in operations? Or of that reduction in absence rates? If fixed costs are this and variable costs are that, at what point do we break even? What will be the profit if we sell so much? What will we lose if we sell only this much? If interest rates are this and expected return on the investment that, is it worth borrowing in order to invest? What if interest rates go up to …? The maths will not tell you what sales figures will be, nor what will happen to interest rates, but it will tell you the likely *results* of different values of these, always assuming that you have chosen an appropriate equation to model the relationships between the factors in question.

In the broad category of use of mathematics described above (loosely, I know) as modelling, that is, in using maths to find an answer to a real or hypothetical question, we are going beyond descriptive language into using *techniques* derived from mathematics. What will 5500 items cost at 50p per hundred? What would it cost to buy 6000, if this means that we can get them at 45p per hundred? Would this be a good buy? Simple techniques give you the answer to the above. If you want to derive, say, an appropriate annual repayment rate for a mortgage of £78 000, borrowed at an annual interest rate of 12 per cent over 20 years, you will need slightly, though not much, more complex techniques. If you want to work out the optimum product mix under varying conditions of labour demand, materials costs, profit margin, etc. you will need more complex techniques still. Mathematics can provide whatever degree of complexity you are likely to want, though you need not learn the techniques yourself. If a problem requires a person with a PhD in Linear Programming, it is probably better to hire one, rather than try to learn the techniques yourself, although it will help you a lot to have a broad understanding of what he/she is doing.

It *is*, however, worth taking the trouble to learn the more basic techniques, as you will find so many opportunities for using them to good effect. They will allow you to make good use of the data generated in profusion in most organisations, and to draw valid conclusions from them. Starting to 'crack the code', and to learn a few basic techniques can thus benefit your performance significantly.

Statistics

Many of the techniques you will need in order to draw conclusions from data fall into the broad category of statistics. Apart from being a branch of mathematics, statistics means sets of data. Statistical techniques are those concerned with making sense of your data. While statistics has had a bad press (e.g. Disraeli's 'lies, damned lies and statistics') this is because many people do not understand the few basic concepts underlying the area.

The most crucial of these is that whereas the mathematical techniques above deal in certainties (the cost of 5500 items at 50p per hundred will always be the same), statistics deals in *probabilities*. Imagine, for example, that two selection methods are compared. Of the 200 candidates selected by one method, 150 are rated as excellent by their bosses five years later, 20 are satisfactory, and the rest have left. Of 100 selected by another method, 50 are rated as excellent, 25 as satisfactory, two as unsatisfactory, and the rest have left. We have no reason to believe that the two groups were treated any differently once they joined the organisation, nor that the pool of applicants was any different in either case.

Most people would be fairly ready to believe, from the above figures, that the first selection method was clearly better. But it is not something about which we can be *certain*. If you spend a day tossing coins, and noting whether you get heads or tails, you will get some stretches when for a long time you get mostly heads, and other stretches when you get mostly tails. Of course most of the time they will be fairly mixed, but you might just happen, purely by chance, if picking two sheets of your results at random, to get one where almost all were heads and one that was almost all tails. Someone not knowing your method of generating the results might be convinced that the two pages referred to quite different situations.

Selection of potential employees is not an exact science. We can expect a degree of random variation to enter into it. It could therefore be that it is this random variation that has accounted for the difference in the results of the two selection methods.

We are very bad at assessing probabilities unaided. That is why we need statistical techniques for assessing them. How likely do you think it is, for example, that in a class of 32 schoolchildren at least two will share a birthday? In fact, the chances are about three to one. Or guess the probability that if you toss a coin just six times you will get either six heads or six tails. Many people think this must be highly unlikely, or even accuse you of using a weighted coin if it happens, but the chance is as high as 1 in 32. So if your class all tossed six pennies, you would not be at all surprised if one of them *did* get six alike.

If straightforward things like this are hard to assess, it is clear we need techniques for assessing the probabilities of more complicated results, so that we know how much significance to attach to them. Such techniques would enable you to assess how likely it is that if the two selection methods described above were equally effective you would get this much difference between your results. Again, a vast battery of statistical techniques exists, and you will almost certainly be introduced to some of them during your course. This chapter will not attempt to cover them. But if you understand the basic idea of probability, you should feel more comfortable with the techniques when you meet them.

You are, in any case, advised to check any research plans with a competent statistician who can advise you on the size of sample you need, and on the sorts of statistical tests you should use to decide whether your results are significant. This will be an important consideration for your dissertation. Many students ignore this advice, and their results are worth very little in consequence, despite their hard work. The problem is not restricted to students. Much organisational research is carried out without sufficient regard for statistical considerations, thereby producing results of dubious validity. But these results are often treated as sound, thus possibly leading the organisation to take unwise decisions.

Probability and statistics can also be used for modelling. This can enable you to find out not what *will* happen, but how likely various outcomes are under different assumptions about the environment.

The above has done no more than sketch out the range of ways in which mathematics can help you, whether by allowing you to calculate the value of something you wish to know, by telling you whether variations in your findings are likely to be meaningful, or by enabling you to answer 'what if?' questions. You can add to this list by becoming more aware of the uses of mathematics around you. Even if you do not understand the fine detail, keep a log of the sorts of things in use, and what they are used for. This will help you make sense of your coursework, and alert you to the techniques which seem to be in common use in your own organisation. It will also probably convince you, if you still need convincing, that it *is* worth trying to learn at least the basics of the language of mathematics, and the simpler techniques, so that you can begin to use them to improve your performance as a manager. You should also then be better able to benefit from (or be more critical of) articles or reports which draw conclusions from numerical evidence.

The first thing that you need to feel comfortable with is the set of symbols that constitute the 'code' of mathematics. Whether you are fairly confident of your abilities, or have always hated mathematics and think you haven't a clue, try Exercise 1 to check your memory of the basics. It is important to work through the whole exercise, doing as much as you can, *and writing down your own answers* before you look at the answers at the end of the chapter.

If this diagnostic exercise suggests that there are things you have forgotten, or perhaps never really grasped, turn to the end of the chapter, pour yourself a drink and/or do some deep breathing, and work your way through the Helpfile, 'Cracking the Code'. You should find that it is really quite simple, and that when you try the exercise again (or similar exercises from sources suggested at the end of the chapter, such as Morris (2000)) your competence surprises you.

EXERCISE 1

(a) Write the following as decimals:

$\frac{3}{4}$ $\frac{6}{7}$ $1\frac{1}{3}$ $1\frac{5}{7}$ $\frac{9}{11}$ $\frac{6}{8}$

—   —   —   —   —   —

(b) Write the following as percentages:

2 $\frac{3}{4}$ $1\frac{1}{3}$ $\frac{10}{11}$ $\frac{1}{4}$ $\frac{2}{3}$

—   —   —   —   —   —

(c) What is the value of:

2^3 14^2 3^4 $3^2 \times 3^2$ 12^3 1^4 6^0

—   —   —   —   —   —   —

(d) Write as a power of a single number:

$2^2 \times 2^5$ $3^4 \div 3^2$ $10^3 \times 10^5 \div 10^8$ $17^5 \times 17^3$ $21^{21} \div 21^3$ $x^3 \times x^2$ $x^y \div x^2$ $z^{2x} \times z^{2y}$

——   ——   ————   ——   ————   ——   ——   ——

(e) Use your calculator to work out the following writing your answers using only two places of decimals.

$\sqrt{16}$ $\sqrt{144}$ $\sqrt{36}$ $\sqrt{38}$ $\sqrt{2}$ $\sqrt{10}$

___   ___   ___   ___   ___   ___

(f) Write as a power of a number

$\sqrt{2^{16}}$ $\sqrt[4]{10^4}$ $\sqrt[3]{3^2}$ $\sqrt{(x^2y^2)}$ $\sqrt[7]{z^{14}}$

___   ___   ___   ___   ___

(g) If $x_1\, x_2\, x_3,\ \dots\ x_r$ represent the numbers 1, 2, 3, ... r, what is the value of $\sum\limits_{r=1}^{3} x_r$?

_____

(h) Which of the following are true?

(i) $7 \neq 7$ (ii) $3 \geq 1$ (iii) $5 > -5$ (iv) $3 < -5$ (v) $x^2 > x$ when $x = 1$

___   ___   ___   ___   _____

(i) Write the following without the bracket:

$2(x + y)$ $3(x - y^2)$ $-3(x - y)$ $(x - y) - (x - y)$ $(x - y) - (x - 2y)$

___   ___   ___   _____   _____

(j) Work out:

$5 + 2 \times 4$ $3 \times 6 - 5 + 4$ $x + x \times x \div y$ $1.2 \times 3.4 - 1.2 \div 6.1$

___ ___   _____   _____   _____

Additional exercises are given on the companion website www.booksites.net/cameron

REPRESENTING NUMBERS

Much of the data with which you will be faced, whether at work or generated by your research for a dissertation, will be in the form of strings of numbers. It has already been pointed out that we are not very good at assessing the chance of getting one set of numbers rather than another. Worse than that, most of us are not very good at making any sort of sense of a string of numbers. This is why you will encounter bar charts, graphs and other ways of presenting sets of data so that aspects of those figures can be seen at a glance.

Suppose you have the following sets of figures giving course scores for two sets of students.

Group 1: 20, 70, 80, 83, 50, 55, 75, 60, 61, 30, 95, 55, 54, 51, 40, 57, 69, 70, 75, 81.

Group 2: 40, 43, 47, 60, 49, 55, 51, 60, 63, 49, 42, 70, 75, 50, 46, 41, 49, 67, 60, 42.

It is very difficult to make sense of these figures when they appear like this. In order to start to draw conclusions, you need to organise the figures in some way. The simplest is to provide a summary of the scores, by giving the *average*, or *mean* score. To do this, you add the numbers for each group, and then divide by the number of students in the group.

EXERCISE 2

Find the mean score for each group using a calculator.

Group 1 _____   Group 2 _____

Sometimes, if the distribution is a bit odd, a mean score can be misleading, and you will find some other measure of the 'middle' of the group useful. One of the two most commonly used is the *median*, which gives you the size of the middle value if you order all the measurements by size and then take the value of the measurement which is in the middle of the list. Thus the median value of 1, 1, 4, 5, 7, 10, 10, 10, 11 is 7. There are 4 values bigger than this, and 4 smaller. The other measure is the *mode*, or the value which occurs most often. The mode for the list given is 10.

EXERCISE 3

Find the mean, median and mode for each of the following sets of values:

(a) 5, 5, 3, 2, 6, 7, 9, 11, 1.   mean _____   median _____   mode _____

(b) 3, 3, 7, 2, 1, 4, 3, 3, 13.   mean _____   median _____   mode _____

To get a better 'feel' for the effect of different sorts of distributors on these measures of central tendency, experiment with writing lists where mean, median and mode all have different values (no anwer given for this part). Try to construct at least one list where the differences are substantial.

RANGE

The mean (or median or mode) may be all you need, but you can see that you lose a lot of information by merely giving the average. One group has a much wider spread of scores than the other, and the average gives no indication of this. One simple way of adding this information is to supplement the mean with information about the *range*, the spread from the highest value to the lowest. In the above, the range for Group 1 would be 20–95, for Group 2, 40–75. You can see that Group 2 scores are more bunched together.

DISTRIBUTIONS AND HISTOGRAMS

Even this information may be misleading. Suppose Group 1 had one student with 20, one with 80 and the rest all scoring 50, whereas in Group 2 half the students had 20 and half had 80. In this case, mean and range would be the same for both groups, yet the groups would obviously be very different. For a start, half of Group 2 are failing, whereas only one of Group 1 is. It would obviously be helpful to see how the scores were distributed within the groups. You can get an idea of this at a glance from the numbers given in the example, so may feel you need not bother about means, etc. But if you had 200 students in each group, or 2000, you would not be able to see the *distribution* of the scores at a glance, and would need the figures to be summarised in a way which showed this.

You will learn more sophisticated techniques on your statistics courses, but a primitive and simple technique, the tally, can be very useful. To produce a tally, you divide your measures into a number of categories. Here 5 categories would do, say 0–20, 21–40, 41–60, 61–80, and 81–100. If you had a larger number of students you could afford to use smaller bands. Then for each score you put a tally mark in the appropriate band, as below. (Adding the fifth mark as a diagonal slash across makes the groups of five stand out more clearly, and aids adding up afterwards.)

Group 1

81–100	///
61–80	JHT //
41–60	JHT //
21–40	//
0–20	/

EXERCISE 4

Complete the tally for Group 2 (no answer given).

Group 2

Often, instead of tally marks, a bar of an appropriate length is drawn. These bar charts, which show how often different values occur, are called *histograms*. As the categories on a histogram should cover all possibilities, with one category starting as the other finishes, the bars are usually drawn as adjacent. They can be drawn horizontally or vertically. Figure 13.1 shows a vertical histogram for Group 2's scores.

These diagrams are extraordinarily useful as a way of summarising data. They are easy to draw, whether by hand or by computer, and give a clear picture of how results are distributed. The only thing you need to beware of is the occasional practice of using categories of different size. In the tally example given, each band was 20 marks. But I could have, for example, amalgamated 0–20 and 21–40, to give a band twice as wide. Where different sizes of category are used, the bars are drawn so that the *area* corresponds to the number of instances, and you have to be careful in interpreting the histogram. Looking at the height of equal width categories is fine. Looking at the height if categories are not of equal width is potentially misleading.

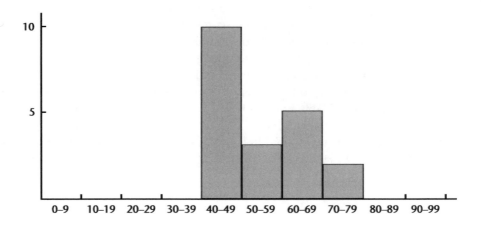

Fig. 13.1 Histogram for Group 2 scores

Note that while each of the above ways of representing data (central tendency measures such as mean, or range, or distribution) tells you *something* about how sets of data compare, you need to be very careful about drawing conclusions about the significance of differences or the reasons for them. In Exercise 2 you found that Group 1 had a higher average score but that this could be the result of a variety of things, including random variation. (Remember the penny tossing example.) Before concluding that Group 1 was better, or that they had a more lenient marker or whatever, you would need first to estimate the probability of such a variation occurring by chance, and second to obtain considerably more information. The statistics that you learn on your course should help you address rather more interesting problems of this nature.

BAR CHARTS

You can use bar charts to show values other than frequency. In this case you will usually be looking at values for different sets of data, say annual rainfall and average temperature for major cities around the world, or various production figures for a number of different plants. Here there is no particular way of ordering the different sets of data. Lima could come before London because it was earlier in the alphabet, or with other South American capitals, before or after Europe, or wherever you choose to put it. The bars or sets of bars are therefore drawn as separate from each other, although if there are several bars for each town, plant or whatever, these bars will often be drawn as touching each other, as then they are more clearly distinct from the other sets of information. The goal is clarity. It would be misleading to imply continuity of data in the same way that it exists on a histogram. Several different types of information can be clearly shown on the same bar chart by using different colours or different forms of cross-hatching to distinguish between the bars, and a key to show what these represent. Figure 13.2 shows an example of a bar chart.

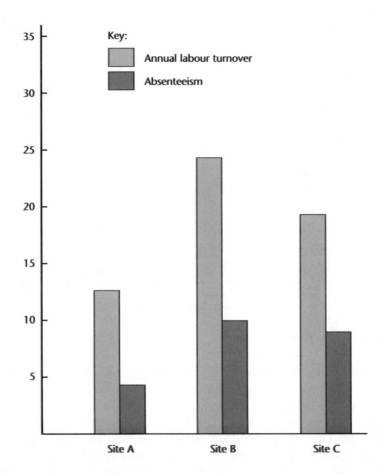

Fig. 13.2 Bar chart showing absenteeism and labour turnover rates at three sites

EXERCISE 5

Represent the following information on a bar chart:

Business school	% entrants with degrees	% women
Aston	62	13
Bradford	88	19
City	88	30
Cranfield	82	11
Durham	71	32
LBS	97	22

(The above figures are for 1983, and taken from Hussey (1988).)

Note: Because of the difference in range of the two sets of figures you may find it helpful to use two scales, one covering the full range for the percentage with degrees, one covering a much smaller range, therefore allowing a wider spread within that range, for the percentage women. Experiment to see what gives you the clearest picture.

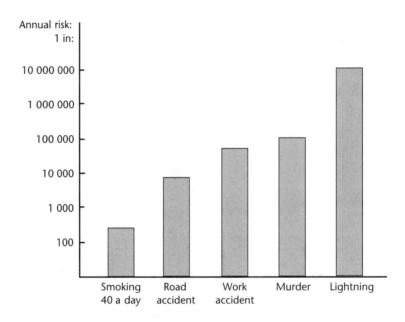

Fig. 13.3 Risk of some causes of death

It can be a tremendous advantage to use different scales to increase clarity. For example, if all the values you are plotting lie between 90 and 95, differences between them will be barely perceptible on a 1–100 scale. But if you use the same distance to represent from 90 to 95, the variations will be much more apparent. Be careful though. Once you stop using 0 as the bottom of your scale a bar that is twice as high as another no longer means that the value is twice as much.

Sometimes it is necessary to use each interval on the scale to represent an increase in size gained not by adding, but by multiplying. This is known as a *logarithmic* or *exponential* scale. It allows you to represent a much wider range of values on a single scale than would be possible with an interval scale, yet still to see how things at the small end relate to each other. You will see an example of such a scale when you come to the next diagram.

You will see that great care is needed in interpreting bar charts, as the use of different scales can be misleading if the differences and their implications are not clearly understood. Using different scales may make your diagrams much clearer, but if the reader is careless in reading them, you may not communicate. If you are using other than a normal interval scale starting at zero, you may wish to point this out in your text to be doubly safe. Sometimes scales seem to have been chosen almost with the intention of misleading. Look at the chart in Fig. 13.3, which is similar to one that appeared in a reputable scientific periodical. What, at first glance, is most likely to kill you?

It is only when you stop to think that surely lightning *can't* be so much more dangerous than smoking that you realise that the scale is dealing in risks, expressed in such a way that unlikely things get a taller bar than likely things. A 1 in 10 chance is much *bigger* than a 1 in 100 chance, yet it comes lower on the scale.

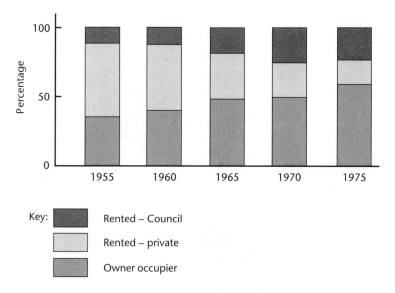

Fig. 13.4 Types of dwelling in a village

Sometimes bars are used to show proportions. In this case the height of each bar will be 100, with a part of each bar devoted to the different quantities that go to make up that whole. Again you will need to differentiate the parts with colour or shading. For example, a survey of a small village over a number of years might show the proportion of owner occupation rising. This could be represented as in Fig. 13.4.

Note that it is not possible to tell from the chart how *many* of any type of dwelling existed in any year, as it would be from the type of bar chart described before. In fact the village was growing quite significantly over the period in question, but there is no way of telling this from the chart above. All that you can say is how the total in any one year was divided between the three categories. You need to be very careful not to draw conclusions about whether actual *numbers* in any category are increasing or decreasing. Although the proportion of privately rented accommodation decreases, the overall growth in housing provision might well mean that the actual numbers of privately rented dwellings are increasing, albeit more slowly than the overall rate of increase. Again you need to be careful when reading the diagram.

PIE CHARTS

The other type of representation commonly used to show proportions of a total in different categories is the *pie chart*. Again, the ease of generating such diagram on a PC has led to a proliferation in their use, often in a multiplicity of colours, sometimes in mock 3D. Such charts have obvious attractions. They *look* good, and are prettier than simple bar charts. They are easy to understand, even by those who are uneasy about fractions. Whereas with proportions of ⅙, ⅓ and ½ some might

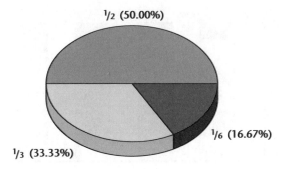

Fig. 13.5 A very simple pie chart . . .

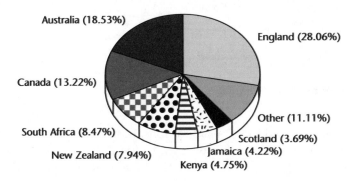

Athletics Gold Medals Commonwealth Games 1930–1970

Fig. 13.6 A pie chart with too many slices . . .

find it hard to say how the parts relate to each other, it is immediately obvious with a pie chart, as Fig. 13.5 shows.

However, pie charts become less useful when there are many 'slices'. We are not very good at judging fine differences between angles by eye, and it can be quite hard to tell whether some of the 'slices' are bigger than others. The picture can be further confused by the 3D effect, professional though this may look. It then becomes necessary to print the % on each slice, and to label it, which rather negates the intended advantage of visual impact, as in Fig. 13.6. When there are more than four or five 'slices' you should normally, in the interests of clarity, use a bar chart, even if it is less attractive.

EXERCISE 6

Convince yourself of the advantage of bar charts by representing the pie chart (in Fig. 13.6) in bar chart form. You will see how much easier it is to compare the size of the different parts (no answer is given).

Note that while bar charts can be used to show either a range of values, or, by fixing the height of the bar at 100%, to show proportions, a pie chart can *only* be used for proportions. It is totally invalid to use it to show, say, sales figures for a number of years.

GRAPHS

It has been pointed out that on bar charts other than histograms, the order of the bars normally does not matter. There is thus a scale along one axis which tells you the value of the height or length of the bar, but not along the other axis. There, you merely have a number of labelled points or bands. Sometimes you will see the top of such bars joined together to give a *graph*, but this is not really valid, as a graph should represent the relationship between *two* variables. Thus it would be perfectly legitimate to show a year's worth of monthly figures as either a set of bars or as a graph, but it would *not* be legitimate to show the figures from 12 factories or 12 sales teams as a graph. There you should use a bar chart. The monthly figures can be plotted against a scale showing time in the first case, whereas there is no second scale available in the second.

It is when you are plotting things over time that you will most frequently encounter graphs, although there are many other uses, costs against volume being a very common one. Just as when you are drawing bar charts, you need to think very carefully about the scale you wish to use, in this case for each axis. This should be such that your range of values uses up most of the available axis. Again, your scale does not need to start at zero, and you may need to use a logarithmic scale.

As with bar charts, you can show several things on a single graph. You can see from Fig. 13.7 that a rough visual comparison can be made of the two sets of figures shown. This would be much more difficult if you were working just from the sets of raw figures.

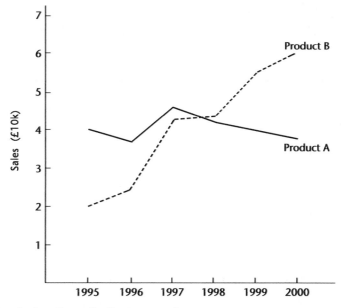

Fig. 13.7 Graph showing sales for two products

You can use a graph to see how two different things are related. For example, if you were to plot weekly average temperatures over a period and ice cream sales using one line for each (and different scales, of course), you might well find that if one line went up, the other one went up too. Or, if you used one line for absence rates, and another for output, you might find the opposite relationship. If you are using more than one line you do need to exercise restraint. If you try to show too many lines your graph will become very difficult to read.

You will easily be able to see trends, too, if your graph shows values over time. Indeed, graphs can be used to provide simple forecasts. By continuing the graph in the direction it seems to be heading, future values can be estimated. As most graphs will show a degree of variation about what seems to be the general direction, you will need to beware of continuing just in the direction of the last section of the graph, as a slightly odd last value might mislead you significantly. You will learn techniques for allowing for this, but try to forecast the future direction of the following graphs by eye.

EXERCISE 7

Extend, or *extrapolate from*, the following graphs to provide an estimate of future trends, putting a dot where you think the next point is most likely to be.

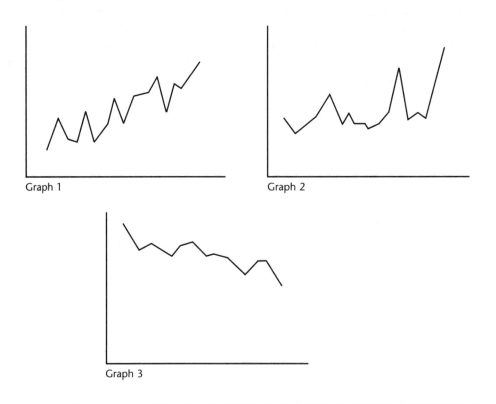

Graph 1

Graph 2

Graph 3

In the above we have concentrated on showing data in a way that makes visual sense. These techniques are likely to be extremely useful to you, but you may well need to supplement them by doing simple sums, or working with equations. This is where it starts to look like maths again, so you may need another drink.

ESTIMATING

You have already seen how a calculator can make things much easier for you, but that it has its weaknesses. Some of these may not be obvious, as the calculator may still give you an answer. For example, the four calculators in our house, when we tried to add 50% to 100 by pressing $\boxed{1}\ \boxed{0}\ \boxed{0}\ \boxed{+}\ \boxed{5}\ \boxed{0}\ \boxed{\%}$ gave 200, 300, 250 and 150. Calculators do not know, either, when you have pressed a wrong button. You therefore need to have a rough idea in your head of what the answer should be so that if it comes out wildly different you know that something is wrong.

The technique for doing this is called *estimating*. For example, if you are adding up 10 numbers in the range 700 to 900, you can estimate that the answer will be somewhere about 8000. If it is more than 9000, or less than 7000, you have done something wrong. Whatever the calculation that you are doing, it is worth getting a ballpark figure in your head, so that you know if some extra noughts have crept in somewhere, or you have pressed a $\boxed{+}$ somewhere instead of a $\boxed{-}$.

EXERCISE 8

Estimate the value of the following before doing the calculation on your calculator.

		Estimate	*Answer*
(a)	2734 + 5955	_____	_____
(b)	40 569 ÷ 9	_____	_____
(c)	25% of 39 400 113	_____	_____
(d)	95 + 15% of 113	_____	_____

ROUNDING

To estimate, you are probably working to the nearest hundred or thousand to get a rough idea of what the answer will be. This technique, called *rounding*, is very important. You will remember that when you used your calculator to work out $1\frac{2}{3}$ it filled up its display with '6's. You will seldom wish to work to so many places of decimals. Total accuracy is often not that important. To work to lots of places of decimals is not only inconvenient: it implies a spurious accuracy, casting doubt on your grasp of what your results really mean.

Suppose that your project involved using a questionnaire to obtain a measure of job satisfaction. Respondents were asked to rate a number of aspects of their jobs on a scale from 1 to 5. If you wanted to work with average scores in this case it would be totally absurd to give these to much more than one decimal place, as the ratings themselves are subjective, and the scale crude.

When rounding, you increase the last number you are using by 1 if the first number you are discarding is greater than 5, leaving it alone if the number you are discarding is less than 5. Opinions vary as to whether you should round up or down if it is 5. It doesn't really matter which you do, but whichever you prefer, you should do this consistently. Thus, 1.5326719 would be 1.5 to one decimal place, or 1.533 to three decimal places.

EXERCISE 9

Round the following to 2 places of decimals:

1.6324	3.9995	7164.2294	51.1111	1.6556
_____	_____	_____	_____	_____

You will see from this exercise that rounding to, say, two decimal places does not provide a consistent level of accuracy. A better measure is the number of *significant figures* in the answer, i.e. the number of digits between the first digit which isn't zero and the number which you round (inclusive). Thus 7 268 893.4 is 7 269 000 to four significant figures, and 0.006038215 is 0.00604 to three significant figures.

FRACTIONS, PERCENTAGES AND RATIOS

While you probably studied fractions at school, you may have paid less attention to ratios. You will encounter a number of key ratios in your accounting and business policy courses, and will need to be happy with the concept. Ratios are a sort of fraction, and fractions will also appear in other contexts, so a quick revision of how to deal with fractions is appropriate. The need for fractions will have already emerged if you have worked through 'division' in the Helpfile. Fractions can be expressed in three forms: as one number divided by another; as a decimal; or as a percentage.

EXERCISE 10

To refresh your memory, try the following. Your garage is offering tyres at 80 per cent of their original selling price. You decide to buy two, which would normally cost £100. You also have a company card, entitling you to a 5 per cent reduction on anything you buy. What should you end up paying, and should you ask for your 5 per cent discount before or after the promotional discount is deducted?

Fractions

With a calculator it is easy to turn fractions into decimals and then to work with them just like any other number. Unfortunately we cannot leave it at that, as many of the equations you will encounter will include letters, and your calculator cannot decimalise those. There are other times when you will not *wish* to turn a fraction into a decimal. Therefore, you need to know a few basic rules for dealing with fractions. Sometimes they will make a calculation so easy that you can dispense with your calculator anyway.

> **Rule 1:** You can multiply or divide top and bottom of a fraction by the same thing, be it number or letter or mixture, without changing the value of the fraction.

Imagine cutting a cake into 2, or 4, or 6, or 10, or 12 pieces. What would be half the cake in each case? Clearly $\frac{1}{2} = \frac{2}{4} = \frac{3}{6} = \frac{5}{10} = \frac{6}{12}$.

Similarly over $\frac{2(3+y)}{3(3+y)} = \frac{2}{3}$, as you can divide top and bottom by $3 + y$. This operation is called *cancelling*, and is very useful in simplifying fractions, so that a sum becomes easier to do.

EXERCISE 11

Simplify the following fractions by dividing top and bottom by the same thing, i.e. a factor common to both.

(a) $\frac{20}{30}$ _____

(b) $\frac{75}{100}$ _____

(c) $\frac{6}{9}$ _____

(d) $\frac{22}{11}$ _____

(e) $\frac{16}{12}$ _____

(f) $\frac{3x}{4x}$ _____

(g) $\frac{4(x+1)}{8(x+1)}$ _____

> **Rule 2:** To multiply a series of fractions you multiply all the numbers (or letters or brackets) on top to get the thing on top (the *numerator*) in your answer, and multiply all the things underneath to get the *denominator* or the thing on the bottom in your answer.

Thus, $\frac{2}{3} \times \frac{4}{5} = \frac{8}{15}$, and $\frac{1}{2} \times \frac{3}{4} = \frac{3}{8}$. You can now see how cancelling comes in very handy. You can cancel out numbers, or letters, or whole brackets, that appear on both top and bottom in a string of things to be multiplied, even if they do not appear in the same fraction. Thus $\frac{1}{2} \times \frac{4}{5}$ can be written as $\frac{2}{5}$, for you can divide both the 2 on the bottom, and the 4 on the top, by 2.

EXERCISE 12

Multiply the following sets of fractions, using cancelling to make the sum easier.

(a) $\frac{2}{3} \times \frac{3}{4} \times \frac{4}{5} \times \frac{1}{2}$ _____

(b) $\frac{1}{(n+1)} \times \frac{(n+1)}{3}$ _____

(c) $\frac{1}{xy} \times \frac{x}{(1+y)}$ _____

(d) $\frac{1}{2} \times \frac{50}{100}$ _____

(e) $\frac{2y}{14} \times \frac{7}{xy}$ _____

(f) $\frac{2}{15} \times \frac{3x}{4y} \times \frac{y(y+1)}{x}$ _____

(g) $\frac{y}{x} \times \frac{7}{y} \times \frac{x^2 y}{14}$ _____

Note that whether or not the bottom line of a fraction is written with a bracket round it, you must treat it as if it had one. It would be quite correct to write $1 + y$ in (c) above, i.e. without a bracket, but you could not divide it by any y that might be in the top line, as this would not go into the whole phrase '$1 + y$'.

Following this same rule, you can see that to square a fraction you square the number on the top and the number on the bottom to get numerator and denominator. Thus $\frac{1}{2}$ squared is $\frac{1}{4}$, $\frac{2}{3}$ cubed would be $\frac{2 \times 2 \times 2}{3 \times 3 \times 3}$ $\;or\;$ $\frac{2^3}{3^3}$, or $\frac{8}{27}$. You can either write the index number against top and bottom figures in a fraction you wish to raise to a certain power, or put a bracket around the whole fraction, and write the index number against the top of the closing bracket. Thus the fifth power of $\frac{2}{7}$ could be written as $(\frac{2}{7})^5$, or the nth power of $\frac{x}{y}$ as $(\frac{x}{y})^n$.

EXERCISE 13

Write out the value of $(\frac{x}{y})^n$

(a) where x is 1, y is 2 and n is 3   (b) when x is 2, y is 6 and n is 2

> *Rule 3:* **To divide something by a fraction you turn the fraction upside down and multiply by the inversion.**

Well, obviously you have to do *something* different, as $4 \div 2$ *can't* be the same as $4 \div \frac{1}{2}$. And it makes a sort of sense. If $4 \div 2$ means dividing it into two equal parts, then $4 \div \frac{1}{2}$ could be seen as dividing it into half a part, in which case a whole part would be twice what you started with, or 8.

So $4 \div \frac{1}{3}$ becomes 12, $\frac{1}{2} \div \frac{3}{4} = \frac{4}{6}$, $\frac{2(x+1)}{3} \div \frac{2}{(x+1)} = \frac{(x+1)^2}{3}$ etc.

Because you are converting a division into a multiplication by inverting it, you can string together multiplications and divisions without problem, provided you remember to write all the divisions upside down and then multiply. So:

$\frac{1}{2} \times \frac{3}{4} \div \frac{5}{7} \times \frac{1}{14} \div \frac{3}{5}$ can be written as
$\frac{1}{2} \times \frac{3}{4} \times \frac{7}{5} \times \frac{1}{14} \times \frac{5}{3}$ which cancels down to $\frac{1}{16}$.

Similarly,

$$\frac{(x+y)}{2y+3} \times \frac{3}{x} \div \frac{2(x+y)}{(2y+5)} \;\; becomes \;\; \frac{(x+y)}{(2y+3)} \times \frac{3}{x} \times \frac{(2y+5)}{2(x+y)}$$

which, as you can divide both top and bottom by $(x + y)$, cancels down to

$$\frac{3(2y+5)}{2x(2y+3)}$$

EXERCISE 14

Work out the following combined multiplications and divisions. Leave the brackets in as was done in the example above. Don't worry that we have not yet learned how to multiply them out.

(a) $\dfrac{1}{2} \times \dfrac{2(x+y)}{3} \div \dfrac{3(x+y)}{2}$ _____

(b) $\dfrac{x}{y} \times \dfrac{y}{x} \div \dfrac{x}{y} \div \dfrac{2}{3}$ _____

(c) $4 \div (x+1) \times \dfrac{3}{4} \div \dfrac{(x+2)}{(x+4)}$ _____

(d) $\dfrac{3}{4} \div \dfrac{3}{5} \div \dfrac{x(x+1)}{(y+1)}$ _____

(e) $1\dfrac{1}{2} \times \dfrac{3}{4} \div \dfrac{y}{x}$ _____

Rule 4: **You can add or subtract only fractions which share a common denominator.**

Percentages

Go back to your cake. It makes sense to *talk* about '½ + ⅓', but would be clumsy to include this expression in, say, a string of multiplications. You cannot say that ½ + ⅔ is ²⁄₂, or ⅔, or ⅖, because it isn't. In order to write the addition as something with a single number on top and bottom, we need to turn each fraction into the same sort of thing. ½ can be written as ³⁄₆, and ⅓ as ²⁄₆. These we *can* add, to give ⅚. Similarly, ½ − ⅓ could have been described as ³⁄₆ − ²⁄₆, or ⅙. You can do the same if you have letters in your fractions. If you wish to add ⅗ and $\dfrac{5x}{y}$ you can turn both into fractions with $5y$ on the bottom line, by multiplying top and bottom of the first one by y, and top and bottom of the second by 5. This will give you the sum $\dfrac{3y}{5y} + \dfrac{25x}{5y}$ or $\dfrac{(3y+25x)}{5y}$. When dealing in percentages you are reducing everything to hundredths, so you have a common denominator and can add and subtract.

Note that you *cannot* cancel between different terms in an addition in the same way that you could for a multiplication. Note also that you cannot cancel between *part* of the numerator and the denominator. You cannot get rid of either the 5 or the y in the answer above by dividing the $3y$ by y or the $25x$ by 5. You have to be able to divide every term on the top line by something on the bottom line to cancel. Thus if the top line had been $5y + 25x$ you would have been able to cancel out the 5 in the bottom line, as the top could have been written as $5(y + 5x)$ and the 5 could have been cancelled with the 5 on the bottom line.

EXERCISE 15

Write the following as single fractions:

(a) $\frac{3}{4} + \frac{7}{8}$ _____

(b) $\dfrac{3}{x} + \dfrac{4}{y}$ _____

(c) $\dfrac{5x}{y} - \dfrac{2(x+1)}{y}$ _____

(d) $\dfrac{2}{3} + \dfrac{3x}{5}$ _____

(e) 50% of ¾ _____

(f) $\dfrac{y(5x+1)}{x} + \dfrac{xy}{(5x+1)}$ _____

(g) $\dfrac{5}{(x-1)} - \dfrac{3}{(x-2)}$ _____

Ratios

Now that you have the basic rules for dealing with fractions at your fingertips, whether these fractions are expressed in letters, numbers, or a mixture, we can move on to ratios which are a form of fraction.

You use ratios when you are more interested in the relative sizes of things than in the absolute differences between them. To say that Part A costs 20p more than Part B may be more or less impressive depending on how much they both cost. If Part A costs £200.20, the difference is less striking than if Part A costs 40p. In the second instance it costs 100% more than Part B, or 200% as much, whereas in the first instance it is 0.1% more, or 100.1% of the Part B price.

Ratios, are obtained by dividing one thing by another. Thus in the above, with Part A at 40p, the ratio of the cost of Part A to Part B is 2:1, or $\frac{2}{1}$, depending on how you prefer to write it. You obtain the ratio of A to B by dividing A by B. Thus the ratio of Part B's cost to Part A's is 1:2, or $\frac{1}{2}$. The thing you are finding the ratio *of* is written first, or on top. The thing you are finding the ratio of it *to* is written second, or underneath. So if there are 500 students on a course and 10 tutors the staff:student ratio is 1:50 or $\frac{1}{50}$. The advantage of the fraction way of writing it, rather than the colon, is that you can then include the ratio in an equation if you want to, and deal with it like any other fraction. Since percentages are just another way of writing fractions, you can, of course, express ratios in percentages, too.

EXERCISE 16

Imagine your departmental budget is £40 000 of which £12 800 is spent on advertising.

(a) What percentage of your budget is spent on advertising?   _____

(b) What is the ratio of your advertising budget to your total budget?   _____

(c) What is the ratio of your advertising budget to your budget for
   everything else?   _____

Any accounting and finance course will introduce you to many ratios. This is because ratios deal in relative values rather than absolutes and so allow you to make meaningful comparisons between operations of different size. Certain key ratios are used to compare an organisation's performance from year to year, and to identify emerging trends.

A key financial ratio which you will encounter is 'Return on Capital Employed' (ROCE), sometimes known as 'Return on Investment' (ROI). While an MBA course will take you through the process of working out which figures should be used in calculating this ratio, you can practise working with ratios by calculating ROCE in a variety of cases.

$$\text{ROCE (or ROI)} = \frac{\text{Operating profit (pre-interest and tax)}}{\text{Capital employed}}$$

EXERCISE 17

Calculate ROCE (as a percentage) in the following cases (figures in £000):

	Operating profit	Capital employed	ROCE
(a)	500	4000	____
(b)	164	83	____
(c)	4.3	13	____
(d)	(10)	256	____

Because capital employed may vary, it is common to calculate an average value, using net assets at the year start and end.

EXERCISE 18

Calculate ROCE as a percentage, using average investment.

	Operating profit	Assets at year start	Assets at year end	Mean investment	ROCE
(a)	45	335	300	____	____
(b)	330	120	160	____	____
(c)	2200	7800	8000	____	____
(d)	(55)	5600	5500	____	____

Profit margin (the ratio of profit before interest and tax to sales) is clearly a major factor in determining ROCE. The other important factor is asset turnover. Asset turnover is a measure of how well the fixed assets and working capital of the firm are utilised. Profit margin multiplied by asset turnover gives ROCE.

EXERCISE 19

Asset turnover must be the ratio of *what* to net assets? (That is, if asset turnover is x:net assets, what is x?)

Another important ratio which can be used for practising working out ratios is liquidity. One measure of this is current assets:current liabilities. This shows the extent to which short-term claims by creditors are covered by assets which are likely to be converted into cash within the same time-scale. This measure of liquidity is called the 'Current Ratio'. It is more likely to be given as a decimal number than as a percentage.

EXERCISE 20

Calculate the current ratio in the following cases (figures are in £000):

	Current assets	Current liabilities	Current ratio
(a)	10 000	5 000	_____
(b)	40	35	_____
(c)	2	3	_____
(d)	3 500	2 000	_____

You will learn many more ratios, and how to interpret them, on your course. Sometimes you will be faced with whole pages of figures from which you will be required to derive the ratios before interpreting them. This may at first sight seem forbidding, but in most cases, as the above exercises go some way to show, all you will need by way of mathematical skill is the ability to add, subtract, multiply and divide appropriate numbers. The greater problem is to keep a clear head!

USING EQUATIONS

Take the simple(?) example of compound interest. Suppose you borrow £1000 for 5 years, at 15% interest p.a., and instead of paying the interest, add it to the amount you owe. Thus at the end of the first year, the amount you owe will be £1000 plus 15% of £1000. That is, the debt at the end of year one (call it D_1) will be 1.15 × the sum borrowed.

Your debt at the end of year two will be $1.15 \times D_1$, or $1.15 \times 1.15 \times$ the original £1000.

EXERCISE 21

Use your calculator to find the debt at the end of year two. Then calculate the debt at the end of year three.

Year two_____   Year three_____

Now you can see why it is useful to replace numbers by letters. It enables us to write a general, all-purpose formula for how to calculate the amount owed, without specifying the actual figures. We can say that after any number of years, call it n, the balance outstanding will be $(1.15)^n \times £1000$. If you want the debt after 10 years, it will be $(1.15)^{10} \times £1000$, and so on. If you have a scientific calculator you will have a key which allows you to do this directly, but otherwise you will need to multiply repeatedly.

We can make the formula more general by using a different letter, say A, for the amount originally borrowed, and even more general by using a further letter, say r, for the percentage interest rate. Thus if we use D_n to indicate the debt at the end of year n, we have a completely general formula:

$$D_n = A(1 + r)^n.$$

Using this formula we can work out the debt for any sum, any interest rate, any sum borrowed, and any length of time, merely by replacing the letters by the numbers that we wish to use in a particular case, and then working out the answer.

EXERCISE 22

Work out the amount that will be owed:

(a) at the end of 1 year on a loan of £2000 at 13%   _____
(b) at the end of 2 years on a loan of £1500 at 25%   _____
(c) at the end of 5 years on a loan of £10 000 at 15%   _____

In this instance we are dealing with the simple case of substituting values in the formula to work out the amount owing after a given period with compound interest. It is simply a question of plugging in the right numbers, as the quantity you wanted, D_n, was sitting neatly by itself on one side of the '=' sign. Often it will be less simple. The value you want, traditionally referred to as x, may be mixed up in the middle of an equation, and you may need to move terms around to get it to itself. Or worse still, you may want to find several terms (x, y and z?) which are all mixed up in the same equations, in which case you will need to work with several equations at once to find solutions.

Note that although classical algebra traditionally dealt in 'x's and 'y's, you can use any letters you choose, and you will usually find it much easier to choose a letter which relates in some way to what it describes, as when we chose D for debt, and r for rate in the example above. This makes it much easier to remember what the equation is all about, and which term relates to which. Indeed, if you are struggling with an equation where the author has steadfastly refused to do this, you can sometimes make more sense of it by translating the 'x's and 'y's into letters that have a more obvious meaning. (If you are quoting a standard equation in an assignment or examination, you should, however, always use the 'official' letters.)

With some equations you will be able to find an answer. In other cases, you may have sets of variables and formulae where there is no answer as such, but where you can learn techniques which will allow you to maximise, or optimise, results. You will learn these when you study courses on Operations Research. Key among these techniques are use of the calculus (differential equations), discovered in the seventeenth century, and linear programming techniques, which date from the Second World War.

Don't panic. These techniques are far beyond the scope of this chapter. All that is attempted here is to show you how you can move terms around in a fairly simple equation, so that you will be able to approach the more complex manipulations, which you will doubtless be taught, without feeling confused.

An equation can best be visualised as two sets of things which are in balance. For example, look at Fig. 13.8.

Here x, and $y + 1$, can be weighed in the pans and found equal, and we can thus write $x = y + 1$. Visualising it in this way makes it very easy to see what you can and cannot do to an equation. Clearly you could add the same quantity to each side,

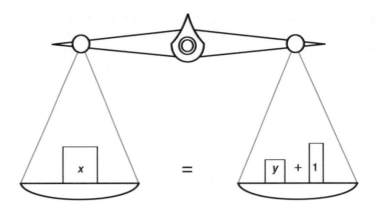

Fig. 13.8 An equation as a balance

and the scales would still balance. Thus in the above case you could write $x + 1 = y + 1 + 1$, or $y + 2$, and it would still be correct. Similarly, $x + z = y + z + 1$ would also be true. You could also take the same quantity away from each side and leave the scales in balance. Thus you could write $x - 1 = y$, or $x - y = 1$.

You could multiply the two sides by the same thing, too. Doubling each side would still produce balance, as would trebling, or anything else. So $2x = 2(y + 1)$, $10x = 10(y + 1)$, or $zx = z(y + 1)$. By the same token, you can divide each side by the same thing. Taking half of what is in each pan will still balance the scales, as will dividing by anything else. Thus:

$$\frac{x}{2} = \frac{(y + 1)}{2}, \text{ and } \frac{x}{z} = \frac{(y + 1)}{z} \text{ and } \frac{x}{(y + 1)} = 1$$

Indeed, whatever you do, as long as you do it equally to both sides, you will be left with a valid equation. What you cannot do is to do something to one side, and do it to only part of the other side. Multiplying all of the right-hand side, but only some of the left, by a quantity would not be valid. Thus you could not write $2x = 2y + 1$ in the above example. (To remember this, you will need to put brackets round each side of the equation if you start multiplying or dividing.)

This is the main rule for manipulating equations. Once you have grasped it, you will be well away. Thus, suppose that you were working with the debt example we used earlier, but you knew the amount owed at the end of the period and the interest rate at which the money had been borrowed. What you did not know, and wanted to find out, was the original debt. Suppose that after 4 years at 20% the debt was £4147. You *could* experiment by trying different original loans, and working out the debt in each case. When you got too big a debt you could try a smaller loan, if that came out too small you could try a bigger one, getting closer to your £4147 debt each time. Alternatively, you could rearrange the equation so that the term you wanted, A, was on the left of the '=', all by itself, and then work out the figure you wanted directly. You do this by using the fact that you can do something to both sides of the equation without affecting its validity.

The original equation was:

$$D_n = A(1 + r)^n$$

Don't worry that this is much more complicated looking than the $x = y + 1$ type of example used above. The principle is exactly the same. In this case, we want to stop the A from being multiplied by $(1 + r)^n$. If you had $2A$ and wanted to have only A you would divide by 2. It is exactly the same here. If we divide $A(1 + r)^n$ by $(1 + r)^n$, then the two $(1 + r)^n$'s cancel out, and leave us with A. But remember, if we did something to one side of the equation, we had to do it to the other, so we must divide the D_n by $(1 + r)^n$ as well. Thus we get the equally valid equation:

$$A = \frac{D_n}{(1 + r)^n}$$

This is a much more useful arrangement of the equation if A is what we are looking for. We know the values of D_n and r and n, so can put these into the equation, giving $A = £4147 \div (1.2)^4$, which your calculator should tell you is near enough £2000. This should be a much quicker, as well as more accurate, way of getting the answer than the trial and error method. (Note, however, that there will be occasions when trial and error is your only option, so do not underestimate that method's potential!)

To use a different equation, suppose you wanted to find x, and you knew $y = 7 + 3x + \frac{1}{y}$. The first thing you could do would be to subtract $7 + \frac{1}{y}$ from each side of the equation, leaving you with $y - 7 - \frac{1}{y} = 3x$. Then, since we usually write what we are trying to find on the left of the '=' sign, we could swap the sides over to give $3x = y - 7 - \frac{1}{y}$. We then need to get rid of the 3, so we divide both sides by 3, giving us:

$$x = \frac{(y - 7 - \frac{1}{y})}{3}$$

If this were to be included in a longer equation, and there might be some chance of further cancelling, we might wish to sort out the rather messy $(y - 7 - \frac{1}{y})$ into a single fraction. To do this we need to express it all in 'y'ths, that is, as something over y. Just as 2 is $\frac{4}{2}$, so y can be written as $\frac{y^2}{y}$, and 7 as $\frac{7y}{y}$, so the whole phrase inside the bracket could just as well have been written as $x = \frac{(y^2 - 7y - 1)}{y}$, or the whole equation written as:

$$x = \frac{(y^2 - 7y - 1)}{3y}$$. If you know y, it is now easy to work out the value of x.

For example, if $y = 2$, $x = \frac{(4 - 14 - 1)}{6}$, or $-\frac{11}{6}$.

EXERCISE 23

Rearrange the following equations to get x on the left, then work out the values of x if:
(i) $y = 2$, (ii) $y = -3$, (iii) $y = 0$

	$x =$	(i) $y = 2$	(ii) $y = -3$	(iii) $y = 0$
(a) $2y = x + 5$	_____	_____	_____	_____
(b) $y + 1 = 3x - 2$	_____	_____	_____	_____
(c) $y + 2x = y - x + 12$	_____	_____	_____	_____
(d) $\frac{y}{4} = \frac{x}{2} + 3$	_____	_____	_____	_____
(e) $xy = 3$	_____	_____	_____	_____

	$x =$	(i) $y = 2$	(ii) $y = -3$	(iii) $y = 0$

(f) $\frac{x}{y} = y + \frac{1}{2}$ _____ _____ _____ _____

(g) $\frac{y}{(x+3)} = 4$ _____ _____ _____ _____

(h) $\frac{x}{(y+2y+1)} = y + 4$ _____ _____ _____ _____

WORKING WITH BRACKETS

In the above, you have often needed to use brackets because this is a way of reminding you either that everything on the top and everything on the bottom of a fraction must be multiplied or divided by the same thing if the fraction is to stay the same, or that everything on each side of an equation must be treated in the same way if the equation is to remain valid. In the exercise above, you could work with the brackets by substituting numbers and then working out the value of the bracket before dealing with it further, but sometimes you will need to work with brackets when you cannot do this. You have already seen that a simple multiplication, say $2(a + b)$, means multiplying *everything* in the bracket, here by 2, giving you $2a + 2b$ in this case. If you want to multiply *two* brackets, you need to multiply everything in the first bracket by everything in the second. Thus

$$(a + b)(c + d) \text{ will give you } ac + ad + bc + bd$$

Note that if two brackets are written side by side it means they are to be multiplied. There is no need to use a 'x' sign to show this. Work out the value of the above where $a = 1$, $b = 2$, $c = 3$ and $d = 4$, and then check that this is the same as if you multiplied 3 by 7.

EXERCISE 24

Work out the value of:

(a) $2a(3b + 2c)$ _____

(b) $\frac{x(6y - 4z)}{2}$ _____

(c) $3r(s + 2t) + 3s(2r + t)$ _____

(d) $(2x + y)(y + 2)$ _____

(e) $\frac{(3z + 4y)\,(2y + z)}{2(4y + 2z)\,(a + b)}$ _____

The above treatment has, I hope, introduced the basics of the maths that you are likely to need. There is no real substitute for practice if you are to become familiar with the techniques involved. Additional exercises can be found on the companion website at www.booksites.net/cameron. Alternatively, make up further equations for yourself, and try using equations you have made up to solve problems. What equation can you construct to tell you how far a car will go on g gallons of petrol if it does 56 mpg? How many miles to the litre will it do if there are 4½ litres to the gallon? There are any number of such small equations that you can construct. Or you can obtain Graham and Sargent, *Countdown to Mathematics* (*see* Further information), a GCSE maths revision book or Morris (2000) to provide further examples. Check that your chosen book provides answers, as you will need feedback on your work. If you do feel particularly weak in this area, and you have time to spare before starting your course, this is one form of preparation that will pay huge dividends. Good luck!

SUMMARY

- Simple techniques such as bar or pie charts or graphs can enable you to represent sets of data in such a way as to make them more meaningful, allowing visual comparison between sets of figures, or the estimation of trends.

- Ratios, fractions or percentages can be used to indicate how parts relate to each other, or to the whole. Ratios or fractions can be multiplied by multiplying numerators to give the new numerator, and multiplying denominators to give the new denominator. They are unchanged if top and bottom are multiplied by the same thing. They can be added or subtracted only if the denominator is the same in all cases.

- Ratios are particularly important in accounting and finance.

- Equations can be used to find unknown values, or to provide a general formula from which values can be calculated in specific cases.

- Equations can be simplified, or rearranged, using the basic rule that an equation remains valid no matter what you do to one side, provided you do it to the other side as well.

- Statistical techniques can be used to provide estimates of the probability of sets of results arising because of random variation, rather than because of a systematic difference. They will tell you only the probability of something, not whether it is true or not.

Further information

Graham, L. and Sargent, D. (1981) *Countdown to Mathematics*, vol. 1, Addison-Wesley with the Open University Press. This covers much the same ground at greater length, and provides many more examples for you to work through, with answers.

Huff, D. (1991) *How to Lie with Statistics*, Penguin.

Moroney, M.J. (1951) *Facts from Figures*, Penguin, is a classic but accessible introduction to statistics.

Morris, C. (2000) *Quantitative Approaches in Business Studies* (5th edn), FT Prentice Hall.

Morris, C. and Thanassoulis, E. (1994) *Essential Mathematics – a refresher course for Business and Social Studies*, Macmillan.

Oakshott, L. (1998) *Essential Quantitative Methods for Business, Management and Finance*, Macmillan Business.

Powell, J. (1991) *Quantitative Decision Making*, Longman.

Rowntree, D. (1987) *Statistics Without Tears: a primer for non-mathematicians*, Penguin.

Sprent, P. (1991) *Management Mathematics*, Penguin.

For further exercises, refer to the companion website at www.booksites.net/cameron.

HELPFILE: CRACKING THE CODE

This section takes you, very gently I promise, through the basic symbols you may find in mathematical equations.

$\boxed{+}$

You will know that in 5 + 3 the '+' is telling you to take the *sum* of 3 and 5, or what you get when you add them together. If you had trouble doing the sum, or would have done if it had larger numbers, you can easily get the answer from your calculator, by pressing the obvious buttons. Here you would need $\boxed{5}$, $\boxed{+}$, $\boxed{3}$, $\boxed{=}$. Note that for additions, the order of the terms does not matter. 5 + 3 is the same as 3 + 5.

$\boxed{-}$

You will also know already that 5 – 3, or 5 minus 3, means what you get when you take 3 away from 5. Again, you can easily do subtractions by pressing the obvious calculator buttons. Note that subtractions are more complicated than additions in two ways. First, the order *does* matter. 5 – 3 is *not* the same as 3 – 5. If you have £3000 in the bank and take out £5000 you are *not* in the same situation as if you have £5000 and take out £3000! In the second case you will have £2000 left, and your bank manager will be happy. In the first case you will have an overdraft of £2000, and unless you cleared this with the bank first, they will probably *not* be happy. You will have –£2000. This may be written as (£2000) in some sets of accounts.

Second, there is the interesting question of what to do when you want to take away an amount that is already negative, i.e. has a – sign in front of it. To 'take away' your overdraft, someone would have to *give* you £2000, and indeed to take away a number that is already negative you *add* that number. Thus 5 – (–3) is 5 + 3, or 8. Note that basic calculators can't do this for you; you have to apply this rule of signs yourself before you press the buttons.

$\boxed{\times}$

This indicates multiplication. 5 × 3 means 5 lots of 3, or 15. Again, the obvious calculator buttons will produce the answer if you have forgotten your tables. And, as with addition, order does not matter. When dealing with negative numbers, you need to count the number of '–' signs in the string of numbers you are multiplying. If you have one, or indeed any odd number of minuses, the answer will be negative. For example, if you owe 5 weeks' garage rent at £3 per week, you have 5 × (–3), or – £15.

If you are multiplying two negative quantities, or any even number of negatives, the answer will be positive. A cheap calculator will not be able to handle a string of mixed signs in a multiplication. When you put in a $\boxed{-}$ it will start to subtract. So you will have to treat the numbers as positive, and again add the right sign yourself, once you get the answer.

Part of the reason for difficulty in working with mixtures of signs on a calculator is that in a string of things to add, subtract, multiply and divide, the signs have different *strengths*. If you see 5 + 3 × 2, this means that you should work out the 3 × 2 *first*, before adding the 5. Thus you get 11, *not* 16. Multiplication and division signs are stronger than addition and subtraction signs, so must be worked on first. Sophisticated calculators are progammed with this rule, but cheap ones are not.

÷

This indicates division. 5 ÷ 3 means what you get when you divide 5 into 3 equal portions. If the second number goes into the first with no problems, for example in the case of 6 ÷ 3 where the answer is 2, life is simple. If it does not, because the first number is not capable of being produced by multiplying the second number by a whole number, you start getting into *fractions*. If I produce 5 cakes, my 3 children will know that they will get less than two each, because there are less than 6 cakes, and more than 1½. To be sure they are happy, I could divide each cake into three equal parts and give them a part of each cake. The *fraction* of each cake that they would get would be ⅓.

Figure 13.9 shows how one share is 5 times ⅓, which could be assembled into 1⅔ cakes. You could write the '1⅔' as ⅗ if you liked. You will see in a minute why this can sometimes be useful.

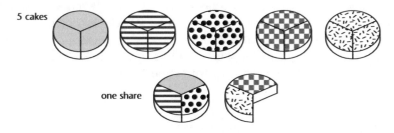

Fig. 13.9 When you have five cakes and three children...

·

This is a decimal point. You will be used to seeing figures written in decimals. 1.5 means 1½. The decimal point divides the whole number from the fraction. Adding fractions can be quite difficult, but if they are expressed as decimals, the sum can be easily done. Press ⟮5⟯, ⟮÷⟯, ⟮3⟯, ⟮=⟯ on your calculator to see what 1⅔ is in decimal notation. The same sort of system works to the right of the decimal point as to the left. You will know that the first place to the left of the decimal point represents units, the next tens, the next hundreds, and so on. As you move one place to the left, you multiply by 10. Once you move to the right of the decimal point, exactly the same applies. But because you are now travelling right instead of left, each shift away from the decimal point means a *division* by 10. Thus 1.5 means 1 and ⁵⁄₁₀, 1.05 means 1 and ⁵⁄₁₀₀, etc.

It is very easy to work with decimals on a calculator, as they work in exactly the same way as whole numbers. As long as you remember to insert a decimal point at the right place in each number, the calculator will do the rest. You merely have to remember that your calculator will not be able to cope with a mixture of additions and multiplications if it is a cheap one, and you will have to work out the multiplications or divisions first, before inserting the result into the sum you give to the machine. If you are working in decimals without your calculator, you must remember to line up the decimal points. Thus in adding 101.75 and 1.003 you will get:

$$101.75 +$$
$$\underline{1.003}$$
$$102.753$$

In this way, you are adding units to units, $\frac{1}{10}$ths to $\frac{1}{10}$ths, and so on.

If you want to add a string of fractions on a cheap calculator, you will again start to confuse it. To get around this, use the memory. Each time you work out a fraction as a decimal, add it into the memory. The button usually says $\boxed{M+}$ for this. If one of the fractions is to be subtracted, press the $\boxed{M-}$ button. When you have finished, you can access the result with the memory recall, probably $\boxed{MR}$, button.

$\boxed{\%}$

Percentage, or per cent. This is a fraction expressed in $\frac{1}{100}$ths. Thus 1 is $\frac{100}{100}$ths or 100%, half is $\frac{50}{100}$ths or 50% etc. This is very similar to working in the first two numbers to the right of the decimal point, and has the same advantages as does using decimals. It is very hard to see how $\frac{11}{13}$, $\frac{27}{31}$, and $\frac{6}{7}$ relate to each other. If you express them as percentages it is very easy to see which is biggest, or to add or subtract them. Use your calculator to find out what a variety of fractions are in percentages. You will probably be able to do this by pressing say $\boxed{1}$, $\boxed{\div}$, $\boxed{4}$, $\boxed{\%}$ to get $\frac{1}{4}$ as a percentage. Start with something you know first, like $\frac{1}{2}$, to check that these are the right buttons.

$\boxed{=}$

You will have been happily using the $\boxed{=}$, or 'equals' button on your calculator if you have been trying out simple sums as suggested above. Equations always contain an equals sign. It means that everything to one side of it is the same as everything to the other side. More of this later.

$\boxed{2}$

The power of two, or squared. Little numbers up in the air to the right of a number or letter mean that it has been multiplied by itself, the number of terms in the multiplication being given by the number. Thus 2^2 means 2×2, and 3^2 means 3×3. We call this 'squared', or 'to the power 2'. If the little number is a 3 we call it 'cubed', or 'to the power 3'. 4^3 is $4 \times 4 \times 4$. 10^3 is 1000. After this we run out of special terms, and are reduced to speaking of 'to the power 7' or whatever. What do you think you get when you multiply two powers of a single number? Try it with $10^2 \times 10^3$. You will find you get 100 000, or 10^5. This always works. You can simply add the powers together if you are multiplying two powers of a single number. Remember this, as it has all sorts of uses. By the same token, you can *divide* a power of a number by another power of that number by subtracting the second index from the first. Thus $2^3 \div 2^2 = 2$, or $10^{12} \div 10^8 = 10^4$.

There are two funny indices, the power 0 and the power 1. Try to work out what these must mean, remembering that to *multiply* powers you *add* the indices. Raising a number to the power 1 must therefore mean using the number as it stands. 5^3 must be the product of 5^1 and 5^2. But you know that 5×5^2 is 5^3, so 5^1 must be 5. By the same token, $5^0 \times 5^2$ should be 5^2. But the only thing that you can multiply 5^2 by to get 5^2 is 1, so 5^0, or indeed anything to the power nought, must be 1.

$\boxed{\surd}$

Square root. This is the number which multiplied by itself gives you the number you first thought of. Thus $\sqrt{9}$ is the number which, when squared, gives the answer 9, i.e. 3. Press $\boxed{8}$, $\boxed{1}$, $\boxed{\surd}$ on your calculator to find the square root of 81. You should be able to work out what the index number, or power, of a square root is. Stop for a minute and try.

If you are stuck, remember that to multiply two powers you *add* the index numbers. And the index for a number itself is 1. This will only work if each index is ½. Thus $\sqrt{4} \times \sqrt{4} = 4 = 4^{1/2} \times 4^{1/2}$.

Just as you can find squares, cubes, fourth powers, etc. so you can find cube roots, fourth roots, etc. Cube roots are written as $^3\sqrt{x}$ or $x^{1/3}$, fourth roots as $^4\sqrt{x}$ or $x^{1/4}$, etc. Work out $^4\sqrt{16}$ on your calculator.

You will not have found a '$^4\sqrt{}$' key, but you knew that a fourth root is the square root of a square root, so if you could not do the sum in your head, you could press $\boxed{1}$, $\boxed{6}$, $\boxed{\surd}$, $\boxed{\surd}$, giving the answer 2.

If you still feel a bit bemused you will find it helpful to find squares, and square roots, and cubes and fourth powers of a variety of numbers, writing down each number with its square or whatever, until you get the feel for how such numbers relate. You can check your squares by finding their square roots to see that these are what they ought to be, or your square roots by multiplying them by themselves.

This exhausts the signs on a cheap calculator. Scientific calculators have a much wider range of keys, offering all sorts of facilities, including the ability to do calculations involving mixed additions and multiplications without getting muddled. Even better are the financial calculators, which allow you to derive values for things like net present value at the press of a button, instead of sweating blood working these out by hand as did earlier generations of students. You will doubtless want to invest in one of these calculators once you start your MBA accounting courses, but while you are just gaining confidence, you might actually be better off with a simple cheap calculator: there is less to confuse you.

Other mathematical signs you will frequently encounter include the following.

$\boxed{x}$

x or indeed any other letter. This is referred to as a variable, and appears in an equation to indicate something that can take a number of values, or whose value you do not know. Although some people are put off by the appearance of a letter in an equation, in fact you treat it just like a number, and can move it around in the same way. Of course, if you want, say, to multiply it by 2, you can't write in a new number, but you can work with, say, $2x$, quite happily. Indeed it is often very much simpler to play with letters in an equation than with numbers, which explains their popularity. When we deal with equations in more detail you will see why.

$\boxed{\Sigma}$

The Greek letter sigma, used to indicate the sum of. You will often see something of the form $\sum_{n=1}^{r} x_n$. This indicates that there are a series of values of x, which have been called for convenience x_1, x_2, x_3, all the way up to x^r. You are to add all these values for x_1 through to x_r. Thus you could express a year's sales figures as the sum of the monthly totals, x_1 to x_{12}, written as $\sum_{n=1}^{12} x_n$, or the second quarter's total as $\sum_{n=4}^{6} x_n$. The notation may look clumsy and forbidding, but is often an economical way of expressing something in an equation.

$\boxed{f}$

This means 'function'. If we say $y = f(x)$ we mean that y varies in some way as x varies, or it is a *function* of x. It could be $2x$, or $x + 10\ 000$, or anything else involving x. You could, for example, write $v = f(l,b)$ to indicate that the volume (v) of a room depends upon its length (l) and breadth (b). (It also depends on its height, which you are choosing not to mention.) This is one of the favourites among those who like to repeat their text in equation form. Unless they specify what the function *is*, their complicated looking expressions are unlikely to communicate more than their verbal description.

$\boxed{\neq}$

This simply means 'not equal to'. If you write $x \neq y$, you are saying that x *cannot* take the same value as y.

$\boxed{<}$

This means 'less than'. If $x < y$, then x is less than y.

$\boxed{>}$

This means 'greater than'. If $x > y$, then x is greater than y. It is easy to remember which is which, as in both signs the wider part of the wedge is pointing to the larger number.

$\boxed{\leq}$

This means 'less than or equal to'. If $x \leq y$, then x cannot be greater than y, though it could be the same value, or smaller.

$\boxed{\geq}$

Obviously this means 'greater than, or equal to'.

$\boxed{(\ )}$

Brackets. These are very important in equations. If things are in a bracket, it means that they must be treated as a whole. $2(7 + 6x + y)$ means that you must multiply *everything in the bracket* by two, for example. Here you would get $14 + 12x + 2y$. Also, $(5+3) \times 2$ tells you to do the addition first.

Answers to Exercises

Exercise 1

(a) 0.75, 0.8571428, 1.3333333, 2.1428571, 0.8181818, 0.75.

(b) 200%, 75%, 133%, 91%, 25%, 67% (taking the nearest whole percentage as the answer).

(c) 8, 196, 81, 81, 1728, 1, 1.

(d) 2^7, 3^2, 10^0, 17^8, 21^{18}, x^5, x^{y-2}, $z^{2(x+y)}$.

(e) 4, 12, 6, 6.16, 1.41, 3.16 (giving answers to two decimal places).

(f) 2^8, 10^1, $3^{2/3}$, xy, z^2.

(g) 6.

(h) ii, iii.

(i) $2x + 2y$, $3x - 3y^2$, $3y - 3x$, 0, y.

(j) 13, 17, $x + \dfrac{x^2}{y}$, 3.88 to two places of decimals.

If you had more than one or two (careless) mistakes you should take time to work through relevant parts of the Helpfile.

Exercise 2

61.55, 52.95.

Exercise 3

(a) mean 5.44, median 5, mode 5

(b) mean 4.33, median 3, mode 3.

Exercise 5

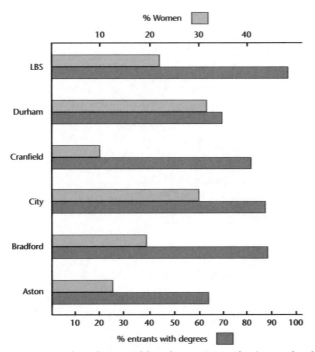

Proportions of graduate and female entrants to business schools, 1983.

Answer to Exercise 5

The chart shows one possibility. But it does give a false impression of the percentage of women, so you might have preferred to use the same scale for both. It would depend on whether you were primarily interested in the differences in each type of percentage *between* the schools, or the differences between the two percentages in each case.

Exercise 7
The shading in the graphs shows the broad areas which are reasonable. If the end of your line lies outside this area, you should ask yourself whether you have been unduly influenced by recent variations in the graph.

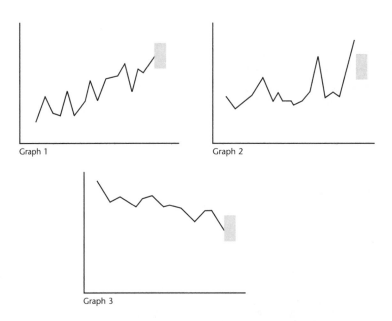

Graph 1   Graph 2

Graph 3

Answer to Exercise 7

Exercise 8
(a) My rough guess was 8600. Actual figure, 8689.

(b) My rough guess was 4100. Actual figure, 4507.7.

(c) My guess was 10 000 000. Actual figure, 9 850 028.3.

(d) My guess was 107. Actual figure, 111.95.

Perhaps your guesses were better!

Exercise 9
1.63, 4.00, 7164.23, 51.11, 1.66.

Exercise 10
£76. It doesn't matter which way round the discounts are calculated. You pay £0.95 × 0.80 × 100 (or £0.80 × 0.95 × 100), and it makes no difference what order numbers appear in a multiplication.

Exercise 11
(a) ⅔ (b) ¾ (c) ⅔ (d) 2 (e) ⅓ or 1⅓ (f) ¾ (g) ½

Exercise 12

(a) $\frac{1}{5}$ (b) $\frac{1}{3}$ (c) $\frac{1}{y(1+y)}$ (d) $\frac{1}{4}$ (e) $\frac{1}{x}$ (f) $\frac{(y+1)}{10}$ (g) $\frac{xy}{2}$

Exercise 13

(a) $\frac{1}{8}$ (b) $\frac{1}{9}$

Exercise 14

(a) $\frac{2}{9}$ (b) $\frac{3y}{2x}$ (c) $\frac{3(x+4)}{(x+1)(x+2)}$ (d) $\frac{5(y+1)}{4x(x+1)}$ (e) $\frac{9x}{8y}$

Exercise 15

(a) $1\frac{3}{8}$ or $1\frac{5}{8}$ (b) $\frac{(3y+4x)}{xy}$ (c) $\frac{(3x-1)}{y}$ (d) $\frac{(9x+10)}{15}$ (e) $\frac{3}{8}$ (f) $\frac{[y(5x+1)^2 + x^2y]}{x(5x+1)}$

(g) $\frac{[5(x-2)-3(x-1)]}{(x-1)(x-2)}$ or $\frac{(2x-7)}{(x-1)(x-2)}$

Exercise 16

(a) 32% (b) 32:100 or $\frac{32}{100}$ (or 32%) (c) 47% or 47:100 (or 128:272)

Exercise 17

(a) 12.5% (b) 198% (c) 33.1% (d) (4%) – a negative return

Exercise 18

	Mean investment	ROCE
(a)	317.5	14%
(b)	140	236%
(c)	7900	28%
(d)	5550	(1%)

Exercise 19

Sales.

Exercise 20

(a) 2 (b) 1.14 (c) 0.67 (d) 1.75

Exercise 21

$D_2 = £1322.50$, $D_3 = £1520.87$

Exercise 22

(a) £2260 (b) £2343.75 (c) £20 113.57

Exercise 23

(a) $x = 2y - 5$ (i) –1 (ii) –11 (iii) –5

(b) $x = \frac{(y+3)}{3}$ (i) $\frac{5}{3}$ (ii) 0 (iii) 1

(c) $x = 4$ (i) 4 (ii) 4 (iii) 4

(d) $x = \frac{y}{2} - 6$ (i) –5 (ii) –$\frac{9}{2}$ (iii) –6

(e) $x = \frac{3}{y}$ (i) $\frac{3}{2}$ (ii) –1 (iii) infinity (or undefined)

(f) $x = y^2 + \frac{1}{2}$ (i) 5 (ii) $7\frac{1}{2}$ (iii) 0

(g) $x = \frac{y}{4} - 3$ (i) $-2\frac{1}{2}$ (ii) $-2\frac{1}{4}$ (iii) -3

(h) $x = (y + 4)(3y + 1)$ (i) 42 (ii) 70 (iii) 4

Exercise 24

(a) $6ab + 4ac$

(b) $3xy - 2xz$

(c) $3rs + 6rt + 6rs + 3st$, or $9rs + 6rt + 3st$

(d) $2xy + 4x + y^2 + 2y$

(e) $\frac{(3z + 4y)}{4(a + b)}$ (note it was possible to divide top and bottom by $2y + z$)

SKILLS FOR ASSESSMENT

14 Scoring well in assessment

Objectives

By the end of this chapter you should:

- understand the objectives of your assessors in setting assignments
- know the most common causes of student failure
- be aware of how to avoid these hazards
- understand the requirements of successful communication.

INTRODUCTION

Thus far you have concentrated on the skills needed to benefit from your studies. But learning that makes you better at your job is not your only likely goal. Gaining a qualification is also probably important. And this means passing the exams and other assessments on your course. Learning is not enough. You have to be able to *demonstrate* to your examiners that you have learned what they intended!

The aim of the next few chapters is to help you to gain grades that are at least as high as your learning deserves. To do this you need to understand the viewpoint of those who are assessing you, and the characteristics of the types of assessment with which you may be faced. You also need to develop some fairly specific skills in being assessed, although most of these will be relevant in work situations as well.

This chapter covers the purposes of assessment, the particular challenge of work-based assignments, the common causes of failure on Master's programmes in management, and the general principles of communication which underlie all types of assessment. Subsequent chapters will deal with more specific types of assessment: written reports; oral presentations; examinations; portfolios and assessment centres; and producing a thesis or dissertation.

ASSESSMENT IN CONTEXT

Assessment is a complex area, with many influences acting upon it. The form of the assessment to which you are subjected will depend upon the nature of the programme in which you are involved, what it is trying to teach and the views about learning that underpin its design. It is also likely to depend upon where the institution is trying to 'position itself' in the management education market. Critics of current forms of management education also see assessment as a vehicle for policing both tutors and students in a system which demands a high level of conformity from both. From a less critical viewpoint assessment is both a vehicle for learning and a necessary means of demonstrating that standards are being maintained.

Institutional objectives for assessment

In choosing your course the likely value of the qualification will have been a factor. You would not want to work hard at gaining a degree which was deemed worthless because it was awarded by an institution which was seen as third rate. All reputable academic institutions are highly concerned that 'standards' are maintained, and with them their own credibility. Therefore they do not wish their graduates to bring the institution into disrepute by their subsequent incompetence or ignorance. They need to be sure that their graduates have reached a standard worthy of the qualification they are to be awarded.

Second, this concern with standards must be perceived by others. Academics want colleagues elsewhere to respect the place where they work. More importantly, institutions want to gain, or keep, accreditation from AMBA, EQUIS or wherever. The recent explosion in postgraduate management education, and in the number of institutions providing it, has made this concern even more pressing.

One of the generally accepted ways of maintaining standards, and thus meeting both these objectives, is to have a rigorous structure of assessment, including unseen examinations, with a system of external examiners to maintain comparability between institutions.

There is a third, and perhaps even more important objective for assessment. Properly designed it can be an 'engine of learning', driving students to exert effort that they would not otherwise exert, providing both carrots (the glow of satisfaction from a good grade) and sticks (the risk of not being allowed to proceed towards a qualification). If the assessment is well designed it will direct that effort into activities that will enhance learning and increase understanding. If students furthermore are given feedback on their efforts they will gain understanding of their strengths and weaknesses and will be able to do better in future work. You may curse the assignment that keeps you up until after midnight to meet a deadline, but the pressure may have been necessary to get you to do the work at all. You may hate getting a fail grade on the first piece of work you submit, but will thank it later, when you have remedied whatever weakness caused it, and gone on to do far better subsequently. (Only last week I received a 'thank-you' email saying, 'You may not remember me, but you gave me 38 on my first assignment. I've just got a distinction on my final MBA course'.)

What is assessed

Traditionally examinations were the most important form of assessment. Where teaching is seen as transmitting knowledge, they are an efficient way of testing that students can remember key information, concepts, techniques and theories. Exams are also good at assessing the ability to construct a reasoned argument from evidence. Whether intentionally or not, written communication skills are also assessed.

Exams were supplemented by a thesis or dissertation, which allowed research skills and a higher level of analytical skills to be assessed, as well as presenting a greater test of writing skills, and challenges in terms of time-management and other management skills.

Both these forms of assessment are still widely used today (and have subsequent chapters devoted to them). But as programmes have moved away from the purely 'academic', and become more concerned to develop the range of skills outlined in Chapter 2, the scope of assessment has correspondingly increased. Thus you may be required (if studying while working) to apply what you have learned to situations you encounter at work. Indeed, the thesis may have been replaced by an internal consultancy project. In either case, 'own-organisation' based assessment presents very specific challenges, dealt with in the next section. You may be required to work on a project as a group, perhaps 'meeting' electronically to do this, and be assessed either on your contribution to the effort, or as a whole group with a single mark. Your competence as a manager may be assessed via a portfolio of work-based evidence. Some assessment may be computer-based, with automatic scoring of multiple choice questions.

Thus 'what is assessed' is changing in two ways. The range of skills which business schools seek to teach, and which therefore needs to be assessed, is widening. And the range of ways in which schools attempt to assess these skills is changing in consequence.

Work-based assessment

Now that part-time students are in the majority, work-based assignments are widely set. They allow assessors to test not only your familiarity with concepts and models in the course, but your ability to *apply* these concepts appropriately and constructively. This requires a higher level of skill than the writing of an academic essay. Many of these concepts are remarkably simple in themselves. But *using* these concepts to make sense of a complex and confusing situation, and to come to creative conclusions as to what to do about it, may be a real challenge. A key part of that challenge is being sufficiently selective.

Being selective

In case study based work, even when the case study is depressingly heavy, the person compiling the case will not have written down more than a fraction of what *could* have been written. Most of the points covered in the case will be important. In a work-based assignment, you are likely to feel you are drowning in a sea of potentially relevant, though perhaps not easily accessible, information. You will frequently experience many uncertainties as to what to consider and what to ignore. 'Hard' information from company records may turn out to be surprisingly unreliable. 'Softer' information from interviews or other sources may present even greater problems of interpretation.

Another problem with own-company work is that it is harder to think up creative options than for a case study. In the case study you will be blessedly unaware of most of the constraints that would apply in reality. In your own organisation you are likely to be all too aware of what has already been tried and failed, or is considered as quite out of the question by significant members of the organisation. Yet your assessors will still be looking for the ability to come up with such options.

As MBAs are concerned with developing strategic skills in managers, and since a prerequisite for successful strategy is sensitivity to the environment, your assessors will be requiring you to demonstrate the ability to look beyond your organisational boundaries. You will also need to adopt the perspective of someone possibly considerably higher in the organisation than yourself in using information about the environment to inform decision taking. It may be necessary for you to check out your perceptions with someone senior to yourself, or to have as your project client someone in such a position. You will therefore develop skills for operating on a different level.

Work-based assignments, especially projects or dissertations, may be longer term than much of the older style of assessment. This, together with the conflicts generated by part-time study, means that you will need a much higher level of time-management skill than may have been required by an earlier generation of students.

Thus, in shifting from an emphasis on examinations to assessment based on work-relevant skills, your assessors may be causing you to develop an even broader range of skills than they intended. In order to produce the assignments that will convince your assessors that you not only know what you have been taught, but know how and when to apply it and can use it to tackle managerial problems in a creative and sound way, you will be using many skills of vital importance to a manager. This will be the case even if these skills are not themselves directly assessed.

COMMON CAUSES OF FAILURE

Outright failure is uncommon on most MBA and related Master's programmes. More frequent is withdrawal prior to completion. But this still represents failure to complete, so will be considered here. Figure 14.1 shows the pattern of interrelated causes most commonly contributing to either form of failure.

ACTIVITY

Add to Fig. 14.1 any additional factors which you feel might threaten your own course completion.

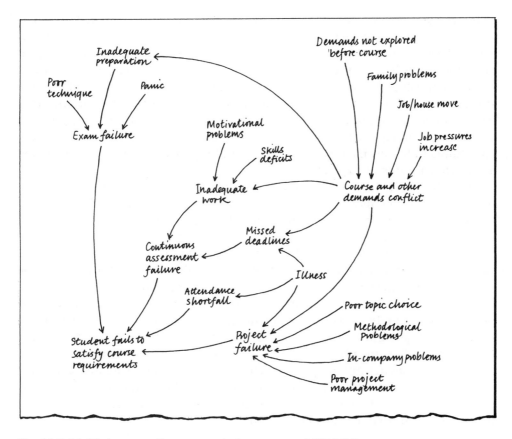

Fig. 14.1 Multiple-cause diagram exploring causes of MBA failure

The factors on the diagram, and presumably any you have added, can be divided into those you can do nothing about, those which with the aid of this book or other assistance you *might* be able to influence, and those where there *is* a remedy, albeit a long-term one.

Environmental changes

In the 'probably unavoidable' category are illness, sudden totally unanticipated change in job demands, redundancy and relationship breakdowns. In some of these cases your studies may themselves be a causal factor. While there is usually little you can do to prevent these disasters, you should take immediate action if they *do* strike. Even if your course is the least of your worries you should inform the college of your problems as soon as they happen.

If warned of problems *before* deadlines are missed, tutors are far more likely to be sympathetic, and may well be able to help you find a way of staying with the course despite your problems. If not, they will probably be able to keep the door open for you so that you can resume your studies when problems are resolved. Most tutors will go to almost any lengths to support and aid students. But if the student does not alert them to problems, there is little they can do, and they may well attribute missing work to lack of organisation. Reasons offered long after the event may be interpreted as excuses. You should therefore do all you can to keep your tutors fully informed from the outset, and to make full use of any help and advice which your college offers.

Avoidable, though you may not choose to avoid them, are such events as finding a better job, moving to a better house, getting married, or adding to your family. All of these events put enormous stress on you if you are a part-time student, stress which is often underestimated beforehand. If you seriously wish to complete your course, and especially if you want to do well on it, you should think very carefully before risking making life more difficult for yourself. Obviously you may still wish to go ahead, but do not underestimate the increase in pressure which will result. Unfortunately(?), the mere fact of studying may increase your chances of a better job, whether in your own organisation or outside. I *have* known students negotiate a delay in promotion until they have finished their course, while others have deliberately suspended their habit of looking at job advertisements, but you may lack this strength of purpose. Whatever you do, think carefully about the strategy that is right for *you*. If you do go ahead, and then run into problems, you should seek advice straight away, as described above. The longer you delay, the fewer the options that may be open to you.

Personal skill deficits

One of the commonest causes of failure, especially in the stress of an examination, is neglecting to answer the particular question asked, or all of the question, or the right number of questions. This can also apply with continuous assessment, though usually less catastrophically, although it is fairly easily avoided if the advice in this chapter is followed. Examinations are dealt with in Chapter 17.

Slightly more difficult to deal with, though manageable, are time-management and communications skills problems, the attainment of a correct balance between theory and 'reality', and dealing with numbers. Although a remedy cannot be guaranteed, there are suggestions on all these areas within this book, and if you are worried about your writing ability or other personal skills you should devote some time to developing these, preferably before the course starts.

If you are planning to enter a postgraduate programme on the strength of your managerial experience rather than your educational qualifications, and feel you may have major problems, you might see whether there are courses locally available that could help you plug the greatest gaps. Before committing yourself, however, check with your intended college as to skill levels they think are required. You may find that you are worrying unnecessarily, as they have much lower expectations than you fear.

In the unlikely event that your educational background does turn out to be more of a handicap than you anticipated, and you do fail, it is very important that you see this failure as a failure on assessment criteria, not as a manager. The point has already been made that institutions are as yet a long way from being able to assess competence with much reliability. I have known several excellent managers fail, even in areas of their own special expertise. Personnel managers have failed human resource management courses, senior marketing managers have failed marketing courses.

This in no sense meant that they were less than good at their job. Rather, they had problems in areas specific to MBA assessment, in particular with exam technique and with developing an argument from evidence and communicating this argument clearly in their writing. In the first area, there is clearly no relationship between this and on-the-job performance. The inability to argue from evidence might be a serious skill deficit in many jobs. However, their weaknesses were in no way interfering with their current job performance.

If you find the MBA very difficult from the outset, you might wish to think about transferring to a Certificate course. You could use that, and a subsequent Diploma course, as a vehicle for developing your skills related to assessment at a more leisurely pace. You could then move on to an MBA afterwards, confident that the skills already developed would make success much more likely. On some programmes a Diploma exempts you from part of the programme.

You may decide to persevere with the MBA hoping that your skills will develop as you go along: there is a reasonable chance that they will. If you are unfortunate enough to fail in the end, it is important to remember that the MBA is not everything. Disappointment will be inevitable, but it should not be accompanied by a sense of personal failure. Rather, you should dwell on what you have *gained* from your studies, which may be even greater than the benefit gained by some of those who passed. Many of Britain's top managers have, after all, reached their positions without benefit of an MBA qualification, and you will have the advantage over them of having *studied* management at a high level.

Fear of failure should not, therefore, discourage you from starting, nor cause you to drop out silently if the course turns out to be tougher than expected. Instead you should discuss your fears before you start, and any subsequent difficulties, with your tutors and, if appropriate, with your employer. You can then decide, in full knowledge of the options available, on the best course of action for *you*, the one which will have the greatest beneficial effect on your personal development as a manager.

Dissertations/projects/theses

As you can see from Fig. 14.1, dissertations are a particularly high-risk part of the programme, with many different factors capable of contributing to failure in this aspect. Even students who have coped well with the earlier part of the course may find difficulty with the greater freedom and longer time-scales involved, and the need for a high level of independence in directing their work.

Dissertations based on in-company research are singularly vulnerable to changes within that company. In the extreme case you can lose your job half way through your research, thereby losing access to further data. Equally devastating to the project, if not to yourself, you may find that the part of the organisation you are researching suddenly closes. Your in-company 'client' may leave, to be replaced by someone antagonistic to the project. Your project topic may suddenly become highly sensitive, or other changes may make for major problems.

The risk of many of these happening may be minimised by careful topic selection. This is dealt with in Chapter 19. If, despite care at this stage, things go wrong, then you should follow the earlier advice of seeking guidance from your tutor or supervisor at once.

Motivation

The remaining major cause of failure is the failure to sustain motivation. You may have the ability to do well, but the whole thing may turn out to require far more effort than you expected, and the prospect of giving up your free time for two or three years may become increasingly unattractive. The immediate excitement of starting the course has worn off, and there seem to be few rewards along what is a very long path.

Even full-time students can find they are suffering from low motivation at times, but it is generally less of a problem for them. They are eating, sleeping (if not a lot) and breathing their MBA, surrounded and supported by other students and faculty. Much of their learning takes place through group work. The course is shorter. The conflicts are simpler, usually between work and sleep, not between work, job and family.

Part-time students are faced with a longer course of study, much of it done in isolation. There will be pressures and conflicts every day, these being subject to unpredictable variation. If these pressures mean that you cannot study as much as you anticipated, and that you are getting lower grades than you hoped, these will be disincentives to further work, rather than rewards.

The three main sources of motivational 'recharging' are your teachers, fellow students and yourself. Institutions vary enormously in the amount of support and contact they offer students, and in the extent to which contact with fellow students is encouraged or even possible. As both types of contact can be great boosts to enthusiasm, ensure that you take full advantage of what *is* available. Make the effort to attend all face-to-face sessions on offer, even if the quality of the lecturer's input is variable: there are other benefits in terms of contact with your fellow students. In any case, merely voting with your feet will not bring about improvements. Remember, you (or your employers) will have paid a considerable sum for your course. If you do not feel you are getting value for that money, you should make your feelings known.

Motivational resources:
- *your teachers*
- *fellow students*
- *yourself.*

If you are dissatisfied with any aspect of your programme you should take steps to make that dissatisfaction known, so that the institution can do something to improve the situation. Many colleges are still poor at monitoring the quality of work of those they employ. It is possible for a lecturer to be appointed with no evidence sought as to lecturing skills, no effective training given and no real feedback on performance levels. Unless students complain, there will be no way for a problem to come to light.

If your institution provides you with a personal counsellor or academic adviser (terms vary), then this person can be very helpful to you if you experience motivational or indeed any sort of problems. You should feel no inhibitions about seeking help. This will not be held against you, nor affect your grades in any way other than positively; if you encounter real problems this adviser can argue for these being taken into consideration when your final marks are decided.

The value of self-help groups

If at all possible, try to develop informal contacts with other students. This possibility has already been raised in Chapter 11, but should be pursued particularly vigorously if you find you are suffering from 'motivation droop'. Informal study groups, often called 'self-help' groups, are one of the most powerful antidotes to this yet discovered. Your institution may be able to help in various ways, such as by releasing student names or giving guidance on how to run such groups. There was a very simple list of such guidelines given at the end of Chapter 11. Your college may also be able to offer a room for your group to meet in.

If you are following a distance learning programme there may well be facilities for computer conferencing. Many students find the more informal conferences the most valuable in terms of making them feel involved, as well as the most enjoyable. (These are often labelled 'pub' or 'cafe' to denote the sorts of conversation taking place there.)

Self-help groups have been popular with undergraduate Open University students for twenty years or more, but are particularly valuable for management students. Much of the excitement of the course will come in seeing how the ideas can make sense of organisational situations, and from seeing how many more options there can be in a situation than you realised. By learning more about other organisations you can broaden your awareness considerably. Other students can be a source of more information on these things than the official course material.

Discussing the application of course concepts with fellow students will make the ideas come alive in a way that relying on your own experience may not. It can also be reassuring to find that when you experience difficulty with a part of the course, you are not alone. A commiseration session when the going gets tough can be highly encouraging, as well as cathartic.

If you have chosen your fellow group members with a view to ensuring a breadth of expertise, there will usually be someone in the group who can help you through any specific difficulty. Most MBA groups contain students with an accounting background, some from marketing, some personnel specialists, and other experts. By becoming part of a mixed group, you are making it possible to obtain (and give in exchange) supplementary tuition. Thus when you do hit a problem and perhaps cannot contact a lecturer for help, you have access to a friendly coach.

If you live too far from other students, or for some other reason cannot join such a group, you may be able to gain some of the benefits by starting a discussion group with interested colleagues at work. They will gain second-hand benefit from your studies, while giving you valuable motivational support. If you are being supported by your employer, your training manager may be interested in setting up such a group, as a way of increasing the return on their investment in your course fees. If not, you might be able to make informal arrangements with other managers with whom you feel comfortable.

If you are on a distance learning programme, and your course uses computer conferencing or other computer-mediated interaction, distance will be no obstacle to interacting with fellow students. It may seem strange to do this via a computer keyboard, rather than face to face, but many students who take part in such conferences find them immensely useful. If tutors also take part, the potential benefits are enormous. You may find it fairly difficult to cope with computer conferencing if you are new to communicating via a PC, but persist. Most conferencing systems are now very easy to use. Increasingly it is becoming possible to incorporate voice contact and shared computer screens into such conferences. Video links are also becoming more available, further enriching remote communications.

The final source of help for drooping motivation lies within yourself. This may sound about as helpful as the suggestion to a depressive that he 'snap out of it', or advice to use your bootstraps for self-elevation. The algorithm shown in Fig. 14.2 summarises the procedure involved. The item 'analyse possibilities for improving the situation' is the key.

Obviously the remedies will depend on the problem identified, but common ones are:

Problem: You have been working far too hard, allowing no time for exercise or relaxation, and are physically and mentally jaded.

Remedy: Build in 'treats', and schedule time off, some of it for enjoyable exercise.

Problem: You have received lower grades than you had hoped, and feel somewhat bruised about the ego.

Remedy: Reassess your objectives. If passing is your main objective, middling grades will get you the qualification just as well as high ones.

Problem: Your studies seem to stretch forward into the distant and dismal future, and you really don't know whether you are making any progress.

Remedy: Assess progress to date. Look at early assignments and see how much better you could do now. Review your personal development diary if you have been keeping one. (If not, start such a log.) Set interim targets for the course.

Problem: You can't see what the course has to do with your job.

Remedy: Talk to your tutor and your training officer, mentor or superior in your organisation. Make active efforts to find links. Talk to other students to see whether they have the same feeling.

Problem: You are being sabotaged by resistance, overt or covert, from colleagues or family.

Remedy: Consider whether you are collaborating in the sabotage. If so, think

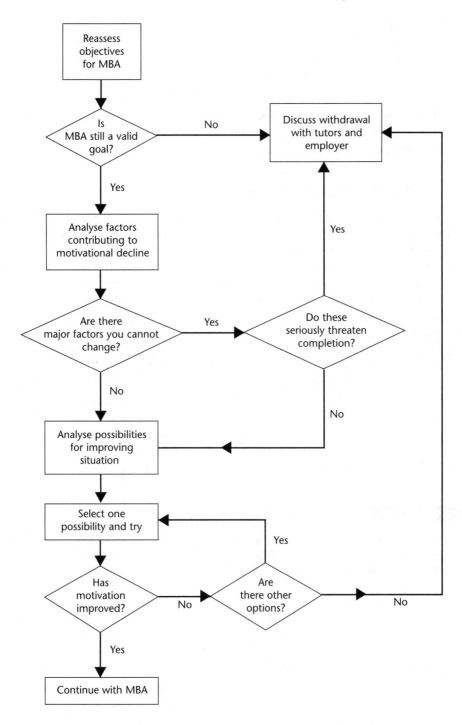

Fig. 14.2 Algorithm for tackling motivational problems on an MBA (or other course)

again about why *you* want an MBA, and be firmer about sticking to your goals. Discuss the problem in a positive way with the sources of the resistance. People may be unaware of it, or of the strength of their feelings. You may be equally unaware of the demands you are making on them, or of other changes in your attitudes.

Motivational problems are among the hardest to solve, but provided your original objectives are still valid, it should be possible to regenerate at least some of your original enthusiasm.

ASSESSMENT AS COMMUNICATION

In doing an assignment or an examination the effectiveness with which you communicate will affect your grade in two ways. First, because communication is an important aspect of management, you will be penalised if you show weakness in this area. Second, if you fail to communicate what you intended as a demon-stration of the extent of your knowledge and understanding of the substance of any assignment, you will gain no marks for that knowledge. It is therefore important that you understand the principles governing any form of communication. You also need to take steps to develop your skills in those types of communication most necessary for the MBA. This will be particularly important if you know (or discover) your communication skills to be weak.

No assessor will be unduly concerned with your literary skills. Examiners are not looking for an ability to use a wide vocabulary or complex grammatical forms, or to evoke depths of emotion in your reader. All that is required is that you can put across the message that you intend, in a manner suitable to your target audience, and in understandable, plain English, supplemented by whatever visual aids will strengthen your message. This point is developed in Chapter 15.

ACTIVITY

Think of the last time that you were unhappy with the effectiveness of a communication, whether one directed to you or originated by you. Jot down the aspects which contributed to your lack of satisfaction.

_____

_____

_____

_____

_____

_____

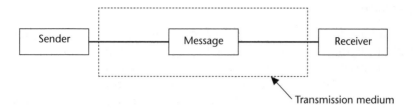

Transmission medium

Fig. 14.3 The elements of communication

The chances are that your dissatisfaction concerned either the substance of the communication, or the manner in which it was communicated. This distinction is worth bearing in mind. It is also worth remembering that there are two distinct parties to any communication, the sender or originator of the message, and the receiver or intended audience. Fig. 14.3 shows these aspects.

This is a simple, even simplistic diagram. But it illustrates the way in which such simple frameworks can act as a sort of shopping list, ensuring that you direct your attention to all of the relevant aspects of a situation. Thus the diagram makes the point that in planning an effective communication, you need to pay attention to these four elements. It does not tell you what to do about them, but can act as a starting point for generating relevant questions. Some examples follow.

Sender

What are your objectives? Unless *you* are clear as to these, they are unlikely to be achieved. Is your goal to impress, inform or influence, or a combination of these? What characteristics or attributes do you have that are relevant to the situation? For example, are you much better at face-to-face spoken communication or writing? Do you tend to overcomplicate matters, assume more knowledge in your audience than is reasonable, or antagonise others without intention? Are you particularly good at explaining the meaning of figures, or making implications of a situation clear, or bringing others to see your view? Once you know your own strengths and weaknesses you can use that information to make your communication more effective.

Receiver

What are the receiver's objectives? Are they congruent with yours, or in conflict with them? Is the receiver happier with some forms of communication than others? At work you may have subordinates who do not read easily, or a boss who insists you put everything in writing. There may be an organisational style of report writing your boss will expect you to follow. Different lecturers will have preferences for one style over another. Is there a constraint on the length of a communication? Many busy managers refuse to look at anything that cannot convince them in a one-page summary that it is worth their time. Assignments may have word limits. Some audiences may have very short attention spans.

The message

Is what you have to communicate simple information, or is it an interpretation of information? If the latter, how compelling is that interpretation? Do the facts 'speak for themselves'? If so, how many of the facts are necessary to achieve this effect? How important is quantitative information as part of the message? Can the form of this be altered to increase its significance? Are relationships a key part of the message? In this case diagrams will probably be necessary. In any course assessment you need to remember that the overall message must be that you have absorbed relevant concepts, techniques and information, and can use these appropriately to perform well as a manager, or at least to take sensible decisions in a real or simulated managerial situation.

The channel

For course assessments, the communication channel will normally be prescribed: a written document of a certain length; an oral presentation; or a written or viva voce examination. These may sometimes be supplemented by examples of work you have produced in your job (*see* Chapter 18), where the prescription may be more general. In communication at work, the range of options may be much greater. If you are unhappy with a superior's decision, do you raise the matter 'in passing', in the course of other discussions, send a brief e-mail saying you are unhappy about certain aspects and would like to discuss them, or write an extensive analysis of why the decision is faulty, sending it to everyone in the organisation right up to the chairman? Indeed, you might deem it wiser to keep quiet.

Whatever your choice, you will need to bear the characteristics of your chosen channel in mind. It is worth recalling that however they are transmitted, messages tend to lose something in the transmission. You probably played 'Chinese whispers' as a child. Any ambiguity in the message received (due in that case to the difficulty of hearing the whisper) will be acted upon by predispositions in the receiver, with additional distortion at each link in the chain. If new working arrangements are communicated in over-sophisticated language by a boss, they may be interpreted by the audience as another attempt to screw the workers, whatever the actual message intended. A message 'cascaded' through several layers of management may be subtly transformed at each stage.

Unfortunately this carries through into assessment, and the lecturer faced with an assignment or exam paper presented in poor handwriting and unclear English is likely to put down an ambiguous statement to failure to understand a key point. The same ambiguity in a clearly typed, well-laid out piece of work might be interpreted much more charitably, with the marker feeling sure that the student *really* knew it, but hasn't made it quite clear.

It is essential to be aware of the likely losses in transmission, and to adopt strategies for overcoming these. For example, underlining key words, including diagrams of key relationships, and making a clear *brief* statement of a complex point before you immerse yourself in the full complexity, can all help to reduce such losses for written messages. Signposting the structure of your argument at the outset and supplementing spoken messages with visual materials can also help. These may be transient, for example displayed slides, or permanent handouts or notices.

If you are aware of the elements that must be considered if you are to communicate successfully, and if you are absolutely clear about your objectives and those of your audience before you start, and if you *plan* your assignments with as much attention to these factors as to the specific points required in each assessment, you should find that your grades are much improved. Subsequent chapters address points specific to particular forms of communication, such as written reports and oral presentations.

SUMMARY

- Your assessors will wish to be convinced that you have absorbed, and can appropriately use, information, skills and techniques taught by the course.

- They will want to know that you can identify significant factors in a situation or its environment, and use what you have learned to solve managerial problems, making sensible recommendations after generating and evaluating a sufficiently broad range of options.

- They will want to be assured that you can communicate your arguments in a clear and convincing fashion, using appropriate communication forms.

- Above all they will not want to give you a qualification if they feel that your competence at the end of the course is so low as to cast doubt on the credibility of their teaching, or of the qualification in general.

- Student failure is uncommon, and more often due to failure to complete the course than failure on assessment.

- If problems do occur, whether caused by external factors, or those arising from your own characteristics, discuss these with your tutor at once, and possibly with your superior or training manager too.

- If you have difficulty sustaining motivation, analyse the reasons and seek all the support you can, from your tutors, your organisation, and, most importantly, from fellow students.

- In the highly unlikely event of your deciding to withdraw or failing on a component of assessment, it is important to see this as something specific to the course, and in no way as casting doubt on your managerial abilities or potential.

- Plan all your assessed work from the perspective of seeking to communicate successfully, bearing in mind your own objectives and characteristics, those of your audience and characteristics of the message intended, and the channel by which it is to be communicated.

15 Writing assignments and reports

Objectives

By the end of this chapter you should:

- understand the importance of clarifying requirements for an assessment
- know how to generate a range of initial ideas
- be able to structure these to produce an initial outline of your report, with appropriate subheadings
- be able to expand these into a first draft, using clear English, ways of showing numbers clearly, and diagrams where appropriate
- be able to develop this into a well-presented final draft.

INTRODUCTION

Much of your assessment is likely to be based upon what you write, so your skills in this area will have a strong influence on your success in your course. Furthermore, written communication (whether paper based or electronic) is still important for managers: skills in this area are likely to contribute significantly to your future career success as well. Things you have written may receive a wide circulation, and bring you to the favourable (or unfavourable) notice of many people at work. The ability to produce a good report is likely to impress both your superiors and your clients.

To do well in written assignments you need to be able correctly to interpret the questions you are asked, and then to construct an answer which is well structured, is clearly argued, covers the necessary ground and is in an appropriate style and format. Reports are still the most common form for substantial management communications, and some of your assignments will probably need to be produced in this format. Even where a report is not asked for, you are likely to find that a similar, clear structure will greatly improve your work.

This chapter covers the interpretation of questions. It deals with assignment planning, written communication in general and the use of a report format. A glossary of terms commonly used in assignments is given as Helpfile 1 at the end. Helpfile 2 covers the basics of spelling, and Helpfile 3, punctuation and grammar.

Work through these if you know that your grammar or spelling is prone to 'wobble', or if tutors or other readers complain that they are not sure what you mean.

Other chapters are also highly relevant to producing good written work. These include those on use of diagrams and on working with case studies. For group assignments the chapter on working in teams will be relevant. For substantial reports, in the context of dissertations or projects, you will also need Chapter 19.

ASSIGNMENT PLANNING

Planning requires that you make sure that you are clear about the administrative side of what is required. For example, what is the submission deadline, the word limit, the required format? But there is a more substantive side to requirements too. What actually is it that you are asked to write, the question that you are to address? Identifying both these aspects of your objectives, and then planning carefully the time, resources and so on needed to meet them, is important for success. Guidelines for such planning are outlined below, and then discussed in more detail in the text that follows.

> *Assignment planning guidelines*
>
> - identify 'administrative' requirements
> - 'deconstruct' the question to identify precisely what is required
> - identify 'strands' or themes
> - identify theory/concepts relevant to themes
> - work out a structure for answer
> - plan time and other resources
> - identify interim targets/review points
> - follow your plan!

Administrative requirements and constraints

It is usually simple to identify administrative requirements, but this does not mean they are unimportant. Failure to submit work on time, or to keep within word limits, or to handwrite when word processing is required, to write an essay when a report is asked for, or to submit the work to the wrong place, probably accounts for as many lost marks as do academic shortcomings. So make sure that you have identified such requirements, and that you plan to meet them. Such planning will be equally important for written assignments at work, so it is a good habit/skill to develop.

Content planning

The first stage here is again to look at what is required. It is not always immediately obvious what a question is asking. Or what may *seem* obvious may be but a small part of what is required. You need to 'deconstruct' the question carefully, making sure you have not only identified all its constituent parts, but also worked out precisely what is required in answer to each part. Take a question I have recently been marking. In essence, the question was:

> As part of a review of your organisation's management and use of information, and the effectiveness of technology use in this, write a report which describes your own use, as a manager, of information and evaluates your organisation's system in terms of meeting your needs.

This is a messy one. First there is an administrative point – a report is asked for. This means identifying a suitable recipient and bearing your specified audience in mind as you write. But there are other potential traps which are far more dangerous than forgetting to write a report. The first is the clear specification of perspective. Students were asked to write about their *own* use of information. Many wrote about the organisation in general, without mentioning how they fitted into it, or giving any idea of what information they used. Second, the main thrust of the question was about management and use of information, not about technology. Technology was clearly seen by the question-setter as part of a wider 'information system'. Yet many students wrote exclusively about technology. Not surprisingly, there was little evaluation (*see* Helpfile 1 at the end of this chapter if you would not have been sure what the word meant in this context), and such as there was tended not to be from the perspective of the writer. As a consequence, many students were surprised at the low marks they received for an assignment which they felt they had done fairly well.

So how might they have done better at identifying what was required? Deconstructing the question they would have realised that the first part – *As part of your organisation's management and use of information, and the effectiveness of technology use within this* – gave important contextual information, but was not the essence of the 'instruction'. (Nevertheless, there was a strong hint here that a wider information system was being considered, with the IT involved being seen as only a part of this wider system.)

What students were actually required to do was, using report format, *describe their use of information* and *evaluate their organisation's [information] system* from the perspective of their own use of, and therefore need for, information.

Several other parts are implicit. You cannot easily evaluate something without making clear just what it is that you are evaluating, and against what criteria you are evaluating it. So in order to evaluate your organisation's information system you need to say what it *is*. Some sort of definition or other representation is called for. Later in the instructions students were recommended to use diagrams where possible, and this is an instance where a systems diagram would be very useful. Then some sort of criteria are needed against which it can be evaluated. Clearly these needed to be derived from the manager's own information use and needs.

If students had gone through this sort of thought process, and tried to take the question apart in this way, they would not have so cheerfully submitted detailed descriptions of organisational IT systems, with virtually no comment as to their appropriateness. Of course it was important to include consideration of IT as part of 'the system', but a wider perspective and evaluation was clearly called for.

To take another, rather simpler example, again of an assignment with which I was involved:

> Evaluate your organisation's approach to recruitment and selection.

ACTIVITY

Before reading further, take a couple of minutes to think about the parts of which this question is made. You might like to sketch these out in the form of a mind map. Don't worry about the fact that you have not yet studied the course for which this was an assignment. Aim at the level of detail – or less – given in the example above.

Again this was a question where many students missed much of the point. They described – often at great length – the detail of their organisation's procedures, though sometimes only those for selection. But for good marks, far more was expected. The question was designed to test the students' ability to relate the theory which they had been taught on this topic to their own situation. To answer it well, students needed to demonstrate that they understood what recruitment and selection were intended to achieve, and the distinction between the two terms. They needed to relate this to the organisation's overall objectives and its staffing plan. They then needed to describe key features of their organisation's policy and practice in this area, evaluating these against relevant legislation and prescriptions of good practice taught in the course. It was important to show an awareness both of the difficulties of implementing that good practice in the real context, and of the problems likely to arise from ignoring it.

There are, thus, many invisible parts to a seemingly simple question. All too often, students seized on the opportunity to describe their organisation's practice at inordinate length, even down to the names of those who sent out letters to candidates or were on interview panels. But amid all this detail there was no reference at all to the effectiveness of this practice in organisational terms, nor to any considerations of equal opportunities legislation, nor indeed to anything else that their course had covered.

Their markers were not particularly interested in the intricacies of the particular organisation. The students' awareness of these was not what was being assessed. Fascinating as these glimpses of organisational life were, there were no marks to be gained from mere description. Where the marks *would* have been available, should the students have chosen to seek them, was in a demonstration of their *understanding* of the relevant course concepts. To show this understanding, they needed to use the concepts to describe and evaluate organisational practice. If the students in question had taken more trouble to clarify what was really required, and had understood their audience's objectives more clearly, they would not have fallen into this trap. Their marks might then have been a pleasant surprise, rather than the reverse. Use the glossary in Helpfile 1 at the end of this chapter to help you work out what an assignment requires. If at any point you are unsure, or seem to be interpreting an assignment differently from other students, check your understanding with the tutor who set it. Misunderstanding the task is in no one's interest, so such checks should be welcome.

Of course, the need to clarify requirements is not limited to course assignments. Any business document must be written with a clear understanding of your audience's objectives, as well as your own. These are often far removed from what they may appear at first sight. It is as well to explore the context of a request for a report, if you possibly can. Although the request may come from your boss, he or she may be planning to circulate your report, under your name or theirs, to a much wider audience. Unless you know of this, and of the debates to which your report is intended to contribute, you are unlikely to direct your efforts as effectively as you might. Time spent finding out what is really required is unlikely to be wasted; it may itself prevent considerable waste of subsequent time and effort.

Having come to a clear understanding of your remit, which may have elements not explicit in the original, write down the expanded version. You will need to check progress against objectives at intervals during your work. You do not wish to forget elements that you have so carefully worked to establish.

Identify themes and relevant concepts

When you 'deconstruct' a question some themes will already be starting to emerge. You probably found this in the previous activity. Your next stage is to develop these further, and identify any which have not emerged. Once you have themes you will have 'hooks' on which to hang concepts. But also, concepts can suggest themes, so at this stage it is worth being fairly open to ideas about both. Individual brainstorming is a good way of coming up with a wide range of possible candidates for inclusion.

If you have been given a group assignment, you should have been working as a group on agreeing objectives, and will obviously be able to do the brainstorming together as well. Even for an individual assignment it can help to do the brainstorming with others, perhaps your self-help group. A group brainstorming will generate many more ideas than an individual one. By bouncing your ideas off other people, and exploring the differences between your views in a constructive way, you will also become more aware of some of your own assumptions and prejudices. Thus a group can help you to take a broader view of the situation than if you are limited to your own perspective. For work-based assignments, collaboration with colleagues has obvious potential benefit. Not only will they hold essential information to which you will need access, but their (different) perspectives are an important part of the situation.

Whatever your approach, make sure that you look at the whole situation, including its context, rather than focusing narrowly on 'the problem'. It is usually easier to narrow down from a broad base than to expand on a narrow one. Breadth of approach, though not superficiality, is one of the things MBAs are trying to develop.

It is important to look as broadly as possible at relevant course concepts. These are just as important as candidates for inclusion as are aspects of the situation under consideration. Many of the frameworks which you will be taught in your course, such as the 'four Ps' in marketing, or the STEP framework for competitor analysis and business planning, or the Expectancy Theory model which you may meet in studying motivation, will themselves provide the basis of a 'shopping list' of potential factors, and of significant relations between them, for inclusion in your analysis.

Ideally, your jottings should be in a form which you can manipulate when moving on to the next stage of trying to impose structure. This is easy with a word processor, but restickable notes or cards which you can move around a table are good low-tech alternatives. Whatever you choose, your aim at this stage should be to assemble your jottings in such a way that you can absorb them all easily, and build up a picture of what is potentially relevant. You can then try various arrangements of this picture to see which way it makes most sense.

This is very similar, if not identical, to the approach suggested for the early stages of case study analysis and similar diagramming techniques, as described in Chapter 10, are relevant. Mind maps can be invaluable, particularly when the basic structure of what is required is fairly obvious. They will enable you to develop this structure by drawing sub-themes out of main ones. Thus your structure generates further ideas, rather than being imposed, perhaps uncomfortably, upon those ideas once they have been produced.

There is a slight danger that you will not be sufficiently experimental with mind maps if structure is *not* self-evident. They can still be extremely useful if you are prepared to experiment with a variety of sets of branches, drawing many possible mind maps before deciding on the best. But if you become prematurely wedded to the first set of major branches that come to mind, the whole of your subsequent work may be locked into an inappropriate structure. Unless you feel no qualms whatsoever about throwing a large proportion of your diagrams into the bin you might be safer to reserve mind maps for the next stage.

Rich pictures are much safer. Because they look childish you are less likely to take them seriously. But you may have difficulty in representing many course concepts in this format, and need to resort to rather more words than would be ideal. Provided you retain the advantage of being able to absorb your whole picture more or less at a glance, this should not be too much of a disadvantage. Figure 15.1 shows three extracts from early notes for an assignment in which first year MBA students were asked to assess the effectiveness of their organisation's human resource policy. (I apologise for the over-emphasis on this type of assignment, but it is likely to be easily understandable even if you have not yet started your course.) These diagrams are not intended as models for a good answer, but merely to demonstrate the sort of thing with which you might like to experiment.

Define or refine structure

How far a structure is already apparent will depend on the nature of the question (some make the necessary structure fairly clear) and on the diagramming or other jotting methods you have used thus far. If you used mind maps, structure should be fairly clear already. If you used notes or rich pictures, then you will now need to start looking for groupings of factors. You may choose to group according to problem themes, by chronology, according to factors such as geography or

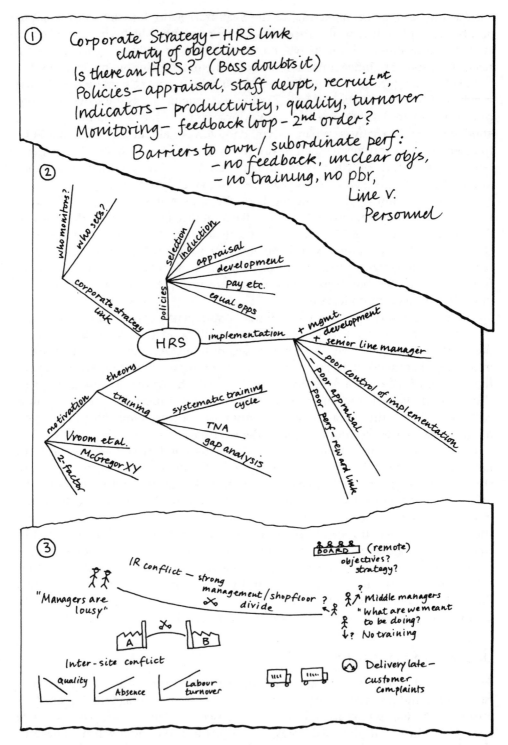

Fig. 15.1 Three specimens of early student assignment notes: 1. Brain dump approach; 2. Mind mapping; 3. Rich picture.

department involved, or organisational level. Your structure may relate to explicitly stated separate question parts, or could be according to conceptual frameworks suggested in your course.

As well as these groupings, if the assignment is based around a problem situation you will normally find the 'Universal Management Paradigm' suggests a useful framework. You should by now have a feel for the stages, but to remind you:

- describe the situation, including relevant elements of context, and indicating why it presents problems
- analyse the problem, using course concepts to help understand the root causes of problems
- decide on measures of effectiveness: what are the criteria for a good solution; what constraints exist
- identify and describe the range of possible solutions
- compare likely costs and benefits in terms of your measures of effectiveness
- recommend, with arguments to support your recommendations, your preferred solutions.

If your report is more action oriented, you may prefer a slight variant on this:

- propose action
- say why the existing situation cannot continue
- describe anticipated costs and benefits of proposed action, to convince the audience of its merit
- outline a plan for implementing the action
- conclude with the inevitability of pursuing the proposed action.

It is clear that both structures are frameworks for arguments. It may help to think of yourself as a lawyer, making a case for the 'guilt' of aspects of the present situation, and then defending your recommendations, or as a doctor making a diagnosis, convincing the patient that the diagnosis is correct, and recommending treatment. Within either framework you can work through the evidence presented by the situation, using relevant concepts as an aid to interpreting these.

Of course, at this preparatory stage your arguments will be tentative and skeletal, as you will not have gathered the evidence to support them. Indeed, if a lot of research is needed, as in major projects, you may be looking for no more at this stage than themes to pursue. But it is not putting the cart before the horse to think about structure before you have all the evidence you need.

There is a serious danger, especially with work-based assignments, of falling into the 'trees hiding the wood' trap. A rough idea of structure before you leap into the details will guard against this. At the same time, it will enable you to be more selective in your information gathering. This is *not* an invitation to limit yourself to information supporting your argument. This would produce a biased case, and unreliable recommendations. But you should direct your effort towards gathering information relevant to your identified themes, rather than collecting a mountain of data in the hope that it might come in useful. There is a powerful reluctance in most of us to discard something on which we have expended effort. You will often *need* to do this in order to sharpen your focus, but there is sense in minimising the necessity.

Check against requirements

Once you have devised an adequate outline structure, your planning stage is well under way. At this point you should check back against the objectives as clarified earlier. Does your proposed structure seem appropriate given the requirements for the assignment? Be as critical as you can in this evaluation. If there are weaknesses in your structure, it may be disappointing to have to rethink it. But it is far better to identify problems at this stage and revise your structure than to have to rewrite a substantial report half way through. Very occasionally this will be necessary, because new information or blinding insight will so alter your perceptions that you can see an infinitely better way of proceeding. But it should not be necessary simply because you were insufficiently critical of your own work at an early stage.

Plan the timing of your work

There is a more detailed treatment of project planning in Chapter 19. For dissertations it constitutes a major consideration. Refer to this if you think planning is a weak point, or if you are uncertain as to your ability to meet deadlines. Otherwise, merely bear in mind that you must plan for 'dead time', such as waiting for replies to letters or getting hold of references to books or articles you do not have in your possession. And do not underestimate the time taken to write at least two drafts of your report, preferably more. (Redrafting still takes significant time, despite the blessed invention of the word processor.)

Once you have submitted a number of assignments you will be better able to make accurate estimates of time requirements. Until you have this experience, allow a large contingency factor. To make sure that you keep to your plan, set yourself clear interim targets for all save the shortest pieces of work, and treat these as real deadlines. (Chapter 6 is relevant here.)

Time planning, and keeping to your plans, is crucial. As an undergraduate you may have survived by working all night when work was due in. As a practising manager you cannot afford this luxury. Furthermore, MBA assignments are often so substantial that a single night would not suffice. You will find that your job will develop a nasty habit of peaking in its demands just when you were planning a major assignment effort. This will not be a catastrophe if you have allowed slack time for just such contingencies and reserved it for genuine emergencies.

If your response is that you are one of those who work best under pressure, remind yourself that as a part-time student you will *always* be under pressure. Your aim is to prevent this pressure from becoming impossible, by careful planning and good time management.

DEVELOPING YOUR MATERIAL

Once you have a skeleton structure, and know how much time you have available, you should have a clear idea as to how to start developing the substance of your assignment. Remember, however, that your structure was intended to provide a firm base for *starting*, not as a concrete cast. It may well need to be amended considerably in the light of the evidence you collect and the way your thoughts about the situation develop as you work on your assignment.

You should not feel discouraged if you do find that you are changing your approach. It does not mean that your initial planning was wasted, but rather that this planning has started a process of conceptual development that is now leading you away from the obvious and into producing a much better assignment. The structure, together with your course concepts and the information you have collected, is leading you to a more creative or penetrating perspective on the situation in question. So treat your initial structure as a working tool which you can deliberately modify (though not inadvertently ignore) when this will lead to better work.

The following guidelines, though by no means exhaustive, may be helpful in your work.

Avoid assertions and opinions

In preparing the substance of your report you need to be sure that all your arguments will be substantiated. Assertions (e.g. 'So-and-so is true', or 'everybody knows…') or opinions (e.g. 'I think…'), no matter how confidently stated, are likely to be poorly regarded by superiors and tutors alike. Your opinions carry no worth by themselves. They need to be supported by reasoning, based on evidence or accepted theories, or preferably both.

Seek your evidence as widely as possible

Obviously the relevant evidence will be determined by the question. For work-based assignments evidence may come from information gathering within your own organisation. As suggested earlier, discussions with colleagues can generate relevant information. An important aspect of many problem situations is that they may be viewed in very different ways by different key people in that situation. Such differences of perspective may be a significant element in a problem.

Subordinates may prove happy to co-operate in your work. Indeed you may be able to make it into a developmental experience for them. This will also serve to reduce any resentment that may be developing towards your course. Superiors or mentors, if they are supporting you in your studies, can also derive benefit from helping you with your assignments. Such help might be in the form of discussions, suggestions as to further sources of information, or comments on ideas and drafts. Being involved will enable them to use your assignments as a form of in-house consultancy, as well as making sure that your learning experience is as rich as possible, increasing the return on their investment in your course. (If you wish to convince them further that such help is a good idea, you might point out that 'customised' company MBAs tend to be much more expensive, if well done, than an off-the-shelf model. By supporting you in your work-based assignments they are, in a sense, doing their own customising, in a way that is both cheap and highly effective.)

Examples of evidence that might be appropriate in an assignment include: results of interviews with key company personnel; company data; records from your own part of the organisation; survey data collected in-company by other consultants; external information such as published market intelligence, government statistics or trade surveys. Relevant literature on the topic culled from management journals, books or even newspapers will also be needed in most cases, together with any course material or lecture notes relevant to the assignment.

Remember that evidence is usually less than perfectly reliable, and you should assess the extent of the unreliability of all the evidence on which you draw. There is more on this in Chapter 19. Look at this if you are planning an assignment based on evidence you have gathered from your company or the environment, rather than using a case study or treating a purely academic topic.

Use theory as much as possible

If writing an in-company report you will need to be careful to use this theory *inconspicuously*. You will thus gain its benefits in making a complicated situation clearer, but will avoid antagonising your readers by making them feel they need to know something which they do not in order to understand your argument, or that you are trying to impress them by using unnecessary jargon. For assignments intended primarily for course assessment you need be less restrained. Remember that the point of your programme is to equip you with a set of conceptual tools and techniques. You are being taught to apply these in a variety of organisational situations in order to cut through complexity and reach valid conclusions as to the best of the strategic alternatives available and how to implement it. The theory which might irritate your superiors in a report for use in your organisation is likely to be just what your tutors are looking for, in order to check that you have absorbed and can use it. Thus theory will almost certainly need to be *explicit* in any report you write for them.

By the end of your course, theory should have become second nature, and *implicit* in everything you do. While you are still studying, you need to take the opportunity to experiment with different ways of using the conceptual tools, and of obtaining feedback from your tutors on this, via your use of these tools in assessment. Many of the marks for assignments may well be allocated to correct use of appropriate theory, so what is good for your learning will also be good for your grades. Part of your preparation will, therefore, be to explore potentially relevant theories and concepts, and experiment with them to determine their usefulness in your particular context.

Use diagrams where possible

If you are analysing a problem situation to see how it arose, *multiple-cause* diagrams are invaluable (*see* Chapter 10). By working back from the event or situation in which you are interested, through contributory factors and factors contributing to those and so on, you should be able to work towards a clear understanding of the web of relationships involved, and see a much wider range of possible interventions than are immediately obvious. Appreciation of these important interrelationships will probably also lead you to avoid recommendations that risk producing unintended consequences worse than the original problem. (These are not as uncommon in real life as you might think!) *Relationship* diagrams will help you to achieve the same benefits for more static situations. Don't forget the basic organisation tree. This was not included as it was assumed that of all diagrams you would know this one, but it can represent one form of relationship very clearly. And, of course, *mind maps* and *fishbone* diagrams have fairly obvious uses, both as frameworks for generating evidence, and for organising evidence into coherent arguments once generated.

Organise the materials you generate as you go along

If your materials are not organised, you will spend a lot of time later trying to sort them out, or to find documents that you know are 'somewhere'. Your outline structure will provide a framework for this, but it is useful, additionally, to keep a log of what you have collected and how you have filed it, and of what is still outstanding, so that you can assess progress at a glance. Such a log serves the important function of giving you a feeling that you are making progress, thus keeping your motivation high, even if the assignment is a long one.

It is particularly important to keep a full reference with each piece of work derived from printed materials (discussed later in the chapter). It is all too tempting to omit this. It seems impossible, at the time, that you could forget where you got something, and the temptation to 'do all the references properly at the writing-up stage' is all too potent. I used to succumb to it myself on occasion, although I should have known better, having wasted countless hours in looking for articles or quotations that were not in the publication I thought. Indeed, some sources seemed to have mysteriously ceased to exist since I last read them!

Fortunately a PC (or even an electronic organiser) makes the storage and retrieval of information so easy that even I have become disciplined in this respect. As you are unlikely to be able to afford to waste *any* time in this way, organise your information from the start. Keep references with the relevant material, and full details in a separate file. Similarly, record all possible details about interviews, letters sent, group discussions held, sources of company data, etc. You need to *know* the mailing list for different letters, or the participants in a particular discussion, not to have to reconstruct these from memory.

Start drafting as soon as possible

This need is discussed more fully in Chapter 19, but briefly, the sooner you start to draft, the clearer you will become about your remaining information needs. Just as moving on to the evidence-gathering stage may have thrown up deficiencies in your structure, so can drafting make you more aware of gaps in evidence. It is, therefore, a mistake to wait until all your evidence is complete before starting your first draft. You should be starting a skeleton draft at the planning stage, developing it as your thoughts become clearer and you gather more evidence. Decisions on major subheadings should be possible by the time you have half your evidence, even for a major assignment requiring substantial research.

DRAFTING WRITTEN ASSIGNMENTS

Getting started should present few problems if you have followed the guidance offered so far. By setting interim deadlines, and starting rough drafting while still collecting evidence, you should be starting your first full-length draft with plenty of time in hand, a clear idea of what you are going to write, and adequate material to hand. The dreaded 'writer's block' should, therefore, be no threat. Indeed, if you have been developing your time-management skills at work and in your studies, even the more common, though potentially equally damaging, vice of pro-crastination should be much diminished.

Drafting guidelines

- Prepare outline structure at outset
- Refine structure when possible
- Set manageable interim targets
- Start a rough draft very early indeed
- If stuck do other study for a (short) while
- If still stuck, consider discarding recent work and changing direction
- If still stuck seek tutor's help
- Check progress against targets.

You may occasionally, for some reason, find it difficult to start, or difficult to restart after a break in your work, and find the coffee cups piling up. Thoughts about the absolute necessity of fixing the roof, cleaning the oven, digging the potatoes, or any other preferred displacement activity, may start to surface, deterring you from starting work on your draft. If so, you have two weapons at your disposal.

First, you must remind yourself that this is only an early draft. It is not the finished product, it does not have to be perfect, and you do not have to start at the beginning and work through to the end. Many people find writing much more stressful than they should because they try to get it right first time, rather than seeing drafting as a process of successive refinements.

Sometimes you will only find out what you want to write by starting. What emerges may be quite a surprise. But once something has emerged, however scrappily, there is something to work with. Re-drafting can allow this to be worked up into a piece that is infinitely better than the original. However, unless you *allow* yourself to produce something that you know to be imperfect as a starting point, the process will not be able to take place. If you know yourself to be a perfectionist, remind yourself constantly that imperfection is a necessary part of the process. A sculptor may saw wood into roughly the right shape before starting detailed carving. Those first rough cuts were nothing in themselves, but produced something which could be developed into a masterpiece.

A second help, if you are in difficulty, is to start with the part of the report with which you feel most comfortable. Introductions are never the best place to start in any case, as it is impossible to introduce a report until you know what that report contains. So start with your evidence, or even your conclusions, if that suits you better. This is only a first draft, and you can modify your initial sections to take account of the content of earlier parts of the report once you get to your second draft.

Sometimes, the resistance to writing stems from the size of the task with which you are faced. If so, draw on time-management techniques, and set very easy targets at first. If you really cannot get started, set the task of drafting any two pages, and schedule this for a specific time. Once you have those two pages, force yourself to stop and indulge in some detailed planning of what parts you will write when. If you set yourself eminently achievable tasks at first, you can get into the habit of writing. Each time you complete a writing task you should find that the resistance to starting work is less next time, until you find you are enjoying the chance to get back to work. This momentum will be sustained only if you treat your report as an 'elephant', and write a little of it every day.

If you are an extreme case, and a mere two pages is enough to induce caffeine poisoning, then you will need an even easier task. Your resistance even to picking up a pen or switching on a PC must be overcome. Start with writing something pleasurable, such as a letter to an old friend, or rude thoughts about your course, before moving on to drafting the assignment. (It is highly unlikely that you will need such tough measures if you have worked through the Handbook thus far.)

If you suddenly become stuck in mid-draft, rather than chewing pencils (what is the PC alternative?) stop what you are working on and start work on a different part of the report. You could even do some other coursework as an alternative. But make a point of coming back the next day, or soon after that, to the place at which you blocked, and try to discover the cause of your difficulty. You will often find that the problem has arisen because you took a wrong turning earlier in your report, but are unwilling to face up to this because it will mean scrapping some of the work you have done. Go back to the last point at which you are totally happy with your draft, and think about how you need to modify it thereafter. You probably know already, if you are honest with yourself!

USING REPORT FORMAT

Uncertainty about correct report format is one source of inhibitions in early assignments. You may feel that there is some mystique to report format, some secret formula that you are not privy to. There are two reasons for the emergence of report formats. The first is the logical necessity to structure your arguments, the second is that the structure is intended to help your readers find their way around what may be a substantial document. Knowing the general order to expect can help. Some organisations seek to maximise this effect by having a standard format for all company reports. If this is the case in your own organisation, make sure that you have a copy of the rules, or one or two reports to act as models, before you start. Your lecturers may also have clear ideas about the structure required, and obviously if your report is for assessment purposes you should meet their requirements.

The following discussion covers what might be seen as the broad range of normal practice, in case neither organisation nor business school offers guidelines or prescription. Even when they do, the guidance may still be useful. Normally a report includes a summary, a title page giving report title, date, addressee and sender, a list of contents, an introduction, a main body which may be divided into numbered sections and subsections, conclusions, recommendations, references and appendices. The function of each will be discussed in turn.

Summary

For any lengthy document a summary or abstract is required. Practice varies as to whether this should be at the end of the report, at the front, even before any contents page, or an introductory part of the report. Many organisations insist on a one-page summary at the very front, arguing that it is possible for a busy manager to decide on the basis of this whether to invest any further time in the report. It is also easily found if at the front, and serves as useful orientation to the reader. It will be much easier to make sense of a complicated argument if you know the overall shape of the report in advance. Putting the summary at the end reflects its purpose of reinforcing key points of the document just read, and probably stems from the fact that it is likely to be the last thing you write. The summary should normally be a summary of the whole report, rather than just of recommendations. You should, therefore, include a brief statement of the original problem, and of the main arguments or evidence that have led you to your conclusions.

Title page

Any report is written, and must be read, in a specific context. It is vital, therefore, that at the start of the report you say who has originated the report, to whom it is addressed, and the date. The report also needs a title, and this should normally be as descriptive as possible. This information is frequently presented on a title page, giving a professional look from the start. An example is given in Fig. 15.2.

In deciding upon a title, think about how it will be used. Is the title going to appear in any listings of reports? If so it will need to indicate the sort of report and coverage in a way that will enable a potential reader, browsing through the list, to know whether your report is worth obtaining. Are there other reports on similar topics in your organisation? If so, you will need a title that distinguishes your report from theirs.

Date is a vital part of the context of a report. Information has a short shelf-life. It may be important for people to know whether your report was written before or after some major event having impact on your topic, or before or after another report. It is, therefore, essential that all reports be clearly dated, usually on the front page, as this may be the first thing a reader will wish to know.

In indicating addressee and sender, it is usually worth indicating a person's title, if this is relevant to their part in the report. Thus, you might be a senior marketing manager but have generated the report in your capacity as chair of a working party on restructuring the organisation's marketing capacity. In that case, it would be the latter title that would be important, and it should be included, with your job title if that is important too.

Contents list

The contents list should show your major and minor section headings, preferably numbered. Figure 15.2 shows a contents page for a student assignment in report format.

You will see that the contents list provides a clear indication to the intending reader of the structure of the report to follow, as well as acting as an index for anyone wishing to refer directly to a specific part of the report, rather than read the work in its entirety. It is helpful to give page numbers as an aid to this index function, although with a short report it is not essential. Some organisations number paragraphs, rather than pages. This allows easy reference to any paragragh but has the disadvantage of confusing any system for numbering major and minor

<table>
<tr><td colspan="2"></td></tr>
</table>

PERFORMANCE
PROBLEMS AT XYZ
COMPANY

To: E. Jones, Production Manager
From: A. Stuart, Plant B Manager
Date: 11.1.20XX

CONTENTS

		page
1	Introduction	1
2	Performance – the problem	2
	2.1 Contextual factors	2
	2.2 Performance-objectives gap	5
	2.3 Cultural factors	8
	2.4 Leadership	9
	2.5 Control	11
	2.6 Communication	12
3	Criteria for a solution	14
	3.1 Objectives	14
	3.2 Constraints	15
4	Possible options	16
5	Evaluation of options	18
6	Recommendations	21

Appendices:
A Organisation chart
B Control loops operating in different plants
C Main communication links

Fig. 15.2 Example of student title and contents pages

sections. Since the latter is such a powerful aid to indicating the structure of your report, you may prefer to use section numbering if given a free choice.

Introduction

This is a crucial part of your report. Although your summary, if at the front, and your contents page will have started the process of reader orientation, the introduction is where such orientation is mainly achieved. If you are not prefacing your report with a summary your introduction will be particularly crucial. Your reader will usually come to the report with a number of questions:

- Why is this topic important?
- What was the remit of the report writer?
- What is the main argument in this report?
- On what evidence is this argument based?
- How is the argument structured?
- What are the implications of the argument?

If your introduction can answer these questions, at least in outline, your reader will be in a much better position to read the subsequent report with interest, and to follow your developing argument with greater ease. Of course, if you have included an initial summary, some of these questions will have been answered already, and you can concentrate in your introduction on the significance of the topic and the aims of the work reported.

It is a great pity, given the above, that too many students use their 'intro- duction', whether in assignments or examinations, to do no more than restate the set question. It *is* important that the remit be established, but you will usually have 'unpicked' a question to discover the various parts implicit in it or otherwise developed your understanding of the question. At the very least, this expanded version should be included in your introduction. Preferably your introduction should go beyond this, as suggested above.

Unfortunately, the only extension of the introduction offered by many students is the inclusion of background information. Again, there is a degree of justification in this. In establishing the significance of the topic, you need to describe the context to some extent. But the introduction should not be seen as 'introduction and background', as it clearly often is. Any detailed background which you feel might be of interest to those reading the report should form a separate section, preferably in an appendix. The only background information which should appear in your text is that essential to understanding your argument.

Main section

As already suggested, you will normally need several major subsections within your main section. These can often be mapped moderately closely onto the stages of the UMP. Thus you might include a more detailed exploration of the background to the problem (this is *not* the same as background information on the organisation), the relationship between problem and other factors, constraints and so on as suggested earlier in the chapter. Sub-topics within each main topic (the twigs on the branches, if you used a mind map) will usually have subheadings, their numbers relating to that of the major heading, as was the case in Fig. 15.2.

Think carefully about what should be included in main text, what relegated to appendices. Normally your aim is to make your main text as clear and interesting as you can for your readers, to increase the chance that they will understand and accept your arguments. It is these considerations that should influence your decision on what to include.

Diagrams frequently serve the function of supporting or clarifying your text, and should therefore be included at the appropriate point. Not only will they reinforce your argument, but they will make the text look less dense and forbidding, and thus help in sustaining your readers' interest. It is also extremely inconvenient for the reader to have to be continually turning between text and appendices in order to follow an argument.

Diagrams which should be placed at the end include any extremely detailed diagrams which only the most dedicated or critical reader would wish to refer to, and any working diagrams produced in the process of developing those which *are* in the text. Your tutor, though not your organisation, may be interested in the thought processes which the latter reveal. When you *do* feel the need to append diagrams, you should always refer to them, and to where they may be found, at the appropriate point in your text. There is nothing more irritating to the reader than to spend a long time thinking about a point, or wanting more evidence on it, only to find, 30 pages later, that the material is in fact there.

Much the same arguments apply to tables or diagrammatic representations of evidence such as graphs or bar charts. Where they are an important part of your argument, they should be in the text. In the appendix you should put the more extensive information summarised in your in-text tables or charts, and any detailed mathematical argument. Those sceptical about your arguments can refer out to the full information on which they are based, while those who are happy to accept your condensed representation of the data will be able to follow the main thread of your argument without interruption.

To summarise, your main section should be self-standing, capable of being understood without reference to appendices. However those not prepared to take your summaries of evidence at face value will find supporting detail in the appendices.

Within the main body of your text, if the report is a long one, you can orient the reader at intervals by including a short introduction to each main section. Just as the structure of the report as a whole should follow the 'Say what you are going to say, say it, then say what you've said' principle, so too can this format be usefully followed within each major section.

Throughout the main body of your report you should be aiming to develop arguments, based on evidence, which build up to your eventual conclusions. It is worth checking at intervals that this is what is happening. If you *cannot* summarise each section in these terms, you should think again about what you have written. It may be that some of the evidence which you have included does not contribute to your argument, or that part of your argument is not substantiated by evidence.

Note: while 'Introduction' and 'Recommendations' are reasonable section headings, 'Main Section' is *not*. In this part of the report your headings will be chosen to describe the particular themes you have decided to cover in your report (*see* Fig. 15.2 for an example).

Conclusions

Your conclusions section should follow naturally from your main body. There should be no new material introduced at this stage, but rather a drawing together of the arguments developed in your main body, so that their implications can be spelled out. Students often have difficulty in distinguishing between conclusions and recommendations, and indeed the distinction can be a fine one. It may help to think of the conclusions as being more to do with logic, while the recommendations deal with the implementation of these conclusions. Thus in an essay you might have 'conclusions' but not recommendations. In a report with a tight word limit and a requirement to 'recommend ...' you might omit conclusions, and include brief logical justification for your recommendations within the recommendations section.

Recommendations

As with the summary, there is debate as to the best location for recommendations. The more action oriented prefer them at the front, as in the second framework suggested earlier. This is the response of the manager who says 'Tell me what you want me to do, and then convince me'. There is a lot of sense to this. Your evaluation of an argument is much helped by the knowledge of the end to which that argument is leading. On the other hand, recommendations cannot be made until the logical process of analysis and conclusion has been gone through, so there are equally powerful arguments for recommendations appearing at the end. Perhaps the best compromise is to have an introductory summary which includes a brief statement of recommendations, and then to have the fuller statement of recommendations, together with any additional arguments needed to justify them, at the end. Check with those requiring the report as to their preferred position.

Wherever you choose to position them, your recommendations should be clearly prioritised, and the priorities justified. Those evaluating your report will be checking that these priorities are appropriate, and that the recommendations are consistent with prevailing conditions in the organisation and its environment. For example, recommendations which call for a massive investment at a time when the organisation has cash flow problems and is already having difficulty in raising money will not be highly regarded. Similarly, if recommendations give a high priority to an interesting but not essential development, and a lower priority to something needed to ensure the continued survival of the organisation, there is likely to be little respect for the writer of the report.

Recommendations should:
- *flow obviously from analysis*
- *be clear proposals for action*
- *be sensible and realistic.*

Appendices

It has already been indicated that appendices are where you include supporting evidence for those wishing for more detail, or those wanting more information before they are prepared to be convinced by your argument. Thus you might include a copy of a questionnaire, or an interview schedule, or the monthly production figures for all departments and sites which you have summarised in tabular form in your text, or detailed organisation charts for the organisation you are studying, in an appendix rather than the text.

Appendices are sometimes used by students as a way of getting around the word limit, as it is generally assumed that appendices do not count against this. While this *may* be true – and you would need to check with your tutor – it is not a good stratagem. If material is essential to your argument it should not be in an appendix. If including it in your text makes you go over the limit, you should consider whether your style is too verbose, or whether the scope of your report needs to be narrowed slightly.

As was mentioned in the context of diagrams, any material in your appendices should be referred to at the appropriate point in your text, so that the reader who *does* wish to refer to the supporting evidence knows that it exists, and where to find it.

In the interests of clarity, letters or Roman numerals may be used to identify the different appendices, to avoid confusion with the numbers used to identify the major and minor sections of your text. (If you have more than 26 appendices, you should in any case be asking yourself whether they are all essential!)

References

Some of your evidence will be in the form of secondary data, information collected by others. You will also be drawing (I hope) on concepts which have been introduced in your courses. In both cases, your reader might wish to reassure himself that you are making appropriate use of information or theory. To do so, he or she would want to look at the information personally, to check that you are not misquoting it, or using it out of context, or go back to the author responsible for the theory you used, to see that you have really represented the concepts correctly.

More positively, your reader might be so fired with enthusiasm by your report as to be inspired to research the topic further, taking up where you left off. In either case, the reader needs to be able to find your sources. You need, therefore, to have made very clear in your text what source you are using at any point, and to include a list, usually at the end, with the full reference to the material in question. Thus in the text you might say 'Handy (1985)', while in your references you would say:

Handy, C.B. (1985) *Understanding Organizations* (3rd edn), Penguin.

There are other styles of giving references, but this is the most widely used in academic circles. You will see that the title of the book is distinguished by the use of italics, but could equally well have been underlined. If you are quoting a journal article, then usually the article title is given in quotation marks, and the journal title italicised or underlined. In the latter case you will also need to show volume and issue numbers of the journal, and the page numbers on which the article appears. Thus:

> Hendry, C. and Pettigrew, A. (1986) 'The practice of strategic human resource management', *Personnel Review*, **15**, 5, pp. 3–8.

If you are referring to more than one publication by an author in a single year, you normally distinguish these by the use of letters, e.g. Handy (1985a), and Handy (1985b).

References should normally include only those sources which have been directly referred to in your text. If you wish to include other items which might be of interest to the reader, but to which no direct reference has been made, the list is normally entitled 'Bibliography'. For direct quotations, as for example when you want to reproduce a whole paragraph from one of your sources, you should always include reference to the page from which the quotation is taken.

THE BASICS OF CLEAR ENGLISH

Even students who are native English speakers lose marks because their use of the language is inadequate. They may write in such a way that their meaning is unclear, and their marker fails to realise what they are trying to say. Grammatical and spelling errors may be serious enough to cost marks. Students for whom English is a second or subsequent language often (though not always!) have greater problems.

In either case it is worth paying attention to your use of language. If you have doubts about your abilities in this respect you should study the following section. After all, the credibility of any report you write at work will be reduced by poor expression. Grammatical or spelling mistakes may create doubt as to your competence in other areas. Lack of clarity in the way you write will imply a lack of clarity in the way you think. Neither will improve your promotion prospects.

Clearly it is beyond the scope of this chapter to teach you the full complexities of the English language. If English is not your first language, and is weak, you should probably take a language course before starting your MBA. But if the problem is minor the following basic guidelines and short explanations of how punctuation can be used may help. A list of words commonly mis-spelled or misused in management assignments is also included.

The following guidelines should help you to improve the style of your assignments, or other reports, at least in terms of increasing the clarity of your communication.

Go for simplicity

While it is possible, if you are thoroughly confident in your use of English, and can keep control of a whole sequence of subordinate clauses, some of which may describe elements of the main clause, others of which may describe phrases which are already subordinate clauses themselves, without forgetting which verb belongs to which clause, or omitting verbs altogether, to construct a sentence that is grammatically correct, the overall effect is usually far from satisfactory, as the reader soon starts to lose track of the main idea, which may have been introduced several lines earlier, and by the end of the sentence it is extremely likely that he will have lost the thread altogether. Is that clear? Probably not! Perhaps you had to read the sentence several times to get the meaning. Yet many students get close to such complexity in their assignments. Often they do *not* keep their grammar under control.

Imagine how much harder the sentence above would have been if it had used long words! If you have a predilection for multisyllabic words, habitually utilising these in preference to equivalent, albeit briefer terms, possibly intending significantly to enhance the impressiveness of your communication by demonstrating the extensiveness of your vocabulary, the capacity for obfuscation is multiplied significantly. So don't indulge yourself! Use short words, and short sentences. Your meaning will almost certainly be far clearer.

If you want to gain a rough assessment of your likely clarity in terms of how you score on these two aspects, there is a measure called the *Fog Index* which you can calculate. Take six sentences at random from what you have written. This is probably best achieved by deciding on the number of the sentences, e.g. second, fifteenth, twenty-eighth, etc. or by throwing a die to generate random numbers. If you look at the text while selecting, the process will not be random. Count the number of words in the selected sentences, and the number which have three or more syllables. Express this as a percentage. Divide your total number of words by six to give average sentence length. Add this average length to the percentage of long words, and multiply by 0.4. If your answer is greater than 12 your writing is 'foggy'. (If you want to work out the Fog Index for a shorter passage, use the whole passage, and adjust your sentence length calculation accordingly.) Your word processor may well have automatic Fog Index calculation. If you want to go even further than this, I have seen an advert for software that not only checks your grammar, but also tells you how close your style comes to one of a number of preferred models ranging from Hemingway to an insurance policy!

EXERCISE 1

Calculate the fog index of the first two paragraphs after the heading 'The basics...', and compare it to the index for the first two paragraphs under 'Go for simplicity' using all the text, rather than a sample, in each case.

> **ACTIVITY**
>
> Find a piece of writing which you did recently, and calculate your own fog index. Check it occasionally in future work.

Reducing your sentence length will almost certainly make your writing clearer. It will also make you far less likely to violate grammatical rules. Shorter sentences are much easier to control. With a long sentence you may inadvertently omit a verb, either from the main part of the sentence or from one of the clauses within it. It is equally easy to use a singular form of verb when it should be plural, or *vice versa*, because you have forgotten what was the subject of that verb. In a short simple sentence such an error would be glaringly obvious.

There are, therefore, clear arguments for keeping words and sentences short. Similarly, you should avoid over-length paragraphs. Paragraphs serve to break a piece of writing into units which the reader can absorb at one go. Ideally, a paragraph will be 75–100 words long. More importantly, it will relate to a single topic or idea. Combining disjointed ideas into a single paragraph will confuse your reader, who will be expecting, and therefore unsuccessfully seeking, connections between them.

If paragraphs are too short, it can make your writing seem disjointed. Check whether the paragraph needs to be expanded, or whether other short paragraphs are in fact devoted to the same idea and could therefore be combined. If not, do not worry too much. The occasional short paragraph will do no harm. Indeed, it can be used to emphasise a point. But if your entire report consists of very short paragraphs, you might wish to rethink the whole thing. Perhaps you are not developing your ideas sufficiently.

If paragraphs are too long, text can seem forbidding and dense, and the reader may find it heavy going. See whether you can split very long paragraphs into shorter ones. I once spent a year as sub-editor of a student newspaper, and most of my job consisted of carving large paragraphs into smaller ones. A report can stand much longer paragraphs than a newspaper, but that year has given me a ruthlessness which I lacked before, and which has stood me in good stead ever since.

Since the carving-up process requires you to think carefully about the points you are making within that section of text, you may find that the paragraph splitting exercise generates significant improvements to your draft. When you think about what you were *really* trying to say, you often find ways of saying it better.

However you split your paragraphs, it is a good idea to link them so as to avoid disjointedness. The first part of the previous sentence constitutes just such a link (see how many more you can identify in previous paragraphs). It relates the idea of linking back to the earlier idea of splitting. Linking needs to be done with a light hand. You do not wish to spend half of each paragraph covering ground covered just before.

At the same time, you want to avoid the floating 'this'. I mean the 'This means ...', or 'This is ...' type of link, where it is totally unclear whether the 'this' is the whole previous paragraph, the last sentence, or the subject (or even the object) of the last sentence. Whether you use 'this' to link sentences or paragraphs, you should always check that it is firmly 'anchored', i.e. that it is absolutely clear to the reader what 'this' is, with no ambiguity possible.

I have a strong suspicion that students are often tempted to use long words, sentences or even paragraphs because they feel that this is the expected academic style. Others think that a simple idea may be made more impressive in this way. There is also a feeling that jargon is necessary. All these feelings are well grounded. There was a depressing piece of research which showed that the same paper given to academic audiences was rated much more highly when the presenter used a high Fog Index delivery than a low one. You may indeed, in the course of your studies, come to the conclusion that many of the 'difficult' papers you read in journals are expressing remarkably simple, even unoriginal, ideas, once you manage to penetrate the language in which they are written. It *is* part of the academic culture to write in a 'learned' style. And you *are* expected to use jargon, to the extent that it expresses course concepts directly relevant to the assignment set.

This guideline is not suggesting that you use only words of one syllable, sentences of no more than five words, and exclude *all* jargon. But it *is* suggesting that you use the simplest language consistent with expressing your ideas adequately, and only those jargon words that are necessary to demonstrate your ability to apply course concepts to problem situations. Almost all MBA assessors, and most managers, will be more impressed by clarity than by unnecessary complexity.

Even with short sentences you may be prone to grammatical errors. If you suspect this to be the case, work your way through Helpfile 3 at the end of this chapter. This covers punctuation and its role in generating grammatically correct sentences, together with other common grammatical mistakes.

Avoid sensational or emotive language

While you want to make whatever you write as interesting as possible, it is best to avoid sounding like a cheap newspaper. For example, if you had surveyed the observance of Health and Safety guidelines in an organisation and found many shortcomings, it would be in order to describe the situation as 'worrying', 'thoroughly unsatisfactory' or 'in breach of legislation'. It would not be appropriate to talk of 'a downright disgrace', 'a thoroughly immoral situation', or 'another example of capitalist managers exploiting the oppressed workers'. It is possible to make your meaning perfectly clear while using slight restraint in your language. Indeed, you may make your point *more* forcibly in this way, as you will avoid reducing your credibility through inappropriate language.

Use the first person with care

You will need to check what the expectations of your audience are on this. For example, I have used the first person in this book, in common with many Open University texts, in order to avoid sounding too distant. Having cut my writing teeth in that context, I find 'the author' sounds pretentious. In any case, much of the text is intended to replace the tutor to whom you may not have ready access, offering the same sort of support. It is not intended as academically authoritative. Suggestions are offered for you to use as you please. 'I' seemed more appropriate therefore. But you may find it grates on you. And it may have a similar effect on your MBA assessors, and be totally inappropriate in many organisational reports, so check before using it.

Check what you have written

Better still, if your spelling or grammar 'wobbles' on occasion, get someone else to check it for you. Your main sources of help are:

- *A dictionary* – keep it on your desk and consult it whenever in the slightest doubt.
- *The spellchecker on your word processor* – this will highlight non-existent spellings and mis-types, but unfortunately will not be smart enough to spot your mistake if your mis-spelling has generated a valid word, such as 'there' when you meant 'their'. Because of this difficulty a list of common mis-spellings (common in student assignments at least) is given in Helpfile 2 at the end of this chapter. This focuses on words where the mis-spelling is a valid, if unintended, word, and therefore not likely to be 'spellchecked'.
- *A secretary* – many (alas not all) secretaries have excellent command of English, and correct everything they type, even if they feel embarrassed at doing so. You can legitimise their efforts by thanking them for any corrections you notice, and asking them to check your spelling when you hand work over. Of course if you dictate, the problem does not arise. You can even encourage them to correct your phrasing if they see things which could be improved. They may be reluctant to do so without permission, but it is a shame if their skills are not exploited.
- *Anyone else* – it is always a good idea to ask someone else to read an important draft. This will enable you to check that your intended meaning is clear throughout, and to see what reaction it produces. Again, make it clear that you would *welcome,* rather than be offended by, corrections to grammar or spelling.

The power of English

The clarity of your English, which in turn depends partly on its correctness, will have a major impact on *all* your written communications. It will help you get good grades for assignments, will make a marked difference to your exam scores and will influence the way people react to reports that you write at work. While content is important, it is not sufficient. The way in which that content is expressed will influence both how much of it is actually communicated, and the way in which readers react to it. This is why your writing skills are so important. Try the following exercise. If you miss some of the possible improvements, work through Helpfiles 2 and 3 at the end of this chapter, and then try some of the additional exercises on the website www.booksites.net/cameron, to see whether your grasp of grammar and spelling has improved. During your course, pay careful attention to feedback from tutors on your writing style. Look for other sources of feedback on your writing, too, both during your course and thereafter, and try, where possible, to critique your own work.

EXERCISE 2

Improve the following text:

The problem in many organisations where labour turnover and absenteeism are high are that their is low moral and the affect of this makes workers less happy. This makes recruiting expences high, looses valuable skills from the organisation, and the staff remaining, who's moral then drops further. This is a viscious circle centred about a deepseeted problem. Yet the managements' disinterest often means that there staff are caught in this trap for year's. This insures a constant decline in affectivness. Personal departments are powerless to, if senior management support is absent. There as frustrated as everyone else are – and everyone knows what that means!

SUMMARY

- Written assignments need to be carefully planned, with the requirements of the intended audience fully considered.

- Seemingly simple questions need to be broken down into their constituent, if implicit, parts.

- Diagrams can be useful in the early stages of planning content and structure.

- Plans need to be checked against requirements at regular intervals.

- Time management is essential if deadlines are to be met.

- Assignments may be asked for in a variety of formats. Clear structure and judicious use of subheadings will almost always improve clarity, even if a 'report' is not required.

- A report should be seen as essentially an argument based on evidence. This evidence includes information about a situation and relevant theory. Your goal is to get your readers to accept your argument and consequent recommendations.

- The drafting process should be started as soon as possible rather than left until evidence collection is complete. Several drafts will be needed, so early drafts can be amended in the light of subsequent findings.

- Reports are normally in a format which includes: a title page with sender, addressee and date, as well as title; a list of contents; a summary; an introduction; the main body of the report, broken into major and minor subsections; conclusions; recommendations; a reference list; and any necessary appendices. Organisations may have house styles varying slightly from this.

- Whatever the format, an appropriate style and correct use of English will enhance the clarity of your arguments. Simplicity of language is usually an advantage, and spelling and punctuation are important.

■ Where possible, diagrams and results important to your argument should be included in the text. More detailed supporting evidence should be included as appendices.

Further information

Adamson, A. (1995) *A Student's Guide for Assignments, Projects and Research in Business and Management* (5th edn), Arthur Adamson.

Bentley, T.J. (1978) *Report Writing in Business,* Kogan Page.

Boden, J. (1997) *Writing a report,* How To Books.

Gowers, E. (1954) *The Complete Plain Words,* HMSO, now available in Penguin. This is the classic work on use of English. It has been regularly updated even since the author's death, and is well worth acquiring.

Joseph, A. (1998) *Put it in writing: learn how to write clearly, quickly and persuasively,* McGraw-Hill. American, but clearly written!

HELPFILE 1: GLOSSARY OF TERMS USED IN EXAMINATION AND ASSESSMENT QUESTIONS

If you are not used to answering assignment questions in social science subjects, the following interpretation of terms commonly used may help you to be sure that you are meeting the requirements of the question.

Analyse

This means to examine part by part. Thus if you are asked to analyse a problem situation, you would be looking for the roots of the problem, rather than merely describing the symptoms which are presented. You would normally be expected to draw heavily on ideas and frameworks in the course being assessed in order to identify the root causes. The analysis may be the basis for suggesting possible ways forward and deciding between them.

Comment

This terse instruction may appear after a quotation or other statement. You are required to respond in a way that shows that you understand the topic to which the statement refers. Thus you might need to define any terms contained, explain the significance of the statement and possibly evaluate it (see below), or state the extent to which you agree and disagree, and give your reasons for this.

Compare

This means look for both similarities and differences between the (usually) two things mentioned. It is very easy to forget one or the other, and safest always to think of 'compare' as shorthand for 'compare and contrast'. You would normally be expected to describe the similarities and differences, and perhaps come down in favour of one or the other. Sometimes it is possible to do this comparison using a table, with one column for each of the things being compared.

Contrast

This is a subset of compare. You are expected to focus only on the differences between the things mentioned.

Critically appraise

This means to discuss the strengths and weaknesses of a proposition or theory (*see* 'criticise' and 'evaluate' below – you will need to incorporate elements of both).

Criticise

This means to judge the merit of a statement or theory, making clear the basis for your judgement. This might be in terms of the evidence on which a theory is based, or the internal consistency of that theory, or the theoretical, logical or factual underpinning of an opinion.

Define

This means to state precisely the meaning of a concept. Normally this will be a definition that you have been given in your course. Sometimes there may be competing definitions, in which case you may need to give both (or all, if more than two), and to discuss the differences between them. You will often be asked to include examples of the thing to be defined, but even if not, doing so may help to establish that you understand the meaning of the term in question.

Describe

This means give a detailed account of the thing referred to, again with a view to establishing that you know what is being referred to, and understand its significance. Diagrams can often help you to describe something, and should be included if they add something to the words.

Discuss

This means to extract the different themes in a subject, and to describe and evaluate them. What are the key factors/aspects? What are the arguments in favour of and against each aspect? What evidence is there in support and against? What is the significance of each aspect?

Evaluate

This means to say what something is worth. If a theory were to be evaluated, you would look at the evidence supporting the theory, and the usefulness of that theory to managers.

Explain

This can mean to make something clear or to give reasons for something, depending on the context. Frequently you would need to do both to answer a question. Remember that your explanation, as with all assessment, is intended to demonstrate your understanding of the concept to your assessor.

Identify

This normally means you are to decide what the important factors are, and describe them briefly.

Illustrate

This sometimes means use a diagram or other graphic aid, but more frequently means give examples to show that you know what you are talking about.

Interpret

This normally means make sense of something, make it clear, usually giving your judgement of the significance of the thing to be interpreted. You might be asked to interpret a set of figures or a graph in which case you would need to describe in words the significant features, or 'messages' contained therein.

List

This needs to be treated with caution. Strictly it means to give single words or phrases. But sometimes the assessor really means you to give a brief description rather than merely a single phrase. If in doubt with written assignments, ask. If in an exam, make a reasoned guess from the number of marks allocated to this part of the question.

Outline

This means give a brief description of key features of whatever.

...?

By this I mean those questions which seem to invite the answer 'Yes' or 'No'. e.g. '...Do you agree?' or 'Are budgets an adequate control mechanism?' It is very rare for the assessor to require a simple yes or no. It is far more likely that you are expected to discuss the statement, and evaluate it.

HELPFILE 2: SPELLING (THE RIGHT WORD)

Because spellcheckers and dictionaries exist, there is no attempt here to list all the words which appear mis-spelled on assignments. Instead the concentration is on those which occur wrongly so often that the student clearly has no doubts about their correctness, and which are valid words in themselves. They would therefore not be picked up by a spellchecker, and presumably do not cause the student to reach for the dictionary. I am assuming that you *do* use the spellchecker! It is an easy and vital tool, even if sometimes irritating.

advice–advise

The noun has a 'c', the verb an 's'. It is clear from the pronunciation which is which in this case, though people still make mistakes. You can use this pair as a model to help you decide in the case of other pairs, e.g. practice–practise, where the pronunciation is no help.

affect–effect

To 'affect' something is to change it, or to have an *effect* on it. As a noun, 'affect' is used by psychologists to mean mood. As a verb, 'to effect' something means to bring it about. Thus 'In order to affect the way recruiters treat minority groups, it may be necessary to effect new legislation. The effect of the legislation should be to make discrimination illegal.'

councillor–counsellor

'Councillors' are elected local authority representatives (among other things). It is 'counsellors' who give advice, or counsel.

disinterested–uninterested

'Disinterested' means impartial or unbiased. If you mean someone shows no interest in something you need 'uninterested'. This mistake is *extremely* common, but highly irritating to more sensitive readers.

ensure–insure

To 'ensure' means to make sure. 'Insure' means to take out an insurance policy.

hear–here

'Hear' has to do with ears, 'here' means in this place (as in 'Here, there, and everywhere').

imply–infer

'Imply' means to hint at. The speaker or writer implies. 'Infer' means to draw a conclusion, or inference, from something, and is done by the reader or listener.

i.e.–e.g.–etc.

'i.e.' means 'that is', i.e. another way of saying the same thing. 'e.g.' means 'for example', so is only a part of the same thing. If you mean 'and so on', you should use 'etc.'. But it is sloppy to use etc. more than sparingly. It can suggest that you haven't bothered to think an argument through. There is a fairly common school of thought (especially among editors) that none of these abbreviations should be used unless absolutely necessary.

it's–its

'It's' is short for 'it is' – the apostrophe stands for the missing letter. 'Its' means 'belonging to it'. The confusion arises because in old English the possessive form used to be 'John his coat', or whatever. So when this was shortened to John's coat, the apostrophe was representing the missing letters. But now it just means belonging to, and its origins are forgotten.

lead–led

The metal is 'lead', as is the present of the verb, as in 'I lead the parade every day'. 'Led' is the past – 'Yesterday I led it, as usual'.

loose–lose

'Loose' means 'to unfasten', or 'not tight'. 'Lose' refers to misplacing something, or not coming first in a race.

moral–morale

When you are talking about job satisfaction, you mean 'morale'. Every time 'moral' is used in this context it conjures up visions of defrauding the customer, or carryings on behind the filing cabinets.

oral–aural–verbal

'Oral' has to do with the mouth, so refers to speaking (or taking medicine), 'aural' has to do with the ears, while 'verbal' means to do with words, which might be written or spoken. (Apparently ear drops labelled 'to be taken aurally' are often misapplied.)

personal–personnel

'Personal' means 'belonging to you', or 'private', while if you mean 'employees', you need 'personnel'.

principal–principle

'Principal' means most important, or the head of something. 'Principle' means an idea, or truth. Or if you are into morality, it can refer to a code of conduct.

stationary–stationery

You buy 'stationery' at a stationers. 'Stationary' means not moving.

their–there–they're–theirs

'There' is the place. (Think of the Beatles again.) 'Their' indicates possession. 'They're' is short for 'they are', with the apostrophe indicating the missing letters again. Note, too, no apostrophe in 'theirs' (as in 'the car was theirs').

to–too–two

The only times you *don't* use 'to' is if you mean excessive ('too'), or the number ('two'). So 'Two of us are going to be too late'.

were–we're–where

'Were' is the past tense, 'we're' is the shortened version of 'we are', 'where' is the place (think of it as getting the answer 'there', which is only one letter different). So 'Over there, where we were, we're almost there'.

who's–whose

Another muddling case, like 'its', where the apostrophe indicates omission not possession. So 'who's' is short for 'who is', and 'whose' means 'belonging to whom'.

your–you're

And again, 'you're' means 'you are', while 'your' indicates 'belonging to you'.

You will see that by remembering the simple rule that an apostrophe stands for letters left out, many of the mis-spellings will be cured. For the rest, you will either need to learn the correct spellings by rote, or use mnemonics. For all other words that cause you doubt, use your dictionary. If you find it embarrassing to consult one openly, get an electronic one!

HELPFILE 3: PUNCTUATION AND GRAMMAR

Once your spelling is under control, the only thing left to worry about is getting the punctuation right. Grammar checks on your word processor are some help here, but the following comments might also be useful. If you keep your sentences short, you will need very few types of punctuation, but are likely to want to use at least:

Full stops (.)

You will need one of these at the end of each of your (short) sentences. Check that your sentence is complete before putting the full stop. It might be a single word, such as 'No'. But if the sentence is longer, check that it makes complete sense. It will usually only do this if it has at least one verb (a 'doing' word, like 'write' and 'go') and a noun (person or thing) to do whatever it is. If the verb needs an object, i.e. is done *to* something, then the object must be in the sentence too. If you do indulge in long and complicated sentences, check that each verb has subjects and objects as required.

... can be used to indicate either that you are breaking off before finishing something or that you are omitting a section of a quotation.

A full stop is also used to indicate an abbreviation, as in co., though is not needed if the abbreviation includes the last letter of the shortened word, as in Dr or many other titles. Remember the earlier caution about the use of abbreviations, however.

Question marks (?)

These are used instead of a full stop at the end of any sentence which asks a direct question, such as 'What are your objectives in seeking to gain an MBA?' But they are not needed if the question is reported, such as 'Many students wonder why they are working for an MBA'.

Exclamation marks (!)

These can be used (sparingly) to denote excitement, or amazement, or to indicate humour or sarcasm.

Commas (,)

These are used to split up parts of a sentence to make the meaning clearer and allow the reader to draw mental breath. They may split strings of nouns, such as 'MBA students need time, self-discipline, organisation and motivation'. You could have added a comma before the *and*. In a longer list this would be preferable, for a short one it is less important.

They may split other lists, such as adverbs or verbs. For example, 'You need to work quickly, efficiently, thoroughly, and with extreme concentration', or 'You will need to think, plan, set deadlines, and monitor your progress'.

Commas are essential to split up more complex sentences with several parts. I shall not give an example, as this book is full of them: my husband says I have an unfortunate tendency towards baroque sentence construction!

When using commas it is essential to check that you have not inadvertently split a verb from its subject. You must not, for example, write 'The courses I am studying, include accountancy and marketing'. In this case *courses* is the subject, and *include* its verb.

Inverted commas ("..."), or ('...')

Use these whenever you are quoting, whether speech or a section of text. You can use single or double inverted commas (if there is a rule, few people are aware of it), but should be consistent. You may sometimes have a quote within a quote, for example if a passage of text you are quoting itself includes a quotation. If so, use double quotation marks to distinguish this if you normally use single, or *vice versa*. Quotation marks may also be used to denote titles of books or articles, although it is equally common to underline these or use italics to distinguish them.

Apostrophes (')

As already indicated, these indicate where a word has been shortened by omitting letters, e.g. 'didn't'. An apostrophe is also used to indicate possession, when s is added to a normal word, as in 'a dog's breakfast'. For plurals, when an s is there already, the apostrophe is added *after* the s, as in 'eight weeks' work'. Note that for odd plurals, where you *do* need still to add an s to indicate possession, as in men's, or women's, then the apostrophe is *before* the added s. Remember that where there is a special word to indicate the possessive, there is no need for an apostrophe. After all, you would never write hi's, so should not use one with its, yours, theirs, hers. Despite this, the use of *it's* to mean the possessive is probably the commonest grammatical mistake seen in assignments.

Brackets

These are used to separate off something that is an addition or insertion (such as an aside which casts light on what you have said). When they occur as the last part of a sentence, close the bracket *before* the full stop. (When a bracket encloses a complete sentence you should put the full stop before the bracket.)

Dashes (–...–)

These can be used instead of brackets to separate off the same sort of thing, or used singly to indicate a break in the train of thought – those occasions when inspiration strikes in mid sentence.

Semi-colon (;)

This is a weaker form of a full stop. It is used to separate things that could be separate sentences, but which are closely linked, thus making the writing less abrupt. Always check before using a semi-colon that what follows it could stand as a sentence in its own right; if it does not, you should probably have used a comma. You also use semi-colons to separate the items in a list, when you started the list with a colon. You can use it before the final item in the list, even if this follows 'and'. You will need many resources for successful study: access to a good library; a place to work in peace; sufficient time; sympathetic family; and a supportive employer.

Colon (:)

This can be used to introduce a list, as in the example above, or in a way similar to a semi-colon, to link two clauses that could stand as sentences in their own right. You would tend to prefer the colon if the second clause explained the first, if you wanted to highlight a strong contrast between them, or if you wanted to draw particular attention to the connection between them. For example, 'He had no trouble getting onto the course: his father was head of department.'

Capital letters

These are used at the start of each sentence, for names (people, places, months, etc.) or adjectives derived from these (Elizabethan, French, Parisian), and for the first and major words in a title (The MBA Handbook).

Other common mistakes

The first is mixing singular verbs with plural subjects, or *vice versa*. So you should say 'one of the students *was* (not 'were') late', and 'the group *was* annoyed'. 'Data' is strictly a plural, but these days it is acceptable among all but extreme purists to refer to it in the singular, 'data is available ...'. To say 'a data' still grates, and should be avoided. Talk about a piece of information if you don't like to use 'datum', the correct singular.

Another fault is using incorrect prepositions. It should be 'different *from*', not to, and 'centre *on*', not round.

Confusing 'shall' and 'will' is also common. You should say 'I shall', or 'we shall' when talking normally about the future. 'Will' is used only to denote strong determination. Thus: 'I shall sit my exam next month. I will work very hard beforehand'.

You should also avoid confusing 'can' and 'may'. 'Can' refers to being able to, 'may' to being permitted to. I can swim, as placed in water I shall not drown. I may swim here, because it is a public beach. 'May' can also mean that something is moderately likely to happen. It may rain tomorrow. 'Might' means less likely, but still possible. There might be a flood, but I should be very surprised.

Confusing 'due to' and 'owing to' is also frequent. 'Owing to' means because of, and usually comes at the start of a sentence. 'Due to' means caused by, and usually comes after the verb 'to be'. Owing to confusion over meanings, words are often used incorrectly. This is often due to poor teaching of English at school.

From all the above, you will see that while it is easy to make mistakes, it is also not difficult to improve the clarity, and correctness, of your writing. If you bear in mind the points covered in this chapter, and always read what you have written, the production of written work for assessment can be a stimulating challenge. It need not be stressful, a chore to be postponed, and something which gives you little satisfaction and low grades, although for too many students, this is sadly the case. Instead, each assignment can be both a vehicle for learning, and an enjoyable and satisfying task.

Answers to Exercises

Exercise 1
(If my counting is right)
The basics...:
Words 151
Words of 3 or more syllables 16
% of such words 10.6 (a)
Sentences 10
Average sentence length 15.1 (b)
Fog Index = 0.4(a + b) = 10.3 (OK)

Go for...:
Words 232
Words of 3 or more syllables 45
% of such words 19.4 (a)
Sentences 7
Average sentence length 33.1 (b)
Fog Index = 0.4(a + b) = 21 (not OK).

Exercise 2
The problem in many organisations where labour turnover and absenteeism are high *is* (subject is 'the problem') that *there* is low *morale*. (This sentence is easily split here.) The *effect* of this is to make workers less happy. (You could argue that this is merely repeating the morale sentence...) *High labour turnover* (otherwise it is not at all clear what 'this' is) makes recruiting *expenses* (I know this word wasn't included, but that doesn't mean you shouldn't look it up in a dictionary if unsure) high, *loses* valuable skills from the *organization* (either this American spelling, or the English organisation is acceptable in most cases, but be consistent) and *puts pressure on* (otherwise this part of the sentence lacks a verb) the staff remaining. (Another place where the sentence can be split, but if you chose not to, I hope you wrote *whose*.) Their *morale* then drops further. This is a *vicious* (dictionary again) circle, centred *on* (*stemming from*, or *caused by* would be better) a *deep seated* (*deeply rooted* better?) problem. Yet

the *management's* (presumably only one management is being discussed in each case) *lack of interest* (surely they are hardly unbiased in this, merely unaware) means that their staff are caught in this trap *for years* (nothing belongs to the years). This *ensures* a constant decline in *effectiveness. Personnel* departments are powerless *too* (or perhaps *to act*, depending on the intended meaning), if senior management support is absent. *They're* (but *They are* would be much better) as frustrated as everyone else *is*. (Omit the rest, as the style is inappropriate, and in any case it adds nothing.)

It still is hardly incisive, or elegant, but it is better …

16 Making presentations

Objectives

By the end of this chapter you should:

■ be aware of the faults common to many poor presentations

■ be able to structure a presentation

■ realise the importance of delivery technique

■ know how to use visual aids effectively

■ be confident in handling questions

■ be able to control 'nerves'.

INTRODUCTION

Standing up in front of a group of people and making a prepared presentation is something most managers have to do occasionally in their careers. Some of them need to do it frequently. As with report writing, it is an area where both success and failure can have a significant effect on your career, being public and highly visible.

Some managers rise to the challenge and thoroughly enjoy speaking in public. Others suffer agonies beforehand, and the relief of having survived the experience is tinged with a sinking feeling that they did themselves less than justice.

It is common for MBA and similar courses to involve frequent group work, and for group members to take turns in presenting their group's results to the whole class. While the exercise is seldom assessed, increasing use of competence-based assessment may change this. Even if you make frequent presentations at work, the chances are that there are areas in which you could improve. If you have little experience of talking to groups, you may be so nervous about making a presentation that this interferes with your enjoyment of, and learning from, the exercise concerned. And the impression which you create, whether this is for assessment or not, may be less than favourable.

While it is beyond the scope of this book to turn you into a brilliant speaker, becoming *good* should be well within your reach. Although *bad* presentations abound, and you will doubtless have sat through many, the basic principles of effective presentation are remarkably simple. By following them, you should be able to create a professional impression that will serve you well on your course and in your job.

THE RISKS OF PRESENTING

Although there are many similarities between written and spoken presentations in that both are designed to communicate in an ordered way, there are additional risks associated with spoken presentations. These stem from the fact that when speaking to an audience you are operating in real time. You cannot afford to go back and correct something you do not like. You cannot afford to go blank. And you have an audience there who will let you know if they do not like what you are saying. If someone starts to read a report that turns out to be inappropriate, they can put it down and waste no more time on it. If they are captive in the middle of a row in a roomful of people, they are more or less forced to hear the presentation through. They may feel strong resentment if it turns out to be a waste of time.

ACTIVITY

Think of an unsatisfactory presentation that you have attended recently. (Lectures are fair game here!) List the factors contributing to your dissatisfaction.

_____

_____

_____

_____

_____

_____

If your experience mirrors mine, you may have listed factors selected from the following list: the speaker was inaudible; slides, OHTs or Powerpoint projections were illegible; the speaker's voice was a hypnotic monotone which had the entire audience asleep; the entire address was read; content was so muddled that it was impossible to follow; the speaker jumbled his or her notes, and spent most of the time trying to find out where they were; half the slides were upside down or out of order; you knew the content already; you didn't *want* to know the content; the room was hot, cold, stuffy or otherwise uncomfortable. The possible list is almost endless, but the above are the commonest faults.

One experience I was once subjected to was at a society's national conference, where the speaker, who had been brought at some expense to address us, gave as his speech a word for word replay of a paper of his that had appeared in the last issue of the society's own journal and which I had read during the train journey there. There was another splendid occasion when the speaker *read* his speech to a hundred people, all of whom had been handed copies beforehand. He was drowned out at intervals by the combined rustle of the audience turning pages in unison.

The working hours lost through audiences sitting through inappropriate or ineffective presentations must be beyond counting. Yet by attention to the principles of communication already covered in Chapter 14, and to the additional factors peculiar to oral presentation, all this could be avoided.

As before, it is essential to be absolutely clear about your objectives, and to have researched these to make sure that they are appropriate to your intended audience. If you are trying to do the wrong thing, it matters little how well you do it.

Once you have avoided the risk of shooting at the wrong target, you can think about your aim. Your delivery must be appropriate to your audience's knowledge and abilities. Your own manner is critical. You must avoid distracting or antagonising your audience by your mannerisms or your style of delivery. Instead you must use your manner to make your message carry a force beyond that possible with the written word. And you must pace your delivery so that your audience can easily absorb what you say. Instead of going slowly through the obvious, with potential soporific effects, then rushing through the more complex and leaving those still awake totally confused, you must adjust your speed to the difficulty of what you are communicating.

You must also work to minimise the problems presented by the location itself. There may be acoustic problems which work against you. You will need to find ways around this, whether by changing the seating pattern, or talking more loudly than usual.

Visual aids can be a problem. Slides may be under the control of someone with whom it is difficult to communicate. An OHP may be so elderly that fine detail or poor contrasts on a slide will be totally lost. Powerpoint projections can be very hard to see in a strong light. Sunny rooms without blinds present real problems. You will need, again, to adapt to what is available, as good visual aids can be invaluable.

The most significant threat is also an opportunity. This is the possibility of audience interaction. Once you have written a report it stays written, even if it does not suit the audience. A live audience can give you many cues as to how well your presentation is going. Are they asking stimulating questions, or aggressive ones? Are they leaning back with their arms folded, or forwards, hanging on your every word? Are they *awake*? Audience interaction may be totally disruptive, making it impossible for you to present in a structured manner unless it is controlled. Or it can make the whole event really stimulating for all concerned, and better than if you had merely given your talk without response.

The remainder of this chapter is devoted to showing you what is necessary if you are to avoid the risks presentations involve, and make the most of the opportunities that they offer.

STRUCTURE

Because an audience cannot turn back the page and check what you wrote earlier, it is very easy for them to lose the thread of your spoken argument. Structure is therefore even more important in presentations than it is in written reports, and needs to be emphasised at frequent intervals. The old advice 'Tell them what you are going to say, say it, and then tell them what you have said' still holds good. You will note the parallel, in a written report, of using an introductory summary, the main report, and then conclusions. It is possible to break these three broad sections down further.

Introductory section

Introduce yourself, explain your objectives, say how long you will be talking for, indicate the main points you will be making and how you will structure these. Make clear the ground rules concerning questions (for example, you may be happy to be interrupted with requests for clarification, but would prefer to take more substantial questions at the end).

Main section

Clarify the problem situation which you are addressing: what are the significant factors in both situation and environment, and the evidence that change is needed? Describe the measures of effectiveness to be used in evaluating options, and how options score on these measures. Make clear what you are recommending.

The above is the same as you would do in a written report. When presenting orally, you will need to give additional pointers to internal structure within your main body. When you have finished dealing with one point, signal this by a brief summary of the point just made, and then a short statement of the point you are about to start on. Visual aids can be useful for this.

Conclusion

Summarise your key points, again using visual aids if appropriate, emphasise your recommendation or conclusion, thank your audience for their patience, and invite questions.

You will find that a simple, and clear structure makes audiences much better able to follow a talk.

DELIVERY TECHNIQUE

Study any brilliant speakers you encounter. They may be using techniques that would be of benefit to your own delivery. If you have yet to meet one, the following commonsense principles, adopted conscientiously, should improve your performance.

Aim to form a relationship with your audience

Try when you introduce yourself to sound human rather than too impersonal. Look at members of the audience. Check at intervals that you are on the right lines. Was that point clear? Can everybody see this slide? Treat questions with courtesy, and thank people for the points they make. Any attempt to make a member of the audience look inadequate will rapidly produce antagonism.

Make it easy for people to hear and understand

Speak clearly, without gabbling, varying your tone. Avoid dropping your voice at the end of each sentence. Don't turn your back on your audience while you are speaking (blackboards are a hazard here). Use short sentences and straightforward language, avoiding any unnecessary jargon. Use the sorts of words and phrases you use for speaking, not those you would use in writing (the large difference between the two explains why read speeches are usually so unsatisfactory).

Try to be interesting

Use visual aids to keep interest, and vary your pace. Relevant jokes can be effective if used sparingly, but avoid overdoing it, or using jokes at all if you know you are bad at telling them. Bad jokes *may* have a place in an after dinner speech, but they are seldom useful in a course or work presentation.

Use detail sparingly

It is far harder to take in a mass of detail from a spoken presentation than from a written report. If detail is important, have a written handout for distribution before or after (*not* during) your presentation, to be used in much the same way as an appendix to a report. If you hand anything out during your talk you will lose your audience. It doesn't matter how many times you tell them not to read it now: the temptation will be irresistible.

Keep any notes brief

Especially if you are nervous, it is reassuring to have notes. Then you know that there is no risk of your 'drying up' completely. But keep them brief, and number them clearly so that if you *do* drop them in your anxiety, or they mysteriously rearrange themselves, you can reorder them easily. Cards are easiest to handle. Resist the temptation to squeeze as much onto each card as is physically possible. You need to be able to refer to your notes at a glance. You do not want to spend minutes peering at them to find where you are.

Mark the point at which you will be using each visual aid. Otherwise it is all too easy to leave one out. If someone else is presenting slides, you will then start getting them out of synch. Some speakers like to use overheads in lieu of notes. While this is frowned upon by purists, and certainly is not very creative, it can help clarify structure provided key points only are included, and thought is given to ensuring that they are useful to audience as well as speaker.

If you are afraid of 'freezing' completely, it may help to write out your entire speech. But keep it in your briefcase. The chances are that your note cards, or what you have prepared with Powerpoint, will mean you do not need it.

Watch the body language

If a glazed look of incomprehension is dawning in the eyes of your audience, you may not be explaining enough. If eyelids are drooping, you may be going too slowly, or they may know it already, or your voice may be becoming monotonous. If feet or fingers are tapping with restrained force, you are being highly irritating. If you start to pick up signals that all is not well, and you are not sure why, *ask* your audience. And adapt your presentation accordingly. This is much safer than assuming you know the answer, and making things even worse.

Don't try to fool people

It seldom works. If you know there is a weakness in your case, admit to it, rather than hoping that nobody will notice. (But do make sure that you have minimised such weaknesses by adequate preparation.)

Allow time for questions

Don't regard this as time which you are free to use by over-running your intended time. Not keeping to your allotted time is a sure sign of ineffectiveness. It is fine to extend into question time if your audience genuinely wishes this, but you should be disciplined about your contribution. Above all, you should avoid over-running the stated time for the session as a whole. Audiences plan their time, and do not like to have these plans disrupted.

VISUAL AIDS

From anyone but a highly gifted speaker, a presentation that consists of straight unbroken talk is hard to take. To maintain your audience's interest, some sort of variety is needed. If you are presenting a group's work then it may be possible for different members to be responsible for different parts of the presentation. Visual aids, skilfully used, can provide this. They can also convey certain things better than can words alone. Relationships, as was noted in the diagramming chapter, are hard to describe in words. A graph or other appropriate diagram can make the point with far more impact and clarity. Video clips can be enormously effective in giving visual impressions of what you are talking about. An object waved in front of the audience can make a point. A faulty item will say a lot about quality, or a pile of thick reports and a sheaf of computer printout will help you convince people that there is too much data and not enough information.

If your presentation is a lengthy one, say in excess of half an hour, then it is worth varying your aids. Some diagrams could be on prepared slides, others drawn on a board or flipchart at an appropriate point in your talk. Handouts that you *do* want people to look at while you talk, such as a detailed table that you wish to discuss at length, can usefully be distributed as people take their seats.

If your talk is shorter, it is probably worth avoiding too much complexity in your aids. Valuable time will be wasted, and the benefits less significant.

It may sound obvious, but it is important that people can *see* your visuals. Even experienced speakers frequently get this wrong. The two commonest problems are barriers between some of the audience and the visual aid, and lack of clarity in the aid itself. Avoid being a barrier yourself. The speaker who obscures half the screen is all too common. Other barriers such as pillars and equipment may be a problem. You may need to ask people to move to where they can see, at least while you are using the screen. This is not at all satisfactory, but better than their sitting in comfortable blindness.

Overloading slides is an even commoner problem. All too often a speaker will project whole tables of figures or pages of text from a book or report, without a hope of any of the audience being able to read them. Your slides need to be capable of being read from the back of the room by someone who is just about ready for a new pair of glasses. This means that any words or numbers need to be *big*, so you will not be able to use many on a single slide. When using colour, be careful that this does not reduce contrast. (I have in my possession some professionally produced slides in tasteful shades of blue on blue. With a small room, and a really powerful projector they are nearly legible.)

Computers make it remarkably easy to produce impressive overheads either for direct projection or for printing on transparencies, so there is little excuse for the hand-scrawled, barely legible exhibits that are still often used. If using a photocopier be sure to use special photocopying acetates – the normal 'write-on' acetates will melt their way into the machine's innards. You can use normal OHP pens to colour key parts of your photocopied slide, or coloured film can be stuck onto larger areas if you do not have access to a colour printer or copier. With computer graphics it is easy to build up from a simple picture to a more complex one. You can superimpose OHTs for a similar effect. (This is more impressive and more flexible than the old trick of sliding a sheet of paper down the slide to reveal a bit at a time.) Apart from being fun, even addictive, the production of good slides will make your whole presentation much more impressive and professional looking.

If you have no access to PowerPoint and projector, or an OHP, then prepared flipchart sheets (again, principles of simplicity and clarity apply) can be used in the same way. If you want to draw any diagrams as you go along, remember to leave blank sheets at appropriate points. An accomplice is useful if you are forced to use a flipchart. Turning the sheets quickly and elegantly is difficult: if you do it yourself it is bound to interrupt your flow.

HANDLING QUESTIONS

Questions can be enormously helpful, or can wreck a presentation entirely. Normally it is safest to restrict questions *during* your presentation to those seeking clarification, reserving more substantive questions to the end. It is all too easy, otherwise, to be sidetracked from your main argument, and to lose both direction and any chance of sticking to your planned timetable. Be sure that in postponing your answer you do so in a positive, courteous way. A questioner who feels 'put down' may go on to be disruptive. If you are holding a question until the end, make a note of it so that you do not forget to deal with it later, or ask the questioner to ask it again at the end.

The most important thing is to understand what is being asked. This is not as easy as it sounds. Careful listening is difficult when you are nervous, and questioners often ask multiple questions, or express themselves less than clearly. It is worth noting down the key parts of the question as it is asked, so that when you come to the end of dealing with the first part you are spared the sickening realisation that there was more, but you have totally forgotten what it was. If you are uncertain as to the meaning of the question, clarify it with the questioner. This will normally be taken as a serious attempt at meeting his or her needs, rather than evidence of your stupidity.

If a question challenges what you have said, resist the temptation to become defensive, or to attack the questioner. Take the contrasting point of view seriously. Unless you are completely sure that the questioner has misunderstood you or is misinformed look for ways in which you can use it to *develop* your position. If they have misunderstood, and simple repetition or correction will not resolve the difference quickly, it is better to offer to discuss it in greater depth *after* the presentation, rather than get into an argument which few of the audience will find interesting.

People ask questions for many reasons, and you are likely to encounter some questions intended to display the questioner's own expertise rather than add to your presentation. Where this is the case, the simplest method is to praise the questioner's knowledge or understanding, agree with as much of the 'question' as you can, and thank the person for their contribution.

Where questions are pointing to a genuine weakness in your presentation, it is usually better to acknowledge, indeed share, the concern, rather than pretend that the problem is less than the questioner rightly thinks. It may, in this case, be helpful to ask the questioner, or other member of the audience, for suggestions as to how the problem might be resolved. You will need, at the same time, to ensure that a small problem is not allowed to grow out of proportion to your main argument.

DEALING WITH NERVES

Most people are nervous the first few times they have to stand up in front of a group of people and talk. Good speakers always retain a slight tinge of nervousness; they find this gives an edge to their performance. Complacency can lead to flatness and boredom all round. So there is no need to eliminate nervousness altogether, merely to reduce it to a level that will enhance rather than detract from your performance. The factors which can help you here are practice, exposure to other similar situations, relaxation techniques, and thorough preparation.

If you are in the minority who view presentations with extreme trepidation, take every chance, whether it be at work, in your leisure activities, or on the course, to force yourself to talk in front of people. It really does get easier the more you do it.

Relaxation techniques were discussed in Chapter 4. They can be enormously helpful immediately prior to a presentation. If you have not practised such techniques, you may need to fall back on chemical substitutes such as a *small* drink or medication. If the latter, experiment beforehand to ensure that it does make you better able to perform. Drugs can have variable effects, and are best avoided if at all possible.

Most important, though, is to be confident that you are well prepared. Knowing exactly what you are trying to convey and how you are going to tackle it, that you have thoroughly researched the topic of your presentation and have supporting evidence and examples at your fingertips is the best possible antidote to nerves. Viewing the presentation not as a problem occasion but as an opportunity for doing something really interesting and worthwhile, as a challenge rather than a threat, should cast the whole thing in a more positive light.

To get you over a possible initial onrush of nerves, make sure that you have memorised your introductory remarks. Take a sip of water and a deep breath, go through your introduction, and by then you should be calm enough to enjoy yourself.

PREPARATION

This is the key to successful presentations. You can *never* afford to cut corners here. It is essential to have researched your audience and the requirements for the presentation so that you are absolutely sure that you are aiming in the right direction. It is vital to have thought carefully about what to include and how to structure it, and about how best to add force to your arguments. It is important to have prepared the most professional-looking visual aids that circumstances allow. It is very helpful, as just suggested, to have learned your introduction by heart.

Unfortunately the necessary work goes beyond this. It is important to rehearse your arguments many times, so that you feel confident in expressing them. Some of this can be done piecemeal. You can work on sections while jogging, or *sotto voce* in the dentist's waiting room. But for an important presentation you *must* allow at least one full-scale rehearsal in conditions as close as possible to the actual presentation.

Arrange furniture to resemble the area from which you will be speaking. Visualise the audience layout. Position a dummy flipchart and OHP (or whatever aids you will be using) as they will be placed on the day, and go through the motions of using them. Look at your non-existent audience, introduce yourself to them, and go through your entire presentation exactly as you plan to do it in reality. Only thus can you be sure that your proposed presentation will fit the time available. If at all possible, find an audience. Family or friends might oblige. Ask for their comments. Failing that, a tape-recording could give you insight into strengths and weaknesses of your proposed presentation. This may all seem like overkill, and for small informal presentations is not necessary, but if you are giving an important formal presentation and it matters that you perform well, and if you do not have a lot of experience, then the effort will be justified.

Another important part of preparation involves arriving at the location early enough to check *everything*. Are seats positioned so that people will be able to see all they need? Is the OHP set up and working and focused? Is the video, if used, working and set up? Are tapes wound to the right point? Are flipcharts correctly positioned, and are there enough working pens? 'If anything *can* go wrong it *will*' applies as much to presentations as to anything else. It is unwise to leave anything to chance.

Finally, though this is often omitted, it is worth coming to an arrangement, perhaps on a reciprocal basis, with a colleague or fellow student, whereby they will give you honest feedback on your performance. Preferably you should schedule this for soon, though not immediately, after the presentation. Immediately after the event you may be in a state unsuited to the receipt of constructive criticism.

This chapter has introduced the basic requirements for effective presentations. You can use a knowledge of these, together with practice, and reflection on that practice, to bring about considerable improvements in your performance. If presentation skills are crucial to your job, and even after trying to put these principles into practice, you still feel you lack skills, you might consider asking your employer whether you could go on one of the many excellent short courses on the topic. There, with intensive video feedback and tutor support, you should be able to develop your skills to a high level.

SUMMARY

- Effective presentations depend on thorough preparation.
- You need to be clear about what you are trying to do, and what your audience needs.
- Structure is even more important than with written reports.
- Good visual aids are easy to produce and very effective.
- Audibility, visibility, and ability to pace your delivery to suit your audience and content are very important.
- Questions can be an asset but must not be allowed to be disruptive.

Further information

Bradley, A. (2000) *Successful Presentation Skills* (2nd edn), Kogan Page.
Collins, J./Video Arts (1998) *Perfect Presentations*, Marshall Publishing.
Manchester Open Learning (1993) *Making Effective Presentations,* Kogan Page.

17 Passing examinations

Objectives

By the end of this chapter you should:

- realise the importance of preparing, and following, a sensible revision plan
- know how to prepare yourself physically for the exam
- be able to control nerves during the exam
- recognise the best questions to answer
- understand the necessity for time management during the exam
- be able to answer your chosen questions fully and effectively.

INTRODUCTION

Examinations are generally recognised as an unsatisfactory way of assessing most of what management education is trying to achieve. Many institutions are now moving away from total reliance on examinations, using continuous assessment as well, with a heavy element of organisation-based project work. But examinations have virtues of convenience, ease of standardisation, and the ability to ensure that what is assessed is indeed the student's own unaided work. Distance institutions in particular find it hard to develop an acceptable substitute for this kind of assessment. It is much harder for them to ensure that students do not receive help with continuous assessment, and an examination is therefore necessary to prevent students gaining undeserved qualifications.

Examinations are also still favoured by accrediting bodies, so you may find you have to sit some exams at least. If so, you will need the relevant skills.

In my experience, examination boards go to extraordinary lengths to *pass* students. But sometimes they cannot help feeling that the student has perversely gone to a similar amount of trouble to thwart their efforts. This chapter examines the main reasons for exam failure, suggests ways in which you can prepare for examinations, and introduces techniques which you may be able to use in the examination itself to ensure success.

TYPES OF WRITTEN EXAMINATION

Probably the commonest form of written examination is an unseen paper of two or three hours' duration, which you are required to answer without access to books or notes. Thus you will be drawing upon your memory of what was in the course, something which can seem quite daunting if you have not sat such an exam for some years, and worry about whether your memory is as good as it once was. If you prepare as suggested in the next section, however, you should have fewer problems than you imagine.

Three other forms of examination are reasonably common. These are computer marked papers, 'open book' exams, and exams based on case studies issued in advance of the exam. Each presents hazards which may not be apparent at first sight. They are therefore discussed briefly here.

Computer marked exams

Although these are more popular at lower levels of study, they are sometimes used at Master's level. They are good at checking factual recall, if carefully constructed can test understanding, and are cheap to administer and mark.

There are two key points to note if you want to do well. First, 'wrong' answers may be penalised. If this is the case it may be safer to miss a question than to guess. Find out what rules are being operated in your case, and adjust your strategy accordingly.

Second, questions may be fairly complicated, and possible answers cunningly chosen to catch you out if you have not fully appreciated what is being asked. (If you have a certain kind of twisted mind it can be great fun setting such questions!) You therefore need to read questions very carefully indeed, making sure you understand the significance of every word, and to think carefully before answering. Obvious answers can be wrong.

If you are not given lots of practice in the sorts of questions you are likely to encounter try to get hold of past questions and spend some time trying to work out how the examiner's mind was working.

Open book exams

In these exams you are allowed to bring course materials and notes into the examination. This may seem infinitely preferable to relying on memory, but beware the following:

1. Any time spent looking things up in your materials will mean less time for writing. If you have a lot of materials and a small exam desk you may spend so long searching that elusive section that you write very little indeed. To avoid this, you still need to be extremely familiar with the course content, so that you need to make minimal reference to materials. It can also help to have a note of where key diagrams or equations can be found.

2. Anything you merely copy from materials will gain you zero marks, as it will not demonstrate anything about what you have gained from the course. You

therefore need to keep quotations to an absolute minimum, giving brief summaries of key points, perhaps with references, rather than extended quotes or reproductions of diagrams. If you have not sat an open book exam before, it is particularly important to do a practice exam under normal time constraints and conditions. This will help you become more aware of how easy it is to fall into the traps outlined, and be more aware of how to avoid them.

Seen case studies

In these exams you are given a case study in advance of the exam, to enable you to study it. You are not, however, usually given the questions that will constitute the exam. You may or may not be able to bring the case into the exam. If you are, there may be limits placed on the amount of annotation allowed. It is important to find out what will be allowed, and work out how best to exploit this. It is possible to write quite a lot in margins, and underlining can be crucial. Cross-references to ideas or other relevant cases could be added.

Whether or not you can take anything in to the exam, spend as much time as possible familiarising yourself with the detail of the case, analysing it, thinking about which course concepts are relevant, predicting possible questions and trying to answer these. You may be able to work with others on case discussion. If so, exploit this. It is probably worth setting each other unseen questions and then marking each other's efforts. This can give you useful insight into the examiner's mind, and into what is meant by 'exam technique', as well as showing aspects of the case that you may not have fully appreciated.

COMMON CAUSES OF FAILURE

Almost all student failure can be put down to a limited number of causes. Some of these are remarkably simple to remedy, others far more difficult.

Not knowing enough

This is the reason students imagine to be most likely to cause them to fail, but it is fairly uncommon for this factor alone to be responsible for failure. It is usually possible to pass an examination with very limited knowledge, certainly knowing far less than the whole of a course being examined, provided that what you *do* know is relevant and put to good use. Conversely, you may 'Know' a great deal – in the sense of being able to reproduce it – but not understand what it means, why it is important, or how to use it. If you devise a revision plan, as suggested later, there should be little chance of your entering an exam not knowing or not understanding enough to pass.

Poor time management

This is by far the commonest apparent cause of failure. In most exams you will be expected to answer a set number of questions. The marking scheme will allocate marks accordingly, and your scriptmarkers will abide by this scheme. The familiar 80:20 rule applies. You can expect to get 80 per cent of the marks with only 20 per cent of the effort that full marks would require. So the pursuit of perfection is a certain route to failure. It is essential that you spend a reasonable time answering each question required. Even if you feel you know nothing about your last choice, still spend time on it. You are likely, despite your ignorance, to gain more marks by attempting it than by spending the time polishing another answer. *Never* inadvertently leave yourself no time to answer one or more questions. Always work out how much time you can afford for each question, and keep a close watch on the clock to ensure that each question gets its fair share. Heavily weighted questions should of course receive a time allocation in proportion to the marks they are worth.

Common causes of failure include:

- *poor time management*
- *answering too few questions*
- *missing out parts of questions*
- *not actually answering the question*
- *not using course ideas.*

To illustrate the importance of this, imagine that you have to answer three equally weighted questions. It will be fairly easy to get 30 per cent, even on a question about which you are very unhappy, whereas if you do not attempt it, you will get 0 per cent. The same time spent working on another question *might* have raised what was already a 65 to a 72, but would be highly unlikely to bring it up to 95. If your overall performance is marginal, the difference between 30 per cent and the additional 7 per cent might turn a fail into a pass.

In working out your time budget you must allow sufficient time for reading the paper and thinking about which questions to answer. Also you will need time to plan your answer. Writing time is therefore very restricted. Do not expect to be able to write a lot. And do *not* feel you have to go beyond your time budget because your answer does not look long enough. Some of the highest marks go to short answers, provided they are relevant and well structured.

Failing to answer the question asked

Of course, those whose time management is awry will fail to answer the question. But there is another significant group of students who allow sufficient time for a question, but then proceed to write what seems to be an answer to something completely different. As examiners will usually be marking to a scheme which allocates so many marks to each sub-part of a question, an answer bearing little relation to what was expected will gain few marks. The only exception to this is when a student has found an original, but still valid, interpretation of the question. Then, if the marker is sufficiently alert to realise that this *is* valid, it may be marked on its merits. There is no guarantee, however, that such an answer will be accepted, so you are not advised to aim for originality.

It is absolutely crucial that you spend some time making sure that you understand what the question is asking for, and identifying all the different parts which may be hidden within a seemingly straightforward question. This is not always easy under exam conditions. It is worth checking, too, that you are not straying away from the question during the course of your answer. Re-read the question at intervals while you are writing your answer, to make sure that you are not drifting away from the main point, or omitting important sub-points. You may find it helpful to refer to the glossary of terms commonly used in exam and assignment questions given in Helpfile 1 at the end of Chapter 15.

Panic

A tiny minority of students find themselves in a state of total panic in the exam. If you are prone to this, you should consult your doctor well in advance, so that the problem may be both registered and addressed. You should also devote time to learning breathing and relaxation exercises, and practise these as much as possible before the exam. Such exercises are also helpful if you do not suffer from outright panic, but are still nervous enough in the exam for it to affect your performance.

Illegible script

Markers may be faced with 100 or more scripts to mark in a very short period. If they cannot read your writing, they may miss many of the points you thought you had made, and you will receive disappointing marks in consequence. If your writing problem has a medical cause, consult your tutor to see whether it would be possible for you to type or dictate your answer. If your writing is simply difficult to read, you should practise writing legibly at speed, well in advance of your first exam.

Other problems

You may anticipate other problems, or encounter them unexpectedly. Perhaps you fall ill shortly before an exam, or suffer a major problem at work or home. If so, as with other problems, it is imperative that you let your tutor or someone else in authority know about the problems, and that your exam performance has been affected in consequence. You should inform appropriate people as soon as it is at all possible. Most institutions will make allowances for such things if they know about them. They cannot take problems into account if they are unaware that anything is wrong.

Having looked at potential problems, it is important not to get these out of perspective. Most students on most MBA courses pass their exams. With only a little attention to the rest of this chapter you should be able to end up in that large majority.

EXAM PREPARATION

In one sense, your exam preparation starts when you begin to study the course. If your note taking was done with revision requirements in mind, then subsequent preparation will be much easier. However, at some point prior to the exam you will wish to focus more specifically on revision, and on developing a strategy for gaining good marks in your exam. As with many of the techniques suggested in this book, the action required is simple and straightforward. But it does require time and planning, and the discipline to start working towards the exam early, well in advance of it being sufficiently imminent to cause anxiety.

You will probably find you use your time more effectively if you go through the following stages.

Identify requirements

It will not surprise you that, as with any other project, you need to know as much as possible about what is required. It should be possible to obtain past exam papers and analyse these for the sorts of topic covered and the type of question asked. Try to put yourself in the examiner's position. It is not easy to think of suitable questions that can be answered in 45 minutes (or whatever the time allocation) under exam conditions. It is even harder to devise questions which will allow students to show that they know, understand and can use parts of the course covered. Some topics will be much easier to write questions on than others. These will naturally predominate. Other topics are so central to understanding a subject that they are almost certain to be needed.

Look at the format of the paper. How many questions are there to choose from? How many topics does this mean you can afford not to revise? With a little research you should be able to identify those areas of the course that it would be dangerous not to know, those which look useful, and those which look less important. You should also have a clear idea of the absolute minimum you must know to have even a chance of passing, the amount that would be fairly safe, and what would give you a comfortable margin of error.

Find out from your tutors what *level* of knowledge is needed. Is it fine detail or broad principles? It is a waste of time learning the finer details of employment legislation if all you are required to know is the broad categories covered. But if you *will* be required to know precisely under what conditions a claim of unfair dismissal can be brought, then broad principles will not be enough. Find out, too, the balance of theory to practice which is required. Many of these finer points will vary from course to course, so you will need to gain information on each course for which there is an examination.

Make sure that you know what, if anything, you can take into the exam room. For some courses you are allowed to bring your notes or a limited amount of printed information. Some courses will issue case studies in advance of the exam to allow prior preparation. Their margins may be usable for other notes too – check whether this is allowed. Programmable calculators provide interesting possibilities; again, institutions have different policies as to whether these are allowable. Electronic organisers, capable of storing *all* your course notes together with outlines of anticipated questions, pose even greater problems for examining bodies. Some courses have totally open-book exams, allowing students to take into the exam any course materials or notes that they wish. Such examinations are dangerous if you are unused to them. There is a strong tendency to waste time looking through materials to find the right place, then to waste more time copying

> *To prepare effectively:*
> - *identify what is required*
> - *plan your revision time*
> - *revise actively*
>   - *summarise*
>   - *diagram*
>   - *test knowledge*
>   - *practise answers*
> - *keep fit.*

a relevant passage. Such copying will gain no marks, as the examiner knows you have access to the original. A good index, prepared with the exam in mind, is essential for an open-book exam and even then you should aim to make minimal use of the book. You will need most of the time for writing. Such exams do *not* reduce the need for revision. While it may be useful to refer to the book for a detailed formula which you will then *use*, the normal time constraints of an exam will mean any other use of books will be severely restricted.

Prepare a revision plan

This is possible once you are clear about requirements. Decide how much of each course you wish to cover in depth, which parts you will give slightly less attention to, and what, if anything, you are going to omit. Think about the time you realistically have available for your preparation, and allow a contingency factor for the disasters that are all too common at critical points like exam time. Think about *how* you wish to work. Do you want to go through the course once, or several times? How *will* you go through it? Clearly you do not have time to read all the books again. Will some parts take longer than others because they do not come easily to you? If you have got into the habit of planning your work earlier in the course, this stage should be almost second nature to you now.

Prepare a chart, showing when you will work on each part of the course. Remember to allow time at the end for overall preparation, and practising with past papers. And do not rely on the night before the exam. That is better used for purposes other than revision. Your chart should have spaces for you to tick off each piece of work completed. Although this is not strictly necessary, you will find that it helps motivation enormously.

If you are revising prior to panic setting in you may need to pay attention to sustaining your motivation.

Revise actively

Once you have allocated your time for preparation, use this time so as to gain maximum benefit. Merely reading through your books and notes in a passive way is unlikely to be of value. As you tackle each topic, you need to bear in mind the following questions:

- What do I need to *learn* (e.g. formulae and diagrams)?
- What do I need to *know* and *understand* (e.g. principles and techniques)?
- What do I need to be able to *do* with the above?

Your exploration of requirements should have put you in a position to answer these questions.

Keep these questions in mind as you work through your materials. You may find it helpful to keep two sorts of notes, those on facts you must learn, including key references, and those on more general points. Even if you followed the advice of taking your course notes with revision in mind, you should still take notes as part of your exam preparation. Condensing your original notes, perhaps progressively, is an excellent way of absorbing material.

I have seen some excellent one-page summaries of entire courses, and students often circulate these electronically. Recipients express almost ecstatic gratitude. This may be misplaced. They do not realise that although such summaries are an invaluable culmination of hours of revision they are no substitute for it. Their value depends upon having gone through the process of producing them. Thus while they will help the person who produced them enormously, their value to others may be very little.

En route to producing such a summary, aim to interact with the materials in as many ways as possible. Draw diagrams of text. Describe course diagrams in words. Try to represent relationships with equations. List possible uses of different techniques. Figure 17.1 shows an example of some notes which have incorporated some of these different things.

Some of your summarising can be done as a kind of test, without looking at materials. You can then go back and see whether there is anything significant that you have left out, or anything you have mis-remembered. You can also test yourself by inventing possible exam questions when you have finished a summary, and then (after a decent interval) trying to answer them. Use past exam papers too, sketching out skeleton answers. Practise going through the following routine:

- analyse the question to see what it is *really* asking, underlining key words (*see* Chapter 14)
- identify key parts of the course which are relevant
- identify relevant concepts, techniques, theories and examples from that part of the course
- sketch out the way in which these could be used to answer the question.

Aim to do this fairly quickly. It will save it from becoming tedious, and will give you valuable practice in organising your thoughts rapidly. Then go back to your course materials to check that you have not omitted other relevant ideas or examples, and that those that you *thought* were relevant do indeed contribute what you thought they would. By *working* on materials in this way, you will find that revision is not boring, and that you will retain material much better.

Of course you will still probably have to *learn* a limited number of things using old fashioned rote learning, unless you were wise enough to identify such things during your course and learn them as you went along. It can be helpful to write such things on index cards so that they are easily portable, and to carry them about with you so that you can learn them on buses, in the bath, or whenever else your brain is not otherwise occupied.

Practise

Unless word processors are allowed in the exam, you are going to have to sit, pen in hand, for much longer than you may have done for years. Many students are now so unused to putting their thoughts directly onto paper that they can no longer do

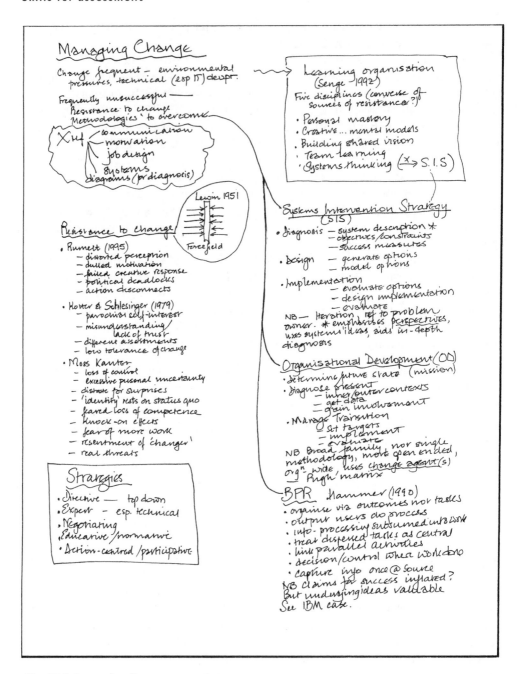

Fig. 17.1 Example of summary notes

this freely. If you are out of the habit of writing with a pen, it really is worth spending some time getting back into it. Otherwise you may find that there is an unwelcome block which inhibits your answering the questions. So start by practising writing anything at all, with a pen! Keep a diary, send old-style paper *letters* to friends, or do a first draft of your written assignments by hand. This will re-open the channel between brain and pen, and make it much easier to answer questions in an exam.

The next thing is to practise writing for the sort of length of time an exam will take. Otherwise you risk developing writer's cramp, and being unable to judge how your time is going without looking at your watch all the time. This practice is probably best combined with the next sort of practice, that in answering real exam questions. You can start by working on individual questions, some of which could be those for which you sketched out answers earlier. Some, though, should be questions which you have not looked at before. Allow yourself an appropriate length of time for each question. Build up to answering whole papers if possible, again working to the time limit that will apply in the exam.

This exercise will be much more useful if you can get feedback on your performance. Ideally, persuade one of your tutors to mark your work and tell you where you went wrong. Alternatives include swapping attempts with a fellow student and marking each other's work, or putting your attempt away for a few days, then trying to work out a marking scheme for the questions attempted. You will need to be very careful to allocate an appropriate ration to *each* part of the question attempted. You can then use the scheme to mark your own work.

Even if you are short of time and cannot do all the practice you would like, it is essential that you write one paper under conditions as close to those of the real exam as you can manage. Not only will this give you a good idea of what you can do within the time, but it will habituate you slightly to the situation, so that the nervousness you suffer will be reduced.

Other preparation

Your remaining preparation should concern more physical matters. You will need a supply of pens that are easy to write with and not likely to go wrong when you most need them. You will probably find pencil and colours useful too, and a ruler and rubber. Check out the calculator situation. Find out whether there is anything else you will need in the exam and make sure it is ready. Remember to take any identification that is required. And if you are allowed to take in refreshments, consider whether a flask of coffee and a snack might revive you during a long exam.

Make sure you know exactly where an exam is to be held: double check this. You might be sure and *wrong*. A friend recently arrived late and breathless at an exam, having run two miles across town from the hall where he had sat *other* exams.

Some of your preparation should concern getting yourself in shape for the exam. Working all the hours there are for the weeks before the exam and keeping yourself going on black coffee is not the way to enter the exam with a functioning brain. The additional stress of being in the exam room may be enough to completely disintegrate you. Very occasionally students will work so hard before the exam that they are barely able to write their names on the paper. This is a tragic waste of effort. It is far better to enter the exam slightly underprepared, but with your brain fresh enough to make good use of what you do know.

So include exercise in your revision plan, and make sure that the night before the exam you get some more exercise, do something relaxing and go to bed early rather than indulging in last minute cramming. I remember feeling terribly guilty just before my finals, because I encountered one of my tutors when I was out on a long walk. But much to my surprise, rather than condemning my laziness, she praised my common sense. I have since come to see that she was right. Exams are not about suffering, but about how best to achieve a desired level of performance.

After all this, it remains only to get to the examination in good time. This means allowing for the worst that the road or rail system can do to you, and for fog, flat tyres, etc. In other words, allow plenty of time, and then some. It can do dreadful things to your concentration if you rush into the exam at the last possible minute, knowing that you have left your car on a double yellow line, and still sweating from the exertion of running to the exam hall.

DURING THE EXAMINATION

If you have followed your revision plan, and prepared yourself adequately for the exam, you should be keyed up enough to give your best performance but not over-anxious. The following guidelines for the day itself may be useful.

Use time before the exam to relax

If you arrived early, as suggested, go for a walk, or get a coffee. Try consciously to relax. Visualise yourself, sitting calmly, feeling clear-headed and in control, writing fluently and confidently.

Read the paper carefully

If you have a choice, much will depend on your choosing the best questions. You will need to read the paper carefully and think about how you might answer each question before making your choice. If there is a compulsory question, you may prefer to answer that first, and then take a coffee break while you think about the rest of the paper. Or you may feel that reading the paper may give you ideas about how to answer the compulsory part. Much will depend on the nature of the paper. It is often useful to highlight the separate parts of compound questions, to ensure that you do not accidentally miss some out.

Work out your time allocation for each question and monitor time usage

You *must* be disciplined about this. The results of poor time budgeting have already been described, and it is essential that you avoid these. Note the time at which you will cease working on one question and move to the next, and keep to these times. Allocate time within questions according to the likely marks allocated to the different question parts. You can work these timings out before the examination if the format is known. When doing your calculations remember to allow some time for reading the paper. Sometimes you will see a question with different weightings attached to each part. Ration your time accordingly. If some questions carry a heavier weighting than others, allocate time accordingly. During the exam make sure that you move to the next question on schedule. If this does not allow you to finish an answer, jot down key points still to make and leave space. You can come back later if you save time on another question. This is a safer strategy (80:20 rule) than aiming to finish but getting behind schedule.

Read each selected question very carefully

It is essential that you understand exactly how the examiner wants the question approached. Do not choose a question simply because you know a lot about the topic to which the question refers. Students often give the impression that they have learned a topic, and then taken the question as the excuse to write down everything they have learned, rather than making their answer relevant to the question asked. Consider the following question (it may be nothing like the sort of questions you will encounter, but the principles remain the same).

> To what extent do accounting techniques provide adequate control mechanisms for an organisation?

This is a seemingly simple question, but consider how much is potentially contained within it. What sort of control mechanisms does an organisation *need*, and what does control *mean* in this context? What is the nature of accounting-based controls? (You would need to give some examples to demonstrate your point.) What, therefore, are their strengths in terms of organisational control? What are their weaknesses? What sorts of problems might arise if control depended solely on accounting techniques?

You can see that a student who wrote down all the accounting techniques he or she knew, complete with all the formulae, would gain few marks. They would have demonstrated that they knew all the techniques, but not that they understood their implications, nor anything about the context in which they were used, which was what the question was all about.

In choosing your questions, it is more important that you understand what the question is driving at, than that you can remember all the details of the topic in question. If the question relating to your pet topic puzzles you, resist the temptation to answer it anyway, unless there is nothing else on the paper that you understand. Avoid what seem to be totally open-ended questions in favour of those that are themselves clearly structured, thus indicating the structure expected in your answer. The former question type may *look* as if it doesn't matter how you approach it, but it is in fact dangerous to assume this. The examiner may have very clear ideas about what is required. Look at the companion website www.booksites.net/cameron for additional questions to 'deconstruct'.

Spend time planning your answer

It is usually essential to spend time thinking about how you will tackle your answer. Mind maps can be very useful here, as they will build on whatever structure is suggested by the question to provide a skeleton for your answer. By following this structure, you will be able to write coherently, and to the point. Time spent planning and making notes is seldom wasted. You may have less time to write your answer, but that time will be used far more efficiently. (There was a student who wrote three pages of notes and half a page of answer, but that is the only time I have known someone suffer from spending too much time planning. He appealed against his fail grade claiming that he had put a note on the exam paper explaining to the examiner that he had run out of time, and that his failure to answer the questions should not therefore be held against him!)

If you are running short of time, do not cross out your notes until you are sure that you have covered everything in them, and even then, cross them out so that they remain legible. Safest of all is to make notes on a separate page, clearly labelled 'Notes' and not cross out at all. Examiners are not supposed to pay attention to work that has been crossed through, but if they are desperately seeking the extra mark you need to pass, they *may* be more charitably inclined if they can see from your notes what you were trying to do.

Use a clear structure

As in your written assignments, you will find subheadings make the structure of your argument clearer. This is particularly important if your *writing* is hard to read. Diagrams can also usefully be included as part of your answer. Be careful though. This is an area where pursuit of perfection is particularly dangerous. Drawing a beautiful diagram can take ages. Aim for quick clarity rather than anything too artistic. Your examiner will expect no more.

If a question asks for a particular form of answer, say a report, make it look right. For a report you will gain easy marks by saying who it is to and from, and titling it, and giving a list of contents (fill these in at the end, having left space). And if it asks for calculations, show your working as well as the result. In this way you will pick up marks for doing it in the right way, even if stress causes you to make an error.

Check at intervals that you are still on course

This applies not only to your time usage, but also to the way that you are answering each question. Once you have worked out what the question is asking, you need to check at intervals that you are still answering this. It is all too easy to get carried away by your flow, and wander off the point. Re-reading the question at intervals, and checking that you are still on target, is essential. A skeleton answer prepared at the question planning stage helps prevent such wandering, as well as increasing your chance of answering *all* of the question.

Remember what you are trying to do

Above all, in writing your answers follow the same rules as you would for continuous assessment. Remember that you are trying to show that you *know*, *understand* and can *apply* the concepts taught in the course. Avoid unjustified assertions, go for reasoned argument instead. Build your argument from evidence and texts you have studied. Give references if you are quoting key authors. And even when report format is not asked for, use *introduction* and *conclusions* sections in your answer.

If, despite your best intentions, your time management goes awry, force yourself to stop the question you are working on, even if not complete, in order to spend 15 minutes jotting down notes on the question you have not had time to answer. Again, it is important to give examiners something on which to exercise their charity, if you are needing it.

Above all, don't worry too much about examinations. As was said earlier, the great majority of students pass, so even if you do not take the advice in this chapter your chances are pretty good, and better if you don't lose sleep worrying. If you do plan your preparation, and follow a sensible strategy during the exam, you should be almost certain of success.

> *To do well in exams:*
> - *budget time carefully*
> - *choose questions you understand*
> - *identify all parts of a question*
> - *plan your answer*
> - *use diagrams where possible*
> - *move to next answer on schedule.*

SUMMARY

- Examinations test a narrow range of skills but have many practical advantages.

- It is important to plan your exam preparation, starting well in advance of the exam date.

- This preparation should be aimed at ensuring that you are physically, as well as academically, in good shape for the exam.

- Active revision is far more effective than passive.

- Use past exam papers if at all possible.

- During the exam it is important to budget time carefully, to read questions thoroughly and only attempt those that you are sure you understand. You should check at intervals that your answer is still relevant.

- If you *do* encounter problems that interfere with your preparation or examination performance, let your college know at once.

- Take heart from the fact that most students at this level pass their exams.

18 Other forms of assessment

Objectives

By the end of this chapter you should:

- understand why alternative forms of assessment may be used
- appreciate your assessors' objectives in each case
- be in a position to work out a strategy for satisfying those objectives, whether assessment is by oral examination, via an assessment centre, or portfolio based
- be starting to assemble material for a portfolio 'just in case'.

INTRODUCTION

Traditional examinations are designed to assess *knowledge*. But management education has been steadily moving away from mere transmission of knowledge, and towards the development of competence, and the ability to apply knowledge to good effect in real situations. With this move has come increasing use of alternative types of assessment. Examinations *are* still used, particularly in institutions concerned to gain or retain accreditation. Hence Chapter 17. Written assignments are common, and have also already been covered. Projects and dissertations are equally prevalent, and dealt with in the next chapter. But you may well encounter a range of other forms of assessment on your programme, and these are dealt with here.

The first, portfolio-based assessment, is increasingly used by professional bodies as part of a case for membership of the profession. Even if your course does not use it, you may need to compile a portfolio in other contexts. The second, the assessment centre approach, is more commonly used as a selection tool within organisations, so again, the skills concerned are highly transferable. The third type of assessment, the face-to-face, or viva voce examination is probably the oldest form of examination. In parts of Europe it is still the prevalent mode. It is increasingly being seen as a necessary supplement to newer forms of assessment, as well as being used in its traditional roles of defending a thesis or dissertation, and giving additional evidence in the case of borderline students.

Obviously you will need to select those parts of the chapter which are relevant to your own programme (or to assessment encountered in your job). Whichever parts of the chapter you are using, you will find an emphasis on the likely objectives of your assessors. If you understand these, you are more likely to be able to satisfy them and to do well.

THE REASONS FOR ALTERNATIVE APPROACHES

There have been several references already to the dissatisfaction felt with current forms of assessment. To be acceptable, assessment needs to be reliable, valid and cost effective, and must contribute to the learning process.

It must be reliable

If the assessment is repeated, or if different assessors are involved, the result should be the same. You would be unhappy if you felt that your exam score depended upon who marked your paper, or on whether you took it this year or last. (Though even examinations are not as reliable as you might suppose, and few institutions are brave enough to double mark papers blind, i.e. without the second marker knowing what the first gave.)

It must be valid

The assessment must measure what you want it to measure. An assessment on a course which depended more on your ability to write coherently than on your understanding of the important parts of the course would hardly be satisfactory. More than *being* valid, it is important that the assessment is *seen* to be valid. If you were assessed by a method that was, in some absolute sense, valid, but which nobody believed to be so, your qualification at the end of the day would be worth very little.

It must be cost-effective

You would not want the cost of your course to be doubled by the use of an enormously sophisticated assessment process.

It should contribute to the learning process

Even an exam does this by providing you with the motivation to work intensively on the course over a finite period. This can help the integration of the concepts taught, as you will be forced to hold them in your brain at the same time. Other forms of assessment are better. For example, doing a project for assessment can be an enormously rich learning experience.

The unease with current forms of assessment on management courses does not stem from inside information concerning inter-marker *reliability* on assignments or examinations, although it well might. It stems from a much deeper questioning of the purpose of management education. If the purpose is not merely to impart knowledge but to develop *competences*, then traditional examinations, which are aimed firmly at testing knowledge, are not *valid*. Competence is more than knowledge. It includes a mixture of skills and attitudes as well. Some form of assessment which tests these is needed.

This argument is clearly very important at lower levels of management. There are basic management skills, such as the ability to interview someone for a job or to chair a meeting effectively, which it would be reasonable to expect of anyone with a management qualification. It is possible to ask a student to write about drawing up person specifications or constructing interview plans. Someone who displays understanding of the processes involved should be in a better position to interview effectively than someone who does not. But it would be quite possible to know what should be done and still be absolutely hopeless at selection interviewing.

Similarly, while an understanding of the principles of running meetings is helpful, it does not ensure effective chairmanship. If assessment is to be *valid*, therefore, some way of assessing such skills is essential. If it is accepted that management education should have a skills development element, then valid ways of assessing skills must be found.

PORTFOLIO ASSESSMENT

Some management programmes are now designed around the performance standards drawn up for National Vocational Qualifications (NVQs) in management. Although this is more common at Certificate and Diploma level, part at least of your chosen programme may be assessed in this way.

Although splitting management skills into a number of discrete competences does present difficulties, portfolio assessment is claimed to be more valid, and more reliable than traditional assessment. Working through a set of competences, reflecting on your strengths and weaknesses, and thinking about suitable evidence of your ability can be a stimulus to considerable learning.

A major drawback of this form of assessment, however, is that it is extremely expensive. There are no economies of scale. Candidates need individual support. Portfolios can take hundreds of hours to assemble, and many hours to assess.

There may be a need to supplement portfolio assessment with observation of behaviour in the workplace, or in a simulation thereof, and by questioning in order to check that the candidate has the necessary understanding and knowledge of the job areas covered.

If you are not currently working as a manager, or are in a very specialist role, you may be able to draw on experience outside of work, for example in a voluntary organisation, but many part-time students find they have no time for this! While simulations may be carried out as part of your course (e.g. a role play of a grievance interview) to provide some evidence, portfolios relying heavily upon simulated evidence are not encouraged.

However, if you are a practising manager and part of your course is based on an NVQ framework, with assignments designed to generate evidence for a portfolio, this can be a useful added bonus. If so, or if you think you may later need to compile a portfolio for professional purposes, it is worth understanding the approach and thinking about the sorts of evidence that you already have access to. You can then ensure that you preserve it.

CONSTRUCTING YOUR PORTFOLIO

In order to develop a portfolio it is essential that you know the standards against which you will be assessed. This presents problems if you are constructing an anticipatory portfolio! Ask your business school as soon as possible for a copy of the relevant standards if you know that they intend to base some of your assessment on these. You can do this as soon as you have decided on a particular course. Alternatively, your organisation might have a copy.

Even if you have only a broad idea of the skills that are relevant, you could start to think about how a 'just in case' portfolio might be assembled. If you have the full list of competence elements and the associated performance criteria, you can plan in more detail the evidence you should collect.

Ask yourself first whether you think you have each skill in question, and then, if you do, when and how you use it. The key question then is what *evidence* you could produce to prove that you have the skill.

The sort of evidence you consider might include, among other things: business plans you have drawn up; policy statements you have drafted; budgets you have constructed; staff development plans you have made; interview plans or records (or even tape-recordings of the interviews); reports you have written; or letters you have sent. Videos you have made, either intended as communications or specifically as a record of some activity such as chairing a meeting, might be suitable evidence. The list is almost endless.

For each piece of evidence note the competence(s) it relates to, and any context helpful for an assessor. Thus, to an interview plan, you could add a note saying what it was about the candidate's application form that made you want to concentrate on these points, or include the form itself, minus any identifying feature. You could also include the person specification for the job. Indeed, if you were responsible for drawing up the person specification yourself, comments giving your reasons would again be helpful. If an activity such as a training session were the basis for demonstrating your skills, you could include not only your plan for the session, and a justification for this, but feedback forms from candidates, and a note as to how future sessions would be modified in the light of feedback.

You can see how a portfolio will rapidly become fairly bulky, but also how it can help you to reflect upon your effectiveness in your job, and how its compilation may be far from a chore. Indeed, the learning diary or study log referred to in Chapter 7 might usefully be incorporated into your portfolio to provide a comprehensive record of skills development and application.

In addition to your supplementary notes, you might think about the ways in which you could prove that work is indeed your own. If you have a sympathetic superior, you might be able to get a signed note saying that work was done by you, or under your supervision. You may occasionally receive a letter thanking you personally for your efforts in a particular endeavour. Add all such evidence to your portfolio.

If you are constructing a 'just in case' portfolio, you should be careful about going to great lengths in generating *new* materials. Your efforts might be misdirected. But there is good reason to think about everything you do, about the skills that it demonstrates, and what, if anything, you could preserve as evidence of that skill. (Remember to remove sensitive pieces of information.) You can then draw on your 'evidence' whenever the need arises, whether for MBA assessment, for use in your annual appraisal, or in support of a job application. You will also be able to retain useful materials should you change jobs.

There should be a secondary and fairly significant benefit. While thinking about the skills you are demonstrating, you may realise that there are skills that you are *not* demonstrating, either because you do not have them or because your job limits what you can do. In either case the information should help you to work out your own personal development plan, if possible in discussion with your training manager or your appraiser.

If you have a gap before your course starts, beginning to plan a portfolio with your training manager or appraiser might be an excellent form of preparation, particularly for a more skills-based course.

ASSESSMENT CENTRES

Many organisations are already using assessment centres as a way of identifying development needs in their managers, or for selecting staff for rapid career progression. Assessment centres put groups of employees through a number of activities, many of which simulate the sort of behaviour that will be required at work. Group problem-solving exercises and in-tray activities are obvious examples. Management games, fact-finding exercises, analysis and presentation (akin to a case study) and simulated (and real) interviews are also used. Trained assessors rate participants against set criteria, and decisions are taken, and feedback given, on the basis of these ratings.

Assessment centre methods also have considerable potential for MBA providers as an adjunct to more conventional assessment forms, and as a supplement to portfolio assessment.

Assessment centres have their critics. They are expensive to run. They have often been set up with only sketchy attempts to validate the process, so that criteria might be questioned. Are they relevant at all? Do they merely replicate existing management styles, thus again being subject to the criticism that they entrench styles and practices that should be improved. Training of assessors is not always as thorough as might be desirable.

Where judgements of your performance at an assessment centre can profoundly affect your career, as when 'failing' forever bars you from promotion, these concerns are extremely important. Where such centres are used as one of several sources of information which is used to construct a development plan for an individual, possible weaknesses in the system may be less critical.

PREPARING FOR ASSESSMENT VIA SIMULATION

As already indicated, assessment centres are widely used in industry, and as some MBAs move further towards being competence based, the attractions of assessment centre methods become more obvious to colleges.

You should not find that such assessment presents you with any serious problems, as it will probably consist of observations of your performance in the sorts of activities to which you have become accustomed during your course, and indeed your career. However, as much of the debate about assessment centres concerns the validity of the criteria against which assessments are made, you would be well advised to do as much research as you can into the sorts of criteria which will be used in your particular case.

For in-company assessment centres, criteria are often derived after consultants have interviewed senior managers in that organisation. From these interviews they extract criteria which are felt to distinguish successful managers within that organisation, as perceived by those senior people. Particularly in an organisation with a strong culture, this may be a reasonable way of proceeding.

'Old faithfuls' are in-tray exercises and leaderless group discussions, planning exercises, where there is access to an overabundance of information requiring the ability to select from this what is needed, simulated consultancy exercises and computer-based management games.

It is difficult to prepare yourself specifically for assessment centre-type assessment, beyond doing all you can to find out as much as possible about the organisation and its culture, and about what is being assessed. If possible, practise the skills identified. You may find that your self-help group can be a useful source of feedback on any group work activities to which you may be subjected. Apart from that, the only preparation you can undertake is the more general preparation described in Chapter 17, aimed at ensuring that you are in good physical and mental shape for the assessment.

VIVA VOCE EXAMINATIONS

Oral assessment is the earliest assessment form of all, and has traditionally been used to help examiners decide upon borderline examination scores and for dissertations. It is also used for assessment which is heavily portfolio based, as a way of checking those areas where the portfolio left doubts either about the candidate's current understanding in an area of competence, or about the extent to which the work is entirely his or her own. Because one-to-one oral examinations can be tailored to each individual candidate, they are more flexible than mass examination, although normally more expensive for an institution to provide.

PREPARING FOR A VIVA VOCE EXAMINATION

You may be given a viva because of a borderline mark in a written examination. Or it may be because your exam mark does not properly reflect your ability, perhaps because you were ill when you sat it. Some institutions routinely examine by viva everyone who submits a dissertation. Some do this only if examiners have concerns about the work. The first thing you need to do is to find out *why* you are being given a viva.

If it is to give you the chance of improving on a mark gained in a written examination, then you should do the same sort of revision that you would normally do for a written exam. You will be tested on your depth and breadth of understanding of the course in question. You could usefully also reflect on what you did in the exam, and any weaknesses that you know you displayed there. It is likely that your examiners will have looked at your paper. If you are already aware of what was wrong with it, it will be a mark in your favour. If you have paid special attention to remedying any weaknesses identified, and are now in full command of the material where you were weak before, you should be in an excellent position. Do not limit your revision to such areas, however, as you may well be asked about other areas of the course as well, and would not wish to reveal weaknesses of which the examiner was not already aware.

If your oral is a routine one, required of all students in support of a project or thesis, then apart from making sure that you can remember what is in the thesis (and given that you will have sweated blood in writing it, it is unlikely that you will have forgotten) little preparation is needed. You might wish to think again about your 'reflections' section and what you learned, and about any areas where you know your research to be weak and how you can explain or defend these. Examiners are fond of focusing on both areas.

But usually, a routine viva for a thesis will be aiming only to assess whether the work is your own. This will be done by testing your understanding of both methods and results. The existence of enough in-depth knowledge to confirm your involvement is normally established very quickly. The exam then usually turns into an interesting discussion on the finer points of your research, presumably a topic dear to your heart.

If the project viva is a non-routine one, find out all you can about the reasons why you have been selected. Your project supervisor should be able to help here. It may be that there are weaknesses of which you are all too aware in your report. If so, think of ways in which you can strengthen your position in the oral. These are likely to involve explaining why the weaknesses were unavoidable, if this was not gone into in depth in your report. Be prepared to say how, if you were starting the project with the benefit of hindsight, you would avoid these weaknesses in future work. Avoid excuses, and instead focus on taking a constructive approach based on the lessons your project has taught you.

Finding out weaknesses

Clearly you will need to know what the weaknesses were felt to be. Check with your supervisor that your list is complete! The weaknesses which you don't know about are the most dangerous! It is important to find out what these are, and to think about how you can strengthen your position. Students often expect to be questioned only about their results, but examiners are equally interested in their methods. Make sure, therefore, that you pay due attention to any weaknesses in your methodology, as well as thinking about your analysis and results.

Whether in finding out your areas of weakness from your supervisor or in answering questions in your oral, it is very important to avoid defensiveness. If your examiner thinks that something about your report is weak, you will not succeed in changing his or her mind by denying the weakness. Nor will you get all the information out of your supervisor that you need if the first hint of criticism causes you to bristle and reject all the points made. It may be hard to accept that the work over which you have laboured so long and so hard is not perfect in every respect. It is particularly hard if you feel insecure about your own qualities, and cannot handle the idea that weakness in your product implies weakness in yourself.

Although avoiding defensiveness *is* particularly difficult if you feel at all insecure, it will be hard to make progress if you cannot accept that there are areas where progress would be a good idea. So try very hard to accept that as nobody is perfect, there is no need for you to be. And because writing a thesis is enormously challenging, some things can be expected to go wrong. Remembering this will make it easier to accept a weakness when the examiner points it out. You can then give further background information on what went wrong, and do everything you can to demonstrate that any weakness in the project has been a source of learning.

You may find it helpful to bring to the examination examples of work you did, or data you obtained, that did not feature in your report. Again, your aim will be to demonstrate not only that this is your own work, but that you went about it in a well thought out manner, and responded to any setbacks in a positive way, so that you learned from the experience.

Whatever the reason for your viva, a lack of defensiveness is to be recommended. This is not to suggest that you should accept any criticisms which are unwarranted. Sometimes an examiner will not have had time to read your report in as much depth as he or she should, and may have misunderstood, or not grasped, key points. If this is the case you *should* defend your position. But where a criticism is deserved, there is seldom much to be gained in pretending that this is not the case. It casts doubt on *your* understanding of what you have done, as well as contributing to an uncomfortable atmosphere in the examination.

If your oral examination is in conjunction with a portfolio rather than a thesis, the same considerations should still apply. The check could again be on understanding or on authenticity. Again, it will help to take a constructive approach to areas of known weakness. Again your preparation could usefully include further thought on these areas. And the following comments apply equally to all types of oral examination.

You should always listen very carefully to the questions the examiner asks. This may sound so obvious as to be not worth saying, but it is even harder to understand all the implications of a spoken question than it is for a written one. And it must be admitted that not all examiners are particularly good at formulating clear questions. If you are not sure of the meaning, avoid guessing. Instead, ask for clarification before proceeding. And stop to think about your answer, if you feel this is necessary. No examiner should mind a short pause while you gather your thoughts. This is far better than giving an irrelevant answer, or one that is only partial.

A sensitive issue concerns how formal you should be during the examination. You will need to take your cues from your examiner, but on the whole anything you do to help the *process* of the interview will not go amiss. Therefore, you should not avoid the occasional smile if the occasion arises, and need not avoid the examiner's eye. The occasion is one for *communication*, and anything which helps communication will help you. So check that the examiner has understood what you say, as well as checking that you have understood the examiner. It may be that there is something else which you could say which would entirely satisfy your examiner, but unless you check whether or not this is needed, you will probably not add it.

SUMMARY

- When emphasis shifts from a knowledge-based MBA programme to a competence-based one, assessment methods may alter to reflect this.
- Portfolio assessment is based on evidence drawn from the workplace, and organised according to the competences required.
- Evidence that might be useful can be assembled even before a list of competences is available, and taken with you if you change jobs.
- Assembling a portfolio is a useful developmental experience in its own right.
- Portfolios may be supplemented by assessment of simulated activities.
- Assessment centres allow you to demonstrate a range of relevant behaviours.
- Oral (viva voce) examinations might be a supplement to either of the above, or used in conjunction with more conventional assessment forms.
- Whatever the form of assessment, it helps to be as clear as possible about the assessors' objectives, and the criteria being used.
- It is also helpful to accept any areas of weakness and attempt to build on these, rather than becoming defensive, and denying that they exist.

19 Projects, theses and dissertations

Objectives

By the end of this chapter you should:

- know how to choose a suitable topic for a dissertation, taking into consideration all relevant factors
- be aware of the steps needed to clear access and gain commitment within your organisation
- appreciate the advantages and disadvantages of different types of information
- be able to identify appropriate sources of information for your proposed topic
- know how to draw up an initial research plan
- understand the distinctive requirements of thesis reports.

INTRODUCTION

Master's level programmes, including MBAs, have traditionally contained a substantial project, thesis or dissertation element. (The words are used almost interchangeably, but if a distinction is to be made, 'project' more commonly refers to work where the practical application predominates, 'thesis' to longer and more academic research-oriented work, and 'dissertation' to something intermediate.) This is a high-risk part of the course, particularly for weaker students, those who have problems with self-direction, and those under particular pressure from competing demands. Potential benefits are also high. A good in-company project can develop valuable research and consultancy skills, and give you valuable insights into your own organisational context. It can also help find solutions to a long-standing organisational problem and bring you to the favourable attention of senior management.

This Handbook cannot give a detailed coverage of research methodology, statistics or any other relevant subject. What it can do is highlight areas where many students have problems and suggest steps which will minimise these, thus reducing the risk and increasing the potential benefits attached to your dissertation. Many of the steps described should be taken well in advance of the research itself. Choice of topic, negotiations with your organisation, and careful planning are critical, and should be commenced at least six months in advance of the 'official' dissertation period.

THE OBJECTIVES OF A MANAGEMENT THESIS OR DISSERTATION

Management research can take a number of different forms. It may be:

- pure research aimed at resolving theoretical questions, or
- aimed at problems of general interest, or
- directed towards evaluating some aspect of an organisation's performance, or
- aimed at solving a practical organisational problem, culminating in a set of recommendations in a report to that company, or
- going beyond recommendations into implementation of the proposed changes, perhaps even to the stage of evaluating the changes.

Despite the aside on possible distinctions between words, a more specialist Master's programme may expect a dissertation somewhere in the academic half of the scale. MBA dissertations (even if called projects or theses) usually lie somewhere in the middle of the dimension from pure research to action research outlined above. This is best understood by looking at the objectives which any MBA thesis serves, over and above the specific objectives of the individual project itself.

Three sets of objectives are important here, those of the educational institution requiring the project, those of your organisational client (if you have one) and your own. Meeting the published requirements for the dissertation will be easier if you understand the reasons for these requirements, so these will be considered first.

While institutions vary in their priorities, and you would be well advised to find out as much as you can about your chosen institution's aims and objectives as soon as possible, the intention is usually to develop the following:

- the ability to carry out investigative work in organisations and arrive at valid results
- the consultancy skills expected of MBA holders
- the ability to manage a substantial piece of work with only minimal guidance
- analytical skills
- report-writing skills
- the ability to integrate and apply what has been learned on a variety of courses
- the ability to assess the value and limitations of information in deciding on future courses of action
- the ability to approach real problems at a strategic level
- research skills that will enable students to progress to a PhD if they so require.

While full-time students may be seconded to willing organisations offering topics intended to meet the above objectives, this is less practical for part-time students, and virtually impossible for distance students, who have chosen that mode of study precisely because it does not make demands upon them during working hours. For such students, a project on their own organisation is likely to be the only choice, apart from the fall-back position of a library-based project for those unable to obtain co-operation from their organisations. (This is usually an option of last resort, as it does not allow the consultancy skills objectives to be met, the problem is likely to be a theoretical one, and a narrower range of research skills is likely to be needed.)

To meet institutional objectives, a fairly broad ranging topic will be needed, with sufficient scope to allow interesting analysis.

Assuming that you will be able to find an in-company project, your organisation's objectives will be important. Many of these will be specific to the topic you finally choose, but general considerations will also be important.

ACTIVITY

Consider what objectives your organisation might have for your project, regardless of the topic chosen. List these here.

_____

_____

_____

_____

_____

Comment

Your list might, for example, have included a desire to give you some in-company training, to minimise use of company time, to be seen to be supporting management development, to support some other company initiative, and to minimise the risk of upsetting anybody. Whatever the likely objectives, and some will be overt, some fairly well hidden, you are more likely to be able to come to a mutually acceptable topic if you are alert to these factors.

Although ideally your company will be giving you considerable support in your project, the main effort will necessarily be your own. Too often students settle on a project topic on the 'Well, I've got to do *something*' principle, and then spend a depressing six months or more working on something which does not interest them at all. Before considering topic choice in more detail, it is worth thinking about your own general objectives, ones that might be served by a well-chosen project. These might include, for example, a desire eventually to specialise in a particular area or to move into a particular part of the organisation, or the wish to incorporate a leisure interest more closely into work.

ACTIVITY

List any personal objectives that your project *might* be made to serve.

_____

_____

_____

_____

THE ROLE OF A SUPERVISOR

Although you are expected to work fairly independently at this stage in your studies, you will almost certainly be allocated a supervisor for your project. This role is interpreted differently by different institutions, and by different supervisors and supervisees within them. Your project supervisor *may* be of immense help to you, but this depends upon your forming a good relationship with him/her. This relationship needs to be maintained, even if you are completing your research after you have finished the taught part of your course and have gone elsewhere.

In order to gain the necessary support, you need to discuss your plans with your supervisor from the start of your thinking about your topic, and to keep in close touch thereafter. Some institutions (wisely) *require* you to meet your supervisor a certain number of times, and to agree certain key points such as project proposal, data plan, report outline and at least one draft chapter. Even if this is not required, you might discuss whether you and your supervisor could usefully aim to reach such agreements, and set target dates for these.

This may seem like an unnecessary constraint on your work. But I have recently examined a set of dissertations where students had *not* been required to agree such things, and had exercised their independence to the full. The result was a set of dissertations that looked beautiful – they showed excellent word-processing and graphic skills, were lengthy and had dedications which referred to the labour involved and support of families through this. But a large proportion of them did not meet the institution's requirements for a dissertation. Project topics were not realistic, data were inadequate and the style of writing quite inappropriate. The resulting work represented a huge waste of student effort, waste which could have been avoided if better use had been made of supervisors. I hate to think, too, of the distress which the inevitable 'fail' grades will have caused the students and their families.

The moral is, therefore, that if it is at all possible, you should agree key milestones with your supervisor, even if this is not required by your institution, and should check your progress at each of these. (It is so easy to communicate electronically that this can be done even if you are doing your project at some distance from your institution.) Checks at intervals are really important because if you become deeply involved in a project for its own sake you may well veer away from meeting academic requirements, even if the project is progressing brilliantly against other objectives.

If you *disagree* with your supervisor, take this very seriously. Other horror stories concern students who resolutely failed to listen to their supervisors, and again produced work which did not meet requirements. Listen very carefully to what your supervisor is saying, and try to work out why you find it difficult to accept. If your disagreements cannot be resolved, or for some reason you cannot get the sort of support that it is reasonable to expect from a supervisor, see whether it is possible to change supervisors. This should not be done lightly, but occasionally may be the only way to get the help which you can reasonably expect.

TOPIC CHOICE

It is perfectly possible to do a poor dissertation on an excellent topic, but the reverse is much more difficult. While some refinement of topic as you progress is possible, even desirable, major change becomes increasingly difficult as your work progresses. It is therefore vital that you start with a suitable topic, and any time spent considering possible projects can be regarded as a wise investment. It can save you hundreds of hours of depressing work directed towards what you by then realise will be at best an adequate result, at worst not even that. In considering possible topics, there will be several factors you will need to evaluate.

> *An ideal project:*
> - *meets academic requirements*
> - *interests you*
> - *is useful to your client*
> - *is feasible*
> - *will be valuable whatever you find*
> - *is low risk.*

Interest

Perhaps the most important criterion is that the topic be of interest to yourself and to your organisation. You will be putting considerable and extended effort into the project, and your organisation will be bearing not only the cost of any working time you devote to the research, but also that of any others in the organisation whose co-operation you need. There may be additional costs such as travel, duplicating, phone calls, postage, information searches, etc.

If you and your organisation (and that usually means an individual within the organisation with the status to act as client for the research) are not equally interested in the topic, there are likely to be problems. If it is your interest that is weak, motivation is likely to slump during the dissertation period, and you will find it an enormous effort to do the necessary work. If your client is not interested, then he or she may not provide you with the support you need, whether this is in terms of refining your project plans, facilitating access to information needed, or sponsoring your final report so that it is taken seriously at an appropriate level within the organisation.

If you are not genuinely interested in a possible topic, therefore, or if you detect a lack of real interest on the part of your likely client, you should keep seeking alternative topics until you do find one of concern to you both.

Scope

It is also important that your chosen topic is potentially broad enough and deep enough for you to exhibit the range of skills your institution will expect. Because the dissertation is expected to develop generalisable investigative skills, you will be expected to evaluate possible research methodologies or approaches as part of your project work, selecting an appropriate one and justifying your choice in your final report. On an MBA you will also be expected to take a reasonably broad perspective, showing the strategic awareness that the course is supposed to develop by researching your topic in such a way as to demonstrate an awareness of the organisational context in which the problem is situated. (On a more specialist Master's course, a narrower topic, studied in greater depth, may be more appropriate.

A narrowly defined topic is less likely to allow you to demonstrate either methodological awareness or strategic thinking. Thus, if your employer asked you to find alternative suppliers of packaging materials and recommend the cheapest, this would not be a suitable research topic. If you had been asked, however, to review the effectiveness of the packaging operation as a whole, and make recommendations as to ways in which it might be redesigned so as to better serve organisational objectives, there would be much more scope. There would be real questions about what constituted measures of effectiveness in this case, and about suitable investigative methods and sources of information. There would need to be a clear understanding of the operation of the rest of the organisation, and its requirements if appropriate recommendations were to be made. Aspects of studies on accounting, operations management, human resource management and other topics could be used to inform the research.

Educational and employer definitions of 'project' may be a long way apart. Your employer may imagine that a course project is the same as other projects in the organisation – a piece of practical work to be done to meet organisational objectives. You may need to spend some time making clear that there are educational objectives to be met too, and explaining what these entail, before you, your college and your organisation can come to a mutually acceptable topic.

Symmetry of research outcomes

This is a less obvious, but important criterion. It means that your research results should be interesting no matter how they turn out. Research to 'prove a point' should be avoided. You are likely to bias the result in your attempt to get the answer you want. There is surprisingly large scope for the unconscious introduction of bias into research. Careful design is needed to minimise this, as biased results are naturally worthless. Worse, you may succeed in designing your research so that bias is eliminated, and then *not* prove your point.

To take an unlikely example, you might have a hunch that gaining an MBA does not, contrary to popular wisdom (and research), improve career prospects. You might carefully design a research study, comparing career patterns of matched groups of managers, the only difference being that one group gained an MBA five years ago and the other didn't. If, as a result, you found that an MBA did nothing to improve career prospects, or positively harmed them, this would be interesting. If you found, however, that those with MBAs did progress faster, the general response might be 'So what?' Demonstrating the obvious has little value on the whole, unless it is an assumption which has *never* been put to the test.

Because overturning received wisdom can be a highly desirable, newsworthy and publishable outcome, you may wish to take risks of this kind. If so, do it with due consideration, and build in enough additional information collection that your resulting thesis is still of interest even if the original assumption was wrong. In this case, what aspects of the MBA were helpful? Which types of career progression were most common or fastest? Is there variation between different types of organisation or different jobs? Is there an age or gender effect? Supplementary questions of this kind can provide the material for an acceptable thesis even if the main question was a risky one and did not turn out as you expected. Of course, it is better to select a main question which itself is characterised by equal interest in possible outcomes.

Feasibility

This is obviously a critical consideration for any proposed project. Attempting the impossible shows lack of judgement. And rather less is possible within the time and resource constraints of an MBA dissertation than many students optimistically assume. If at any time you feel your ideas might be slightly ambitious, stop at once. They are probably wildly unrealistic! All projects have a way of expanding to fill at least twice the time allotted them, so always aim to undershoot, and allow large margins for the unexpected.

As well as checking that the proposed project looks possible within the time constraints of the dissertation, you need to check that it will not require other resources unlikely to be available. These include finance and availability of information. If your project looks as if it will incur costs which neither you nor your sponsor are prepared to bear, then it is unlikely to be feasible unless some other sources of finance can be found. The following also call into question the feasibility of a proposed project: it requires access to classified, or even sensitive, information; you will need information which cannot be obtained without a major investment which neither you nor others in the organisation are prepared to make; it requires the co-operation of those outside the organisation who are highly unlikely to see any reason for co-operating.

The catastrophe factor

This is closely related to aspects of feasibility and should be just as carefully considered. There are less polite ways of describing this aspect of projects, but it stems from the fact that your research is likely to involve a timescale over which considerable change may take place in your organisation. It is impossible to guard against everything. If you are promoted into a job on the other side of the world, or indeed, if you are made redundant, you will have more pressing concerns than whether you will still have access to the information you need to complete your dissertation. Far more improbable catastrophes are still possible, but there are also several fairly likely happenings within any organisation which can seriously impede your project. These include political or personnel change, increase or decrease in workload, and restructuring. You should attempt to assess the probability of such events within your organisation and their likely effect on any proposed topic. Only then can you decide whether the risk is an acceptable one.

If not, could it be reduced by reformulating the topic? You cannot prevent the department you are studying being closed at 24 hours' notice when you are in the midst of collecting your information. If this happens you will need rapidly to change direction. But you can reduce the chances of such disruption by avoiding as a subject for your research any part of the organisation under serious threat.

'Real time' projects, involving ongoing implementation of change or of evaluation of such change as it happens, are particularly vulnerable to catastrophe. Any change to the timescale of the subject of the research can have disastrous effects on a tight project plan. It is far safer to select a topic where data sources already exist. You can then draw upon these within a timescale to suit your project requirements.

Politically sensitive projects are also prone to catastrophe. If the political climate within the organisation shifts, you may find that co-operation is withdrawn and confidentiality restraints placed upon your eventual report.

The above list of factors which should influence your choice of topic will be common to most situations, and should be supplemented by any criteria deriving from your personal list of objectives above.

ACTIVITY

List any personal criteria which are important to you in your choice of topic.

_____

_____

_____

_____

_____

It may seem premature to be thinking about criteria for evaluating project topics before generating possibilities to evaluate, but there is sound methodological sense in this. The argument was outlined in Chapter 12, but will be briefly restated here. If you think about possible options first, and then think about ways of evaluating them, your choice of criteria may be influenced by the characteristics of the option which you at first sight prefer. If you bias the choice in this way, albeit quite unconsciously, it removes the advantage of taking a systematic approach to the choice of option. Many problem-solving methodologies therefore explicitly recommend that measures of effectiveness are specified *before* options are generated, and this is the approach suggested here. You should follow the same pattern in your research if your chosen topic involves recommending a small number of options chosen from a wider range.

GENERATING POSSIBLE TOPICS

You may have a long-standing and burning desire to investigate a particular topic, and regard your dissertation as a heaven-sent opportunity to indulge this wish. But you may instead belong to the larger class of students for whom despair sets in at the prospect of having to find a suitable topic. This may be because you feel your organisation offers no suitable opportunities, or because your boss is antagonistic to the whole thing, or because you still do not really have a clear idea of what is required.

If you are in the first category, you may see topic choice as irrelevant. There is no choice to be considered, and nothing to be gained by generating a range of options which will inevitably be rejected. Nevertheless, you *may* find that there is more value in the exercise than you think. While it is certainly important that a topic interests you, it is equally important that it is of interest to your client, that it will meet your institution's requirements, and that it is 'do-able' within the constraints operating. Your own enthusiasm for a topic may blind you to its shortcomings in these areas, or cause you to underestimate their importance. By forcing yourself to take the generation of alternative topics seriously, and to evaluate your preferred topic against these, you may become more aware of potential hazards. You can then find ways of improving your preferred topic by modifying it to incorporate elements of other options.

If you are in the second, despairing, category, you may have a strong temptation to put off all thought of the project for as long as possible, perhaps hoping that inspiration will occur at some future point. While this *may* happen, it is fairly unusual for a suitable topic to surface by itself. You are far more likely to find yourself in the uncomfortable position of having to choose a project topic in a rush, with your research due to start and no time for proper thought or for discussion with your supervisor and organisation. Under such circumstances it is likely that your chosen topic will not be totally satisfactory to any of you, and you will have difficulties throughout your research in consequence.

If, therefore, you are unhappy about project choice, start work at least six months in advance, giving yourself extra time for this stage, rather than reducing the time available by procrastination.

In any problem situation, your chosen solution will seldom be better than the best option generated. (It can, of course, be worse, if you choose the wrong one!) Your aim at this stage should therefore be to generate as wide a range of possibilities as you can. There are several different things that can help in this. Brainstorming and other creativity techniques were introduced in Chapter 12, and you may have learned more about them during your course. If so, use them!

You can carry out brainstorming of possible topics with fellow students, with colleagues at work, or, ideally, with both. Each group is likely to produce very different options, and by amalgamating two disparate lists you will widen the range. From the lists you can select any item that seems to have in it the germ of a possible project and discuss the most likely with your possible client, perhaps using the successive branching and narrowing approach shown in Fig. 12.1.

ACTIVITY

List the most promising topic areas generated by your brainstorming or other creativity techniques.

_____

_____

_____

_____

_____

_____

Another immensely rich source of possible ideas is the store of past projects submitted. It is customary for universities to keep past successful projects in their libraries. These can be referred to on demand. They form excellent material on which you can practise your scanning and rapid reading techniques. The best ones will give you an idea of how much can be achieved in a dissertation. You may find this inspiring or profoundly depressing! The weaker ones will demonstrate the minimum that is acceptable. If the first category depressed you, this should make you feel better. However, it should not make you complacent. The minimum may be surprisingly low in some institutions, but it would be dangerous to aim for this lowest acceptable level. There may have been extenuating circumstances, or the student may have been extremely lucky not to have had the thesis rejected. In any case, you are unlikely to gain much satisfaction from poor work. Knowing the range of acceptable standards may make the project less threatening: many students find dissertation work unnecessarily stressful because they are aiming for a standard more appropriate to a PhD than a Master's.

Perusing past thesis titles and their abstracts should give you a field of possibilities from which it is possible to select a small number of suitable areas for subsequent development, to be added to those drawn from your brainstorming.

ACTIVITY

Draw a mind map or other diagram to represent the field of recent thesis topics, showing broad areas and sub-areas into which these can be classified.

List thesis titles which suggest projects which would be possible within your own context.

_____

_____

_____

_____

_____

Existing theses can also be used to provide an alternative slant to your search by giving you insight into what it is that makes a project interesting for you.

Select theses which do _not_ strike you as potentially applicable in your own context, but which still look extremely interesting. Analyse these to see whether they have any features in common, or in other ways indicate what your definition of 'interesting' implies. List these features.

_____

_____

_____

_____

_____

The next set of activities involves mapping your organisation and its possibilities. (If an own-company project is absolutely out of the question, you should discuss alternatives with your tutors immediately.) If you are not the first MBA student from your organisation, you may find considerable in-company expertise in the selection of suitable topics. Previous clients of the research and past students will both be good sources, and constitute a valuable resource which you should exploit to the full. If you are breaking new ground and therefore lack this resource, you will need to explain dissertation requirements very carefully to those who will need to approve your plans and to any others whose co-operation will be important.

There are obvious advantages in involving potential clients in topic choice if this is at all possible. They may have many suggestions to make, and these are likely to be topics that are of particular interest to them. If potential clients feel that they were largely responsible for the choice of topic, they will have a much stronger commitment to making the project a success because of their feelings of ownership. The risks attendant on these benefits should, however, be considered, and minimised if possible. Some stem from the very strong organisational meanings attached to 'project', or 'research', meanings which as already indicated may be very different from those prevailing in your institution. You may, therefore, have topics pressed upon you which offer too little or perhaps too much scope for MBA project requirements. It is therefore essential that these requirements are made absolutely clear at the outset of discussions, and that it is understood that the final choice of topic must rest with you and your thesis supervisor.

While many of your discussions will be with superiors, or with an in-company mentor if you have one, or with your training department, do not neglect to seek ideas from colleagues at the same level as yourself or from subordinates. Both groups are likely to have clear ideas about possible problems you might research and can comment usefully on ideas you already have.

ACTIVITY

List three problems of which you have been aware during the last six months, either within your own part of the organisation, or elsewhere.

_____

_____

_____

_____

_____

_____

Use separate pieces of paper to construct multiple-cause diagrams showing contributory factors in each case. Identify common themes between problems, and main causes within each. For each cause or theme, construct a mind map expanding the cause into as many areas as possible. List any project areas suggested by this mapping exercise.

_____

_____

_____

Similarly, think of three changes, either within the organisation or to its environment, which you think will affect the way your job will, or should be, done in the next 12 months. List these.

_____

_____

_____

Again use a mind map to explore related areas for each potential change, and consider whether any of these areas or groups of areas might prove a useful starting point for research. List any which have potential.

_____

_____

_____

An example of a mind map and subsequent thoughts on a possible project in an organisation where it was felt that there might be an absenteeism problem is shown in Fig. 19.1. (Figure 10.2 showed how the related form of diagram, a relevance tree, could be used in much the same way.)

Once you have selected a range of possible topic areas, you need to select a small number for further exploration. It is worth proceeding with several at this stage, as there are a number of criteria to be borne in mind. As your first attempt to assess possibilities against these criteria will necessarily be fairly rough and ready, you should be able to keep anything up to seven possibilities 'live' at this stage. Obviously this will depend to some extent on organisational circumstances.

TOPIC SELECTION

Topic selection is an iterative process, i.e. one that goes round in circles, but progresses a little at each step. You cannot be sure that a topic is suitable until you have invested considerable time and effort into developing your ideas and planning out your research. If at the end of this process you find that the topic is _not_ suitable, you have wasted a lot of time and effort and are back to the start.

To avoid these problems it makes sense to do a very broad-brush, 'quick and dirty' evaluation of a number of projects in parallel, before proceeding to a more

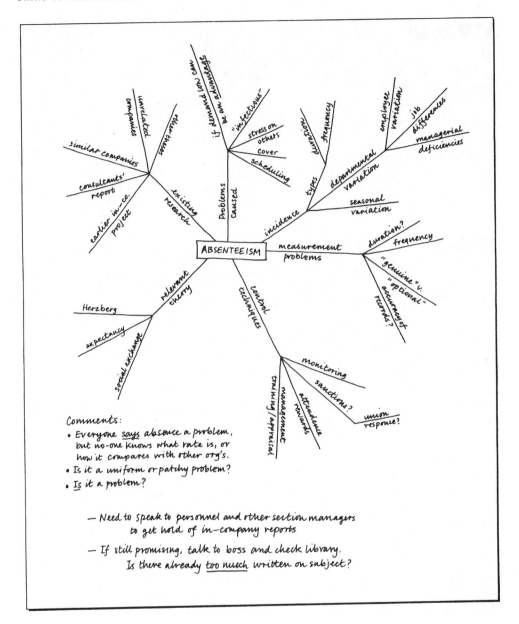

Fig. 19.1 Student's mind map and subsequent thoughts on a possible absenteeism topic

detailed evaluation of a smaller number. After this you will be in a better position to select the option with which to proceed. If you run with enough options at each stage to have a reasonable chance of at least one looking promising by the end of the more detailed pass, then even if a number of possibilities turn out to be unsuitable you will have made progress at each stage.

Figure 19.2 shows a basic algorithm for project choice. This shows the process as

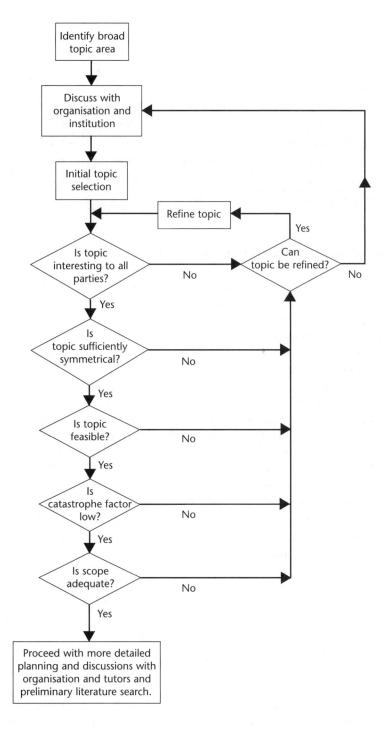

Fig. 19.2 Algorithm for project choice

Criteria	Topic 1	Topic 2	Topic 3	etc.	
Project interests me	● ●	● ● ● ●	● ● ● ● ●		
Client supports project	● ● ●	● ●	● ● ●		
Adequate breadth of topic	● ●	● ● ●	● ● ● ● ●		
Availability of resources	● ● ● ●	● ●	● ● ●		
Absence of political sensitivity	●	● ● ●	✕		
Low reliance on real-time events	●	● ● ●	●		
etc.					

Fig. 19.3 Example of part of a project evaluation table

a series of yes/no decisions for a single topic, which, together with a process of refinement if possible, will enable a single topic to be developed into something which is at least a possibility, or else to be rejected.

If using the suggested broad-brush, multi-topic approach, you would need to use the algorithm on each topic, but of course several topics could be discussed in a single meeting with a potential client.

An alternative approach, or one which could be used to select from those topics which survived the algorithmic approach, would be to construct a *Which?* type diagram (*see* Fig. 19.3), in which you list possible topics and rate them, say from one to five, on each of the criteria which you are using, totalling the points for each option. If you are using such a table *without* using the algorithm first, then you would need a symbol for 'fails to meet criterion', say X. Any option with one or more X's would be rejected, regardless of its 'point' rating.

Two aspects of which you must be particularly aware are real-time dependence and political sensitivity. Both can lead to a high 'catastrophe factor'. If a topic depends upon something happening in real time, avoid it if there is any risk at all that time slippage might occur. It is far, far safer to investigate a situation which already exists.

Be alert, too, to potential political sensitivities. These are harder to spot. Political structures within an organisation may not be immediately obvious, and may change. But think carefully about whether your potential findings could be perceived as a threat by anyone. If so, could this result in difficulties being put in your way at some point during your investigation? Do the people concerned have the power to block access to information or resources, or even to close down your project?

For your second pass you will need to put much more detailed thought into your planning. It is only once your ideas are fairly clear as to how an idea could be developed into a research project that you will be able to see how feasible it is likely to be, given the constraints under which you will be working.

At this stage you will need to be clear as to who your client within the organisation will be for each possible topic. You will need to have detailed discussions with each client, in order to clarify their objectives for the research, and the resources and other support which they could make available to you for your research. It can be extremely helpful to have a written brief from your client at this stage. You will need to make it very clear, however, that you are still at the planning stage, and it may be necessary for the brief to be amended by mutual agreement.

Once your client's objectives are clearly understood, and you have checked these with your project supervisor if this is possible to ensure that a brief of this kind would also allow you to meet institutional objectives, you can analyse the possible topics in more depth. A useful framework for this analysis is to aim to produce a short project proposal for each topic. This should be somewhere in the region of 1000 words, unless your institution specifies something different.

Your proposal should aim to cover:

- *Problem description* – background to the problem, its context and its significance
- *Project aim* – the purpose of the project, its scope and its limitations
- *Value to the organisation* – it is important to establish why the organisation needs to know what the project is intended to establish
- *Likely project design* – possible methodology, timescale and the skills likely to be employed
- *Data requirements* – what information will be needed, how this will be obtained, and what analysis will be carried out.

Obviously there will be scope to alter and develop this proposal as the project develops. Much of your early work will involve detailed consideration of possible methods of carrying out the research to answer whatever question the topic poses and exploring sources of possibly relevant data. But unless you have thought in some detail about these topics at the selection stage you may hit an unexpected block in mid-project. To decide upon a final topic in which to invest your hundreds of hours of work you need to know how the possibilities are likely to compare on the issues described above.

You may have been surprised at the lack of consideration of the need for originality in the above discussion. While good research *is* original in the sense of covering new theoretical or experimental ground – and a PhD thesis would be expected to show considerable originality – this criterion is less important with research at Master's level. Obviously there would be little satisfaction in repeating research already carried out and small value in plagiarising someone else's discussion of methodology, but theoretical originality is not usually expected. The narrow constraints under which you will be operating make it highly unlikely that you will be able to devise and demonstrate some totally new theory of organisational behaviour. An MBA thesis is much better seen as showing creative use of existing theory and techniques to solve a real organisational problem, and this chapter is slanted towards this type of research.

If your final choice of option seems rather less than theoretically revolutionary you should not therefore worry. Your chances of success will be the greater. And there will almost certainly be sufficient challenge in applying existing theory to produce a valid answer to a real problem.

Once you have decided upon a project proposal that is acceptable to your supervisor and your client and of interest to yourself, you should, if at all possible, obtain written agreement to the proposed research and to the necessary access to information required. This may seem unnecessarily legalistic, but it can be a useful precaution. Your client may be wholeheartedly behind your proposal, but there is no guarantee that your client will remain in a position to support you throughout your project. Personnel move, and you might find that someone less sympathetic to your aims takes over. A written agreement will not prevent all the problems this may produce, but can strengthen your case. It is also a useful protection against claims from some quarters that your research is in some sense a failure because it fails to meet the objectives of the complainant. If these were not the agreed objectives of the research, then you will again find the written agreement useful. Even if you hit no such snags, the agreed brief will serve as a useful reference point for yourself, a standard against which you can test any necessary modifications to your plans.

LITERATURE SEARCH

Whatever the type of project you are doing, you are likely to need to make several searches of relevant literature. The first has already been alluded to. In deciding on a suitable topic, you will need to do a fairly superficial trawl of relevant literature. Once the topic has been decided, you will need to do narrower, but more 'in-depth' searches. You will need first to clarify your research question. Then you will need to work out how to approach your own research (this is likely to include searching both the topic and literature on research methodology). Finally, it is important to set your research in context when writing your report – what you do needs to be interpreted in the light of what others have done and found in the area.

How far you need to go will depend upon the type of project you are undertaking. The closer you move to the 'academic' end of the spectrum, the more substantial will be the expected literature review part of your dissertation. Similarly, more in-depth discussion will be expected of how your findings relate to this literature. How far you *can* go will depend upon the resources at your disposal.

Your first problem is knowing where to start, and how. A good first step is to get to know your library and the resources it offers. Libraries contain a wide range of information sources, both traditional print and electronic. This information is systematically and consistently organised and there will be people there who are only too happy to explain the systems to you, and help you to make good use of them. If you are studying by distance learning, find out what electronic resources you can access remotely, and what support is available to you in learning to make use of them. Find out, too, what your local public library offers, and whether there is a convenient university library – students at one university can normally negotiate reader privileges at other university libraries.

Parameters and key words

Once you have at least a rough idea of the question you intend to investigate you can start to set some parameters to help define your search area. You will probably need to know:

- the broad subject area, e.g. marketing, motivation, health and safety legislation
- the language of your search. Note that American and English are different languages! Many words are either completely different (car/automobile) or spelt differently (behaviour/behavior). This is important in electronic searching
- the business sector in which you are interested, e.g. manufacturing, not for profit, defence
- how far back you want to search, e.g. five years
- the type of literature you want to search, e.g. refereed journals only, government publications

You then need to generate a list of *keywords* to drive your search. These are the words you will look up in indexes, or offer a search engine when exploring the World Wide Web. Think about the sorts of words that authors might have used in the title of the kind of article you want to read. A recent review article can be really helpful here, as can the bibliography of a past dissertation in a similar area. Tutors can also be extremely helpful! Try using brainstorming, either individually or with a group of other students or colleagues, to generate possible keywords and phrases. Once you have something to start with, you can use that to generate other possible terms. Suppose you have used a keyword and found a useful-sounding item on the database. If you then display the full entry, it will normally show you 'subject headings' or 'descriptors', or some other term relating to the index terms used. Among these may well be other potentially useful keywords.

Another good technique is to construct a relevance tree (*see* Fig. 10.2). As you draw this, teasing out possible sub-areas, you will be able to think about which you need to search immediately, and which may become the main focus of your research. It can be helpful to highlight each category in a different colour so that you can easily distinguish the 'immediate' from the 'important'.

You can use such a relevance tree as a working document. As you read, you will inevitably refine your thinking about your topic. Update your relevance tree to reflect different ways of looking at the subject which emerge, or new issues which emerge as potentially important.

Using tertiary sources

Indexes are available in print, on microfiche, on CD-ROM and on-line. For a keyword (subject or author name) the index will suggest relevant journal articles or other sources, giving you the full reference for each so that you can look it up, or request it if the library does not own a copy.

Abstracts are indexes which give you not only the reference, but also a brief outline of the content of the article. This may enable you to decide that you do not

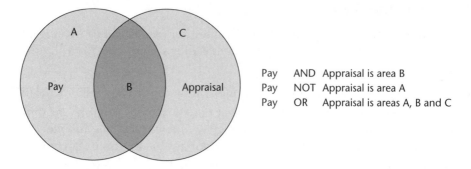

Fig. 19.4 The Boolean logic of searches

need to look at the full article! Electronic forms are taking over from print – CD-ROMs are updated more often than print, and on-line versions are likely to be even more frequently updated, sometimes daily.

Citation indexes are particularly useful if you find a relevant article and want to know how the ideas in it have developed since. A citation index will tell you all the subsequent articles which have referred to that original. (The reference list at the end of the original will give you all the papers which the author used, so between the two you should have good coverage right up to the present.)

You will normally need to use several indexes and abstracts to ensure complete coverage. Consult your librarian if possible over those most likely to be useful.

Print indexes can normally be searched by one word or phrase only. This may produce a frighteningly long list unless your word is newly coined. Electronic indexes offer you the chance to be much more refined in your search, producing a more manageable list of articles, most of which should be relevant provided you have chosen your words and *link terms* carefully. These link terms, derived from Boolean logic, allow you to narrow your search. The terms are AND, OR and NOT (though your system might use '+' and '−' to indicate the same thing, or even some other convention). Figure 19.4 is a pictorial representation of the relationship between these terms.

Thus you could ask for 'pay AND appraisal' (or '+' or whatever) and be offered only references containing both terms, a much shorter list than either 'pay' or 'appraisal' alone. Asking for 'appraisal NOT financial' might spare you hundreds of references on financial appraisal, but still give you a lot of other kinds of appraisal. You might wish to use OR if alternative terms are used for the topic in question, e.g. 'downsizing OR redundancy'. You can also look for part of a word – '*motiv' might generate references on motivation, motivators, etc. Note that the conventions used are yet to be standardised, so you will need to check on the appropriate symbols for each index used.

Merely searching the World Wide Web can take hundreds of hours, so indexes and abstracts can be a more efficient route. They were designed with user needs in mind, and tend to include only reputable sources. The Internet grew, Topsy fashion, and although search engines are becoming more sophisticated all the time, they can still lead you to a wide range of interesting-sounding garbage.

Unfortunately you will almost certainly need to rely on the Internet for some of the information you need, and some up-to-date sources may be accessible only by this route. Be disciplined, though, and avoid pursuing things just because they sound interesting, unless you have hours to spare. And be cautious about the reliance you place on Internet sources. While some (e.g. government sources) are likely to be excellent, others most certainly are not.

If you are searching the World Wide Web for information, it will save you a lot of time if you save references in appropriate directories. Otherwise you may end up with a long list of HTML files which are time consuming to search. When saving, remember to include the copyright statement of the Web page or website and any citation instructions and to note the date on which you last visited the page. You need to give this in your references. If you will be collecting a large number of references, it is much easier if you use a bibliographic software package to help you organise these.

Using what you have found

When you have selected likely sources, and accessed them electronically, or obtained them through a library, you need to remember why you are reading them (*see* Chapter 9), and read, copy and take notes appropriately. If you are planning to include a major literature review section, your notes will need to be fairly detailed. You should normally aim for your literature review to establish current understanding of an area, showing why your research question is worthy of attention. You will also use the fruits of your search at intervals during your report, and particularly in discussion and conclusions sections. Here you will be aiming to show the significance of your own findings in relation to those of others, and may be able to draw on other authors in support of your recommendations. Being aware of these uses while you read will enable you to take more useful notes.

DATA PLANNING

Detailed and realistic project planning is essential, and should begin as soon as you are happy with your project choice, certainly well before you are due to commence your research. This is because you cannot fully assess the feasibility of your proposal until you have a detailed plan of what will be involved. Only then can you start to put timescales to these activities.

No matter how carefully you have done your first two selections, it is still possible to discover snags in a proposed project once detailed planning is carried out, and you need time to go through a third cycle of project choice and develop your second or third choice of option if your first starts to look too risky or is not as feasible as it seemed. Most snags at this stage can be handled by modifications to the proposal, but in the unlikely event of finding that you need to abandon a topic altogether, you do not want this to happen well into the research time. By then it will be a disaster. If it happens before the project is officially due to start, because you are well ahead on your planning, it may be frustrating and annoying, but it is far from catastrophic.

Before you can draw up bar charts or other detailed schedules, you will need to think in considerable detail about your data requirements. For most projects, the bulk of the 'work' consists of data collection and analysis. In conducting your research you will be aiming to collect evidence on the basis of which you can draw convincing conclusions. If your information is deficient, if you do not have enough, if it is not the information you actually need to address your particular issue, or if your information is biased or inaccurate, any subsequent analysis and conclusions will be worthless.

Obviously the data you need will depend upon your chosen topic. Part of your course should be directed towards enabling you to understand how to go about detailed analysis of data requirements, where you can go to find different sorts of data, how, for example, to design a questionnaire that will tell you what you need to know, how big a sample you need in order to obtain a statistically valid result, and so on. However, you may not learn these things until you are starting your research. This is rather late to be indulging in the detailed planning which you cannot do without an understanding of data needs, so you may be caught in a time trap. This chapter aims to indicate, very briefly, the sorts of issues which are important. Suggestions are given for further reading which will allow you to make a more detailed study of data requirements and possibilities if timescales, or the content of your particular course, lead you to feel that this is necessary.

Two important distinctions in considering the data you will need concern primary versus secondary and quantitative versus qualitative data.

Primary data are those that you collect yourself. This might be by direct observation, by interview, by application of a questionnaire, or other means. Primary data can be tailored to your particular requirements. You can design a questionnaire to give you answers to precisely the question of concern to you, administer it to an appropriate sample, and know exactly under what conditions it was administered. You know how accurate the data are, and should have a clear idea of any ways in which inaccuracies might have crept in. Unfortunately you pay a significant price for all these advantages. Collecting valid data tends to be very time-consuming.

Secondary data are those collected by others. These might be the results of surveys carried out by others, government statistics, in-company statistics or records, etc. By using secondary data you will have access to far more information than you could possibly collect yourself, and much more rapidly. But you may not know how much reliance to place upon it, particularly if it was gathered for purposes very different from your own. Even data that might be expected to be perfectly straightforward and reliable, such as a section's weekly production figures, may have been manipulated by those responsible for their compilation. The figures might be compiled in such a way as to keep senior management off the back of the section head by showing output as steady from week to week. Overall total might be right, but some output from a good week might be 'stockpiled', to be used to raise output figures in poor weeks. If your purpose was to explore correlates of variations in output, the figures would be of little use. It is important to be aware of the possible limitations of any data which you have not collected yourself, and to check, if at all possible, what factors may have influenced it. You also need to bear possible unreliabilities in mind when drawing conclusions.

When talking of data it is *quantitative* data, that involving numbers, which readily springs to mind. But important factors in a situation may be very hard to quantify. Attitudes and feelings may be important. Variations in perceptions, for example, the different ways in which different groups of participants in a situation would map the relevant (for them) factors in a situation, may be highly significant. Because techniques for structuring such *qualitative* information, and deciding on the reliance to be placed upon it, are less well-known than the techniques of basic parametric statistics, such factors may be omitted altogether. If not, numbers may be attributed to them, and totally invalid ways of interpreting those numbers attempted.

This may be clearer if you consider data using the classification usually applied in discussions of research. *Textual* data refers to verbal description, for example quotations from an article or an interview. Such data can be a splendid source of ideas and create a vivid picture for the recipient. An interviewee might tell you in all too graphic terms precisely what is wrong with his or her boss, or the organisation, or anything about which you choose to ask. He or she might describe precisely what should be done to solve the organisation's problems. But it is very difficult to know what reliance to place upon this information. Does this interviewee have some axe to grind? How common is this perception? There *are* occasions when such text can itself provide the basis for a more quantitative analysis, for example, in examining the commonest sequences of moves in a large sample of transcripts of negotiations, but this involves fairly specialist techniques. If you are planning to make heavy use of textual data you should consult your thesis supervisor to make sure that you will be using it in a way that will be acceptable to the institution. Some of the qualitative data you will need may well be of a textual kind, until you find some way of at least partially quantifying the information.

Nominal or *categorical* data refers to data where some classification has been made, e.g. into country of origin, or type of first degree held by graduate managers. It is possible to count the members of each category, but even if the categories are identified by numbers, for example you might label the category 'chemists' as 1, 'biologists' as 2, etc., it is impossible to relate categories mathematically. Two chemists would in no meaningful sense equal one biologist!

Again, some of the qualitative information you seek may be capable of being categorised in a nominal fashion.

Ordinal or *ranked* data are those where it is possible to make some comparisons between different categories. Interviewers might, for example, categorise applicants into highly suitable, probably good, acceptable, would need significant training, and non-appointable. If highly suitable was 5 and non-appointable 1 then showing the distribution between the rankings at different appointment panels would carry some information. But you could not suggest that the difference between a '5' candidate and a '4' candidate was in any sense 'equal' to the difference between a '1' and a '2', nor that a '4' was twice as good as a '2'. Equally, it would be invalid to use any sort of statistics that assumed that this was what the numbers meant.

Interval data are those where it *is* possible to assume that differences between numbers mean something. The difference between 25 degrees centigrade and 35 degrees is the same as that between 45 degrees and 55. But there is no real zero on this scale. It was mere convenience that determined that the freezing point of water should be designated zero. So 40 degrees is not twice as hot as 20 degrees. Questionnaire scores on attitude questionnaires might, for example, be capable of being treated as interval data, though more usually they would be ordinal.

Ratio data are those where not only are intervals meaningful, but there is a real zero as well, so that ratios also make sense. 40 people out of work is twice as many as 20. An inflation rate of 12 per cent is three times that of 4 per cent, and it is meaningful to make such a statement. Ratio data are the only ones on which you can use any mathematical technique you wish. Even with ratio data you may not be able to use all statistical techniques, however, as some are more sensitive than others to the distribution of values you are likely to find in the sample you are looking at. With statistics, if you are not an expert it makes excellent sense to discuss your plans with someone who is!

Whatever the type of data you are planning to collect, you should conduct the following checks on your proposals.

How accurate and reliable are the data?

Would a different observer obtain the same result? If there could be a bias, in which direction are the results likely to be influenced? Are all relevant incidents (e.g. accidents) being recorded? If not, are omissions random, or most likely to occur in one particular direction?

Is the sample large enough to warrant the conclusions drawn from it?

Refer to your statistics course notes to decide what size of sample you need if you are planning quantitative data. Remember that you may well end up with less data than you initially think. Return rate on questionnaires usually falls far short of 100 per cent. Interviews may be cancelled at short notice, and so on. Allow for a reasonable rate of attrition, and plan your data collection so that your sample, even after this, is large enough.

Is your sample sufficiently representative of the population in which you are interested?

You would be unwise to predict the election results on the basis of a survey of home-owners, for example. Yet students all too frequently survey one very narrow section of their organisation, and on the basis of their findings go on to make sweeping recommendations concerning the entire organisation, if not the world. I was not impressed by a dissertation I examined recently which reported unstructured interviews with six people, all of whom had a distinctly partial view of the issue in question. On the basis of their expressed opinions the student made recommendations for a complete restructuring of the national sector of which their organisation was a part. This sample was so small, and so unrepresentative of the full range of people affected, that the dissertation demonstrated an ignorance of the rules for drawing conclusions from evidence so staggering as to constitute an academic crime.

Do the data actually measure what they purport to measure?

If you have devised a questionnaire, does it really measure what you think it does? How can you check? Is in-company data to be taken at face value? If at all possible talk to those responsible for putting the figures together. I still remember the difference between the wage clerks and management as to how a bonus scheme actually worked at one of the sites I visited in the course of a research project. I was attempting to answer what I thought was a simple question as to how much people were paid. The clerks' description of how it worked (the better you worked, the less you were paid) was, once they had explained *why* this was the case, the more convincing one. So try to find some way of checking any information. If you ask interviewees to describe an organisation's appraisal scheme they may all tell you that appraisals are carried out annually. Ask them to show you their last appraisal report, or to tell you the date at which their last appraisal interview was carried out, and a very different picture may emerge.

In considering your data requirements you will need to bear all the above factors in mind, and relate them to the particular question which you are trying to answer. This is a difficult task, and one in which you should take advantage of all the help you can get, whether from your project supervisor, fellow students who understand statistics, or those within your organisation in a position to know what information may be available and how it might be obtained.

PROJECT PLANNING AND CONTROL

A detailed project plan will be the key element in your project management. It will provide the standard against which you will monitor your progress for the duration of your research, and through to the point of submitting your completed dissertation. Many dissertations go wrong because of faulty control, yet the use of simple project management techniques, which will almost certainly have been covered in your course, should prevent this. The use of such techniques should provide a fairly tight schedule of tasks, thus avoiding the 'I don't know where to start, so I won't' syndrome that afflicts some students.

Your plan should provide you with a series of planned completion dates for the various tasks involved. This will enable you to be aware immediately of any time slippage, and to take steps to remedy this, seeking help from your thesis supervisor if necessary. Many students *not* using project management techniques realise that something is seriously wrong only when it is far too late to do anything to repair the damage. Interim target dates will do more than merely reassure you that you are on course. They will have a major effect in sustaining your motivation, as each target met will be a source of satisfaction. If the only date towards which you are working is your final submission date, it is all too easy to feel that you are making no progress at all on the project, and to become demotivated in consequence. This is a splendid example of a vicious circle with failure as the most likely outcome.

Now that you have clarified the aims of your research through discussions with your client, and thought in detail about your likely data requirements, you are in a position to think about the activities which will be needed in order to acquire and analyse the data, and to schedule these so as to allow you to complete your dissertation within the time allowed.

By the time you are preparing your dissertation your coursework will almost certainly have covered the use of network analysis for planning and the use of bar charts for schedule control. There is therefore no need for a detailed description of the techniques here. In any case, the basic techniques are straightforward. The difficulty lies, as it would whatever approach you took, in deciding on the best route to your chosen objectives.

Choosing the right methodology

Your first decision will concern choice of an appropriate methodology. Can your question be answered by a search of the literature alone? Do you need to survey a large group of people within the organisation? If so, do you want to do this by postal questionnaires or could you use e-mail for your survey? What about administering questionnaires to groups under your supervision? If the organisation agrees to the loss of working time the latter method improves response rates enormously!

Are questionnaires, in whatever medium, the best approach? Would less formal methods, such as casual observation or conversation be appropriate, perhaps at an initial stage to indicate the shape necessary for more formal approaches? Would research into the history of your own or another company serve your purpose? Do you need to obtain some of your information from external sources? Do you need to involve a group of people within the organisation in joint problem solving, as is the case with some systems methodologies? Do you need to build mathematical models and test your ideas using these? Do you need to experiment with alternative ways of working in order to gain an idea of their relative effectiveness?

Once you are clear on these sorts of issues, you can start to draw up a list of the activities that will be needed to achieve your objectives, and the order in which these will need to be carried out. If your plans include the design and use of a questionnaire, then necessary activities will include informal discussions with a small number of people in order to refine your ideas about the design of the questionnaire, and drafting a first version of this. Piloting the draft on a small sample provides a check that there are no ambiguities, that the questions are interpreted as you intended (you can check this by interviewing the people involved after they have filled in the questionnaire), and that the thing can be completed within a reasonable time.

Possibly in parallel with this, you will have to decide on the size of sample needed and how this should be selected. Once this has been decided you may need to gain organisational approval to your approaching the sample. Then you will probably wish to notify your sample in some way that your research is under way and explain its purpose so that you are more likely to get questionnaires returned and completed in an honest way. You will need to set up some mechanism for distributing and collecting questionnaires, you will need to have your final version duplicated in sufficient quantities, and so on.

Whatever your proposed research design there will be a similar set of inter-related activities, all of which will need to be carried out if the project is to be successful. Once you have listed these activities you can order them, showing which must be completed before any given activity can be commenced, and which can be undertaken in parallel with it.

Estimates can also be made of the time that will be needed to complete each activity. It is important to be realistic, i.e. pessimistic, in these estimates, particularly for activities late in the sequence, where flexibility to compensate for any slippage will be almost non-existent. It is important, too, to allow for less than prompt co-operation from others. You may need to send out one or more reminders to people to return questionnaires, or to wait some time for answers to letters requesting information. Key people may be out of the country at the point when you had planned to interview them. Your supervisor may be prepared to read and comment on your first draft of your thesis, but may need a week or two (or more) to do this.

If you are relying on someone else to type your thesis, you must allow them time to fit it into their schedule, and be prepared for them to be slow if you miss your promised handover date. If you are word processing it yourself, do not underestimate the time that this will entail, especially if you have not followed the advice in Chapter 4 on developing the necessary skills prior to the start of your course, and that in Chapter 15 on starting the drafting process early.

Drawing up a realistic schedule

In scheduling your activities, make reasonable allowance for times when you know that you will be unusually busy in your job, and set yourself a lighter project workload at these points to compensate. Build in some slack for unexpected conflicting demands, too. If your initial schedule cannot be made to allow for such slack then you should revise your objectives to something more modest.

If using a PC for your scheduling you will be able to print out bar charts and revisions of bar charts with relative ease. If scheduling 'by hand' it is still worth the effort of drawing a bar chart. It provides a visible prompt to activity, and an overview of the pattern of your activities. It shows where slippage is possible and where it is critical that it does not occur. As it is almost inevitable that you will need to reschedule, and to add in activities that you omitted first time, it is worth leaving room at the end for extra activities, and then running off a number of blanks before you add the bars. This will make rescheduling less of a chore. Alternatively, you can use re-stickable paper for the bars. Whichever labour-saving device you use, it is important that you can draw up new schedules without wasting time when the need arises. It is not efficient to work from an out-of-date schedule, or one altered beyond the point of legibility.

Figure 19.5 shows an example of part of a hand-drawn schedule. Note that scope for slippage is indicated by the dotted areas after the bars. This should not,

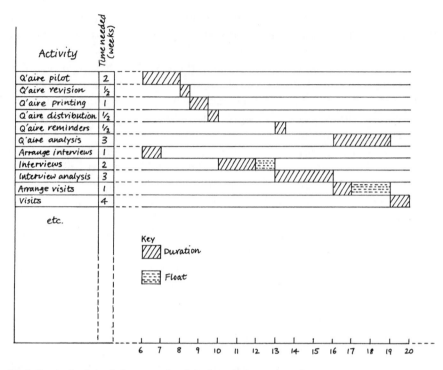

Fig. 19.5 Part of a hand-drawn schedule for project planning

however, be taken as a licence to use the slack whenever you feel a little tired. The knock-on effects of this in terms of unreasonably high workloads in subsequent weeks would make a nonsense of all your planning and seriously threaten your success. Even deliberate slack should be saved for genuine emergencies rather than minor reluctance to work. If you use up your slack early in the project because of slight illness or mild overload at work, there will be none left when the real disaster hits you later on.

ACTIVITY

Work out a bar chart for your proposed project. Once it is complete, perform the following checks.

1. Starting at the end, check that you have included *all* the activities that must take place prior to the end activity. Work back through the chart checking that for *each* activity all the necessary preceding activities are represented.

2. Check that you have indeed scheduled these preceding activities *before* the activities that require their prior completion.

3. Check that you have built any necessary waiting time (e.g. for return of questionnaires, duplication, or data processing by others) into your schedule.

4. Check the workload for each week, to ensure that the total is never excessive.

5. Check that your schedule is compatible with expected peaks in job or other conflicting demands.

6. Look at all activities where the float, or capacity for slippage, is small or non-existent, and check that your time estimates for these activities are realistic.

Comment

If the above activity gives you any cause for concern you should consult with your client and your project supervisor about ways in which the scope of the project could be reduced slightly, to make it more likely that you will be able to complete it successfully within the constraints operating.

Once you have a schedule which seems realistic to you and covers all that you think will be necessary, with sufficient slack for the later inclusion of things that you will subsequently realise are needed or for problems encountered elsewhere, you have your main project control tool. All that you need to do now is to *use* it.

It may be helpful to highlight major milestones in your research, and the dates by which these must be reached. You have already passed two – topic choice and completion of planning! It is likely that others will be completion of your literature search, collection of information, completion of analysis, first draft of your thesis and final submission date. Highlight these points on your chart. (Some students show *only* these activities on their project plans, but such a lack of detail is virtually useless. I hope that the above discussion and activity led you to draw up a far more detailed chart.)

Add any milestones which are important to your particular institution. You may be required to submit revised plans or draft chapters at intervals. If so, submission dates for these should be noted.

Now draw a large version of your chart and put it above your desk and make a smaller version for your diary. Refer to your chart at least once a week to ensure that you are on, or ahead of, target. The whole process can be made more fun, and can provide you with the satisfaction of a visible record of progress, if you colour in activities as they are completed.

If you do encounter an unexpected block, then use your chart to see where you could get ahead to compensate, so that the time scheduled for project work during the period you are blocked is still put to effective use.

Writing the first draft

One activity which can be brought much further ahead than is often realised is the first draft of parts of the thesis. It may seem absurd to start this while data collection is only just beginning and you have little idea of what your conclusions will be, but it can be most enlightening to write a skeleton draft, using guesses at what results might be. Often you will discover a need for additional data, as even if results do turn out as expected, they will support only a weak argument. By trying to construct that argument it becomes clear how additional pieces of information would strengthen your case enormously. If you are finding this out while still at the data collection stage, you can alter your plans and produce a much better piece of research in consequence. By the time you are officially 'writing up', it is usually too late for this.

Thus the project choice phase is not the only one that should be seen as an iterative process. As with any complex problem-solving activity, a constant process of thought, experiment and refining your thought is necessary. This point is made explicit in many of the systems methodologies, some of which you may be taught during your course. The process also reflects the Kolb learning cycle introduced in Chapter 8. We cannot make sense of complexity all at once. But we can make a little sense of it, work with our new ideas, see ways in which they can be improved, try the new ideas, see further weaknesses and ways forward, and so on. Thus step by step we come to an improved understanding.

An MBA project will almost certainly fall into this category of making progressive sense of complexity. You should, therefore, be aware at all times of the possible need to go back and slightly revise earlier thoughts. It is usually by such apparently backward steps that true progress is made. Similarly you should try to make experimental steps forward, as, for example, by trying an early draft, or analysing dummy material, to check out your ideas while there is still time for change.

Many problem-solving methodologies recommend several loops around the whole problem-solving cycle before a satisfactory solution is likely to be reached. You are likely to be operating under such tight time constraints that repeated iterations will not be possible, but you can approximate to this by doing 'quick and dirty' mini-studies to check on your intended directions, and by the sorts of jumps ahead suggested.

Keeping a project log

As well as your chart and its colour scheme, you should keep a more detailed record of progress in the form of a project log. In this you should record all project activity, times taken, details of what happened, snags encountered and insights gained. This can be enormously helpful to you when you come to write up your work, as it can be surprising how easily things which seemed burned into your memory at the time fade into oblivion. Your log can be a source of observations made at the time and eminently quotable at appropriate points in your thesis. Furthermore, many students are asked to include in, or with, their thesis a reflection on lessons learned, and how with hindsight the project could have been improved. This is intended to demonstrate that you have indeed learned something about the process of this kind of research, and how to be critical of such investigations. (It can also be a valuable source of necessary marks for the student for whom everything has gone wrong.) Your project log will be invaluable in writing such a 'reflections' section.

Either in your log or on your computer or somewhere, all together where they could not possibly get lost, you should keep a full record of *all* sources referred to. Chapter 15 highlighted the enormous amount of time which can be wasted by having to hunt for part of a reference which you omitted to note (*which* journal was it in?) or a reference that you had on a piece of paper which somehow seems to have vanished. Even if it seems unlikely that you will need to refer to something, if it is remotely possible that you could use it, note it. It may turn out to be extremely relevant once you have developed your ideas.

With your schedule, your interim dates and your coloured pens, you will have every chance of keeping on target, and of avoiding the stress, even agony, which many less organised students experience. But things can still go wrong. You can encounter unexpected resistance at work, or find the whole place shut down, or hit major problems at home. If this happens, shout for help at once. Discuss your best course of action with your project supervisor, and keep him or her continually informed of the situation. Keep your client informed too. It is not a sign of weakness to admit to things turning out differently from anticipated. The weakness lies in refusing to admit that this has happened until it is too late for plans to be revised or other remedial action taken. A small amount of optimism may be justified. Things may look better tomorrow. But if they are still looking equally bad next week, do something!

WRITING UP

Drafting their thesis is seen by many students as a horrendous task, looming ever closer on the horizon, both dreaded and postponed. In consequence, far too little time is left, revisions cannot be made, some parts are ill thought out, and the resulting thesis is equally depressing to student and examiner. Your client is unlikely to be thrilled by it either.

If you have followed the suggested practice of writing skeleton drafts at an early stage, and are reasonably competent at word processing, the drafting process can be relatively painless. You will know that revisions are easily made, your skeleton drafts can be amended and made use of, your references will be already on the computer, and you will presumably be using your PC for some, at least, of your data analysis, probably using a package which means that figures and graphs can be easily integrated into your report.

The basics of report writing have already been covered in Chapter 15. Refer back to this if you feel the need. This chapter will discuss only those drafting points specific to dissertations and theses.

Who is the audience?

The first, and crucial point is to find out the required audience for your report. Are you expected to submit a thesis addressed to your client, to the academic examiner, or in some way to blur the issue and write a sort of multi-purpose report. This would need to be not so theoretical as to disgust your organisation, who just wanted to know what to do about something that was bothering them. They are not really concerned about the extent to which you have adopted a position that could be described as 'weak logical positivist', or how appropriate a 'grounded theory' approach is to the problem. But it would need to convince your examiners that you *do* understand such methodological considerations, and that you have thoroughly searched the relevant literature to find theories and techniques and data relevant to your chosen problem.

Analysis will present fewer conflicts. Both audiences are likely to need convincing that your analytical techniques are appropriate to the type of data you have collected and to the questions in which you are interested, and that you have used them correctly. Both will want to know that the data you have collected form an adequate basis for the conclusions that you are drawing. And both will require that your presentation is clear, your arguments logical, and your recommendations sensible, unambiguous and ordered according to reasonable priorities.

Both will probably also appreciate suggestions as to future steps to be taken in order to implement your recommendations, though your examiners are likely to be the only ones concerned with your reflections on the progress of the project and the lessons that you learned.

Obviously it is important that your submitted thesis is written for the prime benefit of your examiners. If they do not require the submission of a client report, then you should probably consider 'versioning' your thesis for company use. With a word processor this is a minor task, and well worth the slight effort if you wish your recommendations to be acted on by the organisation, and your own image to be enhanced.

The following broad framework is likely to be appropriate for your examiners:

Title Page
1–2 page summary – you may be required to submit this separately, rather than binding it with the thesis
Preface and acknowledgements
List of contents – numbering should usually reflect major and minor sections, e.g. 4, 4.1, 4.2, etc.
List of tables, figures, etc.
Numbered sub-titled sections – these should include an initial statement of project aims, a short statement of major findings and recommendations, and then detailed descriptions of relevant literature, chosen methodology with justification, data collected, analysis, conclusions, and probably reflections
List of references
Additional bibliography – if needed
Appendices.

Style should be clear, avoiding the use of unnecessary jargon, but using academic concepts where appropriate. Avoid being over-colloquial, and making unsupported assertions. It should be very clear how results are derived, and any shortcomings in the data should be discussed. A short introduction to each section can help make the structure of your arguments clearer to your reader, and the inclusion of relevant diagrams and tables (unless these are very complicated) will help your reader by clarifying points and by breaking up the text. Very detailed or complex information should be included as an appendix. It would interrupt your argument if it was in the main text.

If you can afford it, use good quality paper, as it improves the overall impression given by the report. Pay attention to diagrams, too. These should be either computer generated, or very carefully drawn by hand. Scrappy diagrams do not contribute to a good overall impression. And make sure that you know what type of binding is required. If none is specified, think carefully about the most appropriate and durable way of binding your thesis.

Do check your spelling. Theses have been sent back for correction of spelling errors and this would be disappointing. In any case, spelling mistakes detract from the overall impression created. Check, too, that you have not made mistakes when typing numbers, as errors here are more serious.

Even if you are not *required* to submit a draft of part of your thesis, the point was made earlier that your supervisor's comments on such a draft can be invaluable. It is important to check that your style, level of analysis and use of academic sources is what is required by the institution. There may be simple ways in which major improvements can be made, and you should find out about these at an early stage if at all possible.

If you start your drafting early, have developed your report-writing skills earlier in your course, and have word processing available, then the drafting of your thesis can be one of the most satisfying parts of your whole course. You are creating a substantial piece of work based on your own findings, and are seeing this take shape before your eyes. Far from a chore, this can be enormously exciting.

SUMMARY

- MBA research is usually directed towards a real organisational problem.
- You should start work on your initial planning months in advance of the official project start.
- Topic choice is critical, and should be an iterative process involving yourself, your project supervisor and your organisational client.
- A good topic is interesting to all parties, gives sufficient scope, exhibits symmetry of outcomes, is feasible and not too prone to catastrophe.
- Detailed project planning is essential, and cannot be undertaken until you have a clear idea of how you will proceed and the data that will be required.
- Networks and bar charts are invaluable for project control.
- Work should be as iterative as possible, with dummy analyses of data carried out and skeleton reports drafted well before data collection is complete.
- Analysis should be appropriate to the type of data collected.
- The final report should be clear, well presented and directed towards the right audience.

Further information

Easterby-Smith, M., Thorpe, R. and Lowe, A. (1991) *Management Research: An Introduction*, Sage.

Glaser, B.G. and Strauss, A.L. (1967) *The Discovery of Grounded Theory, strategies for qualitative research*, Weidenfeld & Nicholson. This is a classic text on qualitative approaches.

Howard, K. and Peters, J. (1990) 'Managing Management Research.' This is a special issue of *Management Decision* (Vol. 28, No. 5). It provides a clear, fairly brief coverage of different types of management research, what is involved, and a short but useful bibliography.

Howard, K. and Sharp, J.A. (1983) *The Management of a Student Research Project*, Gower. This is aimed at all types of research, not just management, but covers planning, data collection and analysis in far more detail than was possible here.

Jankovicz, A.D. (1995) *Business Research Projects* (2nd edn), Chapman and Hall. This covers projects from undergraduate through to Master's level, and gives excellent practical guidance.

Lee, T.W. (1999) *Using Qualitative Methods in Organizational Research*, Sage.

AFTERWARDS

20 Beyond your Master's...

Objectives

By the end of this chapter you should:

- have considered how to sustain the learning habit
- have a clear idea of your objectives for the next five years
- appreciate the range of options open to you
- have decided upon your preferred option
- be starting to work towards implementing that option
- know how to go about researching a job opportunity and making an effective application, if this is necessary.

INTRODUCTION

If you have now finished, or are about to finish, your Master's degree, congratulations are due. It is a considerable achievement, the more so if you have been studying part time, and balancing the demands of job and course.

You have two last tasks, if you are to gain the full benefit from your studies. The first is to think about how you can sustain the 'learning habit' into the future. In a rapidly changing world, with 'knowledge management' on everyone's agenda, and the information explosion radically changing the management landscape, lifelong learning is far more than a politician's slick phrase. It is a prerequisite for your continued work success, and for the success of any organisations with which you are connected. Ideas about how managers learn, and what this meant about how best to study, were introduced in Chapter 8. You now need to think about how to consolidate this into the rest of your life.

Your second task is to review your life objectives, and see whether, having gained your qualification, you need to take further steps in order to achieve these. You may already have done this during your programme, but if not, this chapter offers a framework for doing so, and suggestions as to how to implement your chosen strategy. It covers the range of options that may now be open to you, and how to choose between them. There is also guidance on researching job opportunities, preparing an application and making a good impression during an interview.

In going through this process you will in a sense be treating yourself as a live case study, and putting into immediate practice skills which your course will have developed. Furthermore, this will be in a context of obvious personal relevance and importance.

LIFELONG LEARNING

You may by now be 'addicted' to the excitement of learning, of suddenly making sense of a situation in a new way because of a theory or concept, or of knowing that you have done something better than before because of improved skills. On the other hand, you may feel your brain has been stretched for too long, and you just want a rest! Either way, you probably cannot *afford* simply to stop.

As lifelong careers (*see* later in the chapter) become less common, responsibility for management learning is shifting from the employer to the individual manager. Your future employability will depend on your continued learning, so it is very much in your interest to accept this responsibility.

The learning skills you have developed while studying may therefore be among the most valuable things gained from the programme, and it is worth thinking about how to carry these forward into your future. Without the discipline of your course, and the goad of assignments and examinations, it is easy for the pressure of everyday work to drive out all else. You then become trapped in the 'experience' part of the Kolb learning cycle described in Chapter 8, and do not go through the other stages necessary for continued learning.

To avoid this, you need to find a way of continuing to reflect on your experience, of developing your repertoire of useful concepts, and of testing these against the radically changing world in which you are likely to be working. There are thus several elements to a sustained learning habit.

- *Reflection*. Time needs to be scheduled for this, whether daily, weekly, at the end of each significant assignment or all of these. If you have been in the habit of keeping a learning diary, as suggested in Chapter 8, you will find it useful to continue this. If not, starting such a diary may go some way to replacing the course experience. Some reflection can usefully be done in discussion with colleagues. A key strand in the emerging discipline of knowledge management is the need to make tacit knowledge (things that we know, but have not yet put into words, even for ourselves) explicit. This knowledge can then be more easily retained and shared within the organisation. If this is to be achieved, the process needs to be recognised as important, and time scheduled for the necessary thinking and discussion.

- *Theorising*. You already have, as a result of your course, a wide range of theories and concepts at your disposal. Try to continue the habit of applying these to your work experience, applying them in new contexts as part of your process of making sense of what is happening in your organisation, and what you are doing in response to this. Expand your repertoire by judicious reading, surfing, and attendance at professional meetings and conferences. (Remember to keep exercising your critical skills – many management books, papers and presentations are fairly superficial and/or based on inadequate evidence or dubious assumptions.)

- *Testing.* As you encounter new ideas, and develop your own, continue the process of deliberately testing them against your experience as a manager. Only thus can you develop an improved portfolio of conceptual tools.

- *Practise.* In the above you will be practising your learning skills, and some of your critical ones. There will be more concrete skills which you can continue to practise, too. There is probably still room to develop your communication skills in a range of contexts, perhaps IT skills can be extended, or analytical skills and techniques progressed further.

It is worth taking time to think about skills you would still like to develop, as well as how to ensure that your 'reflective practitioner' skills are sustained. Use the following activity as the basis for doing this, deciding on targets and review dates, and noting the latter in your diary.

ACTIVITY

1. If you have not been keeping a learning diary, revisit the section in Chapter 8 on this, and consider whether now would be a good time to start. If so, decide on its form, and take any necessary steps to assemble a framework.
2. Think about suitable times for regular reflection, and any key events after which it would be appropriate to consider learning. Think too about which occasions would be suitable for group reflection. Take steps to ensure that such reflection takes place.
3. List skills which you would like to develop further, and develop a plan (with actions and target dates) for this development. It may be useful to discuss this with your manager, perhaps in the context of an appraisal interview. (Remember the importance of feedback on performance in developing skills.)
4. List areas of interest, where you would like to find out more, and think about ways in which you can achieve this, again developing a plan with target dates. (Update this regularly, as new areas become important.)
5. Whether or not you are keeping a learning diary, make sure that you schedule regular sessions (perhaps three monthly) to spend some time thinking about whether you are continuing to practise your learning skills, and to consolidate what you have learned.

REASSESSING YOUR OBJECTIVES

You should refer to the objectives trees you constructed while working through Chapter 3, and consider the extent they need to be modified now that you have attained at least one of your objectives.

ACTIVITY

If modification is needed, construct a new set of objectives trees showing your goals for the next five years. Do not restrict yourself at this point to career objectives. Start with the wider set of life objectives and nest your career objectives within these. It is important to spend some time thinking carefully about your objectives. They may well have changed significantly as a result of your studies. Unless you acknowledge these changes and their implications, you are unlikely to gain the full potential benefit from your MBA.

EXPLORING OPTIONS

Once you are clear about your medium-term objectives and the shorter-term goals needed to meet them, you can think about ways of achieving these. While your options are likely to be highly personal so that any discussion here will be of limited usefulness, some general points are worth raising.

You may well have broadened your appreciation of the paths available through discussions with fellow students. Perhaps some of them were in jobs which seem attractive to you and which you had never previously considered. You will by now realise that it is important that you generate as wide a range of options as possible, so need to go beyond this chance suggestion of possibilities. You should by now be well aware of the advantages of brainstorming as a technique for doing this. As with so many of the topics in this book, working with a small group of others can be extremely helpful in encouraging creativity and ensuring breadth of approach.

When checking your brainstormed options, you may find it helpful to compare the range of ideas produced with the whole potential field. Logically, the field of options can be divided into:

- making no change
- staying with your present organisation but doing something different, either within your present job or in a different job
- doing a similar job with a different organisation
- doing a different job with a different organisation
- doing something completely different.

It might be well worth looking at all these categories of option to see whether they have potential in relation to your objectives as redefined. Even if you are sure that you *know* the obvious next step for you, it can stimulate your thinking to try to find ways in which, for example, doing something completely different might be made to satisfy your objectives. Sometimes the obvious next step is not necessarily on the shortest path to where you ultimately want to be.

If you favour making no change, do not feel guilty about being unenterprising. If your job is fully satisfying and continues to provide you with all the challenges that you need, then why not stay with it? Provided that your choice is a positive one and not the result of nervousness about the unfamiliar or inability to think of anything different, it can be viewed as a positive course of action.

If your choice is to seek a change in responsibilities within your organisation, you will need to think carefully about the changes that you would ideally like and consult with others in the organisation (perhaps your mentor, a training manager, your own manager and a senior manager in the area you would like to move to) about the best ways in which the desired changes might be brought about. Your focus should be, first, on what it is you want to achieve, given the increased skills and altered perspective gained from your course. Second, you should look at how these might be taken advantage of by your organisation. Only then should you consider specific posts which might be suitable.

It can be fairly limiting to restrict your choice to jobs that are currently vacant, choosing the best from among them. A better route to job enhancement might in many cases be offered by adding additional roles to your current job. You might wish to think about whether getting involved in management development as a trainer offers you scope for using and further enhancing your skills. Are there any major in-company projects starting up in which it would be interesting to be involved? If so, could you persuade your organisation that you could make a worthwhile contribution to one of these? Is there a problem which you know of, and which you might be able to tackle as an in-company consultancy exercise? Would a secondment offer opportunities? This could be to another part of your own organisation or to a different organisation.

If you think that you would like to move to another organisation, then a similar approach to deciding just what you want, and finding the best way of getting it, should be adopted. Again, this is normally preferable to merely scanning vacancies, although there is no reason why you should not do the latter in parallel. You will recognise the arguments from the discussion of how to approach case studies and project work. It was argued there that it was important to look at objectives and measures of effectiveness *before* looking at possible options. Otherwise, a particular option might slant your thinking and limit your choice in consequence. What was important for a case study is even more so when your future is in question.

Research your chosen organisation

If you do think that another organisation would offer you more scope than your present one, research your chosen organisation carefully. It is very easy to write attractive-sounding advertisements, and the job described may sound far more exciting than your own. But recruitment specialists resemble estate agents. A wonderful house on paper may turn out very ordinary when you visit. Your own home may be far better, although you would never have thought of describing it in such glowing terms. Jobs may be similarly distorted in descriptions in advertisements.

It is fairly easy to see many of the merits and demerits of a house at a single visit. It is much more difficult to assess the advantages and disadvantages of a potential job. You may receive a highly edited description in any further particulars you are sent or when you ask questions at an interview. The organisation, after all, may be primarily concerned with selling the vacancy to potential applicants, not realising that lack of honesty at recruitment can lead to expensive labour turnover soon after. You will therefore need to be creative and devious about finding out about what the organisation is like to work for. Are jobs frequently advertised? If so, is growth sufficient to account for this high rate? Do you know anyone who works there, or can you get to speak to someone who does? It is surprising how helpful switchboard operators can be in suggesting people you might like to talk to, and how informative these same people can be when you phone them up as a total stranger, explaining that you are considering applying for a job. The person vacating the advertised job is obviously an excellent source of information, if available for questioning. Can you interact with the organisation as a potential customer and gain insight in that way? Are visits offered to potential candidates? Is there someone suggested in the advert or further particulars that you are invited to contact? If so, take advantage of the offer.

What is the economic strength of the sector in which the organisation is operating and the market position of the organisation? Jobs have been advertised in organisations when preliminary discussions about redundancies were already taking place. Is the organisation ripe for a takeover? Your MBA should have put you in a position to assess the potential company much more effectively than before.

Do something completely different?

In thinking about the possibilities of doing something completely different, you should include consideration of as wide a range of potential areas as possible. What about doing a PhD? Organisations such as the Open University offer opportunities for doing research 'at a distance', so that this could be done without threat to your full-time employment. You might, of course, *wish* to do research full-time, either with your organisation's sponsorship or with the aid of a mature student grant or research fellowship. Again, there is a range of possibilities.

What about writing a book, or at least a series of articles for publication? If you wrote a dissertation as part of your course, this may have distinct possibilities for 'versioning' for other audiences. There may be areas where you realised that you knew more about the topic than your lecturers. What is the potential for using this knowledge in some way?

If you enjoyed working in groups and making presentations on your work, or found the academic side of the work really stimulating, what about starting to teach management studies? This is still an expanding area. As with research, you do not need to give up your full-time job: given current academic salaries you might well not wish to. With the growth in part-time and distance management education, there is considerable demand for part-time teaching staff. Contact your college, any other local institutions and the major distance learning institutions to see what opportunities are available. Your own recent study experience and your MBA should make you in great demand. (You would of course need to check with your employer that such 'moonlighting' was not in breach of your contract, but many employers welcome the continued development opportunities offered by such leisure activities.)

What about consultancy? Again your qualification would be highly relevant and working for a large consulting organisation would rapidly expose you to a wide variety of different organisations and their problems. The breadth of experience so gained could stand you in excellent stead if you wished after a few years to take another managerial job. You might even wish to set up in business on your own as a consultant, although this option can be fairly lonely and carries a high risk. As a one-man consultancy a large proportion of your time may need to be devoted to marketing your skills, and your ability to handle the work you generate will be necessarily restricted. You might consider forming a loose network with others in the same position so that you can help each other out if overload occurs, as well as offering each other support.

What about business journalism, broadcasting, or voluntary work? The list of possibilities is extensive. The suggestions offered so far are not necessarily likely to be suited to you personally. Instead they are intended to give some indication of the range of options available.

The fairly radical restructuring of the 1990s forced many managers into a 'portfolio' lifestyle, at least for a part of their career. Such a portfolio might consist of a mix of activities from the above list. It can offer variety, opportunities for personal development and a more balanced risk than working in a single area.

ACTIVITY

Try to think of at least three further options which differ radically from those already suggested, to ensure that you are casting your net sufficiently broadly:

_____

_____

_____

MAKING AN EFFECTIVE JOB APPLICATION

Whether you are looking for internal promotion, seeking a job in another organisation or aiming to work at something completely different but still as an employee, you are likely to need to make a job application. Your course may have covered this, but if not, you should take this aspect seriously.

Over the last few years, I have dealt with hundreds of job applications from managers, many of whom had MBAs. A significant number of these applications were rejected almost cursorily on the grounds that the applicant did not appear to be serious enough about the job to take a minimum amount of trouble over the application. The following is a list of ways in which you can ensure that you *don't* get the job for which you are applying.

- Send in a hastily scribbled, illegible application form.
  Reaction: this is a person who can't be bothered.

- Omit to send in the required application form, merely submitting a CV that looks as if it was prepared some time previously, and is not tailored in any way to the job in question.
  Reaction: this person doesn't particularly want this job.

- Miss the deadline for applying (except for very good reason).
  Reaction: we have plenty of applications already that *were* in on time. Anyway, it looks as if this applicant is not organised.

- Fail to submit supporting CV and letter giving reasons for wishing to apply for this particular job, and detailing your particular qualities which make you a singularly good applicant.
  Reaction: this person misses opportunities.

■ Fail to name references as required, or to check that your referees are willing to give you a reference and will be in the country at the required time.
Reaction: we don't interview/appoint without good references being received.

■ Give as a referee someone who has a less than favourable view of your qualities and is blessed with an honest nature.
Reaction: if their referee thinks so poorly of this person …
(This one is difficult, as people are often unwilling to say that the reference they are agreeing to write will be a bad one – ask them outright if you have doubts.)

■ Indicate in any way that you have not fully understood the nature of the job for which you are applying.
Reaction: either this person has taken no trouble with their application or they are not very bright.

■ Do anything to suggest that you have not *thought* about what the organisation needs in a successful candidate, and how you can meet these needs.
Reaction: this person has not taken their application seriously, or they are not good at analysing problems.

■ Show up late for interview.
Reaction: if they can't manage to get to an interview on time …

■ Dress inappropriately for the interview. (One person I interviewed for a job involving contacts with senior managers in client organisations showed up wearing jeans!)
Reaction: this shows lack of judgement. Besides, the effect on clients/subordinates/superiors would be bad.

■ Spend the interview cringing and uttering scarcely a word.
Reaction: this candidate lacks presence/communication skills/interpersonal skills.

■ Spend the interview talking incessantly without letting the interviewer get a word in edgeways.
Reaction: this person can't listen/understand what is required. They would be exhausting to work with.

■ Concentrate on proving what a brilliant person you are rather than demonstrating how your skills match job requirements.
Reaction: may be good at selling themselves, but hasn't thought about the job or analysed what is required.

■ Fail to produce one or two penetrating questions when they ask you at the end of the interview if you have any. (How much will I get paid, and when will I hear are *not* penetrating questions.)
Reaction: this person has not thought much about the job.

From the above it is fairly clear how you can increase your chances of making a successful application, provided you want the job sufficiently to put in the necessary homework beforehand. First, it is essential to research the job and organisation as thoroughly as possible. You will have started this process when you were deciding whether or not you wished to apply. Once decided, it is necessary to take it further. Once you *know* enough about the job and the organisation, you need to *think* about how you can use this knowledge to strengthen your application.

Considerable effort needs to be put into preparing your initial application. The impression created must be of a thoughtful, organised applicant, who really wants the job and who can argue for his or her strengths as a candidate succinctly and powerfully. It helps to say something somewhere that makes you stand out from what may be hundreds of other applicants. A slightly original turn of phrase in describing your leisure activities might catch the selector's eye. Or there might be something different in the way you argue why this is precisely the job to which you can make a significant contribution.

Qualities needed in the application

All aspects of your application should show evidence of judgement and selectivity, with everything you write, whether on application form, CV or supporting short letter, tailored to the job in question. The CV which you have obviously pulled off the word processor unaltered since the last application you made will not impress, nor will great detail on your GCSEs or other early experience or qualifications, unless these are particularly relevant.

You should 'version' your CV for each job application, emphasising your most relevant experience. You need to do more than merely list the jobs you have held, or the responsibilities which you had in each. You will produce a much more impressive CV if you highlight the aspects of each job, and the skills which you exercised or developed in consequence, that are particularly important for *this* job. Always give more emphasis to more recent experience than to things you did a long time ago, unless early experience is singularly relevant.

You need to take particular care with your appearance for the interview. Part of your research should cover the sorts of clothes worn by successful people in the organisation. Research suggests that often selection decisions are taken within the first few minutes of an interview. At this point the selector has little to go on beyond appearance, so it is important that your appearance works in your favour. Whether your research suggests leather jackets or designer suits, it is important that you look as if you have taken trouble with your appearance. (It is worth arriving early enough to repair any ravages of travel in the cloakroom.)

Before the interview you should think not only about your strengths in relation to the job, but also about your weaknesses. You may well be asked about these, and will create a much better impression if you admit to at least some potential weaknesses, particularly those which your interviewers are bound to spot. You need to be able to suggest positive steps which could be taken to reduce these as soon as you were in post. If you are really smart you can describe 'weaknesses' that are really strengths, such as becoming *too* involved in your work.

Interview techniques

During the interview it is important to listen very carefully to the questions asked, and to think about how to answer them before opening your mouth. If you are unclear as to what the interviewer wants, ask for clarification. Try not to get bogged down in minutiae. If asked for an example of an occasion on which you had to reprimand a member of staff, don't go into what Fred was wearing and what Maisie had been saying for months before you finally caught him at it. Instead give only as much detail as is necessary to show that you acted appropriately and in accordance with sound principles. In the sort of job you are likely to be seeking, interviewers are likely to be looking for the ability to think clearly, to select relevant factors from a situation, and to take appropriate decisions in the light of available information. Getting into blow-by-blow discussions of things that have happened will not help you to convince them of your strategic ability!

In most managerial jobs interpersonal skills are important. You should have developed such skills on your MBA, but remember to apply them in the interview. Eye contact with your interviewer is important, and occasional smiles can work wonders, though excessive smiling at inappropriate times can be off-putting. You need also to be aware of your body language. Avoid leaning back, crossing your arms, or otherwise looking defensive and, of course, avoid nervous fidgeting.

Also avoid carrying a lot of clutter into the interview. Even if you have to leave bags and coat at reception or in a secretary's office, do not drag them into the interview room. If you wish to take examples of work you have done because you feel your case would be strengthened by these, pack materials in the order you would wish to present them in a neat case. And do not insist on displaying work if the interviewers do not seem eager to see it. The impression created by an interviewee who insists on showing off examples of reports he has written or other 'specimens', is not a positive one.

If you are inexperienced at job interviews, or know that you tend to clam up or spout nervously, practise beforehand. Think of possible questions, and persuade someone to role-play the interviewer and feed you with the questions. Ask them to give you feedback on how you came across. Tape-record the interview and play it back. You should gain two benefits from this. First you will be able to spot habits or weaknesses that impair your performance, and work on reducing these. Second, you should become less nervous with practice, and find that you have the courage to stop and think before replying, and that your replies become more coherent and fluent as well.

Once you do obtain your desired job, you should still be applying the techniques and approaches learned on the MBA to ensuring that you do the job effectively, and that your career needs are met. The application to job content is obvious. The application to your own career management may be less so, but is none the less important for that. Think about your own objectives at intervals, perhaps with reference to the objective trees that you have drawn, and assess progress towards these. Take action if you feel that it is not satisfactory.

TECHNOLOGY AND RECRUITMENT

Jobs are increasingly being advertised on-line, with the expectation of an electronic application in response. This is obviously quicker and cheaper than conventional paper mail based systems, and may attract applications from a wider and/or different field. Sometimes, particularly if large distances are involved, interviews may be held by video-conference link.

While the basic principles of making a successful application are unaltered, you need to think about how you can clearly and effectively demonstrate your suitability for the post in question via these media. The best way to do this may be altered slightly by the technology used. There are also some points where protocol is as yet unclear.

In the case of e-mail applications you may be uncertain as to the level of formality expected. E-mails tend to be less formal than memos or letters. Should your application be similarly informal? While opinions on this vary, unless the advertisement itself is clearly informal it is probably safest to err on the side of greater formality, composing your e-mail as if it were a normal letter of application. However, as span of 'electronic attention' is often slightly less, it is worth paying even more attention than usual to clarity and brevity.

Similarly, it will be important to ensure that your electronic CV is clear and focused. It may be sifted electronically if large numbers of applications are expected, so ensure that the evidence of how you meet essential requirements is clearly signposted. Avoid 'padding' (though you should do this with any CV). It is claimed that electronic CVs are usually scanned for a maximum of three minutes, so your relevant experience needs to make an impact well within that time.

If interviewed by video-conference, you should remember that if a low capacity line is used, rapid movements can make you look as jerky as an early movie star. Try, therefore, to avoid them. Sit in as relaxed a manner as possible, do not fidget or gesticulate, and look directly at the camera. Extremes of sound may be similarly exaggerated by the technology, so avoid these too.

GOING FORWARD

You should now know the direction in which you wish to travel, at least for the next few years, and have thought about how to start moving. You should be aware of some of your weaknesses as a potential candidate for a different job, and have an idea of how to go about reducing these. As with all other types of management, your career management will be helped if you schedule regular, if not necessarily frequent, reviews of your objectives and progress towards these. Only thus can you ensure that you are in control of your career, and directing it towards the objectives which are of greatest importance to you, even when time or experience causes those objectives to change.

It remains only for me to wish you the very best of luck in travelling your chosen path. I hope that this handbook has been of help to you in gaining your qualification, and that the skills you have gained on your course will assist you in attaining your more important life objectives.

SUMMARY

- The skills and approaches you learned on your MBA are equally applicable to the 'case' of planning your own career progression.

- It is important to be clear about your objectives, and about how you will measure progress towards these.

- Consider as wide a range of options as possible before choosing.

- Staying in your present job can be a positive choice.

- If looking for another job, it is important to research possibilities thoroughly.

- If applying for another job, it is important that your application is carefully compiled, relates to the particular job, and is such as to make you stand out from perhaps hundreds of other applicants.

- In interviews your interpersonal skills are being assessed, as well as your other qualities relevant to the job. Again, careful preparation is important.

- Once you are in the job you want, continue to apply what you have learned on your MBA, not only to your job content, but to your own career management and achievement of your life objectives.

Further information

Bridges, W. (1997) *Creating You & Co: be the boss of your own career*, Nicholas Brealey.

Clutterbuck, D. and Dearlove, D. (1999) *The Interim Manager: a new career model for the experienced manager*, Financial Times/Pitman Publishing.

Comfort, M. (1997) *Portfolio people: how to create a workstyle as individual as you are*, Century.

References

Adamson, A. (1995) *A Student's Guide for Assignments, Projects and Research in Business and Management*, Arthur Adamson.

Andreas, S. and Franklin, C. (1996) *NLP: The New Technology of Achievement*, Nicholas Brealey.

Back, K. and Back, K. (1999) *Assertiveness at Work* (3rd edn), McGraw-Hill.

Baumann, B. (1992) 'Master ohne Wert', *Forbes*, 10, pp. 68–72.

Belbin, R.M. (1981) *Management Teams*, Heinemann.

Belbin, R.M. (1993) *Team Roles at Work*, Butterworth-Heinemann.

Bentley, T.J. (1978) *Report Writing in Business*, Kogan Page.

Bickerstaff, G. (1999) *Which MBA? A critical guide to programmes in Europe and the USA* (11th edn), The Economist Publications.

Bird, P. (1998) *Teach yourself Time Management*, Hodder & Stoughton.

Bishop, S. (2000) *Develop Your Assertiveness* (2nd edn), Kogan Page.

Boden, J. (1997) *Writing a report*, How To Books.

Bradley, A. (2000) *Successful Presentation Skills* (2nd edn), Kogan Page.

Bridges, W. (1997) *Creating You & Co: be the boss of your own career*, Nicholas Brealey.

Butler, G. and Hope, T. (1995) *Manage your Mind: The mental fitness guide*, Oxford University Press.

Buzan, T. (1989) *Use Your Head*, BBC Publications.

Buzan, T. (1995) *The Mind Map Book*, BBC Publications.

Buzan, T. (1997) *The Speed Reading Book*, BBC Publications.

Carter, R., Martin, J., Mayblin, B. and Munday, M. (1984) *Systems, Management and Change: a graphic guide,* Harper & Row, in association with the Open University.

Caunt, J. (2000) *Organise Yourself*, Kogan Page.

Checkland, P. (1981) *Systems Thinking, Systems Practice*, Wiley.

Clegg, B. (1999) *Instant Time Management*, Kogan Page.

Clegg, B. (2000) *Instant Stress Management*, Kogan Page.

Clutterbuck, D. and Dearlove, D. (1999) *The Interim Manager: a new career model for the experienced manager*, Financial Times Pitman Publishing.

Clutterbuck, D. and Kernaghan, S. (1990) *The Phoenix Factor,* Weidenfeld & Nicolson.

Colins, J./Video Arts (1998) *Perfect Presentations*, Marshall Publishing.

Comfort, M. (1997) *Portfolio people: how to create a workstyle as individual as you are*, Century.

Constable, J. and McCormick, R. (1987) *The Making of British Managers*, BIM/CBI.

Coopers & Lybrand Associates (1984) *A Challenge to Complacency*, NEDO/MSC.

Cramer, S. (2000) *The Ultimate Business Library: 75 books that made management*, Capstone.

Deloitte, Haskins & Sell (1989) *Management Challenge for the 1990s*, Training Agency.

Easterby-Smith, M., Thorpe, R. and Lowe, A. (1991) *Management Research: An Introduction*, Sage.

Easton, G. (1992) *Learning from Case Studies* (2nd edn), Prentice-Hall.

Forsyth, P. (1994) *First Things First – how to manage your time for maximum performance*, IM/Pitman Publishing.

Gibson, R. (ed.) (1998) *Rethinking the Future*, Nicholas Brealey.

Giles, K. and Hedge, N. (1994) *The Manager's Good Study Guide*, The Open University.

Glaser, B.G. and Strauss, A.L. (1967) *The Discovery of Grounded Theory: strategies for qualitative research*, Weidenfeld & Nicolson.

Glynn, J.J., Murphy, M.P. and Perrin, J. (1998) *Accounting for Managers* (2nd edn), International Thomson Business Press.

Goldsmith, W. and Clutterbuck, D. (1984) *The Winning Streak*, Penguin.

Gowers, E. (1954) *The Complete Plain Words*, Penguin.

Graham, L. and Sargent, D. (1981) *Countdown to Mathematics*, vol. 1, Addison-Wesley with the Open University Press.

Greising, D. (1998) *I'd like the World to Buy a Coke. The life and leadership of Roberto Gorzueta*, Wiley.

Handy, C. (1987) *The Making of Managers*, MSC/NEDC/BIM.

Handy, C. (1993) *Understanding Organizations* (4th edn), Penguin.

Hardingham, A. (1995) *Working in Teams*, Institute of Personnel Development.

Herzberg, F. (1966) *Work and the Nature of Man*, World Publishing Company.

Honey, P. and Mumford, A. (1986) *The Manual of Learning Styles*, Peter Honey.

Howard, K. and Peters, J. (1990) 'Managing Management Research', *Management Decision*, vol. 28, No. 5.

Howard, K. and Sharp, J.A. (1983) *The Management of a Student Research Project*, Gower.

Huczinski, A. (1996) *Management Gurus. What makes them and how to become one*, International Thomson Business Press.

Huff, D. (1954) *How to Lie with Statistics*, Penguin.

Hussey, D.E. (1988) *Management Training and Corporate Strategy*, Pergamon Press.

Institute of Manpower Studies (1984) *Competence and Competition*, NEDO/MSC.

Israel, R., Whitten, H. and Shaffran, C. (2000) *Your Mind at Work: developing self knowledge for business success*, Kogan Page.

Jankovicz, A.D. (1995) *Business Research Projects* (2nd edn), Chapman Hall.

Jantsch, E. (1967) *Technological Forecasting in Perspective*, OECD.

Joseph, A. (1998) *Put it in writing: learn how to write clearly, quickly and persuasively*, McGraw-Hill.

Kakabadse, A., Ludlow, R. and Vinnicombe, S. (1987) *Working in Organisations*, Penguin.

Kellaway, L. (2000) *Sense and Nonsense in the Office*, Financial Times Prentice Hall.

Kelly, F.J. and Kelly, H.M. (1986) *What They Really Teach You at the Harvard Business School*, Grafton.

Kind, J. (1999) *Accounting and Finance for Managers*, Kogan Page.

Kneeland, S. (1999) *Thinking Straight*, Pathways.

Kolb, D.A., Rubin, I.M. and MacIntyre, J.M. (1984) *Organizational Psychology* (4th edn), Prentice-Hall.

Lataif, L.E. (1992) 'MBA: Is the traditional model doomed?', *Harvard Business Review*, Nov–Dec, pp. 128–40.

Lee, T.W. (1999) *Using Qualitative Methods in Organizational Research*, Sage.

Lifeskills International (1999) *Staying Healthy at Work*, Gower.

Management Charter Initiative (1988) *Proposed National Framework for Management Development*, CMED.

Manchester Open Learning (1993) *Making Effective Presentations*, Kogan Page.

MBA Casebook 99 (1999) Hobsons International.

Moroney, M.J. (1951) *Facts from Figures*, Penguin.

Morris, C. (2000) *Quantitative Approaches in Business Studies* (5th edn), Financial Times Prentice Hall.

Morris, C. and Thanassoulis, E. (1994) *Essential Mathematics – a refresher course for Business and Social Studies*, Macmillan.

Morris, S. and Smith, J. (1998) *Understanding Mind Maps in a Week*, Institute of Management.

Nutz, K. and Freiberg, J. (1997) *Southwest Airlines Crazy Recipe for Business and Personal Success*, Orion Business Books.

Oakshott, L. (1998) *Essential Quantitative Methods for Business, Management and Finance*, Macmillan Business.

The Official MBA Handbook 1999/2000 (15th edn) (1999) Financial Times Prentice Hall.

Parkinson, C.N. (1957) *Parkinson's Law or the Pursuit of Progress*, Penguin.

Peters, T.J. and Waterman, R.H. (1984) *In Search of Excellence*, Warner Books.

Pizzey, A. (1998) *Finance and Accounting for Non-Specialist Students*, Financial Times Pitman Publishing.

Powell, J. (1991) *Quantitative Decision Making*, Longman.

Robinson, P. (1994) *Snapshots from Hell: the making of an MBA*, Nicholas Brealey.

Roberts, B. (1999) *Working Memory: Improving Your Memory for the Workplace*, London House.

Rose, C. and Nicholl, M.J. (1997) *Accelerated Learning for the 21st Century*, Piatkus.

Rowntree, D. (1987) *Statistics Without Tears: a primer for non-mathematicians*, Penguin.

Russell, L. (1999) *The Accelerated Learning Field Book*, Jossey-Bass Pfeiffer.

Sprent, P. (1991) *Management Mathematics*, Penguin.

Stratford, S. (1990) 'How Kosher this Hon. Degree?', *British Academy of Management Newsletter*, no. 5.

Tuckman, B.W. (1965) 'Developmental sequence in small groups', *Psychological Bulletin*.

Index

AACSB 22, 38
abstracts 315–16
academic background (yours) 30
accessing information 57
accelerated learning 116
accreditation 22
active learning 100–2
activists 103–5
addition 202
agenda 148–9
algorithm 310–1
AMBA 18, 22, 38
analogy 168
appendices 247
applications (job) 339–41
apostrophe 257–8, 260
arithmetic
  addition 202
  averages 179–80
  brackets 200, 206
  decimals 203–4
  division 192, 203
  equations 175, 196–200
  fractions 190–203
  functions 206
  indices 192, 204
  multiplication 202–3, 204
  percentages 193, 204
  powers 192, 204
  ratios 190, 194–6
  roots 205
  sigma 206
  square roots 205
  squares 192, 204
  subtraction 202
assertions 237

assertiveness 50–6, 75, 151
  behaviours 51–3
  expression 54–5
  preparation for situations 55–6
  rights 53–4
assessment (*see also* examinations) 214–27
  as communication 224–7
  causes of failure 216–21
  forms of 288–96
  glossary of terms used 254–6
  institution's objectives 214
  portfolio 290–2
  work based 215
assessment centres 292
asset turnover 196
assignments 56–7, 229–53
  content 229–32
  deconstructing questions 229–32
  planning 229–36
attitude change 48
average (*see* mean)

bar charts 182–5
barriers to entry 18
Belbin, R.M. 144, 147
biorhythms 64–5, 78, 95
body language 55
Boolean logic 316
brackets
  maths 200, 206
  punctuation 260–1
brain patterns (*see* mind maps)
brain storming 167, 232
Buzan, T. 124, 125, 127

cancelling 191, 193, 199

capital letters 261
case study 155–71
  exams 276
  difficulties 156–8, 162
  groups 158–9
    guidelines 161
    limitations 160–1
    method for analysis 162–70
    teaching method 155
catastrophe factor 303
categorical data 319
CATWOE 116
central tendency (measures of) 179–80
chair (of group) 146–8
channel (of communication) 226
Checkland, P. 94, 116, 128
citation indexes 316
Clutterbuck, D. 160
colon 261
comma 260
communication 132, 159, 224–7
competences 14, 100, 291
completer–finisher 145
complexity 158
compound interest 196–7
computer conferences 24, 57, 221–2
computer-marked examinations 275
concepts 232–3
conclusions 246
consortium MBAs 17
contents (of report) 243, 328
context (see environment)
contextual awareness 159
continuous development 102
conventions 123
co-ordinator (group) 144–5
corporate MBAs 16–7
cost of study 19
course choice 17–25, 26–39
creativity techniques 167–9
critical thinking 94, 158
current ratio 195
curriculum vitae (see CV)
CV 341

deadlines 79
dashes 261

data
  categorical 319
  nominal 319
  ordinal 319
  planning 317–20
  primary 318
  qualitative 319
  quantitative 319
  ranked 319
  reliability 320
  secondary 318–19
  textual 319
  types 318–20
  validity 321
decimals 203–4
deconstructing questions 229–32, 285
delayering 16
delivery
  pattern, teaching 18
  technique, presentations 267–9
denominator 191, 193
description (of problems) 162–4
diagnosis (of problems) 164–5, 235
diagrams 117–18, 120–37, 238–9, 245
  conventions 123
  fishbone 124–7, 239
  importance 121–2
  influence 134
  mind maps 124–7, 232, 239, 285, 310
  multiple-cause 133, 165, 217, 238–9
  relationship 127–8, 163, 165, 239
  relevance trees 124, 126, 315
  rich pictures 128–9, 130, 163, 232, 234
  symbols 123
  systems maps 129–32, 165
  Venn 130
direction (of effort) 73–82
Disraeli, B. 176
dissertation 215, 219, 297–329
  data planning 317–21
  drafting 325–6, 327–9
  literature search 314–17
  log 326–7
  methodology 322–3
  objectives 298–300
  planning 317–21, 321–5
  proposal 313–14

dissertation (*continued*)
  risks 303–5
  style 328
  supervision 300–1
  topic choice 301–14
  topic generation 305–9
distance learning 18, 22, 35–6
distributions 180–2
division 192, 203
drafting 239–41
  guidelines 240
  style 248–52

employers 16–17
English (basics of) 248–53
  spelling 256–9
  punctuation 259–61
entry requirements 19–20
environment
  competitive 94
  effect on study 217–18
  external 94
  internal 94
  organisational 16
  problem 157
  systems 132
EQUAL 22
equations 175, 196–200
EQUIS 22, 38
estimating 189
evaluation (of options) 169
evidence 237–8
exclamation marks 260
examinations 274–87
  failure 276–8
  glossary of terms 254–6
  notes 281, 282
  preparation 278–84
  revision 278–83
  technique 284–7
  types of 275–6
  viva voce 280, 293–6
executive programmes 18, 34
exercise (physical) 49–50, 66, 95–6, 283–4
exponential scale 184
extrapolation 188
eye movements 109–10

face-to-face study 33–6
failure 216–21
feasibility (of project etc.) 303
feedback 151
financing study 19
fishbone diagrams 125–7, 239
Fog Index 249
fractions 190–203
framework (*see* theory)
full stops 259
full-time study 32–3
functions (mathematical) 206

Glossary (terms for assessment) 254–6
GMAT 19
Goldsmith, W. 160
grammar 259–62
graphs 187–9
group working 138–54
  behaviours 140–3
  case study 158–9
  choosing 143
  dangers 149–50
  effectiveness 148–9
  formation 146
  informal 152–3
  process 139–43
  recording interactions 142–3
  roles 144–5
  self-help 152–3
  stages 146
  size 144
  type 144–5
groupthink 149–50, 162

Harvard 12, 14
HEFCE (*see* Higher Educaation Funding Council)
Herzberg, F. 92–3
Higher Education Funding Council 22
histograms 180–2
Honey, P. 100, 102

ICTs 16, 24, 56–8
idea generation techniques 167–9
implementation 170
implementor 145

indexes 315–16
indices 192, 204
influence diagrams 134
informal groups 152–3
information 165
  accessing 57
  search 314–17
Information and Communication
    Technologies (*see* ICT)
institutional variation 37–8
interactions in groups 142–3
internationalisation 20–2
Internet (*see also* World Wide Web) 24
interruptions 81–2
interval data 320
interviews (job) 340
introduction (reports) 244
inverted comma 260
Ishikawa, K. 126
IT (*see* ICTs)

Jantch, E. 124
job enrichment 93
job satisfaction 92–3
job seeking 337–9

Kellaway, L. 175
Kernaghan, S. 160
key words 315
knowledge management 100
Kolb, D.A. 100–2, 105, 326, 334

Lataif, L.E. 14
learning (*see also* study) 87–98
  cycle 100–2
  diary 291, 335
  lifelong 334–5
  styles 102–7
  theory 99–107
length of programme 17–18
lifelong learning 334–5
liquidity 195
literature search 314–17
loans for study 19
logarithmic scale 184

MacIntyre, J.M. 100

Management Charter Initiative 14
Management Development (context)
    13–17
management experience (yours) 31
Master of Business Administration (*see*
    MBA)
mathematics (*see also* arithmetic)
    172–210
  'language' 202–6
  need for 175–8
MBAs
  choice of 26–39
  consortium 17
  corporate 16–17
  delivery pattern 18
  dimensions of variation 17–25
  length of programme 17–18
  Harvard 12, 14
  origins 12–13
  specialist 20–1, 31–2
  teaching approach 23–4
MCI 14
mean 179–80
meaning construction (*see also*
    sense-making) 100
median 180
meetings (*see also* groups) 81, 127, 138,
    143
  agendas 148–9
  stages 149
mentor 45
message 226
metaphor 168
methodologies 93–4
milestones 325
mind maps 124–7, 232, 239, 285, 310
Mintzberg, H. 14
mnemonics 115
mode 180
mode of study 32–7
modelling (mathematical) 175–6
monitor–evaluator 145
Morris, C. 178
motivation
  failure of 220–4
  study 36, 91
  theory 92–3

multiple-cause diagrams 133, 165, 217, 238–9
multiplication 202–3, 204
Mumford, A. 100, 102

National Vocational Qualifications 14, 290
nerves 271–2
Net Present Value 92
Neuro-Linguistic Programming 48
NLP (*see* Neuro-Linguistic Programming)
nominal data 319
nominal group technique 168
notes 117–18, 281–2
  diagrammatic 118
NPV (*see* net present value)
numbers 172–210
  representation of 179–89
numerator 191
NVQs (*see* National Vocational
  Qualifications)

objectives
  assessing 27–9, 335
  career 31
  clarity of 79
  dissertation 298–300
  hierarchy of 27, 29
  study 91–5
  tree 27, 335
open book exams 275–6
Open University 15, 221
opinions 237
oral examinations (*see* viva voce)
ordinal data 219
organisation (of materials) 239
organisational support 44–6
overcommitment 75

panic (in exams) 278
paragraphs 250–1
parameters (for information search) 315
part-time study 18, 33–4
Penrose, R. 175
percentages 193, 204
PEST factors (*see* STEP)
photo-reading 116

pie charts 185–6
planning
  exam answers 285–6
  revision 280
  study 90–5
  time 74–5, 83, 236
  use of book 5–7
plant (group role) 145
political sensitivity 304, 312
portfolio assessment 290–2, 295
PowerPoint 270
powers 192, 204
pragmatists 103, 105, 106
preparation
  assertiveness 55
  IT use 57
  presentations 272–3
  reading 58–9
  study 43–61
presentation 264–73
  case study findings 170–1
  delivery 267–9
  diagrams for 122–3
  nerves 271–2
  preparation 272–3
  risks 265–6
  structure 267–9
  style 266
  visual aids 266, 269–70
primary data 318
prime time 64–5, 78–9
print indexes 316
probability 177–8
problem
  description 163
  diagnosis 164–5
  solution criteria 166
  solving 157–8, 304–5
  statements 165
  themes 164, 232–3
process 139–41
procrastination 78, 90
profit margin 195
project
  evaluation 312–15
  log 326
  planning 321–5

project (*continued*)
    proposal 313–14
    scheduling 323–4
projects (*see* dissertations)
punctuation 259–61

qualitative data 319
quantitative data 319
question marks 259
questions
    answering, in exams 277–8, 285–6
    choice 285
    deconstructing 229–32, 285
    in presentations 269, 271
    terms used in 254–6

range 180
ranked data 319
ratio data 320
ratios 190, 194–6
reading 108–19
    eye movements 109–10
    materials selection 113–14
    practice 112
    speed 111–13, 114–16
receiver 225–6
recommendations 246
recruitment 342
references (in reports) 239, 247–8
reflection 106, 334
reflectors 103–4
relationship diagrams 127–8, 163, 165, 239
relaxation 49, 66
relevance trees 124, 126, 315
report writing 241–52
    guidelines 240
    style 248–52
research (doing – *see* dissertation)
research ratings 38
resource investigator 145
review sessions 102
revision 280–3
Rich Pictures 128–9, 130, 163, 232, 234
ROCE 194–5
ROI (*see* ROCE)
roots 205

rounding 189–90
Rubin, L. M. 100

sampling 320
scales 184–5
scapegoating 150, 162
scope (of project, etc.) 302
Scottish Vocational Qualifications (*see* National Vocational Qualifications)
self-help groups (*see also* study groups) 221–2
semi-colon 261
sender 225
sense-making 100, 106, 157
shaper 145
sigma 206
simplicity (writing style) 248–51
skills
    deficits 23–4, 158–9, 218–19
    transferable 23–4, 158–9
solution tree 168–9
specialist (team role) 145
specialist Master's programmes 20–1, 31–2
spelling 256–9
square 192, 204
square root 205
stakeholders 157
statistics 176–87
STEP Factors 94
strategic focus 21
stress
    causes of 47–8
    managing 44–50
    unavoidable 48–50
study
    groups 152–3
    log 91, 95, 106, 291
    motivation 91
    objectives 91–5
    place 87–9
    plan 90–5
    time 89–90
structure, of book 4–5
subsystem 131
subtraction 202
summary 242

supervision (dissertation) 300
support for study 44–6
SVQs (*see* National Vocational
     Qualifications)
symbols 123
symmetry (of research outcomes) 302–3
synectics 168
system 130–2
systems maps 129–32, 165

taking notes (*see* notes)
tally 180–1
task 139–41
team worker 145
teaching
   approach 23–4
   media 24–5
   quality 38
teams (*see also* groups) 138–54
tertiary sources 315–17
textual data 319
themes (in case study) 232
theory 92–3, 165, 238
theorising 334
theorists 103–6
thesis (*see* dissertation)
time
   in exams 276–7, 284–5
   log 64, 66–8

'making' 65–70
management 71–84
problem 62–70
prime 64–5
requirements for study 63–4
wastage 80–2
title page (reports) 242–3
topic (project, etc.) 301–14
   criteria 301–5
   generation 305–9
transferable skills 23–4, 158–9
Tuckman, B.W. 146
two-factor theory of job satisfaction 92–3

UMP (*see* Universal Management
     Paradigm)
Universal Management Paradigm 27,
     102, 140, 235

validation 22
variable 205
Venn diagrams 130
visual aids 266, 269–70
viva voce 288, 293–6

World Wide Web 24, 316–17
writers' block 240–1
writing (*see also* drafting) 228–53, 327–9
WWW (*see* World Wide Web)